Return to Africa
--a Journal

by

Esther L. Megill

To Linda Schurman
With hope you will enjoy
something of the history of the
Church in Africa.

Esther Megill

AuthorHouse™
1663 Liberty Drive, Suite 200
Bloomington, IN 47403
www.authorhouse.com
Phone: 1-800-839-8640

First published by AuthorHouse 05/14/2008

ISBN: 978-1-4343-7528-3 (sc)

Library of Congress Control Number: 2008902376

Printed in the United States of America
Bloomington, Indiana

This book is printed on acid-free paper.

PREFACE

My life in Africa began in January 1951, when I arrived in Sierra Leone, West Africa, to serve until 1962 as a missionary of the Evangelical United Brethren Church. My primary responsibility was as a medical technologist in a hospital in the interior at Rotifunk, but I also became engaged in many aspects of Christian Education. My experiences during those years are told in the book *Sierra Leone Remembered*.[1]

Africa remained a major part of my life, however, and after graduate study I returned to Africa, first as Area Executive Secretary for North and West Africa for the World Division of the Board of Missions of The United Methodist Church, and in later years as a missionary in Ghana and as a volunteer in other countries. The pages which follow give an account of those years, as recorded in staff reports, letters and a journal during my volunteer year, and my memories. Thus, this book is in one sense a journal of my life from 1968 to 1980 and 1989 to 1990. These were years filled with new experiences, friends, adventure, difficulties and joys. I share them with you in the pages which follow.

I would not do this without the help of others. Dr. Hugh Johnson, Dr. Dean Gilliland and Dr. Robert Carey all contributed information about the years in some of the countries when I was not there, and corrected some of my errors. Dr. David Butler supplied information about Tunisia, and three friends from Ghana, the Rev. Kwaku Asamoah-Okyere, the Rev. Sam Atiemo and Mrs. Mary Kwakye, also helped me with information about that country. I am greatly indebted to those who proofread and edited the material for me: Anne McKenzie, Sylvia Smyth, Elaine Gasser and Dr. Douglas Wingeier.

I met so many new as well as old friends in my "Return to Africa," which added richness to my life. I hope that you will enjoy meeting them also.

Esther Megill, Asheville, NC
January 2008

---

[1]To order call AuthorHouse at 1-888-280-7715 (ask for book #23464) or visit
http://www.authorhouse.com/BookStore/ItemDetail.aspx?bookid=23464

Special thanks are due the following persons,
who added to my story with information which I could not know:

The Rev. Dr. Hugh Johnson

Began language training in 1960, and arrived in Algeria in 1960. He officially retired in 2004, but frequently returns to Algeria as needed. He served in several capacities: pastor to small Christian congregations, teacher in schools, dialogue with Muslims, superintendent of work in North Africa, is part of the Middle East Council of Churches and other ecumenical organizations. He made frequent trips to Tunis for mission business. He and his wife have retired in France.

The Rev. Dr. Dean Gilliland

Served as a missionary in Nigeria, in various capacities, for twenty-two years
Professor of contextualized theology and African studies at Fuller Theological Seminary from 1977 until recent retirement

Dr. Robert Carey

Was in Liberia from 1950-1976, serving as a missionary in the field of education, at the College of West Africa, Cuttington College, and at Ganta, teaching in the secondary schools and also in teacher training.

CONTENTS

Part I. NEW YORK TO AFRICA

AFRICA

From p. 15, *Prayer Calendar 2007*, Daniel Lucardo, ed. Women's Division, General Board of Global Ministries, The United Methodist Church, c. 2006 by the General Board of Global Ministries. Used by permission. (Shading added.)

Chapter 1. North Africa
Introduction

(Maps courtesy of The University of Texas Libraries, The University of Texas at Austin. Provided by the U.S. CIA.)

Algeria and Tunisia are in North Africa, part of the area known as the Maghreb, which is composed of Libya, Tunisia, Algeria, Morocco and Mauritania. Algeria is the second largest country in the African continent, and Tunisia, the smallest in North Africa, is the country farthest north in Africa.

Northern Algeria enjoys a mild, Mediterranean climate. The area just south of the coast has fertile soil; then there are the Tellian Atlas Range and the semiarid to arid high plateau just before reaching the higher Atlas Mountains and then the Sahara Desert. The desert covers seventh-eighths of Algeria. Temperatures vary widely. In the Sahara it can be very hot during the day, but chilly to cold (and occasionally freezing) at night. Petroleum and natural gas are the backbone of the Algerian economy. They also grow and export small quantities of cork, dates, olives, citrus fruits and wine. They grow cereal grains, vegetables, and figs for their own consumption. Forty percent of Tunisia is the Sahara Desert, but much of the rest has very fertile soil. Their economy depends upon agriculture, mining, energy, tourism, petroleum, and manufacturing.

3

Arabic is the official language of both countries, and the religion is Islam. Tamazight (the language of the aboriginal people or Berbers) was recently recognized as a national language in Algeria. French is widely spoken and studied in both countries. English is also gaining in importance.

Both Algeria and Tunisia are Republics. Algeria has a multiparty system, while Tunisia has a single political party.

The Berbers are the indigenous people of both countries, but very few are left in Tunisia. In the second century B.C. Algeria became part of the Roman Republic, and later spent a century under Vandals before becoming part of the Byzantine Empire. It was conquered by the Arabs in the 8th century, and became part of the Ottoman Empire in 1517. The French invaded Algeria in 1830, and after a long and violent war and heavy colonization, Algeria was eventually considered an integral part of France. From 1954-1962 the Algerians fought for independence, and achieved it, proclaiming their independence on July 5, 1962. From 1991 to 2001 there was a violent civil war between radical Islamists and the government. Algeria is now slowly recovering and developing into an emerging economy.

Tunisia became a French Protectorate in 1881, and independent in 1956. In 1942-43, during World War II, Tunisia became the scene of the first major joint operation between the U.S. and the British, who fought–and won–in a major battle with Rommel, general of the German forces.[2]

Rev. David Butler, former missionary in Algeria and Tunisia, wrote the following about Tunisia:

> *Not far from Tunis lie the ancient ruins of Carthage. Founded by the Phoenician traders in the ninth century B.C., capital of the Carthaginian empire, destroyed by Rome in 146 B.C. and then rebuilt as the center of Roman power in North Africa, conquered by the Vandals in the fifth century and reconquered by the Byzantine empire in the sixth, Carthage was finally abandoned at the time of the Muslim conquest in 698. The region of Tunisia has continued to experience the ups and downs of human history throughout its Muslim era. It experienced the colonial period as a French protectorate beginning in 1881 and culminating in independence in 1956.[3]*

Dr. Hugh Johnson, who retired in 2004 after years as a missionary in Algeria, writes the following about Christianity in North Africa:

> *It would be in error if one were to think that Christian presence in Muslim North Africa is a modern phenomenon. What is modern about it is the fact that Islam turns out to be the intermediate development, as an interlude in North African history. Christianity was present in North Africa, both in Algeria and in Tunisia, from the earliest years of Christian history. North Africa has offered several of the great names of Christian history, not the least of which are Augustine, Cyprian, Tertullian, and others, along with a panoply of martyrs to the faith.*

2Information for the above summary was obtained from *Wikipedia, the free encyclopedia*, Algeria and Tunisia, and many helpful comments from the Rev. David Butler.

[3]Butler, David W., "Tunisia," unpublished manuscript. Used by permission of David Butler.

The expansion of the Church in North Africa was rapid and dynamic, but so was division. Willingness to give up articles and practices that put North African Christians at cross currents with their pagan compatriots brought dissension in the ranks of the faithful. Before the conclusion of the fifth century, one found Roman Christians and Donatist Christians practicing violence among themselves, and through violence weakening the Church.

The return of Christianity to the region dates from the mid-nineteenth century, but it was not North American Protestantism that was the prime mover. After Algeria was colonized by the French after the "flyswatter" incident[4] in Algiers, several decades passed before the Protestant faith began to take root. Occasionally, the roots of human migrations were in secular European politics or economics. As for Methodism, the movement was initialized by French Methodists who, having traveled across the countryside, felt called to give witness to their faith to the Muslims of North Africa. With little more than that felt impulsion, they called upon their compatriots to take seriously the evangelical call to faith and conversion.

The entry of world Methodism (with its own roots in expansion to North America) came after the Sunday School Conference in the Middle East in the early twentieth century. A vision grew up whereby properties were purchased and strategies developed for all of North Africa. There would be in every population center of North Africa a church, and beside it orphanages, health care centers and social service centers through which Christian principles would bring expansion. Methodists thus "overspent" for the infrastructure, stretching their resources to the limit before the economic crises and international strife to come later in the twentieth century.

5

---

[4]In 1827, the Ottoman ruler (called a Dey) was accused by the French of insulting the French consul in Algiers by his flyswatter hitting the diplomat's face. As a result France launched a devastating war against Algeria which lasted for fifteen years.

Algeria and Tunisia
1968–Getting Acquainted

My return to Africa began in October of 1968, with a flight first to London, then Zurich and Hanover, Germany. In London I met with leaders of the British Methodists, the Sudan United Mission, and the Church Missionary Society to discuss some of our common concerns in West Africa. I also was able to visit with friends–Betty Beveridge, the nurse midwife with whom I shared a number of years in the hospital at Rotifunk, in Sierra Leone, and Laura Short, a friend and former student at Harford School for Girls.

The stop in Zurich gave an opportunity to meet with Bishop Franz Schaefer, the bishop of North Africa as well as European conferences of The United Methodist Church. In Hannover, Germany, I met with Dr. Immanuel Mohr, secretary of the mission board of the now united churches in Germany. We discussed how we might coordinate our work, as he was seeking personnel to send to Sierra Leone and Nigeria. Finally, on October 31 I flew to Zurich, then Geneva, and on to Algiers.

What can I say of North Africa in a few paragraphs? I knew that this would be a much different Africa from the one I knew, but I still had to keep telling myself that I was in Africa! Algeria and Tunisia are, of course Muslim countries; both were former French colonies, so one has to know French or Arabic to get along in those countries. (How I wished I had the ability to speak other languages as our missionaries had.) In Algeria one still saw signs of the seven years of revolution, as they fought for independence from France. There was massive unemployment, dislocation of peoples, a large population of children and youth for whom there were not enough schools or other facilities. The church was very small in Algeria (and still is). We were (and still are) there as a Christian presence, serving in the name of Christ. Missionaries were serving in boy's and girl's hostels, social service centers, a hospital, kindergarten and nursery, and in the Ecumenical Study Center, where scholars were searching for ways to

Akila Brès, Louise Werder, Shirliann Johnson ,Elizabeth Whittlinger

establish dialogue between Christian and Muslim. In Algiers I visited in the homes of Paul and Akila Brés (Paul is French and Akila Algerian); Hugh and Shirliann (Fritzi) Johnson, who were at that time studying Kabyle, the language of one of the ethnic groups in Algeria; and

Lynn and Jeanne Larson, two "A 3's"(young people who served in an African country for three years).

I was also privileged to share a meal with the girls of the Foyer at Les Aiglons, a hostel for girls who were attending the University. Nearby was a building in which a sewing school had been conducted for girls who had been taken out of school, taught by Louise Werder, a missionary from Switzerland. It was temporarily closed at the time, but later reopened. Sister Ruth Lang, also a Swiss missionary, conducted a small clinic at nearby Villa Elizabeth. She emphasized mostly instruction to mothers and children, and giving immunization with vaccines supplied by the government.

Marcia Henry (center) and Girls at Les Aiglons

The Ecumenical Center for Islamic Studies was a cooperative effort in which we were proud to share. Marston Speight, the United Methodist missionary assigned there, was at that time completing his PhD in Islamics. He and other scholars were collecting a library of materials on Islam and Christianity. They were endeavoring to establish a dialogue with educated Muslims, to share understanding of their faith and ours. Articles were being written, bibliographies compiled, and some materials produced on Islam, written by both Muslims and Christians.

While most of my time on visits on behalf of the Board was spent in meetings with missionaries and visiting various programs and projects, there was also time to relax and do a little sightseeing. In Algiers a visit to the Casbah, the old Arabic section, is a must. The narrow, winding streets are lined with shops of many kinds. Outside a shop one often sees men sitting at small tables drinking the very strong and sweet coffee. (When on a visit to the Casbah with missionaries Sue Robinson and Liv Larsen, we sat down for coffee–even though we were the only women.) It is tempting to buy items made of brass, silver, gold, leather, rugs from a fabulous and exotic array of goods.

Hugh Johnson and Hassan Kabaili, Algerian Christian, in Center

Weaving Prayer Rugs

On another day Paul Brès and I flew to Oran, the second largest city in Algeria, on the shore of the Mediterranean. Markku and Eila Lehto, Norwegian missionaries under our Board, were there to reopen work that had been closed during the Revolution. Already they were engaged enthusiastically in a recreation program for young boys, and had other plans for establishing a reading room for young men, and another room in which women could meet for fellowship and discussion. Eila was a midwife, and hoped to work in a Red Crescent (the Muslim equivalent to the Red Cross) hospital. Through her contacts with women there she hoped to be able to meet with them to give health and religious instruction, if the women were receptive to it. Requests had already been made for services in the small chapel.

Along with the Johnsons and Elizabeth Whittlinger (Swiss midwife), I drove to Les Ouadhias

Lester Griffith in Chapel

on the winding road up into a range of the Atlas mountains. The people in that area are the Kabyle, the largest group of the indigenous Berbers. There Lester and Janice Griffith, veteran missionaries, were engaged in social service and church work. Lester had a sports field which was popular with the young men of the village, a library and reading room, and Bible and craft classes with the boys. Sister Héléne Manz, Swiss (on furlough during my first visit) had a Bible class for women, and supervised the craft classes. A self-help program was run by a Kabyle woman who taught weaving and raffia work in eight-week courses. The women

were given material for their first products, for which they paid when the articles were sold. The government bought all the craft products. That was the only source of income for some of the women and girls.

A dispensary was operated by Gerta Thomas, a Swiss midwife, who was later joined by Elizabeth Whittlinger, when she completed language study.

I was privileged to speak on Sunday to a small Christian congregation, made up almost entirely of women and children.

On Sunday afternoon Gerta Thomas drove me over

to Ft. Nati onal (L'Arbaa ath Iraten), where the Hugh Johnsons were serving on weekends, while they were completing their Kabyle language study, and would later serve full-time. There was a boy's hostel, where boys stayed while attending the nearby government school with about thirty boys at that time. Several were from homes with one parent dead, two were orphans, two were from Christian homes, and some were boys with problems. The director was Maurice Leklou, a Kabyle man, and the boys went home frequently. It seemed to be supplying a real need.

Boys in Dormitory, Ft. National

9

There was also at Ft. National a home economics center for girls, run five days a week. There were girls who had been taken out of school by their parents when they were considered nearly ready for marriage. They learned knitting, embroidery, sewing, and cooking. The school was under the direction of an Algerian woman, Therese Tafat.

Therese Tafat & Hugh Johnson

In the afternoon I met with a few of the Christians from the small church group in the chapel at the hostel. Of course, we had to speak through interpreters, since I did not know French. We discussed how one witnesses as a Christian in that non-Christian culture. The feeling expressed by the most vocal Algerians was that outright evangelism, with preaching and Bible teaching, was not the most effective approach. Rather, the greatest witness was through service in the name of Christ.

Then it was on to Il-Maten, where there was a small hospital with remarkable facilities, and one in which I saw some of the most effective Christian witness in that Muslim land. Dr. Ron Dierwechter built the hospital himself, and he, along with his wife, Jewell, a nurse, and other missionaries had trained the Kabyle staff. A Christian Kabyle served as a clerk and a chaplain for the hospital.

Kabyle Woman and Children

Dr.Ron Dierwechter and Patient

The relationship established by the Dierwechters had resulted in intense loyalty to the hospital by the staff. Some of the young men with whom they had worked from the beginning of the hospital were starting to attend the church services, and to sit and talk with them about important questions concerned with the meaning of life.

It was a pleasure to go with Miss Emma Gisler, a veteran Swiss missionary nurse, into the Kabyle village, where she visited in the homes of the women and talked with them. I was able to see them as they worked in their homes, and they gave me permission to take pictures.

Making Couscous

Making Pottery

I thoroughly enjoyed the long ride to Constantine in the company of Erna Huber, one of the Swiss nurses. The countryside was beautiful, through mountain passes, along the plain, sometimes near the shore of the Mediterranean. It reminded me in many ways of the scenery in New Mexico, one of my former homes, except that the group of migrating Bedouins on their camels gave me the assurance that this was Africa.

In Constantine I enjoyed an evening meal with Elsy Wendle, a Swiss missionary under our Board, and Katherine Holenweg, a Swiss kindergarten teacher. Miss Wendle was in charge of a social center in the midst of the Arabic section of Constantine. There were classes for girls, some who had never gone to school, some who attended until they took a qualifying examination and failed. Those who had some education she tutored to help them pass the exam, so that they could continue in school. For those who had no education, there was practical instruction in such things as mending and knitting. There were also games and handcrafts, Girl Scouts, classes in Arabic,

Elsy Wendle With Girls at Social Center

and Sunday School classes for those who wished to attend.

Katherine Holenweg taught kindergarten, which was held in the Girl's Hostel building. She had trained two Algerian women to help her. She was expecting another teacher soon from Switzerland, and it was planned to begin a training course for other teachers. This was in answer to a request from the community, and had the blessing of the government. I enjoyed my stay with Sue Robinson and Liv Larsen (Norwegian,

Statue of Constantine

Gerhard Schreck, Katherine Holenweg, Herta Schreck , Ward Williams

under our Board) at the Girl's Hostel. There were at that time twenty-seven girls, age 6-14 years, and eleven young women who were University students or working. The home was open all year, because several were orphans (nine girls had no other home). There were also three girls who worked in Algiers, and were in the Les Aiglions hostel, who returned to the Constantine home for vacation periods. There was an acute need for additional help in the hostel. Sue Robinson taught English in a school in Constantine (a form of service which was much appreciated), and so could give only part time to the hostel. This left a great deal of responsibility for Liv Larsen. They felt a need for some mature woman who would be willing to work in the hostel. Both Sue and Liv agreed that the younger children should be phased out, and the number of older girls increased. This seemed to meet the more pressing need of that day. Also, older girls would not require as much care as the younger ones.

Ward and Terry Williams were the directors of the Boy's Home in Constantine, where twenty-four boys, ranging in age from eight to boys who were in their last year in secondary school (equivalent to the first year in college in the United States). An assistant was also needed, probably a woman aged 30-50, to work with Terry as a "mother" for the boys. They felt a young man interested in sports would also be helpful. (All these requests for help were shared with the Board.) Ward Williams spent much time in his job as field treasurer, in addition to his work in the hostel. Herta Schreck (German, under the U.S. Board), who also lived in Constantine, helped Elsy Wendle at the social center. Gerhard was the pastor of the small congregation, and was assistant treasurer.

On to Tunis

Cathedral and Statue of St. Augustine

From Constantine I went on to Tunisia by road. I saw shepherds with their sheep, and a man riding on a donkey while a woman (I presumed to be his wife) followed on foot. I felt that I was in Bible lands. (It made me wonder whether Mary rode the donkey and Joseph followed, as is shown in all our pictures. Perhaps because she was pregnant it made a difference.) We passed through Annaba, the site of the Cathedral of St. Augustine and his statue. He was the well-known early Church Father, and author of *City of God*.

In Tunis I spent three interesting days, including a morning spent shopping in the *souks* of Tunis, where one is tempted to become bankrupt buying brass, silver, gold, leather, rugs–a fabulous and exotic array of goods.

I visited with Thorlief and Thelma Teigland (Norwegian) and David and Carol Butler. They were engaged in work in the church, youth center, social center for women and a nursery school.

Thelma Teigland with Sewing Class

Nursery School Children

Boy's Club

Thorlief took me for a visit to Bizerte, where two Swedish women missionaries, under the Swedish Methodist Missionary Society, had a social center. The work in Tunis was part of the North African Conference. Though there are differences between the two countries, both are Muslim lands, which means that Christian witness must be more in actions than in words.

While in Tunis I also saw the remains of the ancient city of Carthage, and the cemetery where many American soldiers killed in the Africa campaign of World War II are buried.

View of Tunis from Montfleury

View of Bizerte from the ferry

The Christian Mission in North Africa

In order to understand the Christian mission in North Africa, one must have some understanding of what it means to be a Christian presence in a Muslim land, in which Christian missionaries are tolerated if they are rendering some service which is needed and desired. Algeria in 1968 was a nation struggling with the results of seven years of revolution: poverty, destruction, dislocation of whole groups of people, tremendous unemployment, lack of all kinds of facilities for the predominantly youthful population. During the French control of Algeria there were several thousand Christians, most of whom were French, or Algerians greatly influenced by the French culture. When the revolution came, most of these, including many Algerians, left the country. The number of Christians in the Methodist Church (as in all others) dropped to a handful. The Roman Catholics, who had extensive land holdings, turned much of it back to the government. One saw throughout Algeria church buildings which had become reading rooms and cultural centers–one was now a mosque. In Constantine the French Reformed and Methodist Christians had formed one church group, in the Methodist Church. It seemed to me unfortunate that we imposed upon this small group the complicated episcopal structure of the Methodist Church. There was real questioning (and disagreement) among the missionaries as to whether one could properly call the North African United Methodist Church a "church" in any real sense (other than as a fellowship of believers). Certainly, it was felt that for many years into the future–perhaps never–could we expect an institutional church which could become self-supporting, and able to carry on the service centers in which we then operated. If we were to maintain a Christian witness in that land, we should be prepared to continue support with both personnel and money for years to come.

North Africa was an interesting field also because of the international composition of our mission staff. As has been noted, there were Europeans still under appointment by our Board. After World War II the European churches could provide staff but little money for mission work. There were now also missionaries appointed by European boards. There was a great deal of difference in the salary scale between those under appointment by the American and European Boards. It was because of the fine character within the missionary community that there was not more discontent due to this problem.

My greatest concern at that time was a financial one. I was convinced that there was something radically wrong with a system that apparently enabled us to give large grants of money for special projects, but which did not allow us to supply work budgets to continue the work once it was started. During the previous years there had been quite a fluctuation in the work funds allowed. I was very reluctant to approve any more special projects which meant an expansion of work, or of new work, unless some of the present work was discontinued. We had been running on a deficit budget, made possible at that time because of field reserves. However, unless we could use some special funds, there would be some very difficult decisions to make–which of the types of work presently being done were least needed?

I was convinced that one of the most effective types of witness in North Africa was that of the "secular" missionary. The Christian Committee for Service in Algeria (CCSA) was an ecumenical organization which was recruiting and placing Christians in government and other institutions. There was a place for teachers in the universities and secondary schools, medical workers, perhaps social workers, and those with other skills. I urged the Board of Missions to investigate the possibilities for such Christian witness.

There had been some thinking and questioning among the missionaries in recent years as to what form witness should take in a Muslim country. Most had reached the conclusion that it was neither effective nor right to use social services as a "bait" (whether intentionally or only apparently so) to get people to attend Bible classes and church services. Except for a few cases, religious classes were separated from other activities, though an invitation was given to those who came to the centers for other purposes. The amount and kind of religious instruction in the hostels varied. In some, the younger children were not allowed to attend church. When they were older, they might, if they wished. However, young people were not actively encouraged to accept baptism and become church members. To become a Christian was a very serious step; it often meant that one was cut off in many ways from one's family and society. Many missionaries were convinced that it was far better to have a decision to become a Christian made

16

by a mature individual who understood just what that decision would mean, rather than by children who would leave the church as soon as they left the hostel.

A number of missionaries were actively involved in ecumenical relations. It was most unfortunate that a number of small sect groups were giving a divided Christian witness to the Muslims.

As I completed my first trip to North Africa, I was impressed with the missionaries, and with their openness to new forms of mission and to rethinking the present structures. Most of all, I was impressed with their joy and dedication in the difficult and challenging task which was theirs. I felt that we could be proud to have a part in helping to provide such a group. I only hoped that we as a Board of Missions could fulfill our responsibility to them in a more adequate way than we seemed to be able to do at that time.

1969 - 1970 – Trouble in Algeria

On Tuesday, December 30, 1969, the following cable, sent from Geneva, was received in my office at 475 Riverside Drive:

"WITHHOLD EVERYTHING FROM NORTH AFRICA SO FAR EXPELLED
LARSONS WERDER TRYNDAL WIESE EPTINGS OTHERS TO FOLLOW."

I immediately talked with Bishop Schaefer in Zurich and his assistant, Bob Gebhart. During three telephone calls I learned of a shocking incident that happened the weekend before. A seminar for university students (and probably some young people who were working but not in school) was held at the youth center in El Biar (Algiers), under the auspices of Lynn and Jeanne Larson and others who assisted them. (Other information was obtained later when we could speak with those involved.)

This was the third seminar to be held, and was received enthusiastically by the Algerian youth. The conference, which was to last from Friday evening until Sunday noon, was conceived, organized, and prepared for by a committee of A 3's and four Algerians, who were Muslim and university students. Two of the latter had previously studied in the United States for a year, and this was later found to be a cause of suspicion by the police. The theme was "Our Generation Between Yesterday and Tomorrow." There were thirty-five youth, including twenty-eight Algerians, five Americans, one Swiss, and one British. Four of these were A 3's from our Board: Lynn and Jeanne Larson, Shelby Tryndal, and Paul Wiese (in language study in Paris–it had been planned to send him to Algeria in February to replace the Larsons. He went to Algiers for Christmas and to attend the youth seminar). Two were from the Swiss Board: Willie and Marcia Epting (he was Swiss; Marcia was Marcia Henry, who went to Algeria as an A 3; they were serving at Il-Maten Hospital).

The folk dancing had finished and the participants were getting ready to go to their dormitories late Saturday night on December 27, 1969, when about ten policemen, most of them in plain clothes, entered the building and grouped the Algerian boys, the Algerian girls, and the foreigners. This was about 12:15 a.m., Sunday morning. The policemen then started collecting papers and books from around the building and piling them by the door. They ordered Lynn Larson to empty a book case of children's library books, and to put the books on the floor in a pile. Then they asked him to show them the films that they had and to thread one in the projector and project it for them. (It was a UNESCO film of children's drawings from around the world.) Then they loaded the last of the young people into the United Methodist mission car (which was never returned) and took them to the police building. The boys and girls were separated; the boys had to remain standing with their faces to the wall for six hours without putting their hands in their pockets. Periodically different ones were taken for questioning. Lynn

18

Larson was questioned extensively, by fifteen or twenty different people, intermittently during the next sixty-two hours.

The girls were taken to a hall on another floor and also were told to stand in a single file and be quiet. There was a policeman with a machine gun at each end of the line. They were taken one by one for questioning. Jeanne Larson and Shelby Trindal, who had helped to plan the conference, were questioned most extensively. The policemen changed off during the night, and depending on their personalities, the girls were allowed to sit on the floor and whisper at times.

The young people (foreigners) were asked questions about the weekend conference, who had planned it (the questioners could not believe that Algerian youth had done much of the planning and made most of the arrangements), the Methodist Church, the employees of The United Methodist Church in Algeria, Christianity, Israel and their attitude toward the Jews and Arabs, Islam, their early childhood and families, political views, their work in Algeria, how they got to know the participants in the conference, and most of all, their purpose for being in Algeria and the purpose of the conference. Each person eventually had to sign a written report of their statement. There were "mistakes" in some which made them more incriminating. Though protests were made, they were not changed.

Although about three of the Algerian youth were struck by the policemen, none of the foreigners was physically mistreated. In fact, the missionaries in writing their reports more than once spoke of the correctness and courtesy (and even apparent sympathy by some) shown them by the police. Only two or three were harsh with them. Most were obviously obeying orders which they themselves did not understand. Some of the prisoners were given coffee to drink in the morning, and some time in the afternoon they were given bread, cheese and oranges to eat, which they paid for themselves.

Several times some of the Americans and Swiss asked to see a representative of their Consulate, but they were always put off. They were never told what the charges were against them.

Sunday, at about 10:00 p.m., they were all transferred (still in separate groups of boys and girls) to the city jail. There they were told to empty their pockets, turn in their watches, belts and shoe laces, and were searched before being locked in prison cells. The boys were in two different cells, about ten in each. They were 9' x 18', with a Turkish toilet installation in one corner, and a two-foot cement raised shelf for sleeping.

Some of the Algerian girls started crying, and one became hysterical, pulled her hair and beat her head against a wall. After this, the girls were given back their things, and taken back to the central police station, where most of them were allowed to get some sleep. Jeanne Larson spent most of that night also being questioned; she tried to get the police chief to understand the purpose of the conference and their work with youth.

During these two days other events of interest were occurring. Susan Pope, who had been in Algeria for only a few weeks, assigned to the Girl's Home in Constantine, was also at the Saturday evening meeting at La Palmeraie. However, at 10:30 p.m. she decided to go to bed. She woke up once during the night and wondered where the others were, but went back to sleep. During the next day she was in the building, and opened the door for the policemen as they went in and out of the Palmeraie searching the building. But, although she was obviously a foreigner, they never asked who she was or questioned her. Finally, she returned to Constantine with the Algerian girls from the home after they were released on Monday.

Paul Brès, born in Algeria, of French nationality, a missionary of our Board, and the District Superintendent, was in Constantine on business. On Sunday afternoon he received a telephone call from Algiers stating that the entire group from the Youth Seminar had disappeared, and that the only seeming possibility was that they had been taken by the police. There were hurried conversations with colleagues in Algiers (Ulrich Schoen, at the Palmeraie, and Hand Hales, an Algerian United Methodist) and Liv Larsen, Sue Robinson and Ward William's wife, Terry, all missionaries in Constantine. Then Paul and Ward Williams, field treasurer and director of the Boy's Home, took a night plane to Algiers to see whether they could help the young people. They contacted several Algerian friends Monday morning, both Christian and Muslim. At noon the Algerian girls were released, and Paul was to go check on the boys while Ward tried again to see the Director of Indoctrination of the party (FLN), whom he had known in Constantine. The police, however, took Paul from La Palmeraie to the Secret Police Headquarters for questioning, while Ward saw the assistant to the National Liberation Front official. He told Paul, in essence, "We are extremely tired and worried. Put yourself in our place. Here are a lot of students and young foreigners together. Perhaps it is a mistake, but it is now under way. I can assure you the young Algerians will be released tonight. I know, because several of their parents have been here. The worst that can happen to the foreigners is that they will be expelled; the best is that nothing will come of it."

Ward went back to La Palmeraie, and the boys were coming in. He made arrangements for them to return to Constantine, and told them that he would be at the train to see them off after he talked to Paul Brés. However, when he entered La Palmeraie, he was detained by the police, and stayed in the Schoens' apartment under house arrest that night, along with the acting director of CCSA, who walked into the same trap. All during this time Paul Brès was being questioned intermittently. The next morning (Tuesday) Ward Williams and two others were taken for questioning. The other two were released quickly, since they did not belong to our organization, but Ward was questioned thoroughly, especially regarding their funds, the source and amount, the Constantine Boy's Home, and our mission structure, including the names of foreign officials who might visit Algeria in a supervisory capacity. Paul and Ward were eventually reunited and spent Tuesday night in a cell together. They were able to buy food once.

There were thirty-five policemen surrounding La Palmeraie during this time. All property had been sealed off. The Schoens, who lived in an apartment there, were asked to leave. In addition to personal effects, the contents of Paul Brès' and Ulrich Schoen's office and the books and materials in the Ecumenical Study Center were confiscated. The Girl's Hostel in Algiers, Les Aiglons, was closed. Four girls who had not gone home for vacation and the Algerian matron went to Villa Elizabeth, where Louise Werder and Sister Ruth Lang (both Swiss, under our Board) were living. Later, Louise's room was sealed off and the clinic closed. Only the section of the house in which Sister Ruth lived was yet in our possession (at the time of my writing this report). The police were carefully listing all property, and assured the missionaries that their personal property would be returned to the owners. In Paul Brès' office were two of Ward William's briefcases. One of them contained the legal papers for the hospital, which he was preparing to sign over to the local government authorities.

On Monday morning Sister Ruth Lang and Louise Werder were taken by the police and questioned. Sister Ruth was then released. (She asked why she was released and Louise was not, and they told her it was because of the religious habit she wore.) She was told to leave within two days. Later, they told her she did not have to leave, as they discovered she was soon leaving for furlough anyway. They did not keep her alien registration card. This allowed her to return at the end of her furlough. Before she left a friend drove her to a place from where she could call the people at Les Ouhadias. All was quiet there, they said, though naturally they were worried and wondered what would happen next. Paul Brès' thirteen-year-old son was with the Griffiths. He was not able to leave the country with his father, but the French consulate later arranged for his delivery to his father in France. (Akila Brès was in a clinic in France and so was not present when the trouble occurred.)

Back to the story of the original detainees, from information we received later: On Monday morning the time was spent by the young people having "mug shots" (individual pictures) and fingerprints taken, and each one was measured (height, finger length, head size, ear size, etc.) Early in the afternoon they were assembled for a group picture, and at that point Louise Werder was brought in. Louise had been extensively questioned, particularly in regard to her activities and whether she had put pressure upon young people to become Christian. The Algerians were then released, and the foreigners put back into their cells. Two policemen offered to get them some bread and cheese if they would give them money. So they ate their second meal in custody–bread, cheese and an orange. Monday evening they were asked one by one "If you are expelled, where do you want to go?" and how much money they had, for they had to buy their own plane tickets. Louise was asked if she would agree to buy tickets for the other two Swiss with the money she had. She agreed, and also said she would buy tickets for the others as well, if the police would allow her to draw money out of her account. They were amazed that she would offer to buy tickets for the Americans. If the government had had to pay for the tickets, they would have been put on a boat on Thursday to Marseilles, but since Louise would pay, they made arrangements for them to leave by air on Tuesday. (One of the younger missionaries, who did not always agree with Louise, said, "I was never so glad to see her as then!") Finally, at about 12:30 p.m. all of them were called in one by one, given the personal belongings they had checked, and their passports, which the police had gone to get for them when they were given directions of where to find them. All seven of them were then escorted to the police truck, and driven to the airport, accompanied by several men in plain clothes. There they waited in a security police room and their belongings were searched. They allowed Willi to take out a wallet and a briefcase. (This included a camera, with photos he had taken at the conference! We later saw the slides when we all met together.) They were then undressed and searched, and finally, at 2:00 p.m., they were escorted to the field and into the Swiss Air jet bound for Geneva. The young people had been held in custody for a total of sixty-two hours.

While they were waiting to be put on the plane, Elsy Wendle, the Swiss missionary in Constantine under out Board, returned from her Christmas vacation in Switzerland. She thought they had all come to meet her, and began to go up to greet them. Louise Werder spoke to her in German, and said, "Don't come here. You would have been better off to have stayed where you were. If you talk to us, you will be in trouble too." She walked away, but was followed by a policeman. After she had gone through customs and was on the bus, the police took her off

21

and questioned her. They then said she could go She went to La Palmeraie and asked for Paul Brès, because she needed to get money to go on to Constantine. They told her he was no longer there. Finally, they offered to take her to him. A policeman took her to the prison, but she was not allowed to see Paul. Eventually, the police bought her a third class ticket for the train to Constantine. Elsy worked under the direction of the head of the Party in Constantine, teaching girls who were deaf. When he heard of the troubles our groups were having, he came to Elsy and offered to protest. She told him that she appreciated it, but did not want him to get into trouble for their sake.

When the seven who were deported reached Geneva, Willi Epting was able to call his uncle in a bank in Basel, who made it possible for him to get some money. He then sent me the cable, and called the Bishop in Zurich. All six of the young people went to Willi's home in Basel, and lived together in a small apartment for several days. The Eptings made them feel very much at home, and one had the feeling of being in a close community. (I stayed a day and a half with the six of them in Basil.)

Paul Brès and Ward Williams were deported on Wednesday. Paul asked about his little girl, and the police made arrangements for her to accompany him. Because they did not have enough money to go to Switzerland, Paul and Ward went to Lyons, France. There they had a great deal of trouble on New Year's Eve, because they had no money and could get none. Finally, they were given a meal at the Salvation Army, and a taxi driver offered to drive them to Zurich if they could guarantee he would be paid when they arrived there. They arrived at about 9:00 p.m. that evening, and were made welcome at the Methodist Hotel.

After a number of coded messages sent through the American Consulate, Terry Williams arrived in Zurich with their three children on Thursday, January 8, 1970, along with a Swiss kindergarten teacher doing a year of voluntary service at the Girl's Home Kindergarten. She brought news of the uncertainty of the past ten days, as well as the solidarity of Constantine missionaries, other Christians, and Muslim friends, their children's friends, and the American Consul in Constantine. She was able to have all the necessary papers to leave very quickly, and had the impression there was a special effort made to help her and the children. She even received a return visa, with no difficulty. An official investigation of the mission was underway in Constantine, but they knew of only two young people who had been called in by the police. Both had been treated well. One was the son of the Girl's Home cook and a member of our Constantine youth club, and the other was one of the girls who was arrested in Algiers, and who had two brothers in the Home. Both were asked concerning political activity of the missionaries, and both insisted there was none. The police official questioning the young man said, "You mean those people at the Girl's Home are those 'Methodists'? They have my child in their kindergarten, and I know they are doing good work." The veiled, illiterate mother of the young woman went with her and told the police: "They feed, clothe, and send our children to school. Do you know anyone else who will do this?"

Later I was able to report to the Board staff that arrangements had been made for the operation of the Boy's Home for the next few months, with Gerhard Schreck giving some supervision. Gerhard was the assistant treasurer, and was thus able to sign checks, and he had the power of attorney. He was able to check money out of the bank twice (I heard) and was not

22

stopped. We were encouraged to know that payment had not been stopped from our mission accounts.

Police went up to Il-Maten and questioned the Canadian Mennonite couple there. Only Emmy Gisler (Swiss) was left at Il-Maten, along with the couple. The hospital was closed, but the reduced staff had been doing only a minimum of work since Dr. Dierwechter left the middle of December. The Swiss nurse then returned home and brought all of Willi and Marcia Epting's things with her. There were a Mennonite couple, a doctor and a nurse, in language training in France, who had been seconded to us for service at Il-Matin Hospital. At the time I did not know whether they would be admitted in March and the hospital reopened, under Government auspices.

In the midst of this trouble, Laura Chevrin, French, of our Board, retired and left the country after forty years of service. She wrote from France to give the most recent news of Il-Maten. At that time all was quiet at Ft. National, although they expected that there would be an investigation.

Three Algerian Christians (two from our church), two in important government positions, signed a formal protest to the government. This was a courageous act, because their jobs could be in jeopardy. The Roman Catholic Archbishop and the head of the French Reformed Church also made formal protests. The head of the CCSA in Geneva sent the head of the Algerian CCSA, on study leave in France, to Algeria to investigate the situation. He hoped there would be limited publicity, to allow for negotiation with the sensitive Algerians. The American Consul in Switzerland also said that they felt it best not to make an investigation just then. They would make inquiries about the private property of the Americans who were expelled. They, too, hoped there would not be too much publicity.

We heard from two or three sources that the police acted without authority from the government in expelling the missionaries. It seemed doubtful that there would ever be a formal acknowledgment of the error, but it was hoped that Ward Williams, Paul Brès, and Louise Werder would eventually be "forgiven" and readmitted, if there was not too much publicity adverse to the Algerians. (None of those expelled was able to return to Algeria, however; some were assigned to other countries.)

I flew to Zurich on January 1. On January 2 the nine expelled missionaries, Bishop Schaefer, Bob Gebhart, and I had a long consultation. On Monday I traveled to Basel, and had private consultations with each missionary as to their future. On Wednesday, Thursday and Friday, there were more consultations in Zurich, before my return to New York on Friday. I was glad for the opportunity to be there to talk with the "refugees" and to wait together for further news. I was proud of the way in which our missionaries had remained calm during their imprisonment and interrogation and had been drawn closer together. While the two groups (the older and the younger missionaries) had come through the experience with conclusions not much different from their former attitudes about the form our mission should take, I believed there was more understanding among them.

Arrangements were made for furloughs, or transfer to other countries. Emergency funds were given for purchase of necessary clothing, since they arrived in winter in Switzerland with nothing except what they had worn for five days, and not equipped for a Swiss winter.

Exactly half of our missionary force had left Algeria for one reason or another during the period of three weeks. This left only five families in North Africa, two of whom were in Tunis.

Almost all property in Algiers was taken by the police. The Girl's Hostel at Les Aiglons was closed, as was the Ecumenical Study Center, the dispensary, the sewing school, which was to have been reopened in January, the headquarters office, and, of course, the youth center. Il-Maten Hospital was closed. The Constantine Girl's Home and Elsy Wendle's program continued as usual. Gerhard Schreck stopped the youth activities at his center. The Boy's Home continued under obstacles. The Kindergarten and teacher's training program would be able to continue as usual if the kindergarten teacher who was in Switzerland for Christmas vacation returned. Ft. National and Les Ouadhias remained calm. (Oran was closed the August before when the Lehtos had to be withdrawn for medical reasons.) Our mission accounts had not been closed, and we soon began to send small amounts of money at a time to North Africa.

In the months that followed an evaluation of our mission in Algeria continued. The questioning emphasized two aspects: the accusation of proselytizing and of subversive political activity. Particularly in recent years most of our missionaries in North Africa had made the decision that they should put no pressure of any kind on Muslims to become Christians, particularly upon children and youth in our Homes. Attendance at Bible classes and all other activities was voluntary. Although they accused the missionaries of trying to force people to become Christian, the Algerians could understand our distinctly religious activities better than they could those of the younger missionaries who were working with youth. The terminology used by the youth, who avoided the traditional religious vocabulary, was simply not understood and was interpreted as being political by the Algerians. They said themselves that they could not believe that anyone would do anything without desire for some gain for themselves. Presumably, if it had been said that they wanted converts, they would have understood that. But since this was denied, they concluded that the attempt was being made to influence the youth to resist their government. The irony was that the youth who directed the youth program were in sympathy with the socialist government, and more nationalistic than some of the university youth themselves. But for that socialist government the education and training of children and youth was a sensitive point. It was believed that the government should control all such education. They also saw some of the outstanding youth of the country become interested in the program, much more so than in the meetings of the Party. Apparently the mission should have asked for a permit to hold such youth meetings, even though Lynn Larson had been given a work permit for just such activities. One reason given for the raid was that it was after midnight and that was illegal. (Two of the plain clothes men who were at the police station doing some of the questioning had taken part in youth activities at La Palmeraie; it became evident that their activities had been watched for some time.) The Algerians looked at such activities from a completely different frame of reference than we. Also, they had quite a different view of youth, and could not understand why the younger missionaries (of whom two were twenty-six and twenty-seven respectively) were allowed to carry on such activities without supervision. It seemed quite obvious that we dared not engage in such youth activities again under those circumstances.

This experience surely pointed to the absolute necessity of thoroughly understanding a culture, which includes the political system, before we could decide how the Christian faith could best be communicated in relevant terms. What also had to be faced was that no matter how much an American might criticize his own government, he is still judged as an American when in a foreign country.

One or two of the younger missionaries wondered whether there was any way Christians could any longer serve in Algeria as missionaries. They felt that the only legitimate way would be to enter into those programs already being carried out by the State and try to help to improve them. They admitted That would be difficult and in some cases impossible for Americans. On the other hand, missionaries who had been in Algeria longer, knew the respect which the Christian religion had because Christians had expressed their faith in service and felt that their service to people through their institutions was their service to God. They felt that our mission should continue only in service programs and in distinctly religious activities within the churches, as freedom of worship was allowed according to the constitution of the State.

I felt a real concern as to how we could help the small North African church broaden their view of the meaning of the church and the Christian faith. Some felt that if the Christian institutions were closed, the church would be dead; some felt that Christians should not involve themselves in politics at all. What would have happened if all missionaries had been forced to leave, and all institutions closed? Had we helped to create a core of committed Christians who had a firm grounding in the meaning of the faith, so that the Christian fellowship would not die? If not, how could this be done in the months ahead, if indeed we were given the time in which to serve?

My missionary friends who had been interrogated by the Algerians advised that I should not visit Algeria soon, since they had to give my name as one of the persons who supervised their work. Therefore, I was not able to go to Algeria in 1970. I deeply regretted this, because I knew that the missionaries needed to know that they had support. One even wrote a letter saying that they couldn't understand why I had not come. I was able to get word to them of the reason I felt I should not go to Algeria at that time.

However, Dr. Juel Nordby (the secretary for Central and Southern Africa and a Norwegian citizen and therefore able to visit Algeria) was able to visit his sister-in-law (Liv Larsen) in Constantine. He met with all the missionaries and visited the centers which were still open. On February 21 John Schaefer (head of the World Division) and I arrived in Tunis. Bishop Schaefer, and Juel Nordby, Hugh Johnson, Liv Larsen and Sue Robinson arrived from Algeria the next day. For the next days we were able to have consultation with our missionaries from Algeria and Tunisia. Of particular concern to us were the future of C.C.E.M. (The Ecumenical Study Center to which Marston Speight was to return in June), the hospital at Il-Maten, and the future of the whole work in Algeria. I was also privileged to attend a meeting of representatives of ecumenical organizations working in the Maghreb (Morocco, Algeria and Tunisia). All were making contributions to a Christian witness in that area of the Muslim world.

In addition to discussing a number of practical matters, the whole question of the local churches as institutions was raised. Should we continue as before with the same forms of worship services at the same time each week? Or should we experiment with new forms, both in the church buildings and in individual homes? We came to the conclusion that cooperation between different churches and mission groups existed in practical situations, but there was little progress toward organizational unity. Although we realized that our goal was the establishment of a united Algerian church, we did not see the utility of uniting a few churches that were essentially foreign. There was also the problem that most North African Christians were either in conservative groups largely opposed to the ecumenical movement, or in the Methodist Church. So we concluded that we must utilize the existing context, while still keeping a very open stance, and seek functional unity.

We wanted to keep a church that would be open to all, and we hoped that an authentically North African church would be formed one day. However, we looked upon the immediate future of the church as maintaining of the Christian presence and witness. It seemed that it would not be good to abandon our forms of Methodist organization, at least at that time, but we should use them with flexibility and adapt them to the actual situation.

In Algeria the government officially recognized four "religions": Islam, which was the religion of the state; the Catholic Church; Protestantism through the Reformed Church; and Judaism. In some cases we would have to be spoken for and represented by the moderator of the Reformed Church. We were grateful for his willingness to do so. We wanted to continue and increase cooperation with such ecumenical organizations as the CCSA (Christian Committee for Service in Algeria) and CCEM (the ecumenical study center).

On February 26 I was able to write a letter to the missionaries who had been forced to leave Algeria so abruptly and give them up-to-date information. I reported on our meeting in Tunis, and then outlined some of the recent developments regarding our work and the situation in Algeria, as follows:

1. Recently other groups have had trouble with the State because of their involvement with youth. This was true of a fanatical Muslim group as well as a Roman Catholic priest, who was imprisoned and expelled. Articles in the papers state that only the state is to be involved in the education of children and youth.

2. At the same time our missionaries were in prison (and the week before) an Algerian Christian who had been studying in a Bible School in Beirut was imprisoned, interrogated, and treated roughly (questioned with a gun held at his head part of the time). He had been notified in Lebanon previously that the Government wanted him to come home for discussion with them, and they would pay his way. He did not go at that time, but went on his own over the Christmas holiday. They tried to force him to renounce his Christian faith. He has been released, but it is believed his passport has been taken away.

3. Shortly after the expulsion Liv and Sue had to go to the police to renew their residence permits. The police took the opportunity to question them, particularly about what they taught the girls in the hostel. Liv was told that it is against the law to teach the Bible to children and youth. Otherwise, they have not been questioned, although it is obvious that the police have been ordered to investigate all United Methodist work. The two girls at the home who had been imprisoned and the son of the cook at the hostel were questioned earlier. Otherwise, work has continued as usual in Constantine. Gerhard Schreck and his wife have moved to the Boy's Hostel to take charge. We are asking that Liv Larsen be appointed assistant treasurer in order to assist Gerhard and to have more than one person able to sign checks and other papers.

4. At Les Ouadhias Gerta Thomas (nurse-midwife) and Eric (Griffith's thirteen-year-old son) were called in for questioning by the police. Because Eric looks older than he is, and had long hair, they asked him if he was a hippie and whether he took drugs. (He has since cut his hair.) Work is continuing as usual. Lester has stopped his Bible classes with youth. Sour Helene Manz continues hers.

5. At Fort National several people who had formerly worked at the mission were questioned by the secret police. Some had been discharged for various reasons, and told lies about the mission. The Johnson gardener was called in for questioning twice, and was beaten because he kept saying he did not know anything about what happened at the hostel. Finally they told him to steal some books from the library and he did so. They have there only books bought locally, so there was nothing they could find wrong. They beat the gardener again because they thought he was thus ridiculing them. Finally, he went to Hugh and asked to leave the job, and told him what had happened. Hugh went to the head of the party and two officials and complained. They reprimanded the secret police and told them they were not to bother the Methodist missionaries.

6. Il-Maten – The authorities came and took careful inventory, then locked the buildings. They asked the missionaries to name two staff people as guards and turned the keys over to them. Emmy Gisler continues the dispensary work and has many patients coming to her (the authorities gave her permission to do that). The Jesskes remain until we find out what will happen to the hospital.

The test for the hospital will come when Dr. Lopez arrives the middle of March. If the Government accepts him, but says he must be stationed somewhere else, then the hospital will remain closed until such time as the Government might decide to use it for some purpose. If they approve his going there, it means the hospital will open even though papers may not yet be signed. A Norwegian surgical nurse is studying French in preparation for Il-Maten if it opens. The Swiss Board halted any attempt to recruit staff until we know whether we can open the hospital as planned. It is doubtful that papers will be signed to turn over the hospital until when or if the legal status of the Methodist Church is determined. If the hospital remains closed, our concern is whether we can keep some kind of Christian presence there, and what form it can or should take. It seems unwise to leave Emmy Gisler there alone, even though she says she wants to stay.

7. Algiers – Juel Nordby saw the sewing school has been opened. Apparently the young woman who was to have been Louise's assistant is in charge. The Swiss Consul is optimistic that before long Louise will be allowed or even asked to return.

Madame Bouattou is still living in Villa Elizabeth with four girls from the hostel. Places have been found for the others elsewhere.

They have not yet been able to convince the authorities that the study center is distinct from the Methodist Church. I finally was able to get official authorization to Lester Griffith and the American Consul for Lester to receive the personal belongings held at La Palmeraie and Villa Elizabeth, since we had been told the police were ready to release them. However, Lester, accompanied by a representative of the French Embassy, was beginning to pack Paul Brès' belongings when the operation was halted by a higher authority. He was told he was to make a request by letter to the Minister of Interior to get authority to evacuate the goods. On February 23 he was still waiting for telephone calls from either the American or French authorities in Algiers to go and start the operation.

The Swiss Consul is optimistic–for some reason he thinks the police are about finished with their investigation and by next week all the property will be given back to us. Thus, they do not want to give part of it back now. If La Palmeraie is given back, some feel it will be only because there is a church on the property. Others are much more pessimistic about our ever getting it back.

So, I am sorry, but you will have to wait for your personal belongings. Bishop Schaefer has written the Minister of the Interior to ask for an interview with him. He had hoped to go last week before we met in Tunis, but the Minister sent word through Lester and Sue that he was still looking over the situation and would inform the Bishop when he was ready to receive him. Many feel that the whole matter of the property and the future of the United Methodist mission work hinges upon that interview.

Tony Ennis says that the authorities are getting a real introduction to church history through this investigation. They are discovering for the first time the complexity of the various churches, and are quite bewildered.

I believe that these are the essential points. We still live in uncertainty of what the final outcome will be, but in faith that God will continue to guide us if we remain open to His will.

I will try to keep you informed of developments.

In the following months we heard reports of further developments in Algeria. On March 12 it was reported that the property in Algiers, La Palmeraie, had been confiscated by the police. The personal effects of the persons who had lived there had been packed by the government and transported to another part of the city. None had yet been returned to us. Some work was in progress to renovate the buildings. Les Aiglons property was being used for a sewing school under the direction of the city. Louise Werder's belongings were evacuated from the villa, and were under the care of the Swiss embassy.

There seemed to be a real possibility of reopening the hospital. Both Hugh Johnson and Emmy Gisler were told that the hospital was to become a branch of a nearby government hospital, and that between them there would be three doctors. We hoped that Dr. Alberto Lopez, who had been seconded to our Board by the Mennonites, would be allowed to go to Il-Maten, as we had planned. His wife was a nurse. A Norwegian surgical nurse was nearing completion of language study in France, and was to have gone to Il-Maten. We were still waiting, however, to hear whether the hospital was open, and our staff allowed to work.

An effort had been made to procure an audience with the Wali (Governor) of Algiers for Bishop Schaefer. He was told what when the investigation was complete he would be informed of when he could speak with him. On March 26 Sue Robinson, as president of the executive committee of The United Methodist Church in Algeria, and Rev. Gerhard Schreck, treasurer, addressed a letter to the President of the Republic in order to get some type of audience with a responsible person in the Algerian government. Then on April 3 Lester Griffith was received by the First Secretary of the Minister of the Interior, and was very encouraged by his conversation with him. The Secretary said that the Minister planned to receive Bishop Schaefer as soon as he could schedule it. He also said that they had nothing against the Methodists or the Methodist Church. He said that, unfortunately, some individuals among our personnel had acted in such a way as to arouse suspicion and had therefore caused the actions that were taken against us. Lester definitely had the feeling that we were now regarded rather favorably and would be allowed to carry on our work. He also felt that there might be some possibility that the older missionaries would be allowed to return. Sue Robinson reported that they all felt much more relaxed and reassured after this news.

Bishop Schaefer was finally able to meet with the Wali (Governor) of Algiers. He said that the Governor told him that they admired the Methodists because they sent well-qualified people and were working to help the Algerians. He also said that he wanted people of faith, because they really cared about people. But he said, "You are to leave our women and young people alone, and not attempt to make them become Christians." The Bishop asked, "What if they decide on their own to become Christian?" The Governor answered, "Then that is their problem, not yours." [He apparently did not say anything about the men, but expected them to be able to resist any Christian teaching.][5]

It was decided that Marston and Elizabeth Speight would be assigned to Tunis rather than Algiers. He would work out a program of study and research, hopefully with at least some cooperation with the White Fathers. He would stop in Geneva to explore ways in which we could be involved ecumenically in such a study program. Marston would receive his PhD in Islamics from Hartford Seminary Foundation (in Hartford, Connecticut) on May 27, and they planned to leave for Tunisia about June 1.

April 10. In a report written to members of the Africa Area Committee on April 10, I wrote the following:

"For some months there has been concern about the status of the hospital at Il-Maten. There have been talks with various officials about turning it over, to either the Red Crescent (Muslim equivalent of the Red Cross) or the government. Last year, it did not seem possible for either of these things to happen, and have the hospital continue.

"Just recently I have received word that the government told the hospital that all service must be free of charge as of **March 14**. Since they did not offer to pay for these services with government funds, it is obvious that under such conditions the hospital cannot long function. Negotiations are in process either to turn the hospital over to the government, or to remain a private hospital supervised by the Department of Health. The general feeling is that the hospital will sooner or later be taken over by the government. We need to foresee the possibility that our only role there may be one of providing key members of the medical staff working in cooperation with the Algerian government. This would not be easy, but it would give an

---

[5]Hugh Johnson states that the Wali was seeking Methodist help in a program of rehabilitation of handicapped children. The Bishop also met with the Secretary General of the Wilaya, and the leadership of the Algerian Red Cresicent. The Wali expressed the opinion that we should cease to request the return of personal belongings or mission property. The question was "too sensitive."

opportunity for Christian personnel to witness through their lives and words. The Committee on Coordination has recommended to the Board that we offer the hospital free of any compensation if and when the government takes it.

"Sue Robinson, correspondent, writes:

> *I would like to make it clear that the hospital may be nationalized (and, indeed, it seems quite probable that it will be) [but] this does not mean that our work there has suddenly fallen in disfavor with the government. We just happen to be put in the same bag with the other private hospitals in the country. Those three other hospitals have presented the Ministry of Health with certain problems. It seems likely that the Ministry will decide to solve the problems by taking over the hospitals. They have decided that since we fall into the same category, although the personnel at our hospital have made no complaints, our fate will be linked to that of the other three. From an administrative point of view, their decision is understandable, although it seems illogical to many of us that they would want to take over a private hospital that is running well and rendering great service when they haven't enough personnel and funds to meet all their present medical needs."*

April 24. Word was received, in a letter written April 17, that it was expected that within eight to ten days the paper would be signed with the Government to turn Il-Maten Hospital over to them. It was expected that the agreement would be that we would furnish a doctor, medical technologist, and nurses, and would make occasional gifts of equipment and drugs. The Minister of Health had ordered that the agreement be signed as soon as possible. It seemed clear that Dr. Lopez would be allowed to work there. The Norwegian nurse arrived in Algeria on April 18 and was waiting for official recognition and assignment to the hospital. The new director of the hospital was eager for one of the nurses to be a midwife. Hugh Johnson told him that a Swiss nurse had been refused a visa. The director said that if we had a Swiss nurse-midwife he would see that she obtained a visa.

Sue Robinson wrote:

> *We are indeed grateful to God for the doors that seem to be opening at Il-Maten and pray that our personnel will be strengthened to make a faithful and shining witness there. . . . We are all well and in good spirits here in Constantine. We only hope that we and the Church as a whole will not be found lacking in the new forms of witness and service that seem to be opening up. My very best wishes to all of you.*

On **November 4** I received a phone call from David Butler who was in Constantine. He informed me that Liv Larsen and Gerhard Schreck had been ordered to leave Algeria within fifteen days. He also said that missionaries in Algeria were wondering whether this was not the time that we should close or turn over the work in as "graceful" a way as possible, and for all missionaries to leave. I of course consulted with the staff members under whom I worked. We all agreed that we should give the freedom of decision making in the situation to our missionaries in North Africa, if possible in consultation with Bishop Schaefer. I then talked by phone (November 5) with Bishop Schaefer, who had just returned to Zurich from the U.S. He agreed that all preparation should be made for turning over property and funds, but felt that no hasty decision should be made to leave. He, of course, needed to consult with the Swiss and Norwegian Boards, since their missionaries were working along with ours in institutions of the World Division. Anything we would do would affect them. He said he would try to get a visa to visit Algeria. I then sent the following cable to David Butler:

> STAFF SUPPORTS DECISIONS NECESSARY BY YOU. HOPE
> CONSULTATION WITH BISHOP WILL BE POSSIBLE.

I then wrote a discreet letter expressing our support. I also called the Mennonite Central Committee, who had seconded the doctor and his wife, a nurse, to work in Il-Maten. Whether they and the Norwegian nurse would stay on to work under government structures was a decision they would have to make.

I summarized for the World Division staff problems of concern in the situation as follows:

1. The safety of our missionaries (twelve missionaries of the World Division plus about eight from other Boards.)
2. Property of the World and Women's Division (also personal property of all missionaries, including that of those expelled.)
3. Funds, which could not be taken out of the country. Unfortunately, rather large reserves had been allowed to accumulate.
4. Relationships with the small Christian community.
5. Deployment of missionaries after they left Algeria.

On **December 4** I reported good news from Algeria: The expulsion order had been revoked. Liv Larsen and Gerhard Schreck and his family had not yet been given residence cards, but it was possible they would be able to remain in Algeria at least until the end of July.

Bishop Schaefer was able to go to Algeria, and was present for discussions with members of the liaison committee.

Rent contracts had been signed with the Red Crescent for the Girl's and Boy's Homes in Constantine. The transfer had begun; accounts were turned over as of November 18. Liv Larsen and David Butler were still in charge of the homes, but were now considered "technical advisors" to the Red Crescent. The plan was for the Red Crescent to find Algerian directors for the two homes before the end of June 1971. They would be able to work with those people and gradually turn things over to them. [Liv and Sue had just completed turning over the Girl's Home when police arrived at the door to take it over!]

We agreed to continue to furnish the budgets for the homes through July 31, 1971, and to try to second certain personnel to the Red Crescent. They were particularly interested in having Ruth Welti and Katherine Holenweg (Swiss missionaries) continue as teachers in the kindergarten training programs at least through the school year 1971-1972. This action and other influences had prevented the take-over of the buildings by the secret police. It very nearly happened three weeks previously.

It was felt that we should aim at fulfilling our contract at Il-Maten for five years. This meant we would need to look for personnel; a medical technologist was needed soon. We expected to have a nurse by October of 1971, and a doctor to replace Dr. Lopez by March of 1972.

We decided that the Boy's Home at Ft. National and also the home economics courses for girls should be turned over to some Algerian organization, but there would be time to study the possibilities. We hoped that an arrangement could be made for the Algerian nationals who were in charge of these institutions to continue in their jobs.

Hopefully a more official connection could be worked out for the maternity clinic at Les Ouadhias. However, it was felt that it could probably continue in the present status for some time. It was certainly accepted by the authorities.

We wanted to continue our support of the ecumenical literacy program in the Casbah in Algiers as long as it existed.

There were some missionaries who it was hoped could be able to remain and work in Algerian institutions. There was Elsy Wendle at the School for the Deaf, Ruth Lang as a public health nurse, and Sue Robinson at the University. It was felt that we needed some pastors as long as we had personnel there. Even they might eventually have part-time jobs in Algerian institutions. Hugh Johnson, for example, was already teaching seven hours a week in a Catholic school.

The proposed consultation for our mission to Islam would be held in March of 1971 as planned.

And so we continued, with faith and hope!

A Kabyle Village, Algeria

On the road to Constantine– Esther Megill and camels

33

1971
Back to Algeria; Zurich Consultation

Missionaries and national Christians in Algeria had lived through uncertain times since the expulsion of nine United Methodist missionaries in December of 1969. By March of 1971, however, there was a totally different situation. As a result of dialogue between Bishop Franz Schaefer and a missionary representative and high officials in the Algerian government, there was now a better understanding and doors were opening in a remarkable way for service in Algeria.

I was able to make a field visit to Algeria for the first time since 1968 in March before the consultation. I did not go on to Tunisia as originally planned since it seemed important to have more time in Algeria, and I had been in Tunisia the previous year. Also, the two men from Tunis would be at the consultation.

Constantine: One of the creative programs which was begun by the initiative of a missionary even before it became evident that we should work through government structures was the work of Elsy Wendle. It was estimated that there were six thousand deaf persons in the Constantine district, and two thousand in the city itself. Because of the interest of a small group of Algerians, one of them himself being deaf, a beginning had been made in trying to minister to this group of persons. They recognized their lack of experience and training, as well as resources, and were eager for contacts which would enable them to do the work which they themselves had conceived and were struggling to do. The official party of Algeria, the FLN, helped to get the group recognized as an organization, but said they could not be part of the party because they were not political. Thus, they were sponsored by the Health and Social Affairs Department of the government, although they received no financial support from them. The party had given them a building to use, but it needed to be completed in a way useful for their purposes. In 1971 they sponsored a primary school with one hundred sixty students, ages six to twelve. The only teacher was a young woman who had only six years of primary school education, but was doing what she could with very limited background and facilities because she had a deaf sister. The school was divided into two groups. One met from 8-10 and 1-3, the other from 10-12 and 3-5 (with the same

Student at School for Deaf

34

teacher!) The parents paid about $2.00 per month in tuition, and the Red Crescent and some merchants gave a few books and supplies. These, and the very inadequate buildings supplied by the Party and the unfinished building it had offered them, were the available resources. They attempted with other volunteer help to have some sports activities, and drama. There was also a section for young women, who were taught sewing and knitting, so that so that they could make products to sell. Elsy Wendle was teaching in that school, and we supplied some

Committee for School for Deaf

budget. Forty-five women were on the list as possibilities but only seven were then attending.

The three members of the Board for the school met with me. They expressed eagerness for contacts with the Association for the Deaf in America. They would like a chance to get teaching materials and information to help them. They were eager to get training for some teachers. There was a real need, for example, for someone to learn lip reading and the methods for teaching it. I suggested that we might be able to give scholarship help for such a purpose. (This would definitely not be listed as a U.S. grant to a specific person, nor as a Crusade Scholarship, the United Methodist program which usually provided scholarships for persons to study in the U.S. or elsewhere. The word "Crusade" even to this day recalls for the North Africans the "Christian" Crusades which wrought havoc and killed so many Muslims in North Africa in the eleventh to sixteenth centuries.) I promised to explore possibilities for training in France, and to respond

to a request for help if it came through the Liaison Committee. I also recommended a one-time grant, if it was possible.

The Girl's and Boy's Hostels in Constantine were now officially under the auspices of the Red Crescent and I later made a formal request to the Board to allow the ceding of the property when the legal entanglements could be worked out in Algeria. We continued the budget for both institutions for that year only. I met the Executive Secretary of the Constantine Red Crescent, who was also Vice President of the National Society, at an informal evening in the home of Sue Robinson and Liv Larsen. He

Kindergarten Children Enjoy Painting

said that the Girl's Hostel might not be continued after that year (1971) since it was difficult to ask for a budget because many were on scholarship (the young women were students at the University or the school for Kindergarten teachers; a few were working). It would be easier to get a budget for the Boy's Hostel (Algeria was a Muslim country!) The Girl's Hostel might be used for a clinic for the treatment of persons crippled by polio, or perhaps as "polyclinic," since this would not require a budget from the Red Crescent, and yet would meet a great need. He also indicated that the Kindergarten teacher's course would continue. The school was housed in the Girl's Hostel, staffed by missionaries of the Swiss Board, and we contributed something to the recurring budget. However, he indicated that they might not continue the Kindergarten itself.

There was a problem in that we might have to pay a large tax in order to give the property to the Red Crescent. The Secretary felt that when the transfer papers were submitted again (the originals were lost in the office!), he would probably be able to find a way not to pay the taxes. We made it plain that we did not think the Board of Missions would look with favor upon having to pay thousands of dollars in order to give property away.

I expressed my appreciation for his friendliness and support during the difficulties which our missionaries had experienced during the past months, and he expressed hope for continued cooperation for many years to come.

I visited the Kindergarten in the Girl's Home, and the young woman now in charge of the hostel. We had a pleasant time sharing orange juice and Arab pastry. I thought the oranges in Algeria were the best I had ever tasted.

I could write a great deal about a development project of the Algerian government which I visited. It was directed by a Frenchman, M. Jean Carbonare, a committed Christian. He was held in great esteem by the government, and he was one of those who was instrumental in securing the cancellation of deportation orders for Liv and Gerhardt. The project was one of the most exciting development projects I had seen or of which I had heard, and it began with the contribution of church groups, the United Methodist Committee on Relief among them, to a reforestation program. Hans Aurbakken, formerly a missionary in Algeria and at that time a staff member at the Board, had helped develop the early stages of the program.

Tree Nursery–Jean Carbonare

Reforestation

Jean Carbonare with bee hive

They were establishing model villages into which many persons who had moved into the cities were settling; thousands of men were trained in needed skills; and there was experimental agriculture. In the past five years they had received $20,00 and produced $25,000. In addition, they had formulated the whole process, a process in which mistakes were naturally made as they tried new concepts, and had trained many workmen, the value of which would become more profitable later. At one time during our tour Mr. Carbonare said that they had put responsibility on people to the limit of their ability, and sometimes beyond, but that he believed that they must if they were to assist in the development of the nation.

He took me to see the bee hives they were developing, and also the reforestation project. He said, with enthusiasm, as we looked at the small trees just beginning to grow, "We can find insects on the plants now; and when there are insects, birds will come. Life is coming back to the desert."

Ft. National. I was able to have a conference with the Algerian director of the Boy's Home and the woman in charge of the sewing classes for girls. They, along with the few other Algerian Christians, felt that they had been deserted by the Board (which represented the church for them) because of the reduction of income, and our support of turning over property to national organizations. Any change in the institutions of course was a threat to their own positions, and it was a natural reaction. Unfortunately, the time had come that both the circumstances themselves and the concern that we had to meet the challenges to be in mission in the present day in North Africa meant that some radical changes had to be made to our programs.

Les Ouadhias. The government health services wanted us to continue our operation of the maternity clinic, under their auspices, but we were to keep and maintain the property and supply staff. They would eventually supply the recurring budget. However, to fit their policy (the only one within the capabilities of the resources of the government at that time), not to admit maternity patients. They came for delivery, remained a few hours, and then were taken to their homes. Sister Ruth Lang, who had just returned after a medical furlough because of hepatitis, had a baby clinic and dispensary for children as part of her public health work. She had begun the process of being officially recognized as part of the government health program before her illness. There was need for a couple to

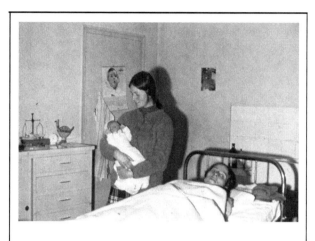

Elizabeth Whittlinger Nurse-Midwife with New Born

*Sr. Ruth Lang,
Public Health*

be stationed there with the single women nurses. We were seeking the right persons, who could teach in the local schools as well as give guidance to the small Christian community.

Algiers. Liv Larsen, who accompanied me as my private interpreter and companion, also went with me to Algiers, where it was hoped that I could meet with two or three Algerian Christians. I did meet Si Hassan Kabaili, but was unable to meet others, although it had been thought that such arrangements had been made. Si Hassan Kebaili was the lay leader of the small Christian community which met for worship at the center of the Casbah, since the church was taken over at La Palmarie. He was in charge of the center for adult education, which we supported along with other churches and groups. There were nearly one hundred adults (men) in the school, held mostly at night, who were being prepared at varying levels for the examinations, based on the French system. This was enabling young men who no longer had the possibility of continuing in a regular school to go further in their education. Si Hassan took us on an interesting tour of the Casbah, but it was not possible to talk with him about our concerns for the church and our work. Neither he nor Maurice Leklou, director of the Boy's Home at Ft. National, were able to obtain the necessary papers to attend the consultation, as had been hoped. If they had been there, the

38

discussions would have taken quite a different turn, for they would have spoken passionately against much of what was raised by the group there.

I talked with missionaries in each place, the largest group of whom were those who met for an evening in Constantine. I came away with a renewed and deep appreciation for our missionaries, who had lived through a very difficult fifteen months. They had made a real witness to the Muslim community by the way they had reacted to the strain and stress. A government official told one of them that he marveled at the way in which our missionaries had reacted to the crisis; most people would have gone home long ago. They recognized that a religious commitment makes a difference in persons, and had asked for more people with the commitment and moral values which our Christian faith gave to them.

A Trip to the Sahara

From a personal viewpoint, the most memorable event of my visit to Algeria in 1971 was a visit to the Sahara. I had asked Sue Robinson and Liv Larsen before I arrived if it would be possible for them to take me into the Sahara, and so they arranged the fascinating trip. We saw a real desert, with great sand dunes, and brisk winds blowing the sand. There were ancient Roman ruins, a few villages and oases. At one place when a child came up to us I noted his red, infected eyes. How difficult it must be to live in such a climate! We saw Bedouins and camels. I was offered a ride on one, but settled for a photograph standing near one. We even found "flowers" in the desert–intricate crystals of sand, from small to very large, called "desert roses." Oil pipes snaked through the desert to the refineries, where streams of flame rose from the burning gas. Oil is one of the most important products of Algeria.

We spent a night at a hotel in the middle of an oasis. We had just gone to bed when we heard a knocking–in fact, a banging–on the door. I was very grateful to be with people who knew the language and the culture, especially since the problems of the last year with the government. The man at the door asked for our passports, and all was well for the rest of the night. Some photographs will give a glimpse of some of what we saw.

Beduoin Tents

39

*Sue Robinson and Liv Larsen, in Roman Ruins
at Tinegad*

A village in the Sahara

Well in the Sahara–Esther Megill

40

Liv Larsen & Sue Robinson selecting
"Desert Roses"

Refinery at Hassi Messaud and burning gas

Scene at Ourgla Showing Contrasts

41

*Sue Robinson & Live Larsen at a Market
in Ouargla
(Note the size of the "Desert Roses")*

Hotel Patio at Ouargla

The Consultation, Mission to Islam in North Africa

The consultation, held at the Methodist Hotel Zelthof, Zurich, March 23-27, was most stimulating and helpful. Thirty-one persons were present, part or all of the time. Represented were missionaries from Tunisia and Algeria; boards of the United Methodist Church in the U.S., Switzerland, Norway and Germany; the French Reformed Church in Algeria; EIRENE, Morocco, CCSA, Algeria, World Council of Churches, the White Fathers (Rome), ACO, France, and Jean Carbonare from Algeria. Present for one evening and a day were two Arab Christians who represented the Palestine Liberation movements. Unfortunately, as stated earlier, the two Algerian members of our church were unable to receive permission to leave the country and were not present.

Background papers were presented by Dr. Elmer Douglas on "The Christian in the World of Islam," and by Dr. Marston Speight, on "The History of Christian-Muslim Relations in Tunisia and Algeria." An analysis was given by Sue Robinson of the present situation in Algeria, with suggestions for the future. These papers stimulated discussion both in small groups and the plenary sessions.

The results of deliberation together were shown in recommendations to the various Boards. It was agreed that:

The church constitutes an abiding testimony to the fact that God created man according to a plan of love. It is by virtue of this living design that we make known the hope of salvation to all men, by word and deed . . . This is the essential justification for our presence and our action in North Africa. Whatever forms our witness might assume, it must be rendered with the the most scrupulous respect for the

42

institutions, laws and religious traditions of the countries concerned. [Report of the Zurich Consultation (March 23-26, 1972) to the World Division and European Boards.]

Recommendations of the Consultation included proposals that social, educational and medical work be carried on only through or in official cooperation with government or other national structures; that we seek new opportunities of service through secular vocations; that the World Division participate in an ecumenical social service to migrants and emigrant North Africans in the area of Strasbourg; and that a program of scholarly research in North African history and culture be continued in order to aid the church in the area in cultivating meaningful relationships, to better inform the churches in Europe and the United States concerning North Africa, for information and orientation of people who go to serve there, and as a means of promoting interreligious communication.

Many people expressed appreciation for the meetings, and more than one said it was the best consultation they had ever attended.

Following the full sessions the North African missionaries met with representatives of the Swiss and Norwegian Boards, and with me, and the Bishop, to make recommendations on administrative matters to the Liaison Committee in North Africa.

At that time, as has been described above, a few institutions remained under the auspices of the church. The Boy's Home in Ft. National, directed by an Algerian Christian, was one of these. However, it was hoped that both the Boy's Home and the Home Economics courses, which were taught by an Algerian Christian, would be recognized and supervised by the appropriate Algerian administration. The maternity clinic at Les Oudhias, with its parallel mother-child care program conducted by a missionary public health nurse, continued as a United Methodist institution. This was done at the request of the Algerian Health Department, although supervised by them. The Health Department furnished medicines and it was planned that they would eventually pay the salaries of the Algerian workers.

Sue Robinson, entering home at 115 Rue Mellah

Even before the events of December 1969-January 1970 some of our missionaries had begun to serve in Algerian and Tunisian institutions. Missionaries in 1971 were now teaching in various kinds of schools–several teaching English in high schools in Algeria; others teaching in adult literacy centers; Elsy Wendle was teaching sewing at a School for the Deaf; and Sue Robinson teaching American studies at the state University of Constantine. The two kindergarten teachers from Switzerland, also missionaries, were training young Algerian women to be kindergarten teachers. This course was begun in cooperation with the Algerian Red Crescent and took place in the Constantine Girl's Home. The two kindergarten classes in the home, which had been rendering great service for a number of years, gave the students in the course an opportunity for practice teaching. Missionaries in Tunisia (Marston and Elizabeth Speight) were cooperating in a Tunisian program for mentally retarded children, and were seeking opportunities for service in that country. Marston was developing a program of Christian-Muslim studies. The Johnsons, in Algeria, had major responsibilities in administration, and pastoral care of both missionary personnel and small groups of scattered North African Christians.

Since Paul Brès could not return to Algeria, he and Akila had spent the year in Strasbourg, France, exploring avenues of service to Algerian migrants, many of whom lived in that city. (This was a new venture for the World Division–to allow some of their missionaries to work in their own country.) The work was under the auspices of an ecumenical committee which worked in Lebanon, Syria, and Algeria. It was hoped that a broad ecumenical base of support could be developed. This did happen in later years, and proved to be an important area of service.

The World Division explored possibilities of recruiting personnel to work through ecumenical agencies in North Africa which were seeking technically skilled persons who could respond to needs expressed by the governments of Algeria, Tunisia, and Morocco. The United Methodist Church was asked to help develop an urgently needed program for physically, socially, and mentally handicapped persons. Liv Larsen was sent to Nashville, Tennessee to work on a master's in social work in order to help fill that need.

One of the Algerian missionaries said:

> What might be called "traditional evangelism" is no longer possible in North Africa, and yet we are called to evangelism as never before–Called to reveal Christ's love and reconciliation in all walks of life, there where man is and where man is in need. Christ said that he came to free the oppressed and to preach good news to the poor. He has set us gloriously free to work with him in this great task, unbound by many of our past traditions and religious taboos–free to follow him in whatever paths he may lead us.

The "Provisional North African Conference"

The members of the North Africa Provisional Annual Conference, meeting in Constantine October 8-10, 1971, under the presidency of Bishop Franz Schaefer, voted to send the following petition to the General Conference of The United Methodist Church:

> The Provisional Annual Conference of North Africa requests permission of the General Conference to negotiate, and upon satisfactory completion of the requirements of the Discipline, to participate in the foundation of a Protestant Church for the territory of Algeria with the Reformed Church of Algeria and other churches and missions.

44

REASONS FOR MAKING THE PETITION:

In Algeria there was a real desire to have a united Protestant church. Protestants in Algeria, of whatever origin, were in very few in number, so few, in fact, that it would be inexact to call them a "minority" in the country. And these few Protestants belonged to a half dozen or so different churches and missions. In 1966 a group of Algerian Christians, belonging to several churches, appealed, first to the Reformed Church of Algeria, then to the Methodist and other churches, to unite in one Protestant Church. They felt that it was only in this way that Algerian Christians could be recognized officially by their government.

In the years following 1966 the number of foreign Protestants living in Algeria decreased, and the number of Algerian Protestants increased very little. The events of years previous to 1971 had caused the Protestant community to feel an even greater need for solidarity and unity. It appeared more than ever imperative to live and witness as a truly united Church.

As far as The United Methodist Church was concerned, it had only a few dozen active members in Algeria, many of whom were foreign missionaries. At the general assembly of The United Methodist Church held in Algiers February 5-6, 1972, only twenty-one United Methodists registered in order to have the right to vote. Of these, no more than ten were Algerians. Of the seven active members of North Africa Provisional Annual Conference, only two were in Algeria and two in Tunisia at that time. None of the seven active members were Algerian.

The majority of United Methodists in Algeria believed that God was calling them to participate in a united church. The legal situation in Algeria made it extremely difficult, if not impossible, for the Provisional Annual Conference to continue as a separate entity. The only United Methodist bodies legally existing in Algeria were the World Division of the Board of Missions and the Women's Division. The Provisional Annual Conference had no legal existence. Theoretically, its statutes could be filed and it could seek to be recognized as an association. However, the government had quite recently published new laws governing all associations. According to these laws, an association must be either Algerian or foreign. If it was to be accepted as an Algerian association, all the officers of its executive council had to be Algerian. Otherwise, it could only be a foreign association. By uniting as many Protestants as possible it was hoped to be able to meet the requirements for an Algerian church. This desire was expressed by a large majority of the United Methodists, Reformed Church members, and other Protestants meeting together in February. Legally, their request would be facilitated because the Reformed Church was willing to allow its statutes (it existed as a legally recognized association) to be modified in the necessary way so that they could be presented as the statutes of the new Protestant Church of Algeria.

All United Methodist property in North Africa belonged either to the World Division of the Board of Missions or the Women's Division. Both of these bodies were represented by the Liaison Committee of The United Methodist Church, which would continue as a separate United Methodist entity in Algeria and would be solely responsible for United Methodist property and institutions. The bylaws of the proposed Protestant Church of Algeria made provision for its members to maintain their membership in the churches from which they came, while belonging also to the Protestant Church of Algeria.

The North Africa Provisional Annual Conference hoped to establish a structural relationship with the Swiss Annual Conference. Although it would be difficult to work out a satisfactory structure, given the ambiguous and complicated situation in Algeria, it was hoped that this could be done through the Liaison Committee.

(Adapted from information sent to the General Conference)

There was not, however, complete agreement among the missionaries, and some of the very few lay Christians (Algerians) said they would not join a united or federated church. Also, it seemed doubtful that the government would recognize any Algerian Christian church. It was felt that the only possibility was to have an officially recognized foreign church (association) to which Algerian Christians might belong. The few Algerians who took part in the discussion were called in for questioning by the police.

1972
A Final Report on North Africa
In Algeria April 6-16

The doors of opportunity for service had opened in North Africa during 1971. There was great interest by the officials of the state of Algiers in a survey to determine the extent and type of handicapped [disabled] persons, particularly children and youth. Mr. Boualem Bousseloub, the coordinator of the governor's committee on youth problems, stressed the importance of the project. The governor's own reputation and position were at stake. We knew that the same was true for our own position in Algeria.

With the help of a medical team from Vanderbilt University School of Medicine and an educational consultant a survey was made with the cooperation of the government in Algiers of the needs of disabled children. Plans were now being made by the government as to ways to begin a program of rehabilitation for the disabled, and the World Division, through the resources of persons and training opportunities at Vanderbilt University, were ready to work with them in this significant program.

Ecumenical Involvement

New emphasis on ecumenical involvement in North Africa was evidenced by continued grants to the "North African Venture" of the World Council of Churches, and the recruitment of an agriculturalist-home economics couple to work for the Algerian government under the auspices of the Christian Committee for Service in Algeria. Work among North African migrants in France had found a firm base in an ecumenical committee in Strasbourg.

Medical Work

Medical services continued at the Maternity Center and public health program in Les Ouadhias, and the hospital at Il Maten, but there was still a crucial need for a doctor, preferably a surgeon, for the hospital by June of that year. At that time the two short-term nurses would also be leaving. If we knew that a doctor would be available at least one nurse would probably return and there would be the possibility of a nurse from France. In the meantime Jay and Judy Bullard had arrived after language training. He was a medical technologist.

We had signed an agreement with the government to supply professional staff for the hospital for five years. It was most unfortunate that our Board had been unable to find any other medical staff person in the previous three years. We had been fortunate in being able to "borrow" personnel from three other small denominations, and in hiring some contract personnel from Europe (not United Methodist). The hospital was serving a real need in the area and was an example of one way in which we could cooperate with the government for the welfare of the people.

Other Institutions and Programs

The one institution still remaining in our hands was the Boy's Home at Ft. National. However, a decision had to be made soon as to the best use of the property in the changing situation in Algeria. Some investigation had been made of the possibility of turning the home over to an Algerian organization (government or Red Crescent), but there had been little progress. Although we hoped the Algerian staff would be employed by whatever group should take over the property, there was a serious question as to whether at that time in history we were serving the greatest need by continuing a home of this kind. The Liaison Committee was urged to continue a serious study of the situation.

The Kindergarten and Kindergarten Teacher's Training School in Constantine, under the direction of the Red Crescent, continued to make a real contribution. The government official in charge of such institutions asked Miss Ruth Welti, missionary of the Swiss Board, to share with them her outline of a teaching program. He had been impressed with the difference between her school and others in Algeria. Unfortunately, both Swiss teachers were to leave in June, and at the time I was there, there was prospect of only one replacement, a Swedish teacher who would continue the Kindergarten but not the teacher-training program.

We met with a committee who was trying to continue a small educational program for the deaf. There had been problems because of lack of knowledge of financial management or education, but the municipality seemed to be showing an interest. It was hoped that Miss Elsy Wendle, who had been working with them, would be able to reopen a class for women and girls. A request would be made for reallocation of Women's Division funds to renovate a Catholic Church building which had been offered for the classes.

Rural Development

A very interesting day was spent visiting the extension government rural development program headed by Jean Carbonare, (described previously). We hoped soon to be able to send a young couple, an agriculturalist and home economist, through the C.C.S.A. to work in a government program. This would be our first venture in recruiting and sending such personnel, who would not be commissioned missionaries, although we trust committed to being in mission in North Africa.

Individual missionaries had found ways of service through teaching at the University of Constantine and in secondary schools. Ministry to the small and scattered Christian community was a concern of pastors in both Algeria and Tunisia.

The small Christian community in Algeria had devoted much time and thought during the year to the future of what had been known as the North Africa Provisional Annual Conference. With enabling action by the General Conference the United Methodist Church in Algeria became a part of the Protestant Church of Algeria. At the same time, the United Methodist Christians wished to be related to world Methodism. It was agreed that the best solution would be for them to be a district of the Swiss Annual Conference, and discussions were continuing on this proposal.

The end of 1969 and the beginning of 1970 had been months of what seemed to be catastrophe; however, Christians involved in mission in North Africa were convinced in 1972 that God was leading to open doors as they sought to understand what it meant to be a Christian in a Muslim society.

A Meeting with Representatives of the PLO

"Our future is not in building houses, in acquiring material things–our future is in the liberation of our country." The Palestinian Arab, speaking earnestly in a language foreign to him, was trying to convey to me some of the depths of the despair and yet the determination of his people.

P.L.O. Headquarters

It was my privilege to meet, at their invitation, with Mr. Abu Messaoud, the assistant to Abu Khalil, who was an assistant to Yassar Arafat, head of the Palestine Liberation Organization. They were hoping that I could help them to have a chance to speak to the American people at the meeting of the Board of Missions, and that the Board would assist them in launching a massive information program to help the people of the United States know some of the facts about the Middle East conflict which were seldom given in our news media. As in so many situations, the position that the United States takes in this conflict is crucial.

With Liv Larsen as interpreter, I was eating dinner in the city of Algiers, guests of the three men who represented the branch of the Palestine Liberation Organization in Algeria. Conversation was somewhat hampered with having to speak through an interpreter of Arabic and French into English, but one could not help but feel the longing within the people for freedom and justice in their desire to have their voices heard in the world.

The young man who spoke talked about his memories as a child of seven in 1948, how there was fighting in their city in Palestine as they hid under the bed while guns were fired. He spoke of his father being put into prison, for since he was young and of an age to fight, "he must be in the army." (He smiled ruefully, "And he didn't even know how to fire a gun.") He remembered when the Israeli soldiers came into their home and ordered them into a truck. They were eventually taken to the Gaza strip where they resettled, but again in 1966 they were driven from that home. He had not returned to Palestine since that time.

The men continued to recount the various injustices which they felt so keenly–the fact that after a limited education Arab students who were frustrated with life in Israel were allowed to leave the country, but their identification papers were confiscated, and they were given only an Israeli pass with no return permit, thereby preventing their future access into any Arab country. Elementary teachers, accused of being *fedayeen* (commandos, or guerilla fighters), were constantly harassed, often imprisoned or expelled. The Arabs felt that these and other methods were used to limit the education given to Arabs, since the aim was to provide only laborers which the Israelis needed to replace their own laborers who were soldiers. They continued to speak of what they saw as a deliberate undermining of the character of their youth, as evidenced by the many bars and casinos being built in and around the city of Jerusalem. "They know we Palestinians are a deeply religious people," said one. "We are not used to having our youth go to such places. But the Israelis want them to go there and accept that type of life, and with no work, no school, and cheap prices, they are attracted."

One of the members of the group arrived late because he had waited for the completion of a radio transmission. He was jubilant over the news that had been received concerning the Palestinian National Congress which was then in progress in Cairo. They explained to us that one hundred fifty-five members were present there; they regarded it as a democratic assembly of the Palestinian nation. Eighty-five of those present were *fedayeen*; the rest were elected delegates of various professional and other groups. For example, there were representatives of doctors, students, and women, the groups who were then living in Algeria, the United States, and other countries. He said that at least one-half million Palestinians were living in the United States. The word which had been received was that there was unity among the various Palestinian groups, that those present had accepted the umbrella organization of the Palestine Liberation Organization, which our hosts represented.

For most Americans, the word "Arab" or "Palestinian" inspired then, and still today, feelings ranging from disapproval to open antagonism; few distinguished between "Israel," "Palestine," and the Arab states. Our President and presidential candidates alike spoke out in favor of aid to Israel (and still do so today). Because of an interpretation of the Bible, some persons applaud what they regard as the fulfillment of prophecy. With a deep sense of guilt because of the persecution of Jews throughout the centuries, often in the name of Christianity, Americans feel deep sympathy for Israel but have little knowledge or sympathy for the persons driven from their homes to make a place for the Jews. When we talk of dialogue between religions, we applaud dialogue between Christians and Jews, as we should, but neglect to go further to speak of dialogue between Christians and Muslims, although this has somewhat improved today. Even worse, we completely ignore the fact that many of the Arabs who were driven out of Palestine, or who continue to live there in brutal conditions, are fellow Christians.

This ignorance on the part of most Americans was, and is, the result of a massive publicity effort by the Zionists. Rare indeed was a newspaper article or an official statement that showed sympathy or even understanding for the Arab cause. For example, the book *The Unholy Land* by A. C. Forrest quickly disappeared from bookstores in the United States when it began to be sold here.

This is not the place to outline the history of the "Israeli-Palestinian Conflict," but much information is available for those who seek it. Suffice it to say that the former struggles of Palestinians to defend their country against the dangers inherent in the massive influx of imported colonists was transformed into a struggle to resist Israeli occupation and to regain lost rights.

It was impossible at that date to get a place on the Board of Missions meeting in Minneapolis in October of 1971 for representatives of the Palestine Liberation Organization, which included some Christians, to speak. They were allowed to speak, however, in an extra "volunteer attendance" session after the Women's Division had met and before the Board of Missions Annual Meeting began. They explained to the group of about eighty persons gathered there that which they called a "revolutionary new idea," their dream of "a progressive, democratic, and non-sectarian Palestine in which Christian, Muslim, and Jew will worship, work, live peacefully, and enjoy equal rights."[6]

The Palestinians acknowledged that this idea had been called "Utopia" and that "few uncommitted people can believe it, let alone support and work for it." For thus they were supporting the concept of a new country that combined the ex-aggressor and persecuted into one, as they believed it was essential if lasting peace and justice were to be achieved in Palestine. These Palestinians were careful to distinguish between Jews and Zionists. They were not anti-Jewish, but were anti-Zionists, because it was they who had insisted upon setting up a separate Jewish state with no regard for the persons who were displaced, whose property was confiscated, and whose lives were lost in order to make a place for massive immigration.

[In the years of struggle since, there are few Palestinians who any longer believe in a one-state solution. Many do wish for two independent states living side by side in peace.]

The Palestine Liberation Organization, through its contact with United Methodist missionaries and World Division staff in Algeria, turned to the churches, and specifically The United Methodist Church, to ask that we help them realize their dream of a democratic, non-sectarian state in Palestine. They turned to us and to the World Council of Churches because when they heard of grants made for humanitarian purposes to some of the liberation movements in Africa, they began to believe that perhaps there were groups concerned about justice. They believed that there was a need for a massive program of information dissemination in the United States because of the strategic role and power of our government in the affairs of the world. As Jean Carbonare, who was committed to the cause of the Palestinians, said, "If the reconciliation Christ taught and came to bring means anything, we must try to bring it to bear upon the Palestine situation."

My experience with the earnest Palestinians in Algiers in 1971 and later a visit to Palestine and Israel in 1989 have inspired my commitment, in any way I can, to joining the struggle for peace and justice for the Palestinians–which will also bring peace to Israel.

---

[6]Quoted from an address by the Al-Fateh Delegation to the Second International Conference in Support of the Arab Peoples, Cairo, January 28, 1969, in *Toward a Democratic State in Palestine*, General Union of Palestine Students, Kuwaiti Graduate Society, p. 1 (pages unnumbered).

Tunisia –April 17-20

A brief visit was made to Tunisia, to visit the Teigland and Speight families. Dr. Marston Speight had been serving as pastor of the "French Reformed Church in Tunisia" during the previous year, and had found the contacts with the English-speaking community meaningful. He also continued his scholarly research in the field of Islamics and Christian-Muslim understanding. He had recently been appointed Research Associate in the Department of Religion, Michigan State University, and a nonresident research fellow of an Institute in Holland. He also served during 1972 as a consultant and contact person for French-speaking West Africa for the Islam in Africa Project,   and took part in the Summer School of the Near East Council of Churches in Beirut.

Dr. Marston Speight

I met with Mr. Jean-Marie Lambert, director of E.S.P.R.I..T. (Ecumenical Service Program in Tunisia), and we discussed possible further involvement of our Board on that program.

In both Algeria and Tunisia it was my privilege to be part of small communities of expatriate Christians who were seeking ways of giving a Christian witness in a Muslim society. In Constantine eight persons met for a Sunday morning service of worship of the United Protestant Church. In that small group there were Americans, Swiss, German, French and Hungarian Christians. There were our missionaries, a French doctor, and two persons working for the Algerian government. In spite of the language barrier, I felt God's presence in a special way as we stood around the altar to receive communion together.

In Tunisia a group of about fourteen persons met one evening for Bible study. Included were American, Canadian, French, Dutch and Italian persons, and Catholic sisters of two different orders, a French Reformed pastor, a research student, teachers, both Protestant and Catholic. There was a spirited two-hour discussion, basically on how one can give a Christian witness in a Muslim state.

In both these countries Protestants and Catholics were taking communion together.

The question of what we meant by "Christian presence" was not an easy one. It was certain that as we began seriously to recruit persons to work in government positions in these countries we must give greater care, not less, to recruiting thoroughly committed Christians, with a missionary calling, and yet a sensitivity to persons of another faith and culture. It seemed to some of us that persons who had only a general desire to work in a developing country, based upon a humanistic concern, should go under other auspices than that of the World Division.

Work Among North African Migrants, Strasbourg, France
April 20-23

Rev. and Mrs. Paul Brès had been working since the end of 1970 in Strasbourg, France to develop a program, in cooperation with other concerned organizations, of ministry to North African migrants. The program involved (1) working directly with migrant workers (visiting hospitals and prisons, work with women and girls, a recreation center, counseling and aid in obtaining employment and housing); (2) a study of migrant problems; (3) an educational program in the churches; and (4) social action (an attempt, in cooperation with other concerned groups, to put pressure upon government to work for improved housing).

During that brief period an ecumenical committee had been formed, made up of representatives of Lutheran, Reformed and United Methodist Churches, and other organizations concerned for North Africans both within and outside France. They had contributed some financial support since 1970, and hoped to be able to take full responsibility for the recurring budget by 1974. The committee expressed appreciation for the work Paul and Akila were doing. They were uniquely able to serve in this ministry since Paul was French (but a foreigner in Alsace, which had some advantages), Akila, Algerian; both spoke Arabic and Kabyle; both had lived most of their lives in Algeria; and both had a deep Christian commitment and concern for social justice.

The Mission in North Africa 1979-2007
Dr. Hugh Johnson

The Protestant Church of Algeria submitted its statutes to the appropriate authorities in Algeria in 1972, and received their approval in 1974. At the same time the Women's Division of The United Methodist Church was recognized, as were CCSA (under the "wing" of the Protestant Church of Algeria), the Roman Catholic Church (Caritas being subjected to the Diocesan authorities), the Jewish Consistory, the Adventist Mission, and the North Africa Mission. Jacques Blanc, a reformed pastor who was the Secretary General of CCSA, was also the first president of the Protestant Church of Algeria. The uneasiness of Algerian authorities with the existence of Christian mission agencies in Algeria led to the withdrawal of recognition of several of the agencies in the late seventies, including the Women's Division. There was at the same time a tolerance of some church organizations as long as they did not engage in proselytism, the latter term being interpreted to mean the unfair use of means of attraction of people to change their faith (convert). The United Bible Societies were allowed to continue their commercial activities in specific recognized locations.

In the late seventies and early eighties, militant "Islamism," probably inspired by the success of the Islamic revolution in Iran, was becoming increasingly active across North Africa, from the Suez Canal to the Atlantic shores. Increasing pressure was brought to bear upon the states to transform relatively secular societies into Islamic states along the lines of the Gulf States.

In the face of social violence as a coercive means of achieving the transformation of society, some citizens of Algeria, and among them Berber strata of society, began to turn away from the state's identification of itself as Muslim and Arab. This fact, along with a rapid growth of cultural identification of Berbers with their civilizational roots, led to a phenomenon of "Berberization" of the Church, mostly in Algeria, but also to some degree throughout the Maghreb. Traditions of fashion from the Middle East were adopted by many Muslims, and other elements of society were becoming more vehemently western in their choices. It is not unusual in the urban areas of the North to see young women walking hand in hand, one dressed in "European" garb and the other in garments coming out of the Arabian Peninsula, or one or another of the Gulf States, or Afghanistan. As the state imposed Arabic language and culture in its schools a number of families who could afford it sent their offspring to English or French language schools operated by the cultural services of Western embassies, until in the late eighties the government decreed that no Algerian citizen could send his children to a foreign school. Thus the cleavage was formalized.

Concurrently, many former emigrants to Europe were returning to North Africa, many among them having attended evangelical services while in Europe, and some of whom had turned to the Christian faith. They were enthusiastic about their faith, and sought to share it with their fellow citizens. A few joined with the recognized churches, but many more, having suffered under the social pressures outlined above during the sixties and seventies, gathered in communities according to their cultural identities. More often than not, the patterns of worship were rather Pentecostal, informal, freewheeling spiritual experiences. It must be said that, initially, there was no official persecution by the authorities of Algerian Christians. Some, of course, were rejected by their families or their villages, some had difficulty in finding employment, or in establishing themselves on friendly terms with their Muslim neighbors. In some cases, they encountered administrative problems, including refusal of travel documents (it was difficult for a time for known Algerian Christians to obtain passports, for instance), but the problems were more individual than official. Although no law decreed that it was a crime to be a North African Christian, state employees had simply taken the law into their own hands.

However, the multiplication of these communities led to other sorts of difficulties which could have been foreseen, but too often were not. These were house churches at the outset, but soon became too large for their "hive," and either split into small communities or joined together to seek larger places of worship (garages, apartments, or dwellings set aside for church activities). As North Africans, they became increasingly preoccupied with witness to their fellow-citizens, often to the exclusion of any other nationalities. They are "mission-minded" in that they seek to witness to their faith among the non-churched of North African origin. At various levels, the church councils which two decades previously were made up of foreigners with token North African participants came to be composed of mostly North Africans with token "international persons." An interesting aspect of this is that they did not tend to become ingrown and self-centered, but increasingly sought relationships with organizations and missions outside the Maghreb. One of the incentives was the financial support that this could provide, but it would be too simple to draw the line there, because there was and is a genuine desire to belong to something greater and to gain themselves international recognition.

And yet, there is a growing international community in North Africa, in all the countries of North Africa, with important numbers of expatriates from sub-Saharan Africa and also from the Middle East. Patterns of worship may be similar, but the language of worship in these (international) communities is neither Arabic nor Berber, and occasionally not even European. Sometimes, these sub-Saharan Africans are simply migrants fleeing lands of limited opportunities for what they have perceived as the El Dorado of Europe (and even – why not? – of North America). The iron curtain which once divided East and West in Europe became a "gold" curtain drawn east- west in the Mediterranean, dividing the North from the South.

The surprising return of North African emigrants to their homeland as evangelists led also to growing opposition to the Church from the fundamentalists in Islam, who became much more vocal and public in their opposition to the fact that Algerians were more and more open to the Christian message. The fundamentalists turned to violent means of repression, and it was in this period that the Church was again subjected to martyrdom. Roman Catholics, being the most visible community, were the targets of predilection. More than two dozen were victims of violent attacks. Many of them were assassinated, and others were encouraged to leave the country or simply lived under threat if they decided to remain. There were, however, some exceptions to this rule. Protestants were also victims of violence, as well as Eastern Europeans (mostly from Russia or from the former Yugoslavia). Only two non-Catholics and nonorthodox, both French Jehovah's Witnesses, were killed by Islamic militants. The male members of the family were stabbed to death in front of the woman and her daughter, and their blood was smeared over the walls and furniture of their apartment in the suburbs of Algiers. Beyond the direct attacks, there was increasing pressure brought to bear upon the fledgling democratic authority of the country. Since the religion of the state was Islam, it was reasoned that the rights of non-Muslims must be severely abridged. A new law was voted in February 2006, in effect outlawing evangelization in Algeria. In what has come to be known as the "somber decade," death threats led to the re-emigration of a disconcertingly large number of recent converts to places of haven North of the Mediterranean. Whereas Church officials had long encouraged North African Christians to remain in their homeland, they had later to adopt more "humane" stances. Emigration was not encouraged, but was a choice increasingly adopted by Christians in a growing hostile environment.

Still another development during this period was the apparent increasing determination of the General Board of Global Ministries (The United Methodist Church) to withdraw its international personnel from Algeria, and eventually from its entire area of service in North Africa. This happened at the same time that opportunities were opening to the East in other predominantly Muslim countries, meaning that North Africa was no longer the only place in the world in which The United Methodist Church was in direct service to Muslim populations. The decision did not seem to be brutal, but more gradual. As missionaries and other international Persons in Mission reached retirement age or withdrew for personal or family reasons, they were not replaced. Today, only two missionaries remain in active service in North Africa, Pastor and Mrs. Kayij in Tunisia. This has left a free hand to more conservative mission agencies which are more than willing to attempt to fill the void.

This period saw as well the rather unexpected opening of new work in the former Eastern European bloc of nations, where the Church had long been severely restricted. The spirit of venture and outreach had been supplanted by what seemed to be the spirit of "cost effectiveness." When funds for outreach became scarce, the natural reaction in the denomination was to redirect funding to invest in areas where results were perceived to be more impressive and therefore more effectively productive if one intends to measure success by statistics.

All the while, from 1970 to the present, there have been incidents of "unfinished business" whereby frequent annoyances occur as a result of measures taken in 1970 and 1971 were rescinded, but remain on the record books, with the result that departures from Algeria and returns to Algeria by those resident there throughout the period are called aside by border police while their "story" is verified. Nearly every time, apologies are offered, along with supplications to "take care of this matter once and for all." In the mid eighties, Paul and Akila Brès were invited to an ecumenical meeting in Algeria, and encountered no difficulties, either on entry or on exit. The conclusion is that their experience of being "taken" to the border had never been ratified by a governmental decree. A side issue in this matter is the difficulty in relations with the "evangelical Christians" when they are advised a cautious and prudent approach to witness to their faith. The whole issue of developing an adequately trained church leadership, aware of the impact of the exercise of their faith and its place in North African history, acquires an increasingly urgent priority.

As recently as March 2007 a Swiss pastor who was president of the Protestant Church of Algeria was invited to leave. This means that the national Church Council is made up entirely of Algerian nationals, including the president.

****

And so, I have taken you with me on a journey to North Africa, and given you a few glimpses of what it means to be in mission in Muslim lands and of the countries in which United Methodists have worked. I hope also that you have enjoyed the trip! And now, to sub-Saharan Africa, a part of Africa much more familiar to me.

CHAPTER 2. NIGERIA
Introduction

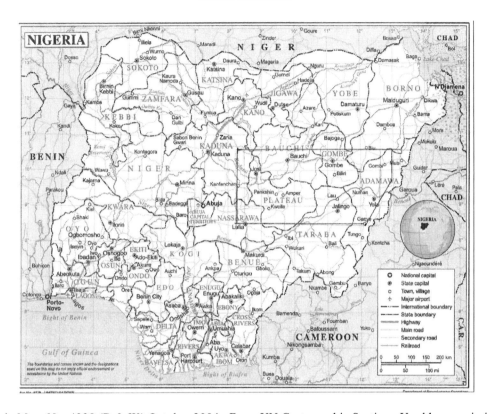

(Nigeria, Map No. 4228 (B & W) October 2004. From UN Cartographic Section. Used by permission.)

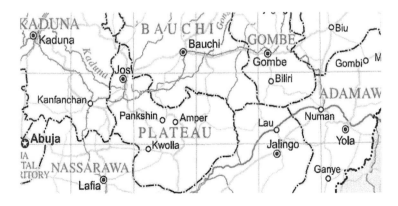

The Part of Nigeria Where The United Methodist Church Works
(Adapted from Map. No. 4228)

The Republic of Nigeria is the most populous country in all of Africa. It covers a land space of 924 sq. kilometers which is slightly more than twice the size of the State of California. It is also the most ethnically diverse nation on the African Continent. There are 200 distinct ethnic or tribal groups and over 400 spoken languages and/or dialects. Nigeria has traditionally been divided into three main cultural regions, (1) the South, both East and West, (2) the so-called Middle Belt and (3) the North. Generally, the ethnic groups that dominate the South are Ibo (Southeast) and Yoruba (Southwest), with the majority religion in this Region being Christian. The Middle Belt is made up of many language groups who in the past were known as the "Minority Tribes," who are mixed Christian and Muslim. The North is home of the historical Muslim peoples. The many African languages are dominated by three: Ibo, Yoruba and Hausa, while English is the official language of all Nigeria. With respect to religion, Christianity has gained over Islam in the "minority" Middle Belt area, so that Nigeria's total population of 130 billion would be about 45% Muslim, 45% Christian and the remaining 10% adherents to African ancestral religions. (This is not an exact enumeration.)

Nigeria was colonized by the British as a Commonwealth in the late 19th Century. Britain granted Nigeria independence in 1960. After a Civil War (The Biafra War) Nigeria was under military rule for 16 years. A new Constitution was adopted in 1999 which completed a peaceful transition to civilian government. The new Federal Capital, Abuja, is located at the geographical center of Nigeria. The nation is made up of 36 States with Abuja as Federal Capital Territory. This oil-rich country has long been handicapped by political instability, poor economic management and generalized corruption but is now undertaking some changes under the reform-minded civilian administration.

The United Methodist Church of Nigeria is in Northeastern Nigeria, centered in Jalingo, capital of Taraba State. The denomination comprises twenty-one church Districts which lie on both the North and South side of the Benue River

–Dr. Dean Gilliland

Getting Acquainted – 1968

Following my first trip to North Africa, I flew to Nigeria, and arrived in Lagos on November 14, 1968. What a contrast! I was back in Sub-Saharan Africa, so many things were familiar to me (the climate, for one), although I also soon found differences. I was very glad to have an afternoon and evening to myself in the hotel. This enabled me to get a "second wind" for what proved to be a very strenuous two weeks in Nigeria.

Jos

I arrived at Jos, in the northern part of the country, at 10:30 the next morning, and was met by Stan and Helen Trebes, old friends from Sierra Leone. Stan was business manager for Hillcrest School, a cooperative school for children of missionaries from many denominations and several countries in West Africa. Helen was the hostess of our guest house in Jos. I met and talked with Martha Underwood, the acting principal of Hillcrest. I found several problems at Hillcrest, but on the whole it was a good school for children of our missionaries. There was some question as to whether they would accept children of our Liberian missionaries.[1] I wrote a letter to the Chairman of the Board of Governors concerning the matter.

Our Board was responsible for supplying the nurse (Delphine Jewell was completing a one-year special assignment until Florence Walter would return from furlough). We also supplied the business manager. We cooperated with the Church of the Brethren in supplying a Junior High math teacher and a Grade 2 teacher. We also cooperated with them in the hostel for our high school children, and shared in the cost of the house parents. All the children of our missionaries from Grade 1 through 12, went to school at Jos, many miles from their parents. High School children of Sierra Leone missionaries also attended there.

Clinic at Hillcrest School

---

[1] A new situation had been created with the union of the Evangelical United Brethren and the Methodist Churches to form The United Methodist Church. Only EUB missionaries had been in Nigeria, and it was that denomination which was part of the arrangement for Hillcrest.

Several missionaries were in Jos, since it was near the end of the school term, when they would get their children, as well as for other reasons. I had conferences there with Gene Westley, the field representative, and his wife Helen, and with Roger and Sylvia Burtner, who were church development missionaries at Pero. On Sunday I visited the Theological College of Northern Nigeria, a cooperative theological school, with two types of four-year courses: a diploma course for students who had secondary school or the equivalent, and a certificate course for those with the equivalent of only a junior high school education. All were mature men.

There was also a school for wives of ministers. They were taught courses in Bible, sewing, nutrition, English, arithmetic, games for children, and instructed about Girl's Brigade.[2] The Rev. and Mrs. Arthur Faust were United Methodist missionaries serving at the College at that time, but were due for terminal furlough in 1969. Dean and Lois Gilliland were to replace them. I met the only United Methodist student, Mazadu Bakila, who was graduating that year after completing the certificate course. He would be the most highly trained minister in our church.

I enjoyed a dinner with the Fausts and Dr. Harry Boer (Christian Reformed), the principal of the school. I felt that our support of the College was one of the most worthwhile contributions we were making to the development of the church in Nigeria, even though our own church had as yet profited very little from it, because of the lack of students.

TCNN Chapel

Art Faust Teaching a Class

---

[2]Girl's and Boy's Brigades are religious organizations for children and young people which originated in the United Kingdom in the nineteenth century They are found in many African countries which were formerly British colonies.

Mazadu Bakila Preaching in Chapel

My Travel Begins

Lois Schmidt, Teacher

On November 18 Gene and Helen Westley drove with me to visit the Waka Schools at Biu, a secondary and teacher-training school maintained by the Church of the Brethren. We cooperated in this school by providing a staff member, Lois Schmidt, in the teacher-training school, and were asked to contribute $4600 a year from 1970-75 for expansion. The school was of definite service to our church. While at Biu I met and talked with Dr. and Mrs. Arnold Thompson, who were seconded to the Church of the Brethren three years previously. They were to take a short furlough in March, and then were planning to return to us at Bambur Hospital for a three-year term.

Baobab Tree

Village in Northern Nigeria

As we traveled in northern Nigeria, we were in semiarid plains and plateaus, with occasional hills or a higher mountain or extinct volcano. The plains were covered with sometimes scanty grass. Occasionally there would be baobab, mango or other trees. Since the rainy season had only recently ended, it was not as dry and hot as it would be later. I noted the villages, made of round huts with grass roofs, arranged in compounds surrounded by corn-stalk fences. In some

Storage Bins for Grain

Place of Sacrifice

places there were cone-shaped storage bins for grain. We saw at one place along the road a place for sacrifice. As is true in many other parts of Africa, the animistic traditional religions were (and are) still common, often mixed with Islam or Christianity. These beliefs were also shown in the charms hung around the neck of a child to ward off disease or evil. In the towns, houses might be square or rectangular, and some made of cement blocks with aluminum roofs.

A Village Well

Later we came across a group of Fulanis, who were migrating to another area. These semi-nomadic people have herds of cattle with long horns, reminding one of Texas "longhorns." One of the missionaries told me that they would sometimes buy milk from them, which they would

Fulanis

boil before using to prevent disease. The Fulanis, along with the Hausas, who are dominant in the North, are primarily Muslim.

Roger Burtner told me that once when he was escorting a group of visitors from the U.S. to the various mission stations they came across some Fulanis. He got out a "finger phone" which was available at the time–a phonograph that was operated by moving it rapidly with one's finger. He had a record in the Fulani language, and played it for them. One of the Americans jokingly remarked to someone that was the only time he had seen Roger do any missionary work. (It is rather difficult to do one's usual work while taking visitors around.)

Occasionally one saw a man riding on a camel.

South of the Benue River

The entire next day was spent in travel from Biu to Lankaviri, where the Westleys were stationed. On the way we stopped at two stations, Zinna[3] and Kassa, where we had mission houses but no missionaries to staff them. Church development missionaries had been requested for several years by the Nigerian church, but we had not yet been able to provide them with even one more.

Pastor Simon's Compound at Kassa

Edna Kline was also stationed at Lankaviri. She had recently come to the field to develop and supervise the program of religious instruction in the primary schools within our church's area. The Native Administration had taken over the schools we started, but we were allowed to supply teachers of religious knowledge both in our former schools and other schools in the area (about thirty in all). It was agreed when the program was started that the local church in each village would help with the cost of the teacher, the rest being subsidized by the Board. Unfortunately, as in several other cases, the churches had done very little.

During my two days at Lankaviri we worked and planned together. We also spent a day at Jalingo, a few miles away, investigating possibilities for a secondary school in Muri Division. The population of that area was a little more than 500,000, with about thirty-six primary schools. There was no secondary school in the area. Students must go to Waka Schools, with which we cooperated (225 miles), Gindiri (400 miles), Yola Government School (100 miles) or Numan Sudan United Mission Secondary (110 miles). We were the only Protestant church in the Muri Division. Duane Dennis had spent many hours in consultation and planning with the hope that the Division would respond to the need for a secondary school. During the time I was in Nigeria on this first trip we met with the Emir of Jalingo, who had made land available for the school.

---

[3]Zinna is now known as Zing.

He and the Native Administration promised their support for the school. He indicated that they would ask permission from the State government to seek public donations, in the form of money or labor. An interesting note: In this first trip to that area of Nigeria, I saw women who wore leaves as clothes, and men with goat skin clothing the size of briefs. The Emir told me that he had passed a law that a woman could not come into the market without at least a cloth tied around her waist. He said, "They complain that they don't have the money to buy a cloth." Gene Westley told me later that he had interfered when he saw one of the Emir's soldiers beating a woman who wore no cloth. I used that example later when a young person challenged me during a mission event by saying, "I suppose you missionaries make people wear European clothing?" (The movie "Hawaii" had recently been shown.)

Mumuye Woman, 1968

The Muri Christian Council of course wanted the school, but it soon became apparent that there was serious disagreement among them as to the site of the school. The leaders were insisting that the school be on the Pero side of the Benue (where we already had Muri Christian Training School and the hospital), rather than at Jalingo, in Mumuye territory. The site at Jalingo had the advantages of being on a road which would allow building materials and supplies to be taken to the area more easily; there were many Christians and some of the strongest churches in Mumuye; and the land was available there. We asked the church leaders to share in the school by giving £1000, in cash, farm produce, or labor. They said that was too much, even though we stressed that it was not necessary to pay in cash. They also accused the missionaries of going secretly to the Emir and government officials and persuading them to put the school at Jalingo.

Another problem was the economic instability of the Nigerian government. Ordinarily the State government would pay 90% of the teachers' salaries and give a boarding grant for each student. Because of the cost of the war[4] the Minister of Education had quite frankly said that he would not approve the beginning of the school until he could be more sure that they could finance it. After long consultation and thought, I made a decision just before I left Nigeria that we could not open a class in January 1969 as had originally been approved by the Board, on a provisional basis. This would have meant moving the Dennises to Jalingo the next week, spending money to make the rented house adequate for them, and more money to repair the temporary buildings offered by the Emir for the school. I sent a letter to the church stating the following reasons for not opening the school as yet:

(1) Official permission had not yet been obtained from the Northeast State Minister of Education and Community Development, because of lack of government funds.
(2) We had no assurance of a teacher to replace Mr. Dennis when he went on furlough.
(3) We did not have certain assurance of funds for the buildings.

---

[4]A civil war began when Biafra declared independence in May of 1967.

(4) We as yet had no builder.

(5) There was no assurance of unanimity in the Church as to the location of the site and the plan of contribution.

A letter was written to the Emir, giving some of the reasons for the delay; we did not list number five, since that would give a very black name to the Christians who were a minority in that Muslim area.

I received word later from Eugene Westley that when that decision was announced by him to the Muri Christian Council they accused the missionaries of telling me what to say, and got up and walked out of the meeting.

There was no doubt that a secondary school was very much needed in that area. There was a possibility of several thousand dollars from the West German government for buildings. But it was quite obvious that much more study and talking were necessary before we could accept the responsibility of a school. We could not carry the entire recurring budget of a school, and we did not start institutions which were not asked for and shared in by the people who were there. Also, we had been told by government officials that when the war was over the government would take over the school, since they felt that education was a government responsibility. We knew, however, the need for a secondary school in the area and were willing to make an investment just to get a school started, if other matters were settled.

North of the Benue

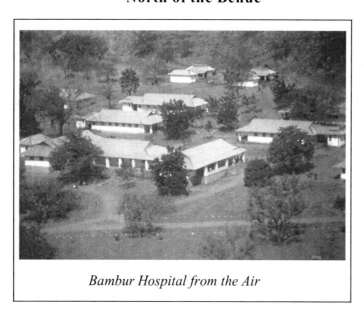

Bambur Hospital from the Air

Travel to Bambur, on the other side of the Benue River, was by plane. I felt truly at home again[5] when I visited the hospital–a one hundred fourteen bed hospital with only two doctors (Dr.

---

[5]I worked as a medical technologist in a mission hospital during the years I was in Sierra Leone.

David Hilton, Dr. Charles Arnett) and one nurse (Vreni Krebbs, from Switzerland), and a nurse teaching in the dispenser's training school (Sister Natalie Mohr, from Germany). The business manager was Dick Hundreisser.

Shortly before I arrived, surgery had been discontinued because the lack of nurses to supervise resulted in too many infections. There was very little laboratory work because there was no medical technologist. Just to continue the general medical and surgical work a minimum of three doctors was needed (there should be at least four, so that there would be three on the field at any one time); four nurses, in addition to the nurse in charge of the dispenser's school; a pharmacist, or someone who could be trained to do this type of work; a medical technologist; a business manager-field treasurer, to replace the Hundreisers, who had asked for transfer to a different type of work. We had a maintenance man (Bill Hinegardner), and I felt that we needed to see that there would continue to be one. He should serve not only at the hospital, where we did have a capable Nigerian at that time, but also in other mission stations. We would have two doctors for only one more year. If at that time we could find no other, we were in danger of having to close the hospital which ministered to a wide area and their supervision by hospital staff and, across the river, by Helen Westley, who was a nurse, were important contributions important contributions to medical care of the area. If we were doing the type of medicine which should be done, we would also have a doctor trained in public health who could devote his/her time to it.

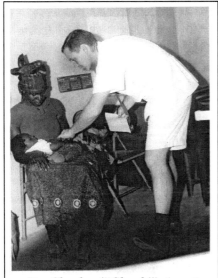

Dr. Charles ("Chuck") Arnett

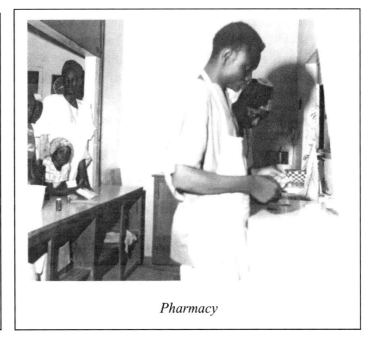

Pharmacy

Sr. Natalie Mohr and Student   *Dick Hundreiser, Business Manager, and Esther Megill*

I also visited the Muri Christian Training School, a pastors' and catechists' training school. Instruction was in Hausa[6], with English taught as a foreign language. The highest education of the pastors in the Muri Church was a primary school education, with one year additional in teachers' training. Many had far less. Few spoke English, an official language for Nigeria. I believed that the school could make an important contribution to the growth of the church. I did, however, direct that the following conditions must be met before further grants could be considered:

(1) Priorities were set within the whole mission program, in staffing and finance. How important was this school considered in the life of the church? If it was to be adequately taught there would have to be, until there was a Nigerian with advanced training, a minimum of two missionaries–one to serve as principal, one as a community development man. (Their wives would also find a place of service within the school.)

(2) A report was to be made of the receipt and expenditure of World Council of Churches funds which had been received. Had some of the projects for which Board funds were requested been cared for by this grant?

(3) Accounts were to be put in order and audited.

(4) Unfinished building and improvement to be completed. This could not be done until we could get more staff.

(5) Work by a qualified committee should be done on a curriculum for the school.

---

[6]Hausa is an official language in Northern Nigeria. The people in the areas where our church worked spoke other languages as their "mother tongue," but Hausa was taught in schools as well as English.

I endorsed the suggestion that had been made some time previously (and the basis upon which the W.C.C. grant had been given) that a threefold program be developed: Biblical and theological training, agriculture and community development, literacy.

Student Housing

Students

Students' wives were also required to attend the school. A maximum of three children could be brought. They were taught by missionary wives and a young Nigerian woman who was a teacher. They were taught to read and write in Hausa, English, arithmetic, health, handwork (such as laundry, "burning" designs on calabashes, sewing), cooking and nutrition, and Bible. They also had a course which was intended to enable the women to assist the Girl's Brigade programs which were found in a number of churches, particularly those where there were schools.

Wives' Class

Women Learning to Read, M.C.T.S.

Another most important contribution to the life the church was that made by Heidy Dennis, who had developed an extensive literacy program. Bathli Hinegardner was assisting her, and she had a young Nigerian, Amadu Biyam, who had learned a great deal and was taking much responsibility. I felt that he should be given additional opportunities for training. Heidy was taking the lead in a cooperative committee (United Methodist, Christian Reformed, and British Sudan United Mission) which was making a study of literature available, with the aim of cooperating on production of Hausa literature. Heidy herself had produced some very practical material on a variety of subjects. Doris Hess, who was Functional Executive Secretary for Mass Communications, was enthusiastic about the project, and gave advice and support to the program.

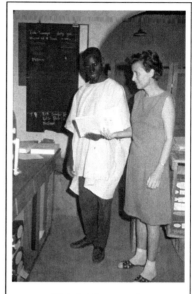

Heidy Dennis &
Amadu Biyam,
Assistant in Training

I reported to World Division staff that I felt it should be decided soon whether we would support an air program with a mission owned plane and a missionary pilot, or whether we would cooperate with Missionary Aviation Fellowship (M.A.F.), which were ready to come into the area. I had conversations with the head of the British branch of the M.A.F and with missionaries about the advantages and disadvantages of such a program. One thing I felt was certain: air transport was very much needed in that isolated area. Bambur Hospital, M.C.T.S., the literacy workers, and the missionaries stationed at Pero were cut off from transport out of the area by road during several months of the year, during the rainy season. Distances were great, and air travel could save hours of time as well as physical wear-and-tear.

A report of my time in Nigeria would not be complete if I did not try to sketch some of the problems which took hours of our time in consultation with both missionaries and church leaders. It was difficult to express in a few paragraphs the situation which faced the church at that time. It had to first be explained that we were not known, except incidentally, as the United Methodist Church. The church was then organized as the Muri Church of Christ in the Sudan. It was part of the greater fellowship of churches which had resulted from the various branches of the Sudan United Mission, known (in English) as the Fellowship of Churches of Christ in the Sudan (TEKAS). Each local Church Council elected from its members four representatives to the District Church Council. All ordained pastors and all licensed catechists were members. The District Council then elected representatives to the Regional Church Council on the basis of one delegate to every one hundred members in the district. This Regional Church Council met twice a year. A chairman, secretary, and treasurer were elected annually. They also elected the standing committees which were to carry on the ongoing work of the church. The Muri Christian Council was made up of representatives of the Regional

Church Council and of missionaries, by virtue of their membership in the Muri Church and their job analysis. The structure thus outlined had evolved since 1961 into the present structure. This had been a learning process. It was obvious that the time had come to do some further thinking and to make some changes in line with the present disciplinary ruling in regard to the Liaison Committee to be established in each field. The church leaders admitted that one of their problems was to know who was the head–the Regional Church Council or the Muri Christian Council. Other conflicts had arisen, due largely to our imposing a western cultural pattern upon the Nigerian church. The function of committees, arriving at conclusions by majority vote, the planning of budgets and use of money were all nearly incomprehensible to the leadership of the church at that time. As mentioned previously, there was limited educational attainment by the pastors. Some of the younger Nigerian Christians were dissatisfied with their leadership. As one of the teachers said to me, while interpreting during my conversation with the church leaders, "These old men who are our leaders do not understand about arriving at decisions by voting. It makes it difficult for us." And, in Africa, it is usual that age, not educational attainment, is the criterion for leadership.

These and other factors had unfortunately resulted in a feeling of suspicion and discontent on the part of the African leaders, and continual frustration and discouragement on the part of the missionaries. It became clear after long consultations that if the church was to grow in responsibility and eventual autonomy it was necessary for the present for the Division to give more direction and guidance. One of the many problems was how the church, in a very underdeveloped and poverty-stricken area, could be helped by our resources without making paupers of them. The feeling of the African leaders was that the Division had an endless amount of money which we wanted to give them; it was only the missionaries who prevented it. They had no understanding of such things as expense accounts (for example, one pastor attended three meetings in one place during one day, and collected three travel allowances), of keeping books (we had been unable so far to have enough missionary staff that one person could devote his time in accounting and teaching of both missionaries and nationals in keeping books), of the use of grants which had been made. Loan funds had been set up with grants from the Division which had been used as a gift by the church. I had not approved their request for further funds to replace them in two different instances. In almost every case where the church had been asked to assume a small portion of the financial responsibility, the budget requests had been set high enough so that Division money was used, and the amount from the church had not been paid.

There were also tribal conflicts, resulting in wrangles over the location of the new church office and the proposed secondary school.

In addition, the chronic shortage of missionary staff had led to discouragement on the part of the missionaries. Northern Nigeria was a very difficult place to work, because of the isolation, the climate, the lack of personnel, the necessity of sending children away to a school miles away, the necessity of becoming fluent in Hausa, and most of all, the problem of lack of communication and understanding between African and missionary. Missionaries are human, and in any case when there are disagreements there are two sides to the question. But I was impressed with the complete dedication of most of the missionaries and their honest effort and desire for the growth of the church. I felt that we should give them moral support, remember them in prayer, and provide more personnel. And there would be a real crisis in personnel by June of 1969 if nothing was done to provide more missionaries.

I painted a rather black picture to the staff, but I could not help but be honest. I felt that we could not at that time sit and do nothing about the situation. We must have more personnel. Together we must think, and pray and plan so that the Gospel of Jesus Christ would be proclaimed in a way that its power for new life might be realized in Nigeria.

The Islam in Africa Project

I also investigated the "Islam in Africa Project" while I was in London and Nigeria. There was a center in Ibadan, Nigeria, in addition to one in East Africa. Our church leaders in Nigeria were hardly aware of it, and most were unable to take advantage of it because of their limited educational background. However, some missionaries had profited, and I felt that others could. The representative in Nigeria, John Crossley, was in Sierra Leone the previous year and conducted a very helpful seminar. It was not a World Council of Churches project, but was recognized by the Commission on World Mission and Evangelism of the W.C.C. The Rev. Hugh Thomas, in England, was taking over as secretary for the project. He and Elliot Kendell discussed the project with me in London, and I received letters from Tom Beetham, former secretary. I felt that it was a very worthwhile program, and requested that our Board help financially with this cooperative project.

1969–More Meetings, and Travel by Boat

April

In April of 1969 I reported to the members of the Africa Area Committee of the Board that there were continued problems with obtaining visas for Nigeria, but if we could get them, we had the possibility for more personnel. I was happy to report that the Rev. and Mrs. Kyle McQuillen were under appointment to go to Nigeria as Church Development missionaries, and should be ready by December. I had a long conversation with them, and they seemed to be a young couple who would be able to fit into a difficult situation. They knew the problems, as much as anyone could know before being there. We had possibilities for a business manager for the hospital who would also act as field treasurer for one year. We still needed a long-term missionary for that position. There was a possibility for a medical technologist for the hospital, and the German church had two nurse-midwives who were prepared to go by fall. Also, in prospect was a couple for the new secondary school at Jalingo. The Rev. and Mrs. Al Bohr were to return early from furlough in order to get into the country before Marianne's visa expired on May 6 (he was a Canadian, so did not require a visa). It was hoped that the Gillilands would be able to get a visa to return in July also.

September

Although I had planned for nearly a year to visit Nigeria in September, I was unable to obtain a visa until I reached Sierra Leone. This was due to the continuing Biafra War. Even Dean Gilliland had trouble getting a visa to return; the ambassador had read articles in our church papers which were sympathetic to Biafra. Dean had to convince him that those who were working in Northern Nigeria would be good ambassadors for the federal government, and should be allowed to return.

I arrived in Lagos, however, as scheduled on September 9, and flew to Jos on the tenth. Gene and Helen Westley had planned to meet me in Jos, but were unable to drive through because of bridges being out, due to the rainy season. The ban against private planes was causing great difficulty for missionaries in the North. While in Jos I talked with Stan and Helen Trebes, and visited with Florence Walter, the nurse at Hillcrest, and the children of our missionaries in Nigeria, Sierra Leone and Liberia.

On September 13 Stan drove me to the place where the first bridge was out; there I waded across the river (being ever mindful that one could contract schistosomiasis from the water), and was met by a missionary of the Danish (Lutheran) Branch of the Sudan United Mission. We

crossed the Benue by ferry, changed drivers, and drove about two more hours to the next river where the bridge was out. Gene Westley met me there and we walked through the river, then drove another hour and a half to Lankaviri. The trip took about twelve hours in all.

The days at Lankaviri were busy ones. Meetings with the Executive Committee of the Regional Church Council were to have begun on the sixteenth at Jalingo, but it was the seventeenth before the Nigerian members arrived, for travel was difficult for them also. We spent two days preparing an agenda for the Council meeting; every item had to be discussed first to see whether it should be put on the agenda, and then thoroughly discussed again (all in Hausa, of course, with interpretation of the essentials for me). This was in spite of the fact that those meetings had been called especially at my request to discuss various matters with the church. On the late afternoon of the eighteenth we began the Council meetings, which lasted until the night of the twentieth. The two most important items discussed were the changes made in the constitution of the Muri Christian Council so that it could function as the liaison committee, which was required by the World Division, and a constitution to form a Board of Governors for the Muri Christian Training School. There had been serious conflicts within the church and between the church and missionaries during the previous year. The hope was that the changes which would come because of the adoption of these constitutions would improve the situation. It was easy to understand why almost all the pastors, who had had no formal education except for two or three years in a vernacular Bible School, were fighting to keep control of the church. They saw the changes which were coming all over the country as those who had even an elementary school education, and especially secondary, were beginning to take the places of those who had little or no opportunity for education. But the church simply could not grow if teachers, dispensers, and students could not begin to have a role in the leadership of the church. There were several teachers and some dispensers who showed insight and were quite vocal in support of the changes which the new constitution would bring. There were also some persons with a limited background who had served to the best of their ability, who were now moving over with a good spirit to give room to those better qualified. I thanked God for them.

We discussed at length the problem with the new secondary school which had opened just that year. We had received no money as promised by the State, and we had not been able to obtain visas for teachers. If these conditions were not changed by the end of the year, we would have to close the school, at least for a time, and try to find places in other schools for the students. The Nigerians found it very difficult to understand why we might not be able to continue, as there was such great need for a secondary school.

Ezra Barawani Jen

During this stormy session I sat while the Rev. Ezra Barawani Jen, (known commonly as "Pastor Ezra"), the Chairman[7], upbraided me for half an hour, all faithfully interpreted by Gene Westley. At the end of the session one of the pastors, younger and the best educated of the group, said to me in an admiring tone, "You didn't even cry! You acted just like a man!"

The Nigerians found it difficult to accept me, a woman, for being in position of authority.

Conditions were becoming more difficult for the people of Nigeria. Prices continued to rise, and many goods were unobtainable. There were high taxes and very little money for development. Soldiers were seen everywhere and the common people (rightfully) were afraid of them. I did not feel that I could tell our church people of the millions we (as a Board) were spending for relief. Even our missionaries sometimes found it difficult to understand why more money was not available for their own work of treating children with kwashiorkor, teaching nutrition, and programs of education and training. They would have been glad for a small part of the relief money.

At the meeting an announcement was made of a representative from the Christian Council relief program who would be available for visiting churches in the North in November to interpret the program of relief for those in the war-torn area and raise money. There was some discussion, which showed the lack of understanding of the situation. The first question was whether he was an Ibo,[8] and then whether the government would approve of his coming. It was finally agreed that he would be invited to come, but that enquiries would be made concerning him from leaders of other churches who knew him.

---

[7]Dean Gilliland writes the following concerning Pastor Ezra:
"EZRA BARAWANI JEN, (Barawani: his father, Jen: his home village) was elected Chairman of the Muri Church (now UMCN) in 1969. Ezra, now an elder among the pastors in UMCN, was elected at a time when Nigeria had received independence. There was much agitation against expatriate authority both in government and institutions, including the church. Ezra was educated at the vernacular level, meaning he had received his education in the African language. Coming up through what was known as the "Adult Literacy Program.". (I remember that as a grown man he actually attended primary school with the children ,as did others during that era). Ezra was trained for church work at two levels; I was his teacher at both. The first was known as Evangelist's Training or Catechist (lay pastor) and secondly, in a three year course as Pastor. He was ordained following this course and soon was elected a Chairman of the Church. As Chairman, he followed one of his own ethnic colleagues, a laymen. Ezra made his name as one who was known for his desire to lead the church into a new kind of autonomy. He was and is a man of personal charisma, physical strength and natural leadership, very strong in his convictions. In the early 1970's there was much criticism of missionaries and policies that had been laid down by missionaries. In this sense he was a popular but polarizing figure."
Pastor Ezra died in April 2007.

[8]The state of Biafra was inhabited principally by the Igbo (Ibo) people. In the mostly Hausa north resentment against the more prosperous and educated Ibgo minority erupted into violence in 1966 and thousands were massacred in the Northern Region, and perhaps a million fled as refugees to the Igbo-dominated east.

(1) Temporary Housing for the Students
(2) Boys Walking to their Quarters
(3) Carrying Water (no well!)

On Monday, September 22 I met with the Muri Christian Council, with some seconded members added to make it a truly representative liaison committee until the new council was formed in December. I explained the new system of Advance Specials (new to them because the Evangelical United Brethren Church Board, when a request was approved, would immediately provide the funds). We also discussed the policy for equipment funds and vehicle requests. We worked out the 1972-73 askings during the meeting. The Council also voted on return of missionaries and stationed the new missionaries. I went through the proposed 1970 budget with them.

In all the meetings I was pleased by the apparently frank discussion, indications of increased understanding, and general friendly feelings. I was sure there would be repercussions at the December meeting, but things could only be better from now on; I thought they couldn't be much worse than they had been during the previous year.

On the next day the newly constituted Board of Governors of Muri Christian Training School met. Dates were set for opening and closing of the school term, the number of students to be admitted agreed upon and other policy matters settled. Because of the provision for better qualified staff two junior staff members would be replaced the following year. After a year of chaos the school was being put into good shape under the leadership of Al and Marianne Bohr, who had returned in May. I visited Banyam (M.C.T.S.) later in the week. Marianne had already accomplished wonders in the wives' training program. She was bubbling with enthusiasm for the program of nutrition education she had introduced, since she had attended the Agricultural Missions seminar the previous February. She recommended that <u>all</u> missionaries to Africa attend the course.

September 14: The Westleys, Chuck Arnett, Al Bohr, and I traveled to Bambur. It was forty-five miles as a plane flies. However, no private planes were allowed to fly, and so it took us thirteen hours. We drove by Landrover eighteen miles to Lau, on the Benue River.

The Benue River

Gene and Helen Westley

Market at the Benue

Esther Megill on Canoe

The Oxcart–Esther Megill & Helen Westley

There we got into large canoes, with mats over the center to give shade. We had an unusually quick trip going, and reached the point on the other side (and down stream) in about five hours. Some of the time we were going through the marshes, with tall grass all around us. Quite literally some of the way was over motor roads, which were there in the dry season. We went as far as we could by canoe, and then transferred all our loads and Helen Westly and me. We had the prize seats on top of the barrels of gasoline – not very comfortable, but better than walking through the mud. We rode that way for about six miles, while the men walked. By that time the oxen were obviously tired, and we got out as we began to come to deeper mud holes and more water. It wasn't long until I took my shoes (sneakers) off, because of the sand in them and blisters on my heels, so I walked about five miles barefooted, and the last mile in the dark in a downpour of rain. Finally, the cart became mired in the mud, so Helen and I walked ahead to the hospital compound, which we were near, to see why the car hadn't come as far as the air strip to meet us. We found that the drivers had taken us on a "short cut" up to the hospital, and we had not seen the car in which Arnie Thompson was waiting. Needless to say, we were soaked and cold at that point. I arrived at the door of the Arnetts' home, where Pearl met me. She looked at me and said, "I think you would like a hot bath!" I agreed, but pointed out that my suitcase was behind in the cart, so I had no clean clothes to change into. Looking me over, Pearl (who is small and slender), said "Perhaps you could wear my maternity dress." And so I did! After a hot bath and a meal we were ready to tumble into bed.

The Walkers: Pastor Jonah, Chuck Arnett, Gene Westley, Al Bohr

I visited the hospital, the Bohrs at Banyam, and the literacy center, where work was being carried on by Amadu Biyam in Heidy Dennis' absence. There were meetings with Nigerian staff, church people, and missionaries.

On September 26 we made our long trip back to Lankaviri, returning the same way we had come. We started back to Jos the afternoon of the twenty-eighth and arrived there on Monday evening, the twenty-ninth.

I had hoped to meet Geoffrey Dearsley, Field Secretary of the Sudan United Mission, but we missed connections all along the way. He was the person who had worked on visas for us, and I would have liked to talk with him. I had planned to meet him in Ibadan, where I also wanted to visit the Pierre Benignu Study Center (Islam in Africa Project), and Immanuel College, where we had sent ministerial students from Sierra Leone in the past. In addition, I wanted to see Eustace Renner (whom I had known in Sierra Leone), and who was there as a secretary of the All Africa Conference of Churches. However, flights were canceled and I was advised not to try to go by road to Ibadan. There were riots in that Yoruba area, and no one was traveling by road unless absolutely necessary. Therefore, I waited in Lagos from October 2-3, until I could get a plane to Accra to catch the Pan Am flight to New York. Pan Am did not stop at Lagos because they were late on the fourth, and no flights landed or took off after dark in the unlighted airport (not lighted because of the war).

Village Scenes

Grinding Guinea Corn

1970–End of the War; Continued Trouble in the Church

I returned to Nigeria in March of 1970. A visa to visit Nigeria was again obtained in Sierra Leone. Because it was the dry season it was very hot, but travel was not nearly as difficult as in the previous September. Cessation of the civil war had brought some changes which were affecting the life of missionaries and Nigerians:

1. Private planes were now allowed to fly. Negotiations had been resumed by Missionary Aviation Fellowship, with which an agreement had been reached by the World Division just before the planes were grounded. It seemed likely that permission would be granted for M.A.F. to import a plane and begin flights by June 1, However, they now had a problem in obtaining experienced staff, so they would have no regular service until March of 1971. In the meantime, some assistance could be given by the Christian Reformed Church and Sudan Interior Mission planes. This would save a great deal of time spent in travel, and would give more security to those who were completely cut off by road during the rains.
2. Night flights had now resumed to Lagos and Kano, and Maiduguri would become an international airport.
3. Shelves were beginning to fill with items which had been scarce during the last years.
4. Building materials were extremely hard to obtain, and the cost was high. The army was buying up most of the available supplies, as they built barracks in various places throughout the country. It was uncertain whether hundreds of soldiers were going to be demobilized, which would cause tremendous social problems, or whether they were being scattered throughout the country to show the power of the government or to keep them occupied.
5. The Northeast State was being divided into "development areas." There was uncertainty as to whether or not these would be administrative areas. It had caused unease among the people of Muri. The Native Administration officials had been removed, and popular elections were to be held for administrative positions. The result would be even less power for the emirs; if it were an honest election, it would be good; but few people believed that it would be any less corrupt than most of the politics of the country.
6. The *New Nigerian* was filled with anti-American sentiment, while Russia was high-lighted and praised as the true friend of Nigeria. There were many Russians in the country. The British were having a difficult time, and permits to enter the country were not easy for them to obtain.

Problems in the Muri Church continued. For the last year and a half we had been trying to help the pastors and evangelists to understand the necessity of a representative liaison committee. Suggestions were made for some changes in the composition of the Muri Christian Council (which served some of the functions of an executive committee for the Regional Church Council, or *Magalissa*), so that it could serve the function of a liaison committee. Many hours had been spent in discussion of proposed changes in the constitution, in 1968 and again in 1969, and they were accepted by both the Muri Christian Council and the *Magalissa*. However, the matter had been brought up again in December of 1969, after a campaign by some of the pastors, and the former action had been revoked. The pastors and evangelists felt threatened because of the provision which would allow church members who were not members of the *Magalissa* to be on committees of the church. Suggested changes would have insured that persons actually engaged in the various parts of the work of the church would be on the committees. Because many of them were teachers or dispensers with more education than the pastors and evangelists, the latter did not want them to have a place of authority in the church. There was unrest, and threats on the part of one segment of the church to withdraw. Protests of those who were not in control were quite valid, but it had to be remembered that this same group was on the other side of the fence only a few years before. There were constant tension and actual fighting among members of different tribes. The missionaries, particularly the Field Representative and those involved in financial matters, were severely criticized. Some of our best missionaries had been Field Representatives and had left the field after they had served in that capacity. After June of 1970 there would be no one for that position, yet it was an absolute necessity to have someone serve at least some of the functions, because of the lack of educated leadership in the church and the structure of the government of the Sudan United Mission, of which we were a part. Because of the lack of experienced missionaries, a plan had been worked out to divide the responsibilities of Field Representative among several missionaries and the Chairman of the church. The church leaders were protesting this bitterly, and were accusing us of deserting the church, even though only two months earlier some were trying to get rid of the Field Representative. They wanted missionaries to act as errand boys and to blame them for things they did not like, and did not want to accept more responsibility for the inner life of the church. Some of the teachers, dispensers and students were dissatisfied and concerned about the state of the church. They understood and accepted the changes in the constitution which had been suggested, but were not in places of authority to bring the changes about.

I was privileged to meet with the annual Field Committee of the Sudan United Mission in Jos, and it was some comfort, though a dubious one, to learn that other branches were having similar problems.

McBride Secondary School

The new secondary school at Jalingo was in its second year, with two classes. Darrell and Anne Spores, who received a visa in December and went immediately to Nigeria, were doing excellent work. Anne had been elected principal, and Darrell was in charge of the building. This, too, was difficult for the Nigerians to understand–that a man should be subordinate to his wife in position. Darrell was having to spend many hours trying to find building materials. Building could not begin, however, until the government officially approved the Certificate of Occupancy. The wheels of government ground very slowly.

*Breaking Stones in
Preparation for Building*

Making Cement Blocks

*Darrell Spores–Digging
a Well*

Muri Christian Training School

Since the establishment of a Board of Governors and the appointment of Al and Marianne Bohr to the Muri Christian Training School, there had been a great improvement in that institution. A new curriculum was being developed, better qualified Nigerian staff had been obtained, and for the first time extension courses for lay people were offered in the villages during vacation period. The greatest need at that time was for an agriculturalist to work in the school, which it was hoped would become an extension center for community development in Muri.

Marianne Bohr in Student Clinic

*Rev. Mazadu Bakila, Staff Member,
Serving Communion*

Rev. Al Bohr, Teaching a Class

*Rev. Walter Erbele, Agriculture Class
(Guinea Corn)*

T.C.N.N.

Dean and Lois Gilliland were now part of the staff at the Theological College of Northern Nigeria, and both were much appreciated. Dean was also engaged in research for his doctoral thesis, a study of the influence of Islam upon the animistic religion of Northern Nigeria.

Other Concerns

New personnel from both our Board and that of the German church were helping to raise morale of a demoralized missionary staff. The need for a field treasurer–hospital business manager and doctors was still crucial. There were candidates available, and we hoped for visas.

There was time during this difficult trip for some relaxation. It happened that the children and young people who were at Hillcrest were at home on vacation during the time I was there. Dick Hundreiser invited me to go with them to the Yankiri Game Reserve. What an interesting and relaxing time! We saw gorillas, wart hogs, and other animals.

I left Nigeria after that trip with concern for the church of Muri.

Relaxation at Yankiri Game Reserve

Other Nigerian Scenes

Bambur Airport Cafe

Jalingo Market–Pharmacy

Jalingo Street

United Methodist Bookshop, Jalingo

1971–Growth and Problems; SUM Meeting

My 1971 report to the World Division staff concerning Nigeria began with "Problems have been many and relationships difficult with the Muri Church of Christ, in the Northeast State, Nigeria, where The United Methodist Church and its predecessors have been in mission for nearly fifty years. In spite of difficulties, however, the church has continued to grow rapidly; membership is now reported as 4,500. Eleven pastors, eight catechists, and two hundred four evangelists take care of thirty organized churches and many more preaching points in five districts. The church membership is located on both sides of the Benue River, in an area of eighteen hundred square miles and made up of representatives of eighteen different tribal groups. These are communities which have linguistic differences matched by different life styles and high levels of ethnocentrism. The problem is compounded by difficulties in transportation and communication."

McBride Secondary School

Ann Spores, Principal, with Teachers

McBride Secondary School was nearing the end of its third year of existence. The building program was continuing against tremendous difficulties of obtaining materials, qualified workmen and funds. However, the school was able to move into its new quarters in May of 1971, even though the first buildings were not yet complete. Hundreds of students applied, but only a few could be taken; many of these would have been without a school if McBride had not been established. The World Division was searching for an experienced, mature principal who could receive orientation and language study in time to take over the school in 1972 when the present principal would return to the U.S. It was hoped that when the school was more adequately staffed a rural ministries program could be established which would reach to adults and "school leavers" in the community. Plans were to teach classes in English, agriculture, technical skills, and others that might be needed.

Classrooms Under Construction

Medical Work

Guinter Memorial Hospital continued to serve a large number of people in the surrounding area. In addition to curative medicine, the hospital served an important function through the Medical Assistants Training School. The graduates would eventually be in charge of medical dispensaries in villages of Muri Division. These clinics were self-supporting and gave basic medical care to many who could never reach a hospital. With the addition of two new doctors and a public health nurse plans were being made for a Rural Health program, by which it was hoped through education and preventive medicine much illness could be prevented.

Drs. Joyce and Jerrell Mathison

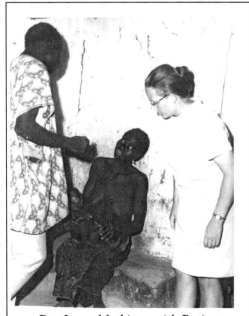

Dr. Joyce Mathison with Patient

The Muri Christian Training School was making an important contribution to the life of Muri Church through the training of evangelists and an extension program in the villages. The recent changes in the curriculum (particularly the addition of the extension program) and upgrading of qualifications of the staff were encouraging. Unfortunately, however, there was a misunderstanding between the church and the World Division. The church leadership refused to allow the institution to be governed by a Board, ordered the discharge of some of the staff, and cessation of the extension program. Because it was impossible to continue an effective school under those conditions, and reduction in funds available made it imperative to set priorities for the use of money, funds and missionary personnel were withdrawn in April of 1971.

The World Division continued to contribute, however, to theological education through the provision of staff and capital funds to the Theological College of Northern Nigeria, a cooperative school of TEKAS. The school continued to offer a certificate course for students who had completed primary school; a diploma course for those who had completed secondary school or its equivalent in teacher training and training for wives in religious knowledge, homemaking, and women's work. An investigation was being made of the possibilities of offering courses which would equip graduates to teach Religious Knowledge classes in primary and secondary schools. Nigerian staff had been added to both the women's and theological sections of the school during the year.

The Division also continued to contribute one staff member to the Church of the Brethren Waka Teacher Training College at Biu.

Amadu Biyam Teaching Women to Read

A literacy program continued in Muri Church under the direction of Amadu Biyam, who continued the work after Heidy Dennis left Nigeria. Classes throughout Muri continued to produce adults who had learned to read Hausa. Many had become Christians as a result.

The World Division continued to contribute proportionately large amounts for scholarships (more than was received for scholarship funds) because of the crucial need for education and training for leadership in the area.

Other missionary personnel continued to make important contributions to Hillcrest School for the children of missionaries.

The report closed with these words: "Those who are concerned for the work in Nigeria need an extra measure of patience, understanding and love; the difficulties are many; the needs are great."

Meeting of the International Committee, Sudan United Mission

On July 2-6, 1971 I attended a meeting of the S.U.M. in St. Legier, Switzerland. The International Committee of the Sudan United Mission, of which we were a part because of the work in Nigeria, had last met five years previously. The S.U.M. was made up of nine autonomous branches: the Christian Reformed Church, South African Branch, Australian and New Zealand Branch, Danish Lutheran Church, French Branch, Swiss Branch, Norwegian Lutheran Church, British Branch, and United Methodists ("American" Branch). The various members emphasized their "evangelical," conservative theology.

Our involvement gave a different perspective to our ecumenical cooperation. Because it meant a more united witness in Nigeria, it was felt that it was a fellowship we should value. Two years previously the Canadian branch had withdrawn because of the involvement of our church and of the Danish Lutherans in the World Council of Churches. The union of the Evangelical United Brethren Church with the Methodists had caused some concern and suspicion by members of the S.U.M. In my report on church union I stressed the evangelical heritage of both our churches, and our flexibility in regard to cooperation with groups with various emphases. Dr. Dean Gilliland and I represented our Board; they had respect and confidence in him, and I believed that our presence there (both of us having been former E.U.B.) was reassuring. Dr. Immanuel Mohr, Secretary of the Mission Board of the Evangelical Methodist Church in Germany, was present as an observer.

Reports were heard from each Branch. Ours was not the only one having problems. Three other branches had experienced tribal conflicts within the church, two of which had resulted in divided churches. The French Branch reported on their work in Tchad, the Swiss, in the Cameroun, and the Australia-New Zealand Branch told of recent contacts with the church in the Sudan which had grown out of their work. (All missionaries were expelled from Sudan eight years before, but the church continued to grow.) The Plateau Church connected with the British Branch was the oldest church and the most developed. That church was now supporting more than twenty-five missionary couples, who were working in a Muslim setting, in an area completely strange to them. They had a school for missionary children, and had more understanding of some of the problems of expatriate staff. One-third of their church's budget of £3000 annually was given for the support of their missionaries. The church had a couple preparing to go to the Kanuri people, a Muslim tribe which had been untouched by Christianity.

Reports were given on various cooperative projects of the S.U.M. and TEKAS. We had shared in a medical evangelistic mission on Lake Chad; the Christian Central Pharmacy in Jos; New Life for All; and Faith and Farm and the Christian Rural Advisory Council (C.R.A.C.).

The question of the doctrinal basis of the S.U.M. was brought up once again, but it was agreed unanimously that we would remain with the current doctrinal statement, one upon which we could agree for cooperation. There was considerable discussion of the future of the International Committee, and whether Nigerian representatives should be included at the next meeting. It was finally agreed that a meeting of the representatives of the boards only would meet together as needed, and that a meeting for fellowship of both S.U.M. and Nigerian representatives might be held in Nigeria in five years, if TEKAS cared to extend an invitation for such a meeting.

1972–Final Report on Nigeria

During 1972 our problems with the Muri Church of Christ in Nigeria continued to be great. It was regrettable that during the year one of the districts felt it necessary to separate from the Muri Church, so that there were now two church groups, Muri Church and Muri East. The World Division was attempting to deal impartially with both groups. In spite of its many problems, however, Muri Church continued to increase in numbers.

There were some positive aspects, particularly in relation to the medical work, and our involvement by means of personnel in cooperative work of various kinds.

Medical Program

Guinter Memorial Hospital continued its service to the people in a large area. Usual problems of meningitis, snake bites from a rare and most dangerous snake, and other tropical diseases were common. The tuberculosis control program was improved, after the return of one of the Nigerian nurses from a special government training program. During the first half of 1972 the patient load was up 25% and the receipts, 35%. The support of the hospital and related program was being sought through Program Project Agreements for three-year periods.

Because new personnel had been obtained, the program of public health was extended in a way which had not been possible before. Dr. Joyce Mathison and Miss Billie Jean Rydberg,

Rural Health Program --Dr. Joyce Mathison, Nurse Billie Jean Rydberg

a nurse, made an excellent team. They made regular visits to the nine dispensaries of the church, and some of the Medical Assistants (dispensers) had been brought into the Medical Assistants Training School at the hospital for refresher courses. The church appointed one of the most experienced and best Assistants to be the treasurer of the dispensaries, and he had asked the field treasurer for help in setting up books. Plans were being finalized for an intensive survey of health needs in the area served by the hospital. Miss Rydberg was planning to spend three weeks in each of four selected villages where there were no dispensaries, in order to learn to know the people, their desires and needs. It would give insight into some of the basic causes of health problems, in addition to helping to have a better understanding and rapport with the village people, and opportunity for Christian witness in word as well as deed. At the end of the three weeks a team of about twelve additional persons was to come from the hospital to conduct laboratory tests and physical examinations, in order to survey the health problems. No major treatments would be given, although immunization would be offered to the children and would be followed up later. The statistics gathered from these four villages, and those from the nine dispensaries, would give a basis for planning what health problems could be attacked with the greatest hope of success for the greatest number of persons. It was expected that it would take the first term before furlough for the Mathisons and Billie Jean to establish the basis for the long-term program of public health. Furloughs had to be staggered so that work could be continued. Dr. Jerrell Mathison was an excellent doctor, but unfortunately had to act as both hospital business manager and maintenance man. Personnel was urgently needed for those positions, so that the doctors could devote their time to medical work. However, with the difficulty of obtaining visas it seemed that the only possibility would be to have a German missionary, and the German Board had not yet been able to find such a person. Dr. Charles "Chuck" Arnett continued his work and concern for the one hundred ten bed hospital, and carried the surgical load as well as other work. Dr. Arnold Thompson would be leaving soon, not to return. A doctor who could do surgery as well as general medicine was urgently needed by 1973, so that the hospital would not again be left with only one doctor. Eventually the State would take over the hospital, as it had others. However, because of its isolation, it did not seem in 1972 that it would be soon, and it was felt that we might be able to continue public health work even then. It seemed, however, that we should not expand hospital facilities, except possibly for another small building for the outpatient clinic, and some renovations. Another staff house would be needed to replace one that had recently been destroyed by fire. Other emphases should be on the public health and church dispensaries program and the Medical Assistants Training School.

We were grateful for the German Church which continued to supply the hospital with nurses. Their Board had for the first time agreed to supply the recurring budget for the Medical Assistants Training School for 1972, and it was hoped, for 1973 as well. A nurse with a degree in nursing education was needed to assist in the school and eventually become the principal.

During the year the nine dispensaries were turned over to the church for direction; a tenth dispensary was added later. A doctor from the hospital gave supervision to the dispensers.

Relationships with Muri Church

There was increasing dissatisfaction within the church over Pastor Ezra's leadership. According to their constitution (which was revised but never officially approved), the chairman should have a three-year term. That meant that Ezra should retire at the end of 1972. However, some time previous to my visit, after some delegates had left the meeting, thinking the business was completed, Ezra proclaimed a nine-year term for the chairman, secretary and treasurer. There was some bitter discussion (and only one who had sat through a meeting of the *Majalissa* could imagine what it was like.), but as usual anyone who disagreed with the chairman was not allowed to speak. No actual vote was taken. When the chairman was queried as to what the minutes stated concerning the action, he said everyone would know when the minutes were distributed. Three of the four districts of the church had threatened to break off, but they were unable to unite in order to present a solid front, and apparently seemed unable to bring about a change. The chairman attempted to have all teachers (lay leaders of the church) in the dissident Kassa District transferred out of the district. That would have effectively stopped the dissent from that area, but the local education authority (which actually controlled the schools) stopped that action. I was told by some Nigerians that they wished we would not continue financial support of the church administration, since it was our money which gave Ezra his power. I was unable to discuss with the executive committee a possible one year agreement for financing. In an attempt not to support dissident groups I wondered whether we were not in fact doing just that when we supported only one out of the four districts of the church, which happened to be in control at that time. I questioned whether it would not be best to disengage completely from the administration of the church itself, to give freedom to work out their own problems. I felt that the World Division staff should consider these questions seriously at the time of budget appropriations.

I had several conversations with other pastors and lay leaders of the church, and there was sincere concern on the part of some at the disunity within the church. Missionaries were struggling to find ways in which they could not only continue the work in their particular areas, but give support to the church in effective ways, and how to develop leadership. Everyone recognized the importance of leadership development, but there seemed to be insurmountable difficulties. Scholarships were given to all students from Muri Church who were in secondary and other schools. However, it was necessary for them to begin to select only those most in need of scholarships and those who would profit most, since the numbers of students had rapidly increased in recent years. There was no longer enough money for everyone to be on scholarship. Pastor Ezra did not allow anyone to take the entrance exam to enter the Theological College of Northern Nigeria in 1971, so there were no pastors in training. We could not give scholarships to the College itself, since their policy was to accept only students who were recommended by their church. Because of constant interference in the Muri Christian Training School we were forced to withdraw support and so there was no training of evangelists or their wives, except for a few who had been accepted in other S.U.M. schools. There was great need for continuing education of the present pastors, but almost no opportunities were open to them because they did not know English, and had no education other than two or three years in vernacular training in Muri Christian Training School some years before. Unfortunately, there seemed to be no facilities for teaching English to adults, since all resources for education in the country were going into education of children and youth, and only a small percentage of them could find a place in a school.

If we could continue the McBride Secondary School and establish an adult education school in connection with it as had been envisioned, perhaps we could offer such help, unless it, too, was hindered by Pastor Ezra.

The Women's Fellowship

Women's Fellowship Group

One of the most encouraging aspects of the work of the church was the Women's Fellowship, or *Zumuntar Mata*. There was a need and an eagerness for Christian nurture as well as help in various aspects of family life. Membership of Muri Church had grown gradually until an annual Women's Fellowship convention might include up to one thousand women if the meeting was centrally located. Most women had to walk over mountains and through rivers, with babies on their backs, to reach a meeting. In 1972 a Leadership Training Course was held with seventy women in attendance, officers of various local organizations. A young woman was also sent on scholarship to the Mindolo Ecumenical Centre at Kitwe, Zambia, for a special program in leadership of women's programs.

I was able to attend the annual meeting of the Fellowship for part of a day during my 1972 visit. Fewer women attended than in previous years (only about three hundred fifty instead of eight hundred to a thousand), partly because the place was very difficult to reach, and also because of lack of communication. (Some thought Pastor Ezra had given instruction that women from his district should not attend, but that might not have been true.) It was hoped that Shirley Mader, after she helped to get the home economics courses started at McBride and learned more Hausa, would be able to give part time to work with women. The women seemed eager for help.

McBride Secondary School

The greatest share of time spent in Nigeria on that trip was devoted to struggling with the difficult situation of the McBride Secondary School. Unfortunately, Dr. Immanuel Mohr, Secretary of the Board of Missions of the Evangelical Methodist Church in Germany, and representative of "Bread for the World" (an organization in Germany that enabled government money to be used for development projects abroad), was unable to obtain a visa. He had planned to be in Nigeria at the same time as I, so that we could deal with the problem together. "Bread for the World" had stopped all funding for the building program until there could be some assurance of the continuation of the school without constant interference (by Pastor Ezra). I had indicated that we could give no more capital funds, and no more recurring funds and personnel after the end of the year, unless some settlement could be made. All possible avenues were explored, including turning the school over to the state immediately, but the only way open seemed to be to have the proprietorship of the school transferred to the Sudan United Mission (United Methodist) until such time as the state desired to take it over. Legally,

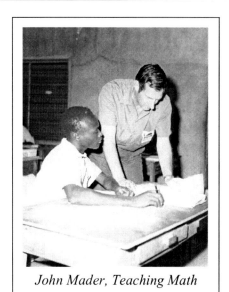

John Mader, Teaching Math

Shirley Mader and Sewing Class

Students in the Library

Teacher Stephen Turah, Leading a Church Service at the School

all that was necessary was for the Board of Trustees of the Muri Church to request such a transfer of the proprietorship. After a long and serious discussion, the three trustees (one of the four was not present) did make such a recommendation. They did so with full recognition of what this would mean for them in their relationship to Pastor Ezra, who had the power. The trustees had recently taken some firm steps in regard to property; there would soon be more in their hands, when the legal requirements could be completed for transfer of housing on two stations. They had frankly stated that Pastor Ezra had sold some property already for which there was no accounting, and for which no approval had been given, and they wanted to safeguard the rights of the church. The request for transfer of the proprietorship was presented at the McBride Board of Governors meeting, but because of Pastor Ezra's protest, it was agreed that the matter would be deferred until the meeting of the *Majalissa* on March 7 and 8. Pastor Ezra assured us that the matter would be approved. However, after long discussion it was not, although no vote was actually taken. Instead, after having told the people in Muri Church they would not have to pay their share of the cost of building the school (£2000 in four years, given in labor, farm products, or money), he had assessed each district some amount, to be paid by March 31. This in spite of our emphasis that the problem was not only in the church's lack of support by being willing to contribute a share, but the interference in the running of the school. £90 was raised by the end of March. Pastor Ezra had told the leaders of the church that when the state took over the school they would pay compensation (which was doubtful), and if the proprietorship remained in their hands they would receive the money. For that reason he was determined to keep the school in their control. He believed that the German church would supply them with money, since the World Division would not do so.

Dr. Mohr and I had a good deal of correspondence, and he supported the action we attempted to take. We met in Frankfurt on April 22 to discuss what the next step should be. He still hoped to be able to visit Nigeria some time between May 3-19. It was decided that he would send a letter written jointly by us to the Board of Governors of the school. We asked that a meeting be called to take action on the recommendations of the trustees for transfer of the proprietorship. We stated that it was felt that if this could not be done the following actions would be taken:

(1) No more funds would be available from "Bread for the World" or the World Division.

(2) Recurring funds would be stopped at the end of 1972.

(3) The present missionary personnel would be withdrawn at the end of the 1972 school term, and no more would be recruited.

(4) We would inform the State that we would be unable to continue support of the school after December 1972, and would ask that they take it over. We expected no compensation.

We told the Board that we would regret having to take such action, but felt it would be necessary if the church did not wish to transfer the proprietorship, since they were unable to take the responsibility of the proprietorship. We would much prefer to be able to complete the basic building and establish a good curriculum so that when the State took the school it would be a good one. Dr. Mohr would inform us (the World Division) of what decision was made by the Board of Governors.

In the meantime long hours were spent in discussion at McBride of how we should plan for a future which was so uncertain. It was agreed that we had a commitment to get the basic building completed, and to staff the school adequately in order to get a good foundation. We tried to plan for minimum capital expenditures and personnel in order to be able to establish the academic West African School Certificate (WASC) courses as required by the government, with emphasis on agricultural science and domestic science.

The Form V class, the last in the full secondary school, was scheduled for admission at the beginning of the new year in February 1973. In addition, if we were allowed to keep the school for even two or three years it was felt that with a minimum expenditure practical courses which would help prepare the large percentage of students who would not be able to go on to the university could be started. This depended, of course, on being able to obtain visas for additional teachers. Perhaps if such persons were able to obtain permits to work within the country an adult school could be continued in the buildings at Banyam (M.C.T.S.), which were then empty, even when the state took over the secondary school. None of this, however, could happen unless the question of the proprietorship could be settled. Members of the church would still be included on the Board of Governors, but it would mean the chairman would be nominated by the S.U.M. and we would nominate the principal. In the meantime, John and Shirley Mader were settling into a difficult situation, after waiting five months for a visa; Jim and Nancy Gulley were in Sierra Leone for practical experience in tropical agriculture and West African education (British pattern); and John and Luella Mallory were in London taking courses at the University while they waited for a visa. He was to take over as principal when the Spores would leave in December. Additional teachers were needed for math, chemistry, commercial courses, and perhaps industrial education, by 1974.

However, toward the end of 1972 word had been received of the probable imminent take-over by the government of the Northeast State. At the time of the writing of my 1972 report the future involvement of the World Division in the school was uncertain.

The Literacy Program

The literacy program also continued. A total of 1,272 students passed tests during the previous four years. New classes opened each year, taught by volunteers. Many not only learned to read and write in Hausa, but confessed Christ as Savior and joined the church during the year.

Ecumenical Relationships

We were perhaps making our best contribution to the church in Nigeria through the secondment of missionary personnel to other groups or institutions. Miss Lois Schmidt continued to make a valuable addition to teacher training at the Waka Schools (Church of the

Brethren). Rev. and Mrs. Al Bohr were much appreciated for their contribution to the Christian Rural Advisory Council (C.R.A.C), organized in the six Northern states to coordinate the rural (agricultural) work of the churches. This organization was independent of the Christian Council of Nigeria, but in fact acted as an advisory council in the North for the C.C.N. Al Bohr was the secretary or director of C.R.A.C.. and also the secretary of the Christian Rural Fellowship, a fellowship of rural workers from all denominations (both Protestant and Catholic) throughout Nigeria. The latter was a C.C.N.-adherent group.

Dr. Dean Gilliland was now principal of the Theological College of Northern Nigeria, and his wife Lois assisted in the school for wives. We also contributed to the staff at Hillcrest School for missionary children.

Conversations were held with the representative of the Missionary Aviation Fellowship (British) concerning continuation of their recently started air service on our behalf. There was some suspicion of our "doctrinal basis," but after some interrogation I believed we had passed the test for the time. It seemed, however, that they would not be able to give the much needed service for our rural health program. Other alternatives would have to be sought. Air service was so necessary in the isolated area in which we worked in Nigeria.

A Visit to a Tiv Village

During this time I had an interesting experience when we went to a Tiv village near the Cameroun border to hold a service. I spoke, with translations from English to Hausa and then to Tiv. I had a long time to think between sentences! An enthusiastic choir of young people sang and played drums and other local instruments. One was made from corn stalks bound together, with seeds or stones inside which made a sound when shaken. I asked if I might buy one, and they gave it to me. Of course we were served a meal before we left.

The Choir

A Girl Drummer

A Woman Preparing Our Food

Bringing Our Food

*The View Through the Window
in the Hut in Which We Were Seated*

I came away from Nigeria disturbed concerning the situation of the Church and missionary church relationships, and yet deeply sympathetic with the real concern of some of the more thoughtful and committed Nigerian Christians, and the overwhelming need in the area for medical care, education, community development and Christian nurture. I also continued to have a deep appreciation for our missionary personnel. Several were working in this very difficult situation at a considerable financial loss. The climate was enervating, the psychological conditions very difficult, and morale was low. They richly deserved whatever support we could give them as we tried to work out together how and where we should be in mission in Nigeria.

And so ended my responsibility for the work in Nigeria. It would be up to others to try to sort out the myriad problems.

WHAT HAS HAPPENED SINCE?
Dr. Dean Gilliland

Schism and Reconstruction 1973-1990

From all that has been written to this point, it is obvious that EKAN Muri (Nigeria Church of Christ in Muri Division: EUB) was headed for serious difficulty in leadership and authority. The central issue lay in the fact that Rev. Ezra Barawani had declared himself as Chairman for nine years. This was in direct opposition to the Constitution of the Church which allowed for three years. A long-awaited Certificate of Incorporation had recently been awarded to Muri Church by the Federal Government, bringing a new self-awareness to the Church and new sensitivity among the trustees to do things in the proper way. Chairman Ezra's leadership style was objectionable to many and his insistence on serving for nine years caused high resentment, especially among the churches connected with the Muri East District.

How the Schism Happened

Muri Church (now UMCN) covers a modest geographical area but in this area there are some eight language groups, bringing always the problems of ethnicity into almost every level of church administration. This factor cannot be missed as an additional problem that Rev. Ezra's chairmanship brought to the Church. Ultimately, the Muri East District declared their separation from the administration of Muri Church which, in effect, was a direct challenge to the Chairmanship of Rev. Ezra and, indirectly an invitation to other churches and districts to show their support or non-support of Rev. Ezra.

A majority of the Muri Church trustees ultimately opposed Ezra's leadership, putting them on the side of the separation action which had been declared by Muri East District. Two of the trustees who sided with the separation were, in fact, from Ezra's own ethnic group.. Missionaries opposed Ezra's demand for nine years and district by district the choice to support or challenge the separation action taken by Muri East developed. In the end, a reversal in perception of the true church evolved. Those who supported Ezra became the so-called separated church and those who supported the trustees became the main church. This quite anomalous situation was brought to the agenda of the annual meeting of TEKAN (The Fellowship of the Churches of Christ in Nigeria) in 1973. TEKAN is the ecumenical Conference of which Muri Church had been a member since 1954.

Representatives from both groups (Ezra's and the Trustees) attended the 1973 TEKAN meeting, both claiming to be the official representatives of Muri Church. After lengthy discussion, the lines were clarified in the eyes of the African churches (six other denominations) when the "separated group," represented by the trustees' delegates, were declared to be the legitimate delegates. Thereupon, the group supporting Ezra and Ezra himself were dismissed from the Conference because they were declared to be in violation of the TEKAN Constitution.

The situation in 1974, therefore, can be summarized in the following way:

Three Trustees who had resisted Rev. Ezra's moves to disrupt the Church were put into leadership of those congregations that now had been designated by TEKAN as the legitimate church. The "church" under Rev. Ezra's chairmanship became more or less confined to one area, that of Jalingo and environs. They had commandeered the Jalingo church building and Ezra was their pastor. He also controlled the Bookshop which was located in Jalingo and a modest headquarters building. Along with this he controlled several rural health centers (dispensaries). The most disputed issue was that the actual Certificate of Incorporation of Muri Church which had recently been issued to the church by the Federal Government was in Ezra's possession. In his mind, the possession of this document authenticated his claim to continue as head of the church.

There was much legal wrangling in secular courts in the months that followed, centering on Ezra's claim to chairmanship, much of which centered on the fact that he worked from the church "headquarters" and that the Certificate of Occupancy was in his possession. As this situation dragged on and on, several attempts were made to bring the groups together but without success. The wider church again became involved when the Chairman of TEKAN came to Jalingo to work for reconciliation. Bishop Todi, the Chairman, was the highly respected head of the Lutheran Church in Nigeria. This protracted meeting ended without change except that some who had been ambivalent about their loyalty, including one entire District, now declared support for the trustees, (that is to say, they abandoned Ezra's group).

The matter of financial support, especially from the U.S.A., began to figure heavily into the ongoing life of the church since the question of authority and legitimacy of the church was in question. In time, funds were released only to the trustees' section of the church. Rev. Ezra's group, in attempting to keep all the work going among his churches, but without funds, complained to the Government with the request that the Government take over the widespread medical work. It was two more years before the medical work was handed over to the Government.

Attempts at Reconciliation

The dissension in the church reached government levels by 1975 due to confrontations between the two factions, touching upon right to properties and legal representation. The Governor of North East State attempted his own intervention by mandating the Provincial Secretary of the State to step in and settle the problem. The anti-Ezra group had now decided on their own candidate for Chairman, Rev. Mazadu by name. Each side was told to come to Jalingo with thirty representatives. On the first round, each side stood firm so the ballot cast was equally divided between the two. Because of this impasse, a second ballot was called for at which time one delegate switched his vote. So the result was 31 for Ezra and 29 for Mazadu. Rev. Ezra was declared by the State government to be the Head of the Muri Church. Of course, this brought further consternation. The problem now was not primarily an ecclesiastical one, rather, it had become an issue of personalities, secular opinion and was heavily conditioned by ethnic prejudice.

In addition to this further offense within the church the ecumenical body (TEKAN) declared that such intervention by the government into church affairs was unacceptable and that the results of the election would not be recognized by the TEKAN churches. TEKAN responded by again calling the two factions together but the Ezra side refused to attend this meeting or even a second one when it was called for. In light of this, TEKAN met with the trustee group and supervised a new election of church officials so that the trustees could get on with the work of the church with some kind of organization. Six officers for the church were elected at this meeting, --a Chairman, a Vice Chairman, a Secretary, an Asst. Secretary, a Treasurer and Asst. Treasurer.

This new roster of officers, put in place by consensus and by those who were seen as the official church, formed a basis for beginning again. The results of the election were sent far and wide, including Government offices, declaring that these persons and these alone were to be recognized by both church and government. These new officers began their work in January, 1977.

As for Rev. Ezra's group and Ezra himself, they continued to function as an independent church but, in time, they began to lose power with the people except for Jalingo town and its environs. Rev. Ezra always claimed he was a representative of the Evangelical United Brethren mission and the African churches founded by the E.U.B. missionaries. He continued to believe this, even though the E.U.B. union with the Methodist Church had taken place in 1968. (We will observe below how slowly the transition to U.M. structure and polity took place.) For Ezra, the E.U.B. was always the "mother church" and developments in the U.S.A. that led to union with Methodists had no effect on his right to leadership.

The action taken by TEKAN provided some clarification as to how to proceed in the interim between the passing of old structures and new arrangements with United Methodists. A consensus was growing among local churches and pastors, and in the districts, that change was inevitable. It had been seven years since Rev. Ezra Barawani had been elected Chairman. In the background, of course, was the long tradition with which leaders and church members were familiar. The way of doing things had been set in place in 1954 when TEKAN was organized with seven autonomous branch denominations; each governed in the traditions of their founding missions from both Europe and America.

Moving Toward a New Church

The "turn-over" from mission to church among the TEKAN constituents began in all seriousness around 1970 with the Lutheran Church of Denmark taking the initial action. The Board of Missions of the United Methodist Church did not make any radical moves toward change in Nigeria during the 70's and into the early 80's. With the newly elected officers set in place by TEKAN and with Rev. Ezra's group becoming less active, the church returned to the familiar organization that they knew best. There were now six Districts, three on the north side of the Benue River and three on the south side. One sticking point continued to come up. The Certificate of Incorporation was still in Ezra's possession even though his legal right to leadership had failed. This ambiguity as to how the church should now be defined resulted in action by the church officers, including three missionaries, to seek full membership in the United Methodist Church. Following the channels of approval, (see below) the Muri Church of Christ (EUB) became officially the United Methodist Church of Nigeria. Of course, this was only the beginning of the fully reconstructed church that was to follow. The years of the 1980s will always be remembered for the re-education of leaders and churches throughout the six districts and for learning how to participate in and govern a new denomination.

To help in the learning process, the GBGM sent two of the transitional church leaders to the U.S.A. Rev. Mazadu Bakila was an ex-officio member to the General Conference of 1984, when the former Muri Church was accepted into the United Methodist Church.

Peter M. Dong learned about church process at the Liberia Annual Conference and returned to teach the Nigerian church leaders about issues related to acceptance into the West Africa Central Conference (1984). The new Provisional Annual Conference of the UMCN was presided over by Bishop Arthur Kulah. This was a time of growth and expansion of the United Methodist Church of Nigeria both in start-ups of new local churches and the opening of new districts.

Bishop Kulah also presided over the election of a new General Superintendent in 1987 which fell to Done Peter Dabale. Dabale had been active in community development and had graduated from the Theological College of Northern Nigeria. Dabale also went to Liberia to take a course in church administration and to study the *Book of Discipline*. Further steps in the transition to becoming a Provisional Conference within the United Methodist Church were carried out by Ms. Ethel Johnson. Professor Johnson carefully worked out a schedule of courses in polity and process, traveling from district to district and to local churches right up to the time when Nigeria became a full Annual Conference in1992.   (The story is continued on p.457.)

Chapter 3. Liberia
Introduction

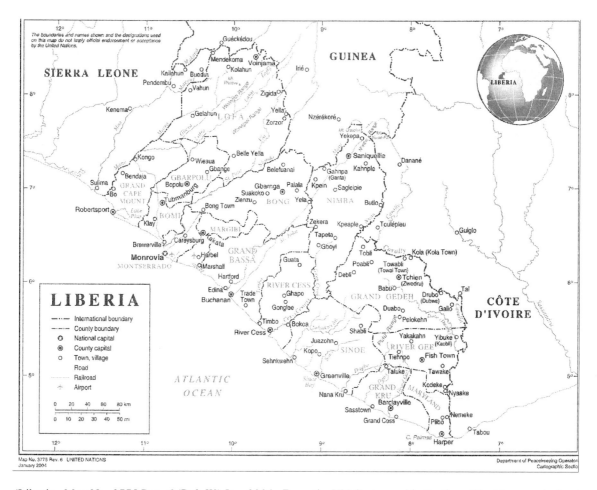

(Liberia, Map No. 3775 Rev. 6 (B & W) Jan. 2004. From the UN Cartographic Section. Used by permission.)

Liberia, a West African nation of 43,000 square miles (slightly larger than Ohio), is at the western end of the rain forest belt that crosses Africa at the equator. Liberia is bordered on the west by the Atlantic Ocean, on the north by Sierra Leone and Guinea, and by the Ivory Coast on the east. The rivers that drain heavy rainfall from interior highlands down to the swamps and lagoons on the coast are formidable to build bridges across, so there is no main cross-country road that links the nation together. A network of country roads, often impassible in the rainy season, bears the brunt of overloaded trucks and mammy wagons shuttling people and animals from village to village. With few natural harbors, the rocky coastline deters access to the interior. A hot, wet climate fosters deadly tropical diseases that sicken newcomers and sap the health and energy of indigenous peoples, hindering progress and development toward a modern nation. The capital and main seaport is Monrovia, with an estimated 1,000,000 residents and more flooding in from rural areas, attracted by bright lights and vain hopes of finding work.

A population of about 3.4 million consists of 16 ethnic groups. The Kpelle in central and western Liberia is the largest ethnic group (20%); the Bassa are 16%, Gio 8% and Kru 7%, with 49% spread over the remaining twelve ethnic groups. Americo-Liberians who are descendants of freed slaves that began returning from America in 1822 make up an estimated 5% of the population. There are also Lebanese, Indians, and other West African nationals who form part of the business community. English is the official language. Religions are estimated as Christian 40%, Muslim 20%, and animist 40%. Unemployment is 80%. Life expectancy is forty-seven years. The largest segment of the work force is agriculture 70%, with industry 15% and services 2%. Food crops are rice, cassava, palm oil, corn, vegetables, bananas, plantain, citrus and some cocoa and coffee. Industry focuses mainly on exporting iron ore, natural rubber, and lumber, with a clandestine trade in diamonds and gold.

History of the area records that the Portuguese first established contact as early as 1461 and named it the Grain Coast because of the abundance of grains of melagueta pepper. In 1663 the British installed trading posts along the coast, but the Dutch destroyed these. As the slave trade began to flourish, French, Spanish, and American slave ships joined in the cruel trade. In 1822 the American Colonization Society, in cooperation with the United States government, established a colony for freed slaves at Cape Mesurado. Thousands of freed American slaves and freed African-Americans arrived in succeeding years and formed more settlements, leading to an experiment in a commonwealth form of government. In 1847, with the blessing of the Society, these settlements joined in declaring their independence and establishing the Republic of Liberia, fashioned after the United States' executive, legislative and judicial government structure, with its capital at Monrovia. The Society's members and their agents were men of faith who had sought to help freed slaves by securing an asylum in Africa where they could be free of oppression, establish their own government, and reap the rewards of their own work. It was also hoped that the colonists would stamp out the slave trade on their coast and present the Christian religion to the Africans. The colonists who assumed responsibilities in the new nation were also men of faith. J.J. Roberts, their first President, and many who followed after him, helped to fulfill those dreams.

In the early years of the Republic, the Americo-Liberian settlers sometimes encountered violent opposition from indigenous Africans due to cultural differences, but also because the indigenes were excluded from citizenship until 1904. In addition, the settlers had to contend with British and French colonial expansionists who took over some of Liberia's territory. The political system became a one-party state ruled by the True Whig Party (TWP) and the Americo-Liberians monopolized political power and restricted voting rights of the indigenous peoples until 1980.

–Dr. Robert Carey

Exploration and Orientation
November 29-December 12, 1968

After some delay in leaving Jos because of plane cancellations, I arrived in Lagos on November 29 just in time to catch the West African plane for Monrovia. B.B. Cofield met me at Robertsfield. I enjoyed staying in the home of B.B. and Martha Cofield, who had lived in Liberia for many years. Martha was a gracious hostess, and B.B. served as field treasurer in addition to being the pastor in one of the churches near Monrovia.

UMC Conference Office

The two weeks spent in Liberia were largely in the nature of an exploratory trip, one to acquaint me with the people and institutions of The United Methodist Church in that country. Although I had visited Liberia when I was a missionary in Sierra Leone (an Evangelical United Brethren) and had met some of the Methodist missionaries, I had much to learn about the church in 1968.

I was privileged to share a meal, and also to attend a reception at the home of Bishop S. Trowen Nagbe, Sr. and Melvina Nagbe. The Liberia Conference was very fortunate to have the leadership of those two outstanding Christians. The Bishop was also fortunate to have as his secretary Sue Cohen, a LOAS worker

Dinner With Some of the Missionaries

B.B. & Martha Cofield, Elaine & Oliver Clark,
Don & Kay Weaver

Tom Tucker, Karey Joseph, Sue Cohen,
John & Mira Pipkin, Shirley & John Mader

The Kru Coast

Bishop Nagbe and I traveled together to the Kru Coast in the mission plane, "The Methodist Circuit Rider," and were entertained by President Tubman at the Executive Mansion at Cape Palmas. (I soon discovered that for all practical purposes The United Methodist Church in Liberia was a "state" church. There could be no criticism of the state in Liberia, and very little criticism of the church. The "state" was controlled by President Tubman, himself a United Methodist.)

President Tubman's
Mansion

I will never forget that Sunday morning when we were driven to the local church, as part of a procession, headed by the President and his cabinet, with flags fluttering in the breeze and martial music by the Army band. During the service President Tubman announced the amount of money he was giving to the church, I believe $100, although I do not remember exactly. Pointing to each of the Cabinet members in turn who were sitting on the front row, he announced, "and you . . . and you . . . will give (the same amount) too." Then, as the custom was, various persons came to the front and put their offering into the container, announcing how much it was. I noted, at the end of that time, that an elderly woman–obviously a village woman, bending low, came to the table and put a small sum of money in the offering plate. No fanfare for her! Needless to say, I remembered the account of Jesus and the widow's mite (*Mark 12:41-44*).

President Tubman Leaving

The Band Playing as the President Leaves

Return to Monrovia

On Monday we returned to Monrovia. There I visited the Girls' Hostel, where girls in grade and high school live while attending the United Methodist schools. The directress was a Liberian, Mrs. Nancy Nah. She was assisted by a matron part-time (a university student) and Jackie Jenkins, an A3, who also taught twelve hours at the College of West Africa.

The Monrovia Girls' Hostel

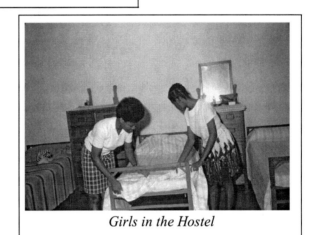
Girls in the Hostel

The College of West Africa was a secondary school of the church, which had a long history and a good standing in Liberia. Plans for expansion were being proposed, but I personally felt that three things needed to be done before further expansion was considered: (1) Find some way to pay for the deficit budgeting; (2) concentrate on quality rather than quantity (classes were too large for good teaching; equipment was not adequate); and (3) wait for the results of a recent educational survey (The Bosserman Survey). Dr. Bob Carey was the president of the school; Rev. Oliver Clark was the chaplain, a teacher of religion, and also the pastor of a church. His wife, Elaine, taught in a United Methodist elementary school. Don Weaver taught science; John Mader was the industrial arts teacher, and his wife, Shirley, at the Bishop's request was working with Mrs. Nagbe on suggestions for leadership training for women, including wives of ministers. The Bishop planned to appoint her Director of Women's Work.

I also enjoyed meeting Dr. Robert Kingsbury, who was under special appointment to the University of Liberia as a W.S.C.F. (World Student Christian Federation) and S.C.M. (Student Christian Movement) chaplain. Shirley Kingsbury was a nurse and had found useful work to do as school nurse at C.W.A. and holding clinics in one of the U.M. churches near Monrovia.

In Monrovia I also met and had opportunities for conversation with two A 3s. Tom Tucker had served as a youth worker, but at that time was carrying much of the responsibility of Tony Fadley, Director of Christian Education, who was on furlough. Tom had begun a good youth program. It was hoped that we could find another A-3 to take his place when he left in July.

Karey Joseph was doing outstanding work in literacy and literature production. She was working with Liberians, and was hopeful that the Conference would assign at least one person full time to work with her, so that he could be trained before she left. There was great need for a linguist who would work in Liberia for several months on an analysis of the Kru language. Until that was done, not much else could be done in the literacy program. Bishop Nagbe was very interested in the Kru literacy program and the help it could give to the life of the churches on the Kru Coast.

John and Mira Pipkin also lived in Monrovia. John was the pilot for the "Methodist Circuit Rider," which carried the Bishop, doctors, missionaries and church leaders to various parts of the country, particularly to the Kru Coast, otherwise almost inaccessible.

Gbarnga

On November 30 B.B. Cofield drove me to Gbarnga. I enjoyed learning to know U.S. and Vivienne Gray, who had served for many years in Liberia, and appreciated staying in their home. U.S. had done much of the building, served as station manager, and in the past had an extensive agricultural program, which served as a stimulus to better farming in the surrounding area. He also had been appointed as pastor of the Voinjama church. Vivienne was educational director of the elementary and high school, supervised, worked with the principal on budget and taught Home Economics and Christian Education in the Junior High classes. She also supervised the two hostels, and helped in Methodist Youth Fellowship and was on religious education curriculum committees of the Conference.

U.S. Gray Supervising Building

U.S. Gray and a Green Mamba

The Secondary School

Boys in Gym

Principal and Boys in the Library

The Pastor's School at Gbarnga was a Conference project, though staffed partly by missionary personnel. There were at that time eight pastors (the number was limited because of lack of housing for pastors' families). Dr. Wickstrom was acting as principal for one year, while the Paul and Sigren Sundar were on furlough. After talking with him and looking at the curriculum, I had come to some general conclusions concerning the school. I had come to feel that the area of pastoral training was one which had been neglected by the World Division. There were widely varied types of curricula and plans for pastoral training. It was very difficult to find suitable material for theological training for students with only a few years of education (reading abilities of the students at Gbarnga ranged from third to eighth grade, although all of them had been through high school). I felt that a thorough study needed to be made of the curriculum at Gbarnga. It seemed to me at that time that it was not meeting the needs of pastors of village churches. I felt that in Liberia, as in Nigeria, the curriculum should feature biblical and theological training, community development, and literacy. The program for wives also had serious defects. If the proposals made by Shirley Mader and Melvina Nagbe could be implemented, there could be great improvement. Another church development missionary was needed on the staff, although I believed that some classes could be put together. It seemed a great expense for training of only eight men a year.

Pastor Guanu (from Ganta), Student in Pastor's School

111

Ganta

The largest mission station in Liberia was at Ganta. The Ganta Hospital had thirty-two beds (it was hoped to expand it to fifty), and four doctors (one always home on furlough). It was the one hospital in the area for which I was responsible that had at least a minimum staff, though at least one more nurse was needed. Jenny Larsen (Norwegian) was a nurse-midwife. Loretta Gruver and Vera Hughlett were in charge of the School of Nursing, which was recognized by the Liberian government. There were at that time eleven students. It was hoped that the school could expand to a maximum of twenty-five students. One requirement for this was a fifty-bed hospital. Uniola Adams, also a nurse, had served at Ganta since 1939, when she came from China. She had worked in the leprosy colony, and helped in various other capacities.

Helen Day, an A 3, had set up a well-equipped laboratory, and trained young men to do the work. Shirley Hickman was also a medical technologist, and would continue to give some supervision to the laboratory when Helen left in March. Dr. Max Hickman and Dr. Paul Getty were at that time the only doctors, although Dr. William Wallace was to complete his study in public health within a few months and return to the field. Dr. Robert Kingsbury would prepare to become Board certified in surgery during his furlough, which would begin in January

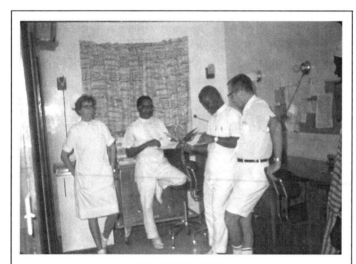

Ganta Hospital
Jenny Larsen & Dr. Max Hickman with Liberian Staff

Dr. Getty had just returned from a study of special surgical techniques for leprosy patients, and after Dr. Wallace returned, was planning for much increased service to persons with leprosy. Paye Nelson, a young Liberian man, had just returned from training in physiotherapy in Ethiopia, and would be a valuable asset in the expanded program. There had been a marked improvement in the leprosy colony in the last few years. Much of this was due to the dedicated work of two missionaries of the Swedish Board, Arnie and Ula-Britt Hansen. He was a builder, and had also helped to organize and supervise the agricultural program at the colony. Ula-Britt used her nursing skills. Both were very interested in the leprosy program. Outstation clinics were held regularly for treatment of patients with leprosy. The American Leprosy Missions contributed most of the budget for leprosy work.

Leprosy Rehab and Control Center

School at the Leprosy Center

Uniola Adams Holding an Outpatient Leprosy Clinic

Taking Smears for Leprosy

There was an elementary school at Ganta, in which some of the missionary wives taught. Doretha Brown was director of the Girls' Hostel, where forty-fifty girls lived while attending school. Another woman was needed to assist her.

Harold Crow was in charge of the industrial program at Ganta. In addition to supervising the maintenance work, he taught mechanics and supervised the carpenter shop. His wife, Anna Margaret, taught part-time in the school and helped in church work.

Jim Hankins was serving as station chairman and had some responsibility for helping pastors of the district. Eleanor Hankins was doing a great deal of enthusiastic work in Christian education: taught in the elementary school, supervised the Sunday School, trained high school boys to hold Vacation Church School, provided curriculum, etc.

The Conference asked that we help to support a modern cooperative hospital at Phoebe. They asked for $5,000 annually.

Back to the Kru Coast

Bishop Nagbe took me on a brief tour of the churches on the Kru Coast (by plane, with John Pipkin as pilot). He was quite interested in the area (he himself was a Kru) where the mission work first began. A tombstone for Jane Lewis, a missionary who died in the early years, reminded me that Liberia was one of the countries in West Africa known as "The White Man's Graveyard."

I saw decaying church buildings, and visited briefly with some of the pastors. The Bishop asked for a missionary couple to be stationed at one of the villages. The "flying doctors" program was giving some medical help. If the Kru literacy program could be developed, there were real possibilities for the strengthening of the church. I was impressed with the attempt by some of the people to help themselves (they were building a girl's hostel, for example). To me, the spontaneous song which was sung by the group of Christians as we left was more impressive than the robed choir in the large church in Cape Palmas.

Seen from the plane:
Burning farms in preparation for planting

*Bishop Nagbe and the
"Methodist Circuit Rider"*

A Hostel for Girls Being Built in Nana Kru

The Proposed Seminary

One of the questions I discussed at some length with a few of the missionaries, and particularly Bishop Nagbe, was that of the proposed United Seminary. The Lutheran Church had offered land near Cuttington College and Phoebe Hospital. There had been a good deal of exploratory work done, but the question of just what type of curriculum, what academic standards should be maintained, and what type of buildings there should be were as yet undecided. The Protestant Episcopal Church had given rather lukewarm support to the project.

Before the union of the Evangelical United Brethren Church with The Methodist Church, Sierra Leone had also been exploring the possibility of starting a seminary. Obviously, since we were now one church, we would not be building two seminaries (we probably would not have done so anyway). For a number of reasons the Sierra Leone Church was reluctant to join in a seminary which was located in Liberia. The financial requirements for such a seminary would be large; I felt that we must explore all possible sources of cooperation if we were to enter the program. It seemed to me that the time had come for a seminary in that part of West Africa, but only if a number of denominational groups would cooperate in it.

I also did some exploration concerning the education of children of missionaries, and asked for further information about the various possibilities.

At the conclusion of my first trip to Liberia I made the following statements to the staff of the Board:

(1) While there were obvious personnel needs in some of the institutions as maintained by the mission and church, Liberia had forty-four missionaries–far more than the other fields in Africa I (North and West Africa).

(2) There was an obvious separation of "mission" and "church" which I did not feel was good. The stations at Gbarnga and Ganta were too isolated from the community. The

churches there were established by the "mission," paid for by Board money, and were not considered "their" churches by the local community.

(3) It was unfortunate that after more than one hundred thirty years of mission work it was still felt necessary to use missionaries as pastors of local churches.

(4) There were almost no self-supporting churches in Liberia. Almost every pastor had another job which was his chief means of support.

(5) There was little sense of stewardship. Money was raised mostly at annual "rallies" in which the gifts were given and announced ostentatiously.

(6) The standard of education of ordained ministers and district superintendents was very low.

(7) Work among women was very inadequate.

(8) There was a great gulf between the residents of Monrovia (often still called the "Americo-Liberians") and the tribal peoples. This was also obvious in the church.

(9) In common with other West African countries there were problems of lack of integrity and laxness in sexual morality, which plagued the church also.

(10) The work had been greatly handicapped by the fluctuation of recurring budget grants. It seemed to me that there was something radically wrong with a system of financing which did not allow for better planning and use of staff which was provided.

(11) Apparently it had not been the policy of the Division to supply money in the budget of the institutions which would allow for hiring of Liberian staff (at least the best qualified Liberians). This was working contrary to our stated purpose of turning over the work in the church and institutions to national leadership. More than once missionaries had been asked for because it was known that money was not available to pay qualified Liberians. I felt that we should be able to channel money that would pay for missionaries through institutions in order to pay for nationals to replace them.

(12) There were a number of strong points in the church: the outstanding Bishop; the developing work in Christian Education; the possibilities in the Kru literacy program, if adequate help could be obtained; the planning in process for a program of leadership training for women; the nurses' training program at the hospital; and the possibility for a unique contribution to the healing of leprosy.

1969
Educational and Community Development Concerns

Dr. Samuel Smith, Functional Executive Secretary, General Education, and I traveled to Liberia together on July 21, 1969. I well remember that I had stayed up most of the night before we left to watch the historic landing on the moon. Then we had the long overnight trip with little sleep, and by the time we reached Monrovia the next morning, we were both very tired. There was just time for a shower and something to eat before we were to meet with the committee.

Seminary Education

We had come primarily to meet with the Lutheran Church of America executives, the Liberian Lutheran and United Methodist Church leaders, and those of The United Methodist Church in Sierra Leone, in a consultation on theological education. Reuben Pederson, Africa secretary, Dr. A. Sovik, executive secretary, and two members of the Board of the L.C.A. were present. The Rev. Leslie Wallace of the Sierra Leone Methodist Church (British) was present as an observer.

The consultation was the culmination of several years' discussion separately and some months of consultation together by the Liberian and Sierra Leone churches on a proposed seminary. I had become increasingly concerned in the past months, knowing our financial problems, with the ambitiousness of the plans. It became obvious also that there was not likely to be real ecumenical cooperation. I had several times warned Bishop Nagbe that there would be no increase in recurring budgets, and probably decreases. The plans projected for the seminary, however, called for a recurring budget of $81,800 a year, and a capital grant of $300,000 to $400,000.

Sam and I at first listened to the discussion among the representatives present. When asked for our opinion, we attempted to raise some questions concerning the number of theological students available and the cost when only two denominations (three churches) were involved. Finally, I repeated what I had already indicated to the Bishop and Dr. Carew (Bishop of the Sierra Leone church), that recurring costs must come within the present reduced budget.

The Sierra Leone delegation reported that there was a change in the attitude of the staff of the theological school at Fourah Bay College, University of Sierra Leone. They now seemed eager for ecumenical cooperation, and offered an opportunity for influencing the curriculum and supplying staff. The Sierra Leoneans urged further investigation. At that meeting the Liberians agreed to send a delegation to Sierra Leone to share in a consultation with Fourah Bay. After the close of the meeting and the return of the Sierra Leoneans, however, we were informed by the Liberians that they would not go to Sierra Leone. They felt betrayed by both the Sierra Leoneans and by us–"the Board."

Before the end of the Liberia visit, Sam and I presented to a small group of United Methodists our proposals for Christian leadership training in Liberia and Sierra Leone. We presented a program gathered from suggestions made during the discussions which seemed more feasible in the light of resources available. Emphasis was upon the broader base of lay and pastoral training of about high school level, using extension courses, seminars, workshops, etc. A theological hall for practical training of students who had received a Diploma of Theology or B.D. elsewhere was included in the plan. B.D. or diploma courses for a selected few were to be obtained for some time elsewhere, whenever possible, in Africa. Occasional graduate scholarships would continue to be made available in the U.S., U.K., or elsewhere. Cooperation between Liberia and Sierra Leone was suggested through interchange of staff and in producing curriculum materials.

The Liberian United Methodists agreed to investigate the plan further. They would present it to the Lutherans, who I believed would welcome it. When presented in Sierra Leone, the plan was accepted in principle with enthusiasm. Actually, it embodied much of what they were already doing or planning in Sierra Leone. There was already cooperation with the Sierra Leone Methodist and Sierra Leone Church (Anglican), and there probably could be more. The Sierra Leoneans would continue a study (ecumenically) of the Fourah Bay situation.

Community Development

A major part of our time in Liberia was also spent in discussion of a rural development program which had been embodied as "Point 14" in the Bosserman education survey. We were sorry to discover that this proposal had dominated the report to the Conference and to President Tubman, and that the Liberians had been told that large sums of money were available for such a project from quadrennial funds. Land had already been given for a center in Gbasontown area (Greenville) on the Kru Coast. By the time we reached there we found that the funds reported to be available had risen to ten million dollars, and that we were expected to build a technical school. People walked for long distances to greet us in a mass meeting, because of what they had been told.

Dean Freudenberger, Agricultural Consultant for the World Division, and Bob Wilson, a Peace Corps director from Togo with several years of community development experience in Africa, were present during the days of consultation on "Point 14." It can be imagined the diplomacy which was necessary in the long discussions that took place. In the end, there was the beginning of a better understanding of what rural development means and a more realistic view of resources available. A request was made for a specialist who would spend six months to a year in Liberia. The University of Liberia and the government agricultural department (on which we had representatives in The United Methodist Church) would make their resources available. We would be asked for further staff and funds later. It was hoped that some quadrennial funds as well as Advance Special[9] funds would be available. It would also be necessary to tap other resources, such as the World Council of Churches, for development funds.

---

[9]Advance Specials are projects for which money is designated by churches in the United States.

Other Educational Programs

At a subsequent meeting of the Board of Education there was discussion of the implications of the educational survey for the World Division. We would be involved in the type of personnel we would provide. Also, in the future we would be asked to make a block grant to education, to be divided by the Board of Education more equally among all the schools rather than giving only to the support of the traditional "mission" schools, the College of West Africa and the schools at Ganta and Gbarnga. Another problem discussed was that of providing salaries for nationals who would take the place of a missionary. Both Dr. Smith and I were concerned that it did not seem possible to have funds which would ordinarily be used for a missionary diverted to a recurring budget to pay the salary of one (or more) qualified national who would take his place, at least for a time.

In addition to the two major problems, I also had to present a 20% budget cut (from 1969) to Liberia. The executive committee of the coordinating (liaison) committee made some changes in the amounts allocated to the various program categories, as was their privilege. They chose to make further cuts in the education budget and add more than I had allowed for church development (which includes a subsidy to evangelists and district superintendents).

Liberia requested a "Partnership in Mission Consultation" in 1970.

Meetings were held with missionaries at Ganta, Gbarnga, and Monrovia. The budget cuts, new furlough regulations and salaries were among subjects discussed. I was reminded some years later by one of the (then former) missionaries that in our discussion of the many problems in the church I made the statement that "If the church were purely a human organization it would have long since died. But since it isn't, it will continue in some form." He said that statement had been of comfort to him. So often we don't realize how what we say affects others.

Sam and I also met with Lutheran executives and representatives of Lutheran and United Methodist missionaries to discuss the problem of education of children of missionaries.

The days spent in Liberia often were tense, but before we left I believed we had worked through our problems and reached a better understanding. I was grateful for Sam's presence because of his long experience in Liberia and his acceptance by the people, as well, of course, as his valuable counsel in the field of education.

1970
No Consultation!

Although the Liberian church had requested a Partnership in Mission Consultation with the Board in 1970, they cancelled it abruptly. Because time had been set aside by board and staff members some months before, it seemed to the Assistant General Secretary and others that members of the team should be allowed to make a shorter visit to become somewhat acquainted with the work in Liberia. It was impossible to arrange for visits to other African countries instead because of the time limit, except for Dick Nesmith (National Division staff, in research), who made a short trip to the Congo by extending his stay in Africa. It was with some concern that I visited Liberia. Actually, however, the visits of John Schaefer (Associate General Secretary, World Division) and Jervis Cooke (Board member) for four days, Marian Derby (Assistant General Secretary, Long Range Planning, World Division) for three days, and Dick Nesmith for one day, were appreciated. Bishop Nagbe arranged for John Schaefer and Jervis Cooke to meet with the Board of Education and the Committee on Coordination (liaison committee). They also met with a group of missionaries from various places. It gave an opportunity for discussion of issues, particularly that of the new salary scale and the very real concern of both missionaries and Liberians for salaries for qualified nationals.

My week in Liberia was spent in Monrovia, Gbarnga, and Ganta, in consultation with missionaries and a few of the national leaders, including Bishop Nagbe. The usual matters of personal nature concerning missionaries, such as furlough plans, etc., were cared for. A matter of vital concern with which the World Division had to deal was that of salaries for nationals. I was beginning to hear statements about shortage of missionary staff as several were leaving during the year, some not to return, and I was sorry that it was not possible to discuss the role of the missionary as planned in the consultation.

At my request, I had a two-hour conversation with Bishop Nagbe the day before I left. He was quite friendly and cordial, and we discussed some of the routine "housekeeping" matters of common concern. However, even though I attempted by questioning and a rather frank statement of my feelings to get at the bottom of the reason for the cancellation, I did not feel that we dealt with real feelings or issues. He thanked me for the extra copies of the position papers which I left with him to distribute. He also said that he thought the Liberian Conference would ask for a consultation in the future. I said we would welcome such an invitation, but that it must be given some months ahead, and we must be assured that there would be no cancellation again.

My assessment of the reasons for the cancellation follows:

(1) More than one person told me that the decision to cancel was a unilateral one. However, one did say that he was present at the Board of Education meeting when the matter of preparation for it was brought up (obviously very close to the time), and that some of the members there protested that it was impossible at the time. Yet,

when they were consulted about it the year before they had agreed on the date suggested. The reasons given me by the Bishop were that the time was a busy one, with Conference having just been completed, the school term beginning, and some of the leaders of the church were out of the country.

(2) Probably more basic reasons are the following:
a. In spite of agreement to the date and planning on our part (with occasional letters to the field) no advance preparation was done, and when suddenly it was realized that the time was nearly there, it was felt that they were not prepared and couldn't go ahead.
b. The Bishop is having problems with some of the other younger, educated men. There have been some quite underhanded and false statements made against him. On the other hand, he is following the rather typical African authoritarian pattern of administration, and is not involving some of the more able men in the decision-making process. Some of the people away from the Monrovia area are quite aware of the problems; some (including Liberians) spoke to me definitely about the control of the church by the Monrovia-based Americo-Liberians, who knew little about the problems and concerns of the rest of the country. One Liberian also spoke very freely in criticism of the control of the church by the state. Some believed that the Bishop felt too insecure at that time to have an open consultation of issues. Others were concerned that even if they did have a consultation the group would be hand-picked so that the Monrovia interests and those who were satisfied with the status quo would be the only factions well represented.
c. The Bishop is deeply hurt and confused by the series of events of the last months, such as the results of the plan for the seminary, the big rural development center which they had envisioned, the 20% budget cut in the World Division appropriationsto Liberia, my insistence that most grants for various special projects could not come from special reserves, but be within the Advance Special askings, etc.

One of the disturbing recent events which was not told me by the Bishop, but by two missionaries and two nationals, was that concerning the implementation of the recommendations of the Bosserman report. The Board of Education had been engaged in a slow but careful study of the recommendations, and had begun to implement the recommendation that seven of the elementary schools should be turned over to the community or the government or closed so that resources could be concentrated on the nine remaining schools to improve their quality. The Board of Education sent out letters informing the schools of the change in their status. Unfortunately, they did not first go to President Tubman to explain their plans to him and to get his approval. (President Tubman was in Annual Conference when the recommendations were read and accepted, but said nothing at the time.) Immediately the people in the communities sent delegations to the President, and he then told the church that they could not close the schools. He said he would help to find money to pay the teachers that year. With budget cuts the Conference was absolutely unable to keep the schools going, let alone try to upgrade the quality of the others. It meant that little else could be done to implement the Bosserman recommendations. Several people were wondering whether the Bishop was going to have the courage to say the schools would close anyway. He did not tell me about this situation, although other members of the team who were in Liberia were told by Dr. Weeks, Chairman of the Board of Education.

The proposed rural development program which was worked out while Rene Ryter (an expert who was sent as had been agreed after the 1969 meeting) was in Liberia was apparently a dead issue.

Although I thoroughly enjoyed personal contacts with people in Liberia, I was increasingly concerned and pessimistic about the state of the church in that country.

1971
Encouragement
June 11-18, 1971

As a result of eight days spent in Liberia in June of 1971, I felt much encouraged. During the previous year some Liberian leadership had come to the fore which was not so apparent before. Several good programs were in progress or envisioned. The leadership of Bishop Nagbe was beginning to have an effect on the whole church. I felt a warm welcome by both nationals and missionaries and some of our conversations helped our mutual understanding.

Some of the outstanding programs were:

Kru Literacy Program

Two men who worked with Karey Joseph to develop the new program were continuing the work in a fine way. The Conference asked, however, for some person experienced in the field of adult basic education to be assigned for another three years, as a member of the team already working. The whole Conference program needed to be coordinated, including the work in literacy in which the women were also very much interested. The name of a short-termer had been submitted and approved. If she would accept and was appointed, she would need some specialized training and experience. Also, one of the Liberian team would be given opportunity for more training.

Christian Education

The Rev. Arthur Kulah, who had just completed his master's degree in Christian Education, was doing a good job in carrying on the work which had been started by a missionary. His emphasis was on leadership education, and the Board wanted to support him in every way possible, within the limits of their resources. The White Plains Retreat Center was being used very often, and was appreciated by everyone. Other groups were also beginning to use the facilities, and it was hoped the charges made would pay for the maintenance if the center continued to be used as often as it was at that time. The provision of a small cottage for the Youth Director at the site would make closer supervision possible, and save a good deal of travel time and expense.

Gbarnga Pastor's School

The curriculum of the school was much improved. The most interesting development was that of the correspondence courses offered, which were taking an increasing amount of staff time (and justified the presence of four staff members for such a small school). An extension program would probably eventually be developed, as well as continuation of refresher courses for pastors. The women's program had been very poor, but there were plans for improvement, and for opening the course not only to wives of the pastors but to other women also. The projected enlargement of the school (for which the Advance Project had been accepted by the Conference) would provide additional facilities for women as well as men.

Elwyn Hulett, the reading specialist, was teaching remedial reading to the pastoral students. He found that even though he was using third grade level materials, many were struggling with it. Remedial reading and English had long been recognized as a real need, but it was only now that they were able to do something about it.

Reading Program

Elwyn Hulett was developing a very fine program of teaching teachers of reading. An Advance Special project which would allow him to hold an intensive two-week seminar at the Retreat Center had been approved. His wife, Cynthia, was assisting with art work to illustrate the materials they were creating. Cynthia also taught at the Campus School at Phoebe which children of our missionaries were now attending.

Ganta Hospital and Leprosy Rehabilitation Center

This hospital continued to be one of the most effective medical programs in Africa because of the School of Nursing, the public health work of Dr. Wallace in cooperation with the government, and the program of rehabilitation for leprosy patients. Their problem was to maintain a balance between curative medicine, which could not be abandoned and the other programs, valuable as they were. A steady decrease in funds made it very difficult.

Jenny Larsen's Work

A number of us had mixed feelings about this program since it was first proposed. But I determined to go with an open mind. On this trip I had a more positive feeling than before. However, we had to be aware of some of the shortcomings of this type of program. When the program was first conceived, Jenny did not place a public health program very high on her list of priorities. She was primarily concerned about the forgotten people – those who had lived at the "colony" for years, and were so disabled that they could not earn a living. They no longer had ties with a village so that they could return to their families. She was also concerned for those who could not afford to pay for treatment at the hospital. (The hospital, with decreasing support from the World Division, had to increase charges in order to keep in operation; little help was received or was likely to come from the government.)

Jenny conceived of her program largely as one of social service. The Medical Board of the Conference did approve it, and the World Division was continuing to supply her salary as she started the new program. It had been made quite clear that the World Division could not support a new program at the very time we were having to cut down on funds to the other valuable medical programs. She had succeeded in getting support of $6,000 a year, and a car, from the Scandinavian churches. She at first started the program without much consultation with the doctors, and did not consider her program part of the overall medical program. However, there had recently been consultation together, and some agreements reached on working relationships.

Dr. Getty, who was involved in the program of leprosy rehabilitation, was skeptical of the program. This was natural, since most of his support was from American Leprosy Missions. Their philosophy, and that of forward-looking leprosy specialists of the day, was that patients should not be allowed to settle down for long terms in the old type of "colony." With the new drugs, and modern techniques of surgery, physiotherapy, and foot wear, the type of deformation which had resulted in so many disabled people could now be prevented or alleviated. It was the old problem of establishing priorities. Within the resources available, how was it best to spend one's time, energy, and money–trying to get at the root of the problem, or treating the results when it was too late to do anything? This problem explained the reluctance of the doctor to accept wholeheartedly the program which Jenny proposed. She was putting back into the condition the houses at the colony which had been abandoned, and had built new ones. On the other hand, there was still a place for compassion and service to those in need; and the persons who had had leprosy for years, and were often beyond rehabilitation, were the outcasts for whom no one seemed to care. Dr. Hasselbad of American Leprosy Missions after he saw her work acknowledged that helping persons to feel human again was also part of rehabilitation. The problem continued, of course, of how to keep a balance between the two programs. Jenny had wisely insisted that the pastor of the Ganta and Leprosarium churches should be the person who decided what individuals should receive financial help in order to enable them to go to the hospital. That is where the largest amount of her money went.

As the program developed, there was an increasing amount of time spent in holding baby clinics and in public health education. Many disabled persons, those with leprosy and those without, were referred to the rehabilitation center for physiotherapy, foot care, braces and artificial limbs. She transported such persons to and from the center.

Recently Miss Larsen had been requested by some village midwives to give them training. She was going to offer such courses, and would see that they were supplied with simple kits which were available through the government (World Health Organization).

One drawback was that this was another example of a missionary starting a new program which would probably survive as long as she was there and able to appeal for money, but not long after she left. However, no expensive buildings were being built, and if the program were eventually discontinued there would be no loss of money; what good had been done would be an asset.

Some women from the Board had visited the program, and would recommend a grant from the Women's Division.

Rural Development Program

 The Bishop was ready to begin specific planning for the proposed rural development program on the Kru Coast, for which money had been granted. He had approved the appointment of Don Cobb as the coordinator of the project. It was understood that he would work as part of the team which was also working on the Kru adult basic education program. There was a Sierra Leonean who was a student at the Gbarnga Pastors' School who had a year at Njala University (an agricultural school) in Sierra Leone, and also had some training as a dispenser. The Bishop was hoping that he could work as a counterpart to Mr. Cobb as they developed the new program.

Financial Problems

 Liberia's biggest problem was that of finance. I was able to talk with the Liaison Committee and some missionaries about our financial problems. I told them what the amount would probably be for 1972, and offered them a block grant, as had been agreed by the Africa Regional Committee. They would have a struggle to know where to cut to meet the 13% decrease in appropriations. The news that there was a possibility for support of nationals for a time was welcomed; this had meant a different feeling toward the World Division. Leaders were now appearing in Liberia; the problem of the church was how to support them. This was partly the result of the very American pattern which had been transported to Liberia, and was most difficult to support in developing countries. It was also due to the fact that government gave little financial aid to education or medical work, so they had to depend upon the World Division for a larger proportion of the cost than was true in some other countries.
 I discussed with them the possibility of a smaller block grant and specific agreements for 1973. They responded favorably. There would be more thinking about that during the next year. However, I felt that the World Division must be much clearer than we were of how such a program could be administered. For example, what was the relationship of such projects to the Advance Special Projects? There were many aspects which I did not feel we had yet clarified in our staff discussion of the subject.
 I found it helpful to be in Liberia at the same time as Doris Hess (Functional Executive Secretary, Mass Communications), as we were able to consult together on the spot, and I learned more about the literacy and literature programs than I would have alone.

Annual Report, 1971

 In my Annual Report for 1971 I stated that "The Liberia Conference, under the leadership of Bishop S. Trowen Nagbe, Sr., has done some significant work during the past year. Outstanding programs and advancements include the following":

 1. Education. The Board of Education was continuing study, and had taken some action which has grown out of the education survey of 1968-69. Recommendations had been made

for changes in structure of the Board to give clearer perspectives and guidance to the educational work of the church. There had been increasing local support of some of the schools. In some communities schools would be discontinued and the buildings used for other purposes, since government was now providing educational opportunities in other places. A growing Reading Development program was providing opportunities for teachers not only in United Methodist Schools but in government and other church schools for instruction in remedial reading techniques. Boy's and Girl's Hostels continued to serve needs, but were struggling with problems of financing and staff. Some felt a need for reevaluation of those institutions.

2. The Department of Christian Education, for the first time under the direction of a Liberian, continued to give guidance and provide resources for a wide variety of Christian education experiences: seminars for church school teachers, pastors, and lay leaders; continued work on the joint United Methodist-Lutheran Church School Curriculum Project; cooperation in a Lutheran-United Methodist T.V. program; and a joint bookstore with the Lutherans. Special classes had been held in church music, and hymns and hymn tunes composed by Liberians were being collected. The Director of Youth Work had helped to organize fourteen new United Methodist Youth Fellowships during the year; youth camps had continued; literature and resources were being produced; youth were being trained to conduct Vacation Bible Schools in the villages. The White Plains Conference Center during its first year had been used by many different groups, United Methodists and others, and was serving a real need.

3. Women's Work. The year 1970 marked a milestone in the Women's Work of the Liberia Annual Conference, for three women had become the first Area Workers of the Department of Women's Work (each working part-time). There had been workshops and seminars for leadership development; the Department of Women's Work sponsored a Ministers' Wives Retreat in October. The Women's Division had been asked to provide a staff member to assist the Liberian women in the development of their training program. Ms. Helen Swett, a regional staff member of the Women's Division, was at that time in Liberia, through a cooperative effort of the Women's Division, World Division and Liberia Conference.

The women were especially concerned that an effective literacy program would be organized for women of the Conference.

4. Literacy and Literature. The Kru Literacy Program had continued to develop. The World Division was planning to make additional financial resources and personnel available, to work with the team already in Liberia, as the program reached a crucial point in development. The staff was attempting to maintain a balance between teacher training and literature production. The programs had been made possible because of work which had recently been done in linguistic analysis and production of a teacher's manual and primer in Kru. The pastors in the Ministerial Training School at Gbarnga were being taught how to teach non literates to read Kru, or train others to become teachers. The Conference Committee felt that there needed to be further coordination of all literacy programs in the Conference.

5. Medical. In line with the plan to move in closer coordination with the Government of Liberia's Public Health service, the prenatal and under 5's clinic had been moved from the hospital into the town of Ganta. The government was supplying the building, and Ganta Hospital the staff, supervision and administration. Supplies would be jointly supplied by the government and hospital. It was hoped that the clinic would be a model for other clinics in the country to follow. Dr. William Wallace had been appointed as County Public Health Officer by the government, and spent part of his time supervising clinics and health centers throughout the country.

The program of Rehabilitation and Leprosy Control of the hospital (formerly the Leprosarium) continued to develop. During the year two, three months' courses in paramedical training had trained workers who were now working in government and mission leprosaria as well as in village areas. They were finding new leprosy cases, and were starting local treatment of patients, since it was the goal of leprosy control to treat patients as close to their homes as possible so as not to upset their normal living and working conditions. Work in reconstructive surgery and foot ulcer treatment also continued. A Medical-Social Work program was administering to disabled leprosy patients who had no one to care for them.

The School of Nursing continued, with a student body of fifteen. The school spirit was high and all were working hard to achieve their goal of becoming registered nurses. The hospital nursing service was almost completely in the hands of Liberian staff. The first Liberian doctor had recently joined the staff of the hospital.

The Ganta Leprosarium Clinic

Wood Carvers Outside the Leprosarium

5. <u>Ministerial Training School, Gbarnga</u>. By employing a combination of resident training and extension training programs, the United Methodist Ministerial Training School at Gbarnga was now reaching more than four hundred persons each year with a variety of training and educational experiences. Married residential students brought their wives and children so that the whole family could develop educationally together. It was hoped that as additional facilities were provided other women might enter the training school as well as wives of students.

6. <u>Rural Development</u>. Plans were being made for a pilot rural development program at Gbasontown on the Kru Coast. The program envisioned would involve the School at Gbarnga and agricultural resources there, as well as the Kru Literacy Program.

7. <u>Industrial education</u>. Industrial education for boys continued at Ganta, with practical "on the job" training for boys in carpentry, garage mechanics, machine shop work, electricity and plumbing. It was hoped that a home economics course could be added for girls, especially for those who would not go further in school.

Harold Crow and Mechanics in Training

130

8. Church Development. The Church Development program at Ganta had made steady progress under the direction of a Swedish missionary and with the cooperation of the pastors in the area. A breakthrough had occurred in the evangelistic work. New areas had been opened as new roads had made villages more accessible. Two of the pastors were teaching Bible classes in public schools. The United Methodist Youth Fellowship evangelistic team held Sunday services in nearby villages. Emphasis was being given to stewardship. New churches had also been organized in the Gbarnga and other districts of the Conference. Continuous literacy work and leadership training had helped the growth and development in some of the churches.

A Lay Pastor Gives the Benediction

A Christmas Pageant in Ganta Church

Ministry in 1972
Annual Report

By the end of 1972 The United Methodist Church in Liberia, which had reported 20,924 members at the end of 1971, was engaged in a number of special programs of ministry. Evangelism continued to be of concern, and planning was in progress for a special emphasis, "God Power '73." Jim and Eleanor Hankins were making an effective witness in the Firestone Plantation Ministry. The United Methodist Ministerial Training School at Gbarnga was continuing to search for new ways of providing theological education to both ministerial students and active ministers. New programs in 1971 included sponsorship of Lord's Acre agricultural projects at several village churches, and a six-week clinical training course for chaplains at Phoebe Hospital. The extension training program

Tony Fadely Teaches at the Ministerial Training School

consisted of the District Pastor's Institutes and a growing number of correspondence courses. An Intern Training Year was introduced as a third year program for ministerial students. Lay training also received emphasis by the Department of Christian Education. About forty lay leaders of districts and larger churches met for a week in a "Churchmanship Institute." Church school seminars for schools and lay leaders were held in eight of the fourteen districts of the Conference. Junior High School students who volunteered to serve the church were trained as Vacation Bible School teachers. A number of workshops for youth officers and sponsors were conducted by the Youth Department.

The Women's Work Board concentrated on officer training workshops during the first part of the year. They also sponsored the annual Ministers' Wives Retreat. A significant part of Women's work was the four district women's workers. They supervised women's societies on the district and local levels and planned and coordinated institutes and workshops. Of particular importance during the last year was the secondment for four months of Ms Helen Swett, a regional staff member of the Women's Division, to the Women's Work Board of the Conference. Her major contribution was the direction given to the development of program materials, and various workshops and other training events.

Melvina Nagbe in Literature Room

The Board of Education continued its study of the Bosserman Report of the educational survey. The Board had been reorganized, and some schools which had not been adequately provided for and which did not meet the purpose and needs for which they were built were converted to other uses. The Conference Reading Program was further developed. The Reading Institute which provided opportunity for concentrated study and experiences for teachers of reading was a highlight of the year.

College of West Africa Students

Student in Library

The College of West Africa (a high school) continued to make a major contribution to education in Liberia

133

Cynthia Hullett (back, left)

Reading Institutes

Literacy and literature production in Kru, Mano and Kpelle continued. The Kru literacy program had halted for a time to give opportunity for special training experiences for Nancy Lightfoot, the new missionary appointee, and her Liberian co-worker, in East Africa and Israel. It was expected that this program would be improved and accelerated when they returned to the work in Liberia.

The healing ministry continued to be an important part of the overall program of The United Methodist Church in Liberia. Ganta continued to be the center of the largest part of the medical activities, with the hospital as the institutional base of operation. The School of Nursing continued its successful operation; projected new dormitory facilities for female students would encourage an increase in applications from women. The Department of Rehabilitation and Leprosy Control continued to expand its activities during the year, with the official opening of the Edith Hill Memorial Building for footwear and prosthetics, and the completion of the second annual paramedical leprosy workers' course in cooperation with the National Public Health Service and WHO (World Health Organization). A week-long leprosy conference was also held, with more than fifty participants from Liberia and Sierra Leone. From this conference the leprosy control program in the Ganta-Nimba County area would begin soon. The Department of Public Health expanded its activities during the year with the official appointment by the National Public Health Service of Dr. Wallace as the Nimba County Public Health Officer, and the establishment of the Church-Government Community Health Center. The Department of Medical-Social Services funded primarily by The United Methodist Church in Norway continued its program of preaching, healing and public health education. Phoebe Hospital and School of Nursing, an ecumenical institution to which the World Division had contributed some funds and a member of the teaching staff, was beginning to explore ways to move into the surrounding areas in an extensive public health program, as well as continuing its schools of Practical

Nursing, Midwifery, Operating Room Techniques, Laboratory Technology, and Professional Nursing.

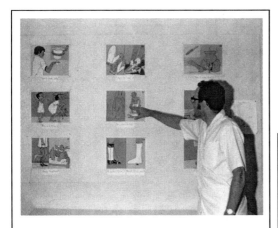

Dr. Paul Getty, Leprosy Rehab

Dr. Getty, Patient Review and Teaching

Paye Nelson, Physiotherapy

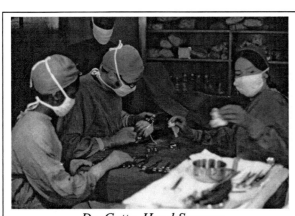

Dr. Getty, Hand Surgery

Prenatal Clinic, Ganta Hospital

Student Nurses (Loretta Gruver in back)

Dr. Kingsbury, School of Nursing

136

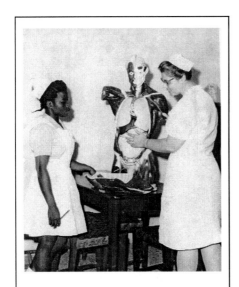

Loretta Gruver and a Student

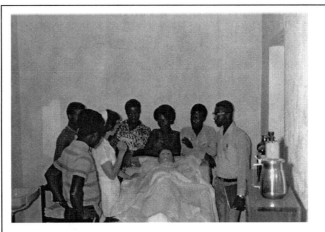

Vera Hughlett Demonstrating a Bed Bath

Student Nurse

Helen Day, Medical Technologist, and Trainee

137

A Student at the Girls' Hostel, Ganta

A new venture in rural development at Gbasontown on the Kru Coast was in its early stages under the direction of Don Cobb, the new agricultural missionary. The program was to be supported by the Norwegian church. It was planned to include agricultural development, literacy, and a program of medical care and education in community development.

One of the achievements of the Liberia Conference during the last months of the year had been the addition of several well-qualified Liberians to the staff of the Conference Christian Education program, Ganta Hospital, and in administration.

A experiment in methods of funding was introduced for 1973, with a block grant and several Program Project Agreements between the Conference and the World Division. It was hoped that this would lead to better planning, more self-direction on the part of the Liberia Conference, and that U.S. Conferences would be interested and challenged to join in partnership with the Liberian Church in the many forms of ministry in which it was now engaged.

Missionaries in Liberia March 1972

Bishop Nagbe and Missionaries

Doretha Brown, Vera Bennett, Vivienne Gray

Carolyn Kingsbury, Eleanor Hankins, Vera Hughlett, Sigrin and Paul Sundar

Elwyn Hulett, Martha Cofield, Cynthia Hulett

139

The Liberia Missionary Family March 1972

Bishop Nagbe and Esther Megill

*Susan Pope, Dr. Paul Getty, Tony Fadely,
Betty Getty*

*Karen Fadley, Mildred Black,
Vera Hughlett, Tony Fadely*

Martha Cofield, B.B. Cofield, Doretha Brown

Sigrun Sundar, Jim Hankins, Vivienne Gray

B.B. Cofield, Sue Cohen, Vivienne & U.S. Gray,
Hjordis. Wickstrom, Martha Cofield,
Werna Wickstrom

And thus ended my four years' experience with the Liberian Annual Conference as Area Secretary of the World Division. Unfortunately in the years since Liberia has been ravaged by a civil war. But I will let someone who is more familiar with Liberia in recent years outline those events briefly.

Liberia Since 1972
Dr. Robert Carey

Because of discontent among many, an indigenous Master Sergeant Samuel K. Doe (Krahn) in 1980 led soldiers in a coup d'etat and executed President William R. Tolbert and the entire cabinet who were of Americo-Liberian descent. Doe's military junta ended 133 years of Americo-Liberian political domination by forming the People's Redemption Council (PRC). But Doe promoted his own Krahn ethnic group, and after highly fraudulent 1985 elections, Doe solidified his control and fostered human rights abuses, corruption, and ethnic tensions.

Executing an opposition leader, Doe's troops also carried out reprisals on other ethnic groups. In 1989, a rival leader, Charles Taylor, and his rebel National Patriotic Front (NPF) attacked Doe and gained support from many Liberians. From 1989 to 1996 as other rebels broke away and began their own forces, a bloody civil war ensued, killing more than 200,000 and displacing more than a million others into refugee camps in nearby countries. Doe was killed in 1990, and ECOWAS intervened, sponsoring a peace accord in Gambia that was soon broken by Taylor and other rebel groups. They continued fighting in spite of an Interim Government headed by Dr. Amos Sawyer, and a five-man transitional government after that, until another election in 1997, which Taylor won because he threatened to continue war unless he was elected. For the next six years he ruled Liberia while promoting a rebel group in Sierra Leone with money from so-called "blood diamonds." Taylor's misrule resulted in resumption of war from other armed groups that had fought him previously.

In 2003, under intense US and international pressure, Taylor resigned office and went into exile in Nigeria. A UN-sponsored 3,600 strong peacekeeping mission laid the groundwork for a two-year National Transitional Government headed by businessman Gyude Bryant. The UN took over security in Liberia with a force that increased to 15,000. Disarmament, retraining of rebel soldiers, and peaceful presidential and legislative elections took place. In 2005 Ellen Johnson Sirleaf defeated international soccer star George Weah 59% to 40 % to become Africa's first democratically elected female president. A graduate in Economics from Harvard, with years of experience on national and international levels, she is leading Liberia in reconstructing its shattered economy. Both President Johnson and Vice President Joseph Boakai are graduates of the United Methodist College of West Africa in Monrovia (Bob & LaDonna Carey remember them as students there.) Ellen is a longtime member of First United Methodist Church in Monrovia. Taylor is imprisoned at the International Court of Justice and is to be tried for his role in the hideous butchering that rebels in Sierra Leone carried out on women and children, dismembering their arms and legs.

The Methodist Church in Liberia was established in 1833. In 2004 it (now The United Methodist Church) has a membership of 168,300 with 700 local churches and 980 local and ordained pastors in 19 districts. The church in Liberia remains alive, yet fourteen years of civil war has undermined the programs and ministries of the church. Its mission stations, the Ganta Hospital, clinics, schools, church edifices, offices and homes are damaged, destroyed and looted.

There are 121 schools (87 primaries, 23 junior high, 11 senior high) with a student population of 45,000 and 2,000 teachers.

Also, United Methodist University (UMU), established in 1998 in Monrovia, offers three colleges: Health Science, Management and Administration, and a School of Theology. The University had its first commencement convocation on February 9, 2004 when ninety-eight students received various degrees. Bishop Ray Chamberlain of the Holston Conference was the commencement speaker. UMU needs scholarships for students. US$500 is the annual tuition per student. UMU is building a new campus, to include an assembly hall and new classrooms.[10]

Bishop Trowen Nagbe, Jr., who was the bishop during the time described here, tragically died on February 2, 1973[11]–the youngest bishop in The United Methodist Church. He was followed by Bishop Bennie D. Warner, 1972-1980, then Arthur F. Kullah, 1980-2000, and the present bishop is Bishop John G. Innis.[12]

---

[10] Dr. Carey took the information about the church from a report by Bishop Innes at the Liberia Reunion in 2005.

[11]*The Encyclopedia of World Mathodism, Vol. II,* p. 1697. Nolan B. Harmon, General Editor. United Methodist Publishing House, Nashville, TN, c. 1974.

[12]*The Book of Discipline of The United Methodist Church 2004,* pp. 5-7. United Methodist Publishing House, Nashville, TN, c.2004

Chapter 4. Sierra Leone
Introduction

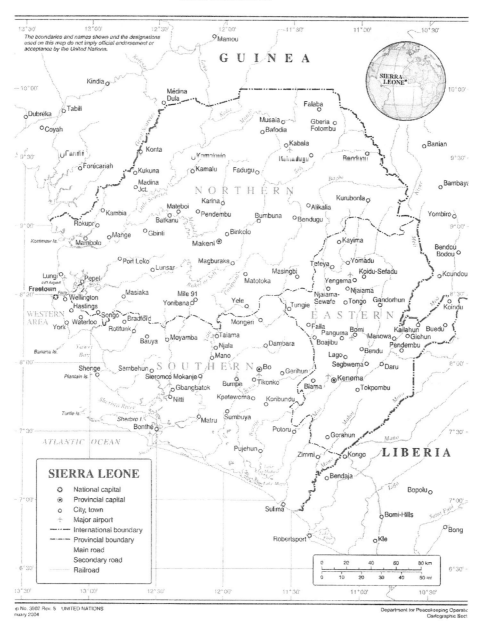

(Sierra Leone, Map No. 3902. Rev. 5 (B & W) Jan. 2004. From the UN Cartographic Section. Used by permission.)

Sierra Leone is located on the West Coast of Africa and covers an area of almost 28,000 miles, a little smaller than Indiana. The population is composed of many ethnic (tribal) groups, which speak a total of fourteen languages and many more dialects. English is the official language and Krio (the language of the Creoles), is widely spoken. It is a mixture of English with smatterings of French and Portuguese, and is often a literal translation of the vernacular.

Little is known about the early history, or exactly when the various tribes came to Sierra Leone. The Portuguese sighted the coast of Sierra Leone in 1446, but it was sixteen years before the coastline was mapped by Pedro de Sintra. He called the country *Serra Lyoa*, or Wild Mountain. Others have said that *Sierra Leone*, as it became known, means "Lion Mountain," but the Portuguese Governor of Elmina Castle, Ghana, disputed that fact, saying that de Sintra himself told him that he called it *Serra Lyoa* because the land looked so rough and wild, not because it was inhabited by lions.

The Portuguese settled at Port Loko, and traded kola nuts, ivory, and slaves. The ships of other European nations began to arrive. Although they were rivals, the Portuguese, French, Dutch, and English were interested in trade rather than in settling in the country. During the eighteenth century about three thousand slaves were sold every year from the area around Sierra Leone. The modern history of Sierra Leone began when slaves who had been persuaded by the British to leave their masters in America and go to England were settled in 1787 on a hill near the "watering place." For many years ships paused here on their journey up the Sierra Leone River to take on water and supplies. There was little shelter, and many died when the rains began.

The Sierra Leone Company was founded in England in 1791. The purpose of the trading company was to provide Africa with European goods rather than to perpetuate the slave trade. They began to govern the settlement which they renamed "Freetown." After the Revolutionary War in America many slaves, freed by the British army, were taken to Nova Scotia. They were dissatisfied with the bitter cold and harsh conditions. The Sierra Leone Company sent a ship for them, and they too settled in Freetown. Thus, the Colony was formed. Later, slaves who escaped from Jamaica joined them. After the British outlawed slavery the Royal Navy would stop slave ships from other countries, and take the slaves they released to the Colony. However, the Temne rulers resented their land being taken, and a war resulted. The Colony expanded into Sherbro territory.

As traders extended into the interior, the British sent soldiers to protect them. After prolonged fighting the Protectorate was proclaimed in 1896. Thus, until independence, Sierra Leone was divided into the Colony, inhabited mostly by the Creoles, descendants of the settlers, and Protectorate, where the peoples native to the country lived. However, in 1924 the Colony and the Protectorate were made jointly responsible for government, allowing three Chiefs from the Protectorate to sit in the legislature. By 1957 there was a House of Representatives, which included members elected directly from the Colony and the Protectorate. In April 1961 Sierra Leone became independent.

Sierra Leone is in the tropical forest belt, although most of the original forest no longer exists. It is 18 degrees north of the equator. There are two seasons, the dry season from November to April and the wet or rainy season for the rest of the year. Freetown has as much as 75 inches of rain a year. The mean temperature is about 80° F. It is a land of small farmers. The chief exports were (until the civil war) piassava, fibers from a particular kind of palm tree used to make brushes; palm kernels; ginger; coffee and cocoa; and diamonds. There are three religions: traditional African religion, Islam, and Christianity.[1] In 1999 the percentages were given as 75% Muslim, 23% Christian and 2% animist and other.[2]

---

[1]Information was obtained from *Independence!, Daily Mail Guide*, 1961, pp. 3-6; Christopher Fyfe, *A Short History of Sierra Leone*, London: Longman's, Green & Co. Ltd, c.1962, Chaps. 5 & 6; *Sierra Leone*, produced by the Director of Information, Sierra Leone Government, n.d., pp. 1-6, and personal experience.

[2]*The United Methodist Reporter*, Jan. 29, 1999.

Home Again!
December 12-27, 1968

Arriving in Sierra Leone was like a homecoming to me.[3] I received a royal welcome everywhere I went. Although there were serious problems in Sierra Leone (many related to lack of personnel), I was glad to be in a situation I knew so well at the end of my tour when I was very tired.

Impressions of the Church in Sierra Leone

Although I was well aware of problems within the church in Sierra Leone, I was much more encouraged with the situation there after seeing the churches in the other three fields. There was much more leadership than in the other churches. Although there was a nonresident bishop (Bishop J. Gordon Howard, Philadelphia), he gave only minimal supervision and acted more in an advisory capacity. That meant that more responsibility had been given to the conference superintendents. For the first time in 1968 there was one full-time superintendent, Dr. B. A. Carew. The Rev. J. K. Fergusson was the conference treasurer, handling all money except that directly related to missionary support and housing.

The church was beginning to understand the meaning of stewardship, after several years of intensive work in this respect. There were, however, many problems. Growth was needed in taking financial responsibility, in facing moral problems within the church, and its witness to youth, particularly those in the university communities. Opportunities for training for leadership were continuing to develop.

The time from December 12-22 was filled with conferences and meetings and visiting various areas of work. I met with the Council of Administration and a special committee to discuss, among other things, the problems in finance and budgeting. It was hoped that the Conference leaders would accept help from Bill Sims, the business manager for the Conference, in changing the form of budget requests, which was necessary as a result of the church union in the United States. Financial reports had to be made regularly. A good deal of friction could be avoided if payments were made promptly to the various institutions. Part of this was due to the irregular payments which had been made from Dayton (the E.U.B. mission headquarters). It was hoped that the New York office of The United Methodist Church would be more prompt with their payments.

There was a good relationship between missionaries and nationals. Clyde Galow, field representative, was a member of the Council of Administration, and was often referred to for advice. Other missionaries also served on the Council by virtue of their functions and Conference

---

[3]I had lived and worked in Sierra Leone as a missionary from 1951-1962. See *Sierra Leone Remembered* (cited previously) for the story of my years there.

appointments. I had one question that I wanted to take to staff–how the disciplinary ruling on the liaison committee could be adapted to different situations. It seemed to me that it would be a backward step to form a separate committee, similar to the Joint Council which they formerly had, that had never worked well and which we felt was outgrown in Sierra Leone. It seemed that the Council of Administration, with slight adjustments, could serve also as the liaison committee. I was also concerned with the position of field representative in the former Evangelical United Brethren fields. I did not see how the function of such a person could be done away with, whatever the name given to the position. Church union in the United States caused problems for overseas churches with which we were connected.

Most of the churches in Sierra Leone which had ordained ministers were self-supporting, though salaries were often not adequate. The World Division supplemented the salaries of a number of evangelists and a few of the pastors. A legitimate subsidy, it seemed, was that which had been given on a decreasing basis to enable three of our ministers who had a B.D. or a Master's degree to serve a church part-time (in addition to their jobs in government, the United Christian Council, United Bible Society). A problem which was (and is) universal in Africa is that of the "brain drain." Answers needed to be found to the problem of how to enable educated men to return to the local church, to break the cycle of weak churches with weak leadership.

Educational Program

The Sierra Leone conference was involved in an extensive educational program. There were one hundred twenty-five primary schools and eight secondary schools (nine, if Rotifunk Secondary School was accepted by the conference). The salary and administrative expenses of the Education Director, Mr. A.M. Bailor, were paid by the Division. Otherwise, a small amount in the recurring budget and occasional capital grants were the only financial involvement of the Division. Grants from the Sierra Leone government plus school fees supported the schools. The chief problem was that the church could not supervise adequately and staff with Christian teachers so many schools. Far too much time was taken by pastors in their jobs as school managers. School chaplains and teachers of Religious Knowledge were needed in the secondary schools. Some materials had been written for the teaching of Religious Knowledge in the primary schools. Some yet remained to be duplicated; others needed to be revised. Most of all, training of religious knowledge teachers and their supervision appeared to be a priority. The conference was requesting missionary personnel for such positions. It was hoped by some that the three young men who were currently in theological school in England could be chaplains of secondary schools and serve the church near the school. That would provide them a living wage and should help both the church and the school.

After they had seen the report of the study of the educational system in Liberia, the conference would consider whether to ask for such a survey in Sierra Leone. When the Council of Administration heard of the possibilities of youth teams and A 3s (something new to former E.U.Bs), they were enthusiastic about it, and planned to make requests for youth for several different positions.

The scholarship program in Sierra Leone was unique in that the Division of World Mission of the former E.U.B. Church had recently adopted the policy of giving block grants for scholarships, to be administered by the Conference Scholarship Committee. The Rev. Eustace Renner, principal of the Bible Training Institute and Conference Director of Christian Education, was chairman. While there were still details to be worked out for smoother functioning, it seemed to me that step was in line with the Division's goals for long-range planning, and should be continued. Grants had not yet been approved for 1968, and I planned to bring the matter to the staff.

Bible Training Institute

One of the encouraging aspects of the work in Sierra Leone was the development in the Bible Training Institute during the seven years since I had left Sierra Leone. Under the direction of Eustace Renner the curriculum had been changed and a different type of student enrolled. The school was now training evangelists or teachers who had been serving the church, giving them three years of training. This included biblical and theological studies, methods of Christian education, preaching practice, English, simple bookkeeping, and training in a skill (chiefly carpentry at that time). It was hoped to develop an agricultural course also. There was a school for wives of married students. The men who finished the three-year course were not ordained, but served as evangelists. Some might go on to a reading course and ordination if desired. The Sierra Leone Methodist Church (British) and Church of Sierra Leone (Anglican) were cooperating in this school

A grant had recently been made to construct another building, to enable the development of a Fourth Year Theological Training program. The building would be used as a center where probationers would come for one year after their theological training and before ordination for study and practical work in the Sierra Leone situation (this applied to those who took a B.D. or Diploma of Theology in the U.S., England, or elsewhere in Africa). It would also serve as a center for ordained ministers to go for a month's study every two or three years. It would be a retreat center for ministers of the Conference.

Proposal for a United Seminary

The Sierra Leone Conference Board of Evangelism and Mission and the Council of Administration, on hearing the proposal made in Liberia for a united seminary, were not convinced that a seminary was needed. They felt that Wesley University in England, where three students were then in training, and Immanuel College in Ibadan (when hostilities had ceased in Nigeria) could serve their needs for some time to come, with the addition of the Fourth Year Theological Training Program. They were not impressed with the standard of education of ministers in Liberia, and were reluctant to enter into a seminary located there. However, they agreed to send a committee in January to meet with Bishop Nagbe and other Liberians to discuss the proposal. Pastor Carew, Clyde Galow and I also met with the Rev. E. A. Pratt, President of the United Christian Council, and a Methodist, the Rev. Leslie Wallace, to explain the progress of the plans for a united seminary. The Methodists in Sierra Leone were involved in straightening their own affairs since achieving full autonomy. They were not much interested in a seminary at that point, but I felt that they would send one person along with The United Methodist committee to Liberia, if we could provide travel funds for all. It seemed important to explore the possibilities for a seminary, but not to go into such a large project unless we had full backing and cooperation from several different church groups. The churches needed to consider very carefully whether West Africa could support another seminary. If it was seen to fill a need, then priority would have to be given if we were to be able to supply staff and the recurring budget. The Lutheran and Episcopal churches in Liberia were cooperating. They hoped that some Sierra Leone churches would become interested.

Urban Work

During my visit to Sierra Leone, Negail Riley, head of the urban work for the National Division of the Board of Missions, arrived for a conference on the urban situation in Freetown and the challenge to the churches. Unfortunately, he was delayed in his arrival, so we had one evening meeting, and part of a day the next day. We had a fruitful discussion with representatives of the United Christian Council and several of our church leaders, including one of our ordained ministers who worked in the government Department of Social Welfare. It was hoped that the church would begin to do something to help meet the needs of the people in the city. Dr. Riley later reported to the Board on the discussion and possibilities for the future.

Women's Work

I was privileged to attend one morning session of the W.S.W.S. (Women's Society of World Service) at the annual convention in Bo. It was good to be among many friends with whom I had worked in years past. It was fortunate that I was there to talk with them about the use of a grant which we had recently given for women's work. The women had a well-organized ministry, with a scholarship program for girls and seven full-time women's workers in the Conference.

Medical Work

The most pressing problem in Sierra Leone was the question of the medical program. In the past few years there had been serious problems with personnel, which resulted in Rotifunk Hospital (where I had worked for twelve years) being closed for a short time. This had been an involved situation, but the hospital had been reopened, and the number of patients was steadily growing. However, we were faced with a severe shortage of staff. The days were past when one could get a general practitioner who would run a dispensary-type program. Our doctors were specialists, and one could not blame a doctor for not wanting to waste his years of training by working in a one or two doctor "hospital" with no lab or x-ray facilities. As of June 1969 we would have no doctors for Sierra Leone. Dr. Donald Megill, internist, was terminating his services; Dr. David Stephenson, a board-certified surgeon, had asked to be transferred to a place where he could do surgery, or he would submit his resignation. There was one nurse for the forty bed hospital, and she, unfortunately, had given very inadequate service. There were a number of Sierra Leone staff persons, with varying levels of training. But it was difficult to get an English or American-trained nurse to work at an upcountry hospital. There was no one to give anaesthesia. Nursing care was completely inadequate. The hospital was filled with expensive equipment with no one to use it. Some equipment was unusable in any case.

There were two maternity centers, one at Taiama and one at Jaiama, with a missionary nurse-midwife at each. The Conference had not seen fit to close these centers and transfer the nurses to Rotifunk to try to help that situation. One nurse-midwife, Brunhilde Goebel (from Germany) was due for furlough in March. That left Metra Heisler as the one medical person on the field. The maternity centers could not be maintained if there was no doctor to supervise them.

It was my unhappy task to inform the Board of Medical Services and the Council of Administration that as of June 1969 we would have only one nurse as medical staff. There were no possibilities in sight for doctors or nurses. Obtaining <u>one</u> doctor would not solve the problem; we needed three more if we were to have an adequately staffed hospital. I advised the Conference to appoint a committee to investigate all possible means of continuing medical service in those places. That meant approaching government to see whether they could and would make use of the facilities for maternity centers and/or dispensaries if the buildings were turned over to them; searching for private doctors who might be interested in setting up their own practice; other private groups, such as the Seventh Day Adventists or Roman Catholics. (Other groups in Sierra Leone were having the same problem as we had in staffing and financing, however.) The Conference leaders asked whether the Board would continue to support the hospital financially if they could find Sierra Leoneans to staff it. I told them I could not say without consultation, but that they had the right to explore the possibility. However, Dr. Renner himself stressed that we needed to look at the reason why the church should have a medical program. If we did not have staff who would give a Christian witness, we had better not be involved. (Actually, there was very little chance that such staff could be found. Dr. Megill had tried hard to get qualified Sierra Leone staff for Rotifunk, but was not successful.) I suggested that we would be willing to finance a survey of all Protestant medical institutions if they would cooperate, so that we could determine how to pool our resources. I doubted, however, that we could convince the other groups that this should be done.

I urgently requested Dr. Reeve Betts, Functional Executive Secretary, Medicine, to go to Sierra Leone as soon as possible (about the middle of March), to guide in turning over the medical work, or closing the facilities. There were only two good things which could come out of such a measure. First, it would enable us to strengthen the staff at Guinter Memorial Hospital in Nigeria; otherwise within a year we were going to be faced with the same situation which we then had at Rotifunk. Both Dave Stevenson and Metra Heisler had said that they would be willing to be transferred there. I was not able to see Brunhilde Goebel, the nurse-midwife at Jaiama, who was out of the country, so did not know how she felt about it. Also, the buildings could be turned over to the secondary schools in Rotifunk, Taiama and Jaiama, and supply some very much needed staff housing as well as extra buildings. Some of the equipment could be transferred to Nigeria, if it was considered worth the cost of transport; others, to Ganta Hospital, or perhaps Phoebe, in Liberia, or given to mission or government hospitals in Sierra Leone.

Needless to say, these decisions about medical work were some of the most difficult I had ever made. I had put twelve years of my life into the work at Rotifunk.

Missionaries

There were several missionaries in Sierra Leone. In Freetown I stayed with friends of several years, Clyde and Gladys Galow. Clyde was doing an excellent job as field representative for the Division. Gladys found several useful things to do in addition to caring for her family and acting as hostess for frequent visitors. Bill and Peggy Sims also lived in Freetown. Bill was business manager, chiefly for the hospital. He was helping with the books at Taiama Secondary School, at the request of the principal. So far, other help had not been solicited by the Conference, though he came at their request.

At Rotifunk at that time the missionaries were Dr. and Mrs. Donald Megill, Dr. and Mrs. David Stevenson, and Miss Margit Forseth. Metra Heisler was in charge of the maternity center at Taiama. Ed and Jane Heyer had recently arrived in Moyamba, where Ed taught Religious Knowledge at Harford School for Girls, and served as chaplain for Harford, Taiama and Yonibana Secondary Schools. He was also the first former Methodist to be assigned to a previously E.U.B. field—the beginning of a mixture that we hoped would soon be universal. Also at Moyamba were Don and Joyce Appleman. Don served as maintenance man for the mission. In Bo at that time were Gilbert and Beverly Olson, having moved there recently from his work in church development at Mendema. Gilbert would serve as acting principal of the Bible Training Institute until a qualified Sierra Leonean could be found to replace Eustace Renner, who would be going in a few months to serve in the A.A.C.C. (All Africa Conference of Churches) at Ibadan, Nigeria. Another church development person was needed very much to teach in the school. Kurt and Hilde Hein, from Germany, also served at B.T.I. He was an expert cabinet maker, taught the carpentry courses, and also made a fine Christian witness in village work nearby. Fred and Margaret Gaston were in church development work in Kono country, at Yekier, though they were not there during my time in Sierra Leone. Jane Eberle was principal of the school at Kabala where the children of our missionaries attended school, grades 1-9. Children in grades 10-12 went to Hillcrest in Jos, Nigeria.

Community Development Program

An important area of work which had begun since I lived in Sierra Leone was the community development program under the direction of Don Pletsch, at Yonibana. He worked with farmers on their own farms to help them improve their yields. They had a tractor with which they plowed smaller areas than the government tractors could do. He helped in a cooperative farm nearby. He had developed a 4-H program among boys and girls who were no longer in school, and experimented with a farmer's training school for boys unable to go on to secondary schools. It was a good program, but needed more supervision than he was able to give. Don was also studying a reading course and hoped soon to be ordained, and was supervising churches in the area. His hope was that the Yonibana program could be turned over to a qualified Sierra Leonean when he went on furlough in 1970, so that he could begin a project elsewhere when he returned. Helen Pletsch was a nurse, and was able to care for people who came to the house. She had small children to care for, and so was unable to have a more extensive program at that time.

School Farm

Don Pletsch, 4-H Rice Farm

Missionary Personnel

As in Nigeria, there would be an acute staff shortage in Sierra Leone by the middle of 1969 unless more personnel could be found. At that time two couples and one single person would terminate their services. Another couple and another single person would go on furlough. The only ones who would be returning from furlough were Vivian Olson, to teach at B.T.I. and work with women, and Virginia Pickarts, to teach at Harford School. That meant that only sixteen missionaries would be left on the field, and probably only thirteen, if medical personnel were withdrawn. Requests had been made to the Personnel Department for several persons. So far, there were no definite promises of more staff.

Personal Time

December 23-26 I spent with my brother Don and his family at Rotifunk. David, age seven months, was a new addition to the family. I enjoyed learning to know Kevin (age 6) and Andy (4). We had an early Christmas on the evening of the twenty-third, and then the next day drove to Shenge, where I had spent many happy vacation days when I lived in Sierra Leone. We were greeted by Paramount Chief Madame Honoria Bailor-Caulker and her family and other friends. We returned to Rotifunk laden with gifts of goat meat, chickens, eggs, plantains, oranges, tangerines, fresh fish and pineapple, and full of Jollof rice!

153

Crossing on the Ribi Ferry–on the way to Rotifunk

*Renovated Martyrs
Memorial Church
Rotifunk*

*Plaques on and in the church, in memory of the
Martyrs of 1898*

Dr. Donald Megill & wife, Mary Alice

Andrew & Kevin Megill Playing "Devil"

155

Adjustments After Church Union
August 1969

Following the intensive meeting in Liberia in 1969, Dr. Sam Smith and I traveled to Sierra Leone. There we met in consultations on the school for missionary children in Kabala, scholarships, theological education and the educational program. I met with the Council of Administration to discuss the formation of a liaison committee (as required by the *Discipline* of The United Methodist Church), the responsibilities of the treasurer, the use of funds now being marked "equipment," support of pastors and evangelists, the budget for 1970, the proposed new literacy and adult education program, and plans for a new urban ministry.

Doris Hess had made a number of suggestions for a strengthened literacy program, and we hoped that the Conference would act upon some of them. We were requested to supply a missionary with skills in literacy and adult education.

The Rev. Randolph Nugent of MUST in New York (an urban ministries program of the denomination) was in Sierra Leone August 9-11, and I sat in a meeting he had with representatives of the five United Methodist Churches in Freetown. They were working on proposals for a cooperative urban ministry. A request was made for a missionary couple to organize the new programs in Freetown.

The Sierra Leone Conference had to make a number of adjustments as a result of new policies which had come with church union. Some of our discussions centered on such situations. The changes were most felt in the scholarship program and in accounting and reporting procedures.

Medical Work

There were still problems in connection with the change in the medical program. Dr. David Stephenson left the day we arrived. We had expected that an inventory had been made of all hospital equipment; and that which would not be needed in a maternity-health center (could not be used by a nurse) would be sold. A committee made up of Ed Heyer, Bill Sims, and Pastor Challe was appointed by the Council of Administration to take an inventory and store things safely. The Council did not like having any items sold, for they still had dreams of the government furnishing a doctor, and thereby miraculously converting Rotifunk into a hospital. I agreed not to have much sold until their October meeting, but said rather plainly that I had real misgivings about having a partnership with the government. If the government wanted to take over the hospital, staff and finance it, fine. But I really didn't see their doing it. I questioned the church's being involved in running an institution on the principles by which the government seemed to run their medical work. In any case we could not continue to support a hospital financially. It was only because of the reduction in the cost of medical service that the

Conference had not been hurt more than it was from the considerable reduction in recurring budget, which would probably be even lower in the years to come.

Otherwise, the medical picture was encouraging. The Conference had decided to make Rotifunk Hospital into a Maternity-Health Center, and to keep it, in addition to the three maternity-child welfare clinics we already had (Taiama, Jaiama, Manjama). We planned to continue to supply at least a few nurse-midwives, and it was hoped that more qualified Sierra Leonean staff could be found. The health centers were now partially staffed by Sierra Leoneans, and could be nearly self-supporting. The church was much more able to carry them because they were of a size and nature that the economy of the country could almost support. They still had not settled the question of supervision by doctors, however, and I wondered how long the government was going to allow this to continue, since we now had no doctor on the staff.

Trips Canceled

I had not asked Clyde Galow to include Shenge in our itinerary, but was of course pleased when he did so. The real purpose was for Sam Smith to see the new secondary school. Paramount Chief Madam Honoria Bailor-Caulker, my longtime friend, had arranged for our entertainment. Her husband, A. M. Bailor, the Education Secretary for the Conference, was to accompany us on the trip, and would be with Sam throughout his tour of schools in the Conference.

We went to Moyamba (to visit Harford School and the missionaries and other staff there) and had planned to go on to Shenge from there. However, we heard that the road to Shenge was impassable. We were going to try it, hoping there would be a lorry or car on the other side to take us on to Shenge. Then it started pouring down rain. It would have been dark in an hour, so we decided at that point not to risk it. We got up early the next morning, a beautiful day with no rain, and went as far as the impassable spot. We could have passed it if it hadn't been for three lorries (trucks) blocking the road beyond. The drivers had returned to Moyamba, so it was impossible to move them. Therefore, we went back to Moyamba. From there I went to Bo with Kurt Hein, and a few days later flew back to Freetown for meetings. Later in the week Sam and I were to fly to Kono, where I would have visited with Metra Heisler and Lois Olsen, who was visiting Sierra Leone. Unfortunately, the Sierra Leone Airways canceled their flight because of the weather, so I was unable to go. I was disappointed not to see them, or to visit Jaiama again. I had not been there for a number of years.

Honoria (Bailor-Caulker) came to Freetown as soon as she could get over the roads in order to see me. I had met several of her children at different times. Also, I had a chance for visits with Mary Cobinah Davies, a former student of mine at Harford, and Doris Caulker, now Lenga-Kroma. When I finally met her husband I was surprised to discover that he was the James Kroma who used to teach at Rotifunk.

While in Freetown, I was able to get a visa for Nigeria. Clyde knew the Nigerian Ambassador. Also, he was from Jos, and had attended one of the Sudan United Mission secondary schools. Word came to me in Freetown that the Mallerys had obtained visas in Liberia. (They were waiting for him in Nigeria to take over as principal of McBride Secondary

School.) I also learned that the Gilliland visas were approved, so things looked a little more hopeful for Nigeria.

Church Growth

An encouraging aspect of the Sierra Leone situation was the growth of the church. In 1968 there was a net gain of 2, 456 communicant members, more than a 10% increase. That was probably the largest annual net gain in membership in all the one-hundred fourteen years of our work in Sierra Leone.

From Sierra Leone I went on to other countries in Africa, not part of my area of responsibility (to be described later).

Partnership in Mission Consultation
February 27 -- March 11, 1970

Dr. John Schaefer, Associate General Secretary, World Division, and I flew from Tunis (where we had been meeting with missionaries) to Frankfurt, Germany on February 26, 1970. There we were able to have conversations with Dr. Immanuel Mohr, secretary of the mission board of the Evangelical Methodist Church, and also with Bishop Sommer. Brunhilde Goebel, on furlough at the time, came to Frankfurt to meet me. On February 27 Dr. Schaefer and I flew to Freetown, where we joined Marian Derby, Assistant General Secretary, Jervis Cooke, Board member, and Dick Nesmith, National Division, the other members of the team for the Consultation. Bishop Maynard Sparks, Bishop of Sierra Leone, had been there for some time in order to attend committee meetings and Annual Conference. During the closing days of Conference members of the team attended some of the sessions and met together for orientation and consultation in preparation for the Partnership meetings which began on March 1.

At the Consultation papers were presented on the following subjects: "The Future of the Sierra Leone Conference," "The Place of Institutions in the Life of the Church," "Financial Dependency of the Sierra Leone Conference on the World Division," and "The Use of Funds." Members of the Sierra Leone delegation presented papers on some of the subjects, and gave an oral report on others. Following their presentation on each subject, the World Division report was read and discussion followed. It was felt that before the Consultation was over there had been frank discussion of some of the issues, and it was hoped, better understanding on the part of both groups of the concerns and problems of the other. Papers on "The Role of the Missionary" and "Liaison with the World Division" were distributed but not discussed for lack of time.

Members of the consultation from Sierra Leone were:

Dr. B. A. Carew, Conference Superintendent
Rev. J. K. Fergusson, treasurer
Mr. A. M. Bailor, Education Secretary
Mrs. Mary Johnson, president, W.S.C.S., and Conference women's worker
Rev. A. J. Smith, pastor, Jaiama, and secretary of the Board of Stewardship and
      Community Development
Mr. Max A. Bailor, principal, Albert Academy
Mrs. Betty Carew
Mr. Bartheloi Warritie and Mr. Christian Karimu, youth representatives
Mr. J. S. Bendu and Mr. R. E. Lagawo, headmasters of primary schools
Rev. Clyde Galow, Field Representative
Miss Vivian Olson, acting principal, Bible Training Institute

Rev. Ed Heyer, chaplain and religion teacher, Harford and other secondary
        schools
Miss Metra Heisler, nurse-midwife, Jaiama
Mr. Bill Hunter, Conference Director of Christian Education

Those who attended part-time were:

Dr. S. M. Renner, pastor, King Memorial Church, Freetown, and former
        Conference Superintendent
Rev. Crispin Renner, associate pastor, King Memorial Church, conference
        secretary (has an important post in the Ministry of Social Welfare)
Rev. S. E. Warratie, head of the Bible Society of Sierra Leone and Gambia,
        pastor of Ginger Hall Church, Freetown
Dr. W. H. Fitzjohn, principal, Harford School; Secretary of Evangelism of
        Conference
The Honorable F. S. Anthony, former secondary school principal, now a Minister
        of Government
Dr. A. V. Howland, missionary on special assignment for building

Bishop Sparks presided at all sessions.

The above group included ten pastors (including missionaries); five teachers; two youths; two women; six missionaries. Fifteen attended full time and six part time.

Representatives of the World Division were: John Schaefer, Marian Derby, Esther Megill, Dick Nesmith (National Division) and Jervis Cooke.

The group recommended that another consultation be held in June of 1971.

Medical Work

A major concern was still that of the future of the medical services. The government had announced that they would send a doctor to Rotifunk Hospital and reopen it under their auspices on January 1. We had continued a staff, including a qualified dispenser and nurse-midwife, since our last doctor left in July of 1969. Because the government had so far not taken over the hospital, however, all funds for medical services were stopped on April 15. The centers at Jaiama, Taiama and Manjama were self-supporting (profit from Jaiama paid a deficit in the Taiama budget). We were spending a great deal of money at Rotifunk, with little service to the community. It was hoped that an agreement could be worked out with the government so that they would reopen the hospital and begin medical service again to the community and the surrounding area.

The government had also announced that it would take over the health and maternity centers at Jaiama and Taiama. There was not a consensus during the consultation. Some were urging that the Conference make a real effort to find a private or government doctor to give supervision to the nurses, as required by government, so that we might be allowed to continue medical service in those areas. Others felt that it was too late, and because of political pressures, the centers would eventually be taken over. Some questioned whether the government had the staff or money to do it, but in the meantime both Sierra Leone and missionary staff were living in uncertainty as to the future.

I remained in Sierra Leone for five days following the Consultation to meet with missionaries in Freetown, Rotifunk, Moyamba, Bo and Jaiama.

More Consultation
Autonomy?
June 18 to July 1, 1971

<u>Meeting with Missionaries</u>

The time spent in Sierra Leone at this time was for me a combined field trip and participation in the second "Partnership in Mission" Consultation. At 8:00 p.m. I stepped from the airport bus into a car which took me to a meeting with missionaries who had gathered in Freetown for that purpose. Originally I had hoped to have at least a night and a day apart with the missionary family, in an effort to get at some of their problems and frustrations within their own group and with their relationship to the church (and for a few, with the Board). The short meeting on Friday night did not achieve what a longer meeting might have done; it did serve a useful purpose in discussing together some of the practical concerns and explanations of policy changes in regard to missionary service. Dr. B. A. Carew, the Conference Superintendent, met with us.

It was an increasingly frustrating time for missionaries in Sierra Leone, as in other places around the world. There was a "generation gap" between a few of the younger missionaries and those who had been there for a number of years. A number of the missionaries had little part in the decision making of the Conference, and in fact were not kept very well informed, except through the Missionary Affairs Office. Others who would like not to be in the position of determining Conference policy found themselves constantly turned to by some of the leadership for help; or, in their frustration they finally would initiate plans or programs which no one else had gotten around to do. One stated that, because of his position in the Conference, he had written a proposal to be presented to the Conference committee. He had hoped it would be discussed and studied. Instead, they accepted it with very little discussion, and it remained another good paper which was not implemented.

The Consultation

A second Partnership in Mission Consultation was held in Freetown in June 1971, between leaders of the Conference and representatives of the staff and Board of Managers of the World Division. Eugene Stockwell, Assistant General Secretary for Program Coordination, and Doris Handy, Women's Division Director, replaced John Schaefer and Dick Nesmith who were part of the 1970 consultation. Problems of finance, missionary personnel, property and the office of the Field Representative and Field Treasurer were chief topics of conversation.

I personally felt a sense of disappointment and frustration because of our inability to get at some of the basic issues. There had as yet been no real facing by the Conference of the

162

financial problems, the type of ministry the church could support, or the kind of theological education and lay training needed to prepare the church for ministry in Sierra Leone. There was a lack of communication from the top. There was a broad base of potential leadership in the Conference who were not allowed in the small, select group which made the policy. There seemed to be real appreciation for information shared from the World Division in an attempt to increase understanding for our situation; however, the request still came to us for large sums of money, with an expression of trust that we would "do what we could."

What came through very clearly was a desire to be given funds with no interference from the World Division as to their use; new projects were to be initiated only by the Sierra Leone Conference, not the World Division; the support of pastors and evangelists was their number one priority; there was to be no education survey as had been suggested by the World Division.

Major decisions were as follow:

(1) There would be no further attempt to recruit missionary personnel until a new request came from the Conference through the liaison committee. Those requests would include the current form used by the JCMP (Joint Committee on Missionary Personnel), filled in with full information, including a clear job description. Biographical information on possible candidates would be sent to the superintendent. It was explained that there were times when a decision had to be made quickly when personnel became available. They promised that such matters would be dealt with more quickly than in the past, because of the recent formation of an executive committee which could act between sessions of the Council of Administration (liaison committee).

(2) The Conference would receive a block grant for the recurring budget in 1972.

(3) The request for a guaranteed block grant for five years was accepted, with the understanding that there would need to be careful study by the World Division. There was some openness to specific agreements for a limited time, but probably only one in 1973. (This would be limited because we could not guarantee a block grant and also make other large special agreements.)

(4) We would try to raise about $47,000 for the proposed Conference office building, as a result of readjustment of Advance Special Project askings for 1971-1972. No decision about additional funds requested could be made until the problem between the United Methodists and the United Christian Council could be worked out locally, and a new proposal made to the World Division.

(5) The new Conference treasurer would submit quarterly reports, beginning with the end of September. He would receive help from the present missionary field treasurer during 1972, and the situation would be reviewed to see whether he would then receive

all funds directly from the World Division. It was hoped that he would be able to give guidance to the Conference as to budgeting and financial planning.

Autonomy?

The chief concern of members of the Sierra Leone United Methodist Church in 1971 was that of autonomy. At the Annual Conference in February, the delegates voted to request autonomy in 1973. Leaders of the church were aware that a great deal of work needed to be done before that time in order to prepare themselves for such an important step. They were somewhat fearful, and it was difficult to assure them of conditions of support, and at the same time be realistic about the resources available. They requested $600,000 as a contribution by the World Division to an investment fund which they would administer. However, with the increasingly difficult financial situation of the World Division we had to be honest to say that we did not see any likelihood of our securing funds of that magnitude.

Theological Education

The Sierra Leoneans indicated their desire that a Theological Hall be established in Freetown. We welcomed their continuing concern for the preparation of the Sierra Leone ministry and hoped that we would be able to provide wise support for any valid program of ministerial training that might be developed. It was suggested that such a program might well be the subject of a special funding agreement between the Sierra Leone Conference and the World Division. We indicated that a careful analysis was needed of the theological training possibilities in Sierra Leone which would be most helpful for the preparation of their ministry. At that time the needs of staffing, budget, capital funds, etc. were not clear. We suggested that it might be wise to secure competent technical assistance for the development of whatever plan seemed best, perhaps with the assistance of the Theological Education Fund which had developed considerable experience in African theological education. The release of funds held in New York for such theological education would await development of the specific plans necessary for initiation of the program.

Cost of Property Transfers

The Conference requested the World Division to assist with the cost of transferring properties held in the name of the World Division to the Sierra Leone Conference. We acknowledged our responsibility to share the cost, and stated that following receipt of a detailed budget we would indicate what our financial response could be.

Missionary Residences

The Conference had requested annual maintenance grants from the World Division for missionary residences turned over to the Sierra Leone Conference. We suggested two steps in response:

(a) That the Sierra Leone Conference carefully study the action of the World Division in October 1970 with reference to missionary residences, with a view of expressing the will of the Conference with regard to the Division action, and

(b) That consideration particularly be given to the development at an early date of a rental arrangement whereby the occupant of the residences pay a rental amount, the proceeds of which would go into the maintenance account to maintain the properties involved.

Continuing Committee

We agreed together that a Continuing Committee of six people, three from Sierra Leone and three from the World Division, should engage in any necessary correspondence to perfect any follow-up recommendations springing from the Consultation.

At the close of the consultation I, as Area Secretary, and Isaac Bivens, Assistant General Secretary, Africa Affairs, met with the liaison committee to work out some administrative details. Much time was given to additional explanation of the function of the liaison committee, the policy in regard to funds for equipment and gift slips, and other details which were still puzzling in spite of frequent attempts to interpret these and other changes which had come with church union. The men seemed appreciative of the explanations, and it was hoped that there would be more understanding and fewer tensions as a result.

Urban Ministries

In my 1971 Annual Report I wrote about some of the projects and programs. Two of the most encouraging aspects of the work of the church in Sierra Leone at that time were the new urban ministries in Freetown and the cooperative ministry in Koidu, in the diamond area. Literacy classes had been started in Freetown with cooperation from the government. It was planned that the courses being taught would be expanded into such fields as health education, home economics, sewing and bookkeeping. Teams of community workers would be trained to work in Freetown to serve their neighbors in the many problems of urban life. Community centers would be developed; a youth hostel built for students who came to the city for education; low income housing constructed; and eventually, it was hoped, there could be some industrial development for the handicapped [disabled] and unemployed of Sierra Leone. Quadrennial funds had assisted in the establishment of that new ministry.

Literacy Program

Literacy Program, Freetown

Rob Dietrich and L. Hamilton
Looking at a site for a future hostel

The Koidu Joint Methodist Parish was a "first," in that it was a combined ministry between the Sierra Leone Methodist Church (British) and the United Methodists. The new church building was dedicated in October of 1971. The program ministered to youth, men and women among the approximately 100,000 persons in Koidu Town and the surrounding villages, as well as the crowded National Diamond Mining camps and townships. Each of the two programs described was headed by a term composed of a missionary and a Sierra Leone national.

Koidu Church Interior

Rural Development

Quadrennial funds were also contributed to the rural development program in Yoni Chiefdom. During 1971 approximately thirty fertilizer demonstrations were set up on local farms in cooperation with F.A.O.; a citrus nursery was started so that sufficient planting material would be available for a primary school and village extension program; assistance was given to a number of local farmers who were starting small plantations, and to others starting poultry flocks. A start was made in helping interested churches in the agricultural development of lands they owned. The construction of the local parsonage was completed, and a primary school class room block was also built. There was some informal training of mothers of small children concerning child care and nutrition. The local farmers seemed more concerned than ever before about agricultural development; a program emphasizing primary education and village agricultural extension was just getting started. There were more requests for help than the staff could process. This program was also headed by a missionary and a Sierra Leone national.

Don Pletsch and Danial Fungbahun, Assistant

Don Pletsch and Poultry

Christian Education

The program of Christian education was also expanding. Two youth camps (junior and senior) were held in July; representative youth and their sponsors attended the Liberian youth camp, and Liberian youth in turn took part in the Sierra Leone camp. The Religious Education Committee spent a good deal of time during the year in a thorough evaluation of the religious education program of the Conference. Concern had been expressed for the need for committed and prepared teachers of Religious Knowledge in the primary and secondary schools. It was also felt that there should be emphasis on church school programs and meaningful education for adults.

Medical Work

During the year Rotifunk Hospital was reopened by the government, and a doctor, dispenser and midwife were providing medical care. Three Maternity-Child Health Centers continued to operate under the auspices of the church at Jaiama, Taiama and Manjama, and rendered significant service to the surrounding communities.

Education

The Conference continued to operate ten secondary schools and one hundred forty-seven primary schools. The Bible Training Institute at Bo was training lay workers to serve as evangelists. The whole program of theological education and preparation for the ministry needed a thorough study, however. Crucial issues of the support and training of the ministry were of primary importance as the Sierra Leone Conference moved to autonomy.

In 1970 the Consultation Team had attempted to go to Shenge but were prevented from doing so because of the condition of the roads during the rainy season. However, this time the team did go, and received a royal welcome from Paramount Chief Madam Honoria Bailor-Caulker and her subjects. The secondary school students entertained us with drama. There was drumming and dancing, and of course, food.

The Team in Shenge: Marian Derby, Gene Stockwell, (two Sierra Leoneans),
Esther Megill, P.C. Madam Honoria Bailor-Caulker, Doris Handy,
Pastor Shenge UMC, Jervis Cooke

Drama,
Secondary School

Dancers and "Devils"

Singers

Women's Work

The women continued an active ministry with nine full-time women's workers.

<u>A message from the Children's Church, Rotifunk</u>

After I left Sierra Leone I received a letter written by three of the Sunday School children, their Coordinator, and Leader:

```
                              Children's Church
                              Rotifunk
                              Sierra Leone
                              25th. June, 1971
Dear Dr. Megill,
    We were expecting our co-ordinator to arrive from Freetown in time
to inform us of your arrival.  But due to transportation difficulties
he arrived after you had departed.
    We were shocked to know that you and your party had traveled
to Shenge by the time we had assembled on Saterday 25th. June, 1971
to welcome you and express our appreciation for your good work here.
We had hoped to illustrate to you the numerous talents concentrated
in our small church.  Even the remaining party was thrilled with delight
on hearing one of our songs.
    We trust you will be interested enough to read and consider our
welcome address to you now attached to this letter.
    Special greetings are sent to you from all of us here.  Remember
us to your family, and may God bless you all.
    We are looking forward to hearing from you sooner than later.

                         Yours in Christ
                         Miss Letitia Mahoi
                         Miss Iye Fullah
                         Master Thomas Pratt
                         Children

                         Co-ordinator

                         Leader
```

From: Children's Church, Rotifunk, Sierra Leone

To: Dr. Esther Megill

This is our finest hour because God has given us the opportunity once again of being in company with the pioneer of our children's church commonly known to us as Miss Megill.

The purpose of this gathering is to welcome, thank and express our sincere appreciation to you, Dr. Megill, for your personal contribution in helping to bring this knowledge of Jesus Christ to us children in this part of the world.

The words 'thank you' are familiar words, but we utter them with a deep sense of gratitude.

These delightful children you now see are the result of a great deal of hard work on the part of many people. Notable among these are our pastor, Rev. W. B. Challe; many missionaries; our two headmasters, Messrs. J. Conteh-Morgan and J. S. Bendu; and some teachers in the persons of Mrs. F. B. Wallace, Mrs. J. M. Kargbo-Labor, Messrs I.H. Caulker, A. M. Koroma, E. K. Kargbo a promising young pastor and indeed the pillar of our church and B. F. Vandi who gives so much of his time to ensure the smooth running of our programmes. We would like to state also that the Johnson family has supported our church morally and otherwise. We owe our greatest debt of gratitude to this family for the splendid appearance of our parent church--Martyrs Memorial Church.

We should like to assure you that in our relations with our fellow churchmates we show friendliness, a willingness to help and always treat others as we would have them treat us.

Though we are small children, we know that you American missionaries are people whose friendship is worth maintaining if for nothing at all at least for the Bible which your predecessors sacrificed their lives to bring to us. We know that to ask you to help send us a doctor to assist in our hospital would be asking too much. But for our sake, please tell your counterparts to forgive us. Take us back and you will know no regrets now or ever.

Please extend our compliment and best wishes to children of the United States. "God go with you, yah."

Yours in Christ,

Miss Letitia Mahoi
Miss Iye Fullah
Master Thomas Pratt
Children

gogbo E.K. (Edward) Kargbo

Vandi

(Helpers)

171

Farewell Again
1972

Preparation for Autonomy

A chief concern for the Sierra Leone Conference during 1972 continued to be preparation for autonomy. February 1973 would mark the beginning of the autonomous United Methodist Church of Sierra Leone.

Ministry to Women

Betty Carew

An effective and widespread program of ministry to women continued under the auspices of the Women's Work Board. Two women attended a training course at Mindolo Ecumenical Institute in Zambia during the year, and others took part in a World Council of Churches conference in Monrovia. Many in Sierra Leone, but especially the women of The United Methodist Church, mourned the death in an automobile accident of Mrs. Betty Carew, wife of the Conference Superintendent. She had contributed so much to the work of women.

Urban Ministry

Ministry continued in the Kono diamond mining area through the Koidu Joint Methodist Parish.

The Freetown Urban Ministry Committee during the year started the construction of two community centers, established several adult education courses, and used funds from the Women's Division to aid in the economic development of women. An Urban/Industrial Ecumenical Ministry Committee had been formed as a cooperative effort between The United Methodist Church and the Sierra Leone Church (Anglican). It was hoped that ecumenical funds could be found to continue and expand the urban/industrial ministry in Freetown.

Rural Development

The program of rural development in the Yonibana area continued to establish roots and was becoming an effective agent for community development in that area.

Medical Work

Dr. Mabel I. Silver

The Maternity and Health Centers at Jaiama, Taiama and Manjama continued to serve the needs of women and children. The government took over the running of the hospital at Rotifunk in 1970, and an official agreement was signed between the government and the Conference on April 7, 1972.

The death of Dr. Mabel I. Silver on Easter Day of 1972 was mourned throughout Sierra Leone. Memorial services to honor her thirty years of service to that country were held in Rotifunk and Freetown.

Christian Education

The program of Christian Education in the Conference was strengthened during the year with the return of two young people from special training programs for children's and youth work. The untimely death of Mr. Vidal Renner, who was the Conference Director of Youth Ministry on a volunteer basis, was a blow to the work among youth in the Conference. One of his dreams was the completion of enough buildings at the new Pa Lokko Conference Campsite by July of 1973 so that the senior camp could be held there. Youth of Sierra Leone were raising money for the project, and contributed time and effort to work camps. Training workshops and youth camps made a contribution to the life of youth in the church.

The Religious Education Committee recommended, and the Conference Council of Administration approved, joining with the Church School Curriculum project in Liberia. Thus, the Sierra Leone Conference would contribute writers to the curriculum, and workshops would be held in Sierra Leone as well as Liberia to train teachers to use the new curriculum as it developed.

The training and support of lay evangelists continued to be a concern of the Conference. There was still a need for a thorough study of theological and lay training and the forms they should take in Sierra Leone.

Thus ended my four years as Area Secretary of Sierra Leone. Once again I left the country which had been home to me for so many years, but I continued contact with many of my friends there.

Chapter 5. Visits to Other Countries in Africa

The Congo and Zambia
August 13-29, 1969

Due to my position as Area Secretary, I was privileged to make trips to other parts of Africa not within my area. Jucl Nordby, my co-worker in Africa (he was Area Secretary for South and East Africa) had suggested that we should each get acquainted with some of the countries in the other's area. He went to Algeria because I was unable to go at the time, and later to Nigeria. At his suggestion I traveled to the Congo after my field trip to Sierra Leone in 1969. I looked forward to becoming acquainted with it, and more of the extensive work of The United Methodist Church. I was particularly interested in some of the training programs for women and the medical work.

I had expected to be on my way by August 10, but when traveling in Africa one must not be surprised if plans are changed. I went to the hotel where I was to board a bus to take me to the ferry that would go to Lungi, where we again would catch a bus to the airport. However, I discovered that the flight to Accra had been canceled. In letters written to my family I describe some of my experiences.

Luluabourg[4], Congo
August 18, 1969

Dear Family,

"I flew from Sierra Leone by KLM on Monday evening, and stayed in a hotel at Robertsfield, Liberia, for a day and two nights. That gave me an opportunity to write some letters and reports. I was thankful that the Pan Am strike was settled in time for the once weekly flight to Kinshasa to proceed as scheduled. This meant that I arrived at Kinshasa on Wednesday instead of Sunday. Because of the delay I felt that I should not stay in Kinshasa, but go on to Luluabourg as planned. However, since I have been here, I have done little. Three of the mission planes are not in working order, so that makes it difficult to take me to the various stations and institutions. Tomorrow a missionary who owns a plane privately . . . will fly here and take me on Tuesday, Wednesday and Thursday to other stations. On Thursday I will go to Lumbumbashi. Mary Ruth Reitz, whom I knew when she was working in the accounting department in the Board in New York . . . is there, and I will be staying with her.

"I am staying in the guest house here. A missionary on vacation was here for a while, and two new Swiss missionaries have been here. I am enjoying learning to know two of the missionaries here. There is a very good women's training program in Luluabourg. Wives of

---

[4]Now Kananga.

174

nurses, government officials, etc. come for a four-month course. They must be literate in the vernacular, and may bring their youngest child with them. They pay a fee to attend, and buy books and materials. Their husbands are eager for them to attend. A number have told the people in charge of the school what a difference it has made in their home life since their wives attended the Institute. It has been a factor in helping to keep homes together. As men in recent years have been put into government and other positions, they

have found that their wives did not have the education or training to make the kind of home they need in the positions they now have. The women have courses in sewing, cooking and nutrition, Bible, French, homemaking, Christian family life, and hygiene and health, including family planning.

"The Congo is a country with a military dictatorship, but at least there now seems to be less tension and peace after so many years of war and trouble. Those who have been here through the years say that a good deal has been done since Independence to begin to improve the situation over what it was during the war. Many of the tasks are new for the Congolese, and so it will take time, as in all developing nations, for life to be much better for those who live here."

Lumbumbashi, Congo
August 23, 1969

Dear Family,

"I am thoroughly enjoying my stay here in Lumbumbashi with Mary Ruth Reitz and Pat Rothrock. I had met Pat in New York, and Mary Ruth stayed in my apartment during my last field visit. We have had some time together in New York and I enjoy her very much. She was working in the accounting department at 475, and has come out to the Congo for a second time to help out in an emergency situation. She is the Branch treasurer, who handles all World Division funds for three conferences, so it is a big job.

"On Tuesday of this week Ken Enright, a pilot and evangelist, flew to Luluabourg to pick me up and take me to Wembo Nyama. This is a station in an isolated party of the country. As one flies in a small plane over the dense forests in the Congo, one can understand the problem of transportation and communication. At Wembo Nyama there is a primary and secondary school, an industrial section (bricks

A Group at the Hospital, Wembo Nyama

175

are made, lumber sawed, etc. for all the building; there is a machine shop for maintenance) and a hospital. It is a typical African bush hospital, with little equipment and inadequate staff. There is at present one Congolese doctor, with a Dutch surgeon coming soon. The hospital still shows the effects of the evacuation a few years ago. Whenever a station had to be evacuated, it was looted so that one had to start all over again.

"One of the Methodist missionaries, Burleigh Law, was killed at Wembo Nyama by rebels in 1964. He is buried there. Now his son, who was evacuated with his mother at the time, is back with his young wife, a special term missionary. He speaks the language perfectly, as well as French, and is very much a part of the people. They have a special fatherly interest in him because of their respect for his father and because he grew up among them.

"On Wednesday we flew to Kapanga. Here we have quite a different hospital—well equipped, orderly, but still only one doctor for about 150 beds. It is in a different situation because they never had to evacuate here, and because there is a doctor who raises thousands of dollars for his work. He is at present on furlough, and a woman, Dr. Pauline Chambers, is in charge. I suppose at times there are two of them there at the same time.

Hospital and Chapel, Kapanga

"Late Wednesday afternoon we flew to a beautiful spot, at Kafakumba. The missionary's house and a guest house are right on a large lake. There is boating and fishing, and even swimming (in a fenced- in area to protect from crocodiles). Unfortunately, I didn't bring my swimming suit on this trip. There is a school there to which pastors are brought for short training courses about twice a year. The whole family comes, and it seems to be an excellent program. The pastors (with a very limited educational background) work together on the Conference reading course. Other retreats and institutes are planned for both missionaries and Congolese.

"I spoke to the pastors' institute early Thursday morning, and then we flew to Mulungwishi, another large center of work. There we have a women's training school, similar to the one in Luluabourg, a theological school, and primary and teacher's training school. The church had beautiful stained glass windows, with African figures depicting the life of Christ. The Congolese artist had learned the art at Mindolo Ecumenical Centre.

"I had dinner at the home of missionaries, and was driven (about two hours) to Lubumbashi by a Greek man (who speaks a little English), who is a contractor for the church. On the way he needed to stop in one of the towns on business, so he took me to the home of his cousin. She is from Cyprus, and so speaks English. She was shy, because she said she hadn't spoken English for several years, since she came to the Congo. We managed to communicate quite well, however. She of course served me Middle Eastern coffee, which is extremely strong and sweet, and some kind of sweet preserve which she says they like very much. It tasted like watermelon preserves, but I don't know what kind of vegetable it was.

Kafakumba Lake

Pastor's School

Stained Glass Windows in the Mulungwishi Church

"As we flew over parts of the Congo this week, I was told some interesting things by Ken Enright. He flew low so that I could see antelope and get a picture. I hoped we would see elephants, but all we saw were the many trails they had made. Whenever they need meat he or his son goes out to hunt. He showed me a spot where he has built an airstrip. He says within twenty minutes after landing there they can have an antelope. I had antelope meat two or three times, and it was very good. I'm sorry I left Wembo Nyama when I did; they were bringing in a hippo that afternoon which one of the men had killed. They say the meat is delicious. Ken also showed me the vast areas of forest, in one section of which there are still cannibals. He said during the uprisings they became absolutely ferocious.

"The missionaries in the Congo have lived through trying times in the last few years. The situation is much better now, but there is still restlessness. Just this last month a family of "faith" missionaries had to be evacuated from one place. Whenever there is trouble and the soldiers are sent in, it causes much trouble. They take all the goats and chickens, rape the women, and even demand money from the people. This is not a happy country.

"Yesterday I saw a little of Lumbumbashi, which is a rather modern city. This is one of the twelve cities chosen for urban work as part of the quadrennial emphasis. (Freetown is one also.) There are about seven United Methodist churches here, four social centers, some schools, and another women's training center similar to the two others I have seen.

"I had my hair done in a beauty parlor yesterday. Methods are similar in all the places I have been. Since I'm not very particular, it didn't matter that I couldn't speak French and she knew only a few words of English.

"Tomorrow Pat and Mary Ruth will drive me to Kitwe, in Zambia. It is about a four-hour drive. They are going to take two or three days' vacation there. Last night they took me to a very nice Belgian restaurant, where we had fondue, their speciality. It was delicious. As you can see, even though I stop for letter writing, this is more of a time for rest and vacation than work for me . . ."

Love,
Esther

A Church at Kasumbelesa, Congo

Curious Children

178

Mindolo Ecumenical Centre, Zambia
August 24-29, 1969

Hotel Continental
Accra, Ghana
August 31, 1969

Dear Family,

"I am sitting on the terrace of a rather nice hotel near the airport in Accra, overlooking a water fountain and landscaped grounds with palm trees, banana trees, bougainvillea and Cana lilies. It's cloudy because it's rainy season here in West Africa. I set my watch back three hours last evening, and so I've already eaten breakfast some time ago, although it is only 7:30 Ghana time.

"This last week has been most interesting. Last Sunday Mary Ruth Reitz and Pat Rochrock drove from Lumbumbashi, Congo (Katanga) to Kitwe, Zambia. I had conversations with directors of several programs at Mindolo Ecumenical Centre. Bishop and Mrs. Ralph Dodge, of our church, are on the staff. He serves as chaplain. Our United Methodist Church has contributed a good deal toward Mindolo. This is one of the best training centers in all Africa. I was interested in first, becoming acquainted with it, and second, investigating possibilities for training for English-speaking West Africans.

"I will describe briefly the various training programs:

(1) A seven-month youth leaders' training course. I hope to have a Sierra Leonean there next year and a Liberian in another year or two.

(2) An excellent agricultural program. This takes men who have had only an elementary school education and gives them a two-year training program. In the second year they are given a loan from Barclays Bank, and under supervision earn a living for themselves and perhaps by then for a wife also. Most are single when they start the course, and no wives are allowed. During the second year they may have their wives with them, and many marry at that time.

They are taught intensive vegetable farming, pigs, cattle, poultry (for eggs and broilers). There is a good market for all these things. One hard-working young man cleared $1600 last year, in eight months. The average is about $480-$700. That is a good income in Zambia, especially for someone in the second year of a training program. I presume they raised a good deal of their own food also.

179

This next year they are beginning a course for ranch managers, at the government's request. They also have a course in farm mechanics.

After finishing a second year they may go back either to their own villages or into a settlement. The government has asked Mindolo to supervise this project for them. Mary Ruth Reitz's brother will head the program (he will be seconded by our Board). The men are given land, which they must clear. They will build their own houses and other buildings, plant their crops, and care for them. Irrigation is necessary during the dry season.

This is a program of getting young people back to the land, which is essential for the economy of African nations, but very difficult to do.

(3) Women's training program. The course is in progress now for young girls who are preparing for marriage. The most usual course, however, is for wives and mothers. It is a four-month course in Christian homemaking. The women are taught sewing, cooking and nutrition, child care, Christian home life, Bible, how to act as a hostess, etc. This is very important, as young African men are becoming educated and put into top positions. They are eager for their wives to take such training. Women want the course because they hope it will keep their men from going off with mistresses, and will make them proud of them. During the last week the men attend school with their wives. President Kauanda's wife is a graduate of this course.

(4) Barclays Bank uses the facilities of Mindolo to train Zambians for various jobs in their banks.

(5) There was a community development course, but it has now been discontinued because it is felt that government is now doing the job.

Student Writing at the Literature Centre

"Closely associated with the Ecumenical Centre, and on the same grounds, is the Africa Literature Centre. They have both English and French courses in journalism, which include news writing, writing articles and short stories and broadcasting. They also serve as a research center to discover literature useful for Africa (particularly religious literature), and an art course, in which Africans are developing African art. I met the young man who designed the beautiful windows of the church in Mulungwishi, Congo, on the campus of our theological school there.

"The Y.W.C.A. nearby has a course for women in which they learn handcrafts which can become a home industry.

"On the campus also is the Hammarskjold Library, built by the Swedish government as a memorial to Däg Hammarskjold, who lost his life in a helicopter crash near here. You can imagine it was pleasing to my ego to discover my little book, *Father, We Thank Thee* in the

Africa Literature Centre

library, and listed by the Africa Literature Centre. I also visited a youth camp which was in progress at the youth leaders' training program and found the East African edition being displayed there among other books for sale.

"It may be that Mindolo will form a course to train trainers of women, with our cooperation, so that some of our women from Sierra Leone, Liberia and Nigeria can attend. Or, Essie Johnson, a United Church of Canada missionary who started the Mindolo women's training program, may go to West Africa to hold a workshop. We've only begun discussion of the possibilities

A Worker on the Farm

Barclays Bank Course

181

Women's Training Centre

Hammarskjold Library

"At Mindolo I met Dr. Newell Booth and his eleven-year-old son, Edwin. He is a professor of comparative religions at Miami University in Ohio, the son of Bishop Newell S. Booth, formerly of the Congo. Dr. Booth grew up in the Congo. He's on quite an extended Africa tour. It just happened that they were scheduled on the same flight to Dar-es-Salaam, so we traveled together and spent some time together there.

Dar-es-Salaam, Tanzania

View of the Harbor

"Dar-es-Salaam is an interesting city. I wish I could have spent much more time there. We got in at about 4:30, and I left at 11:45 the next morning. The city has a marked Muslim atmosphere, and has characteristics of the Arab Middle East. The view of the harbor was beautiful. There are old buildings in which the sultan used to live, with a building for his harem next door. These buildings are now occupied by the White Fathers.

The Old Sultan's Residence (right) and Harem (left)

I also saw the headquarters of ZANU, the Zimbabwe African National Union, founded in 1963 as the people of Southern Rhodesia struggled for independence from the British.

ZANU Headquarters

"Yesterday I crossed Africa from east to west by plane. We flew over Mt. Kilimanjaro and I tried some pictures. We stopped briefly at Nairobi (Kenya) and Entebbe (Uganda) airports. Then we went to Lagos, where we did not get out of the plane, and finally here to Accra. I found that my name is not on the list for the plane to Abidjan today, in spite of having reservations confirmed in New York. So, I may be here another day, at Pan Am expense. There are many traveling, as I am, to the All Africa Conference of Churches meeting. I have seen a number of clerical collars, and at least one A.A.C.C. pin.

"If I weren't tired of writing, I could tell of a conversation we had at Mindolo with Father Michael Scott, an Anglican priest no longer allowed into South Africa, who has had a part in a number of U.N. peacemaking ventures; and Father Adrian Hastings, Catholic, and author and particularly knowledgeable about Southern Africa (as is Michael Scott). But I think this letter will keep you busy long enough."

Love,
Esther

184

Abidjan, Ivory Coast
August 31-September 9, 1969

Abidjan, Ivory Coast
September 7, 1969

Dear Family,

"This has been a leisurely afternoon after a busy week of meetings. Besides sleeping and reading an Agatha Christie book, I've been sorting out and reading materials which I've collected this week.

"I was able to get on a plane from Accra to Abidjan last Sunday, and arrived with a number of delegates for the Second Assembly of the All Africa Conference of Churches. Joy (Thede) Beanland was among the committee which met us. Joy was a nurse-midwife in Sierra Leone in Jaiama during several years while I was in Sierra Leone. Her husband, Gayle, is on the A.A.C.C. staff, in audiovisuals, radio and television. They are Presbyterian missionaries. [Joy's first husband was killed, I believe, while they were still college students. She met Gayle on a trip by ship to Sierra Leone.]

"We are staying at the University of Abidjan. We each have a separate room, small but adequate. We don't have all the comforts of home, but it's good enough for a time. We eat in the University cafeteria, a mixture of African and European foods.

"The people one meets here and contacts made are both interesting and valuable. I am one of five representatives of the National Council of Churches, U.S.A. We, along with others, are labeled "consultants," though it actually means that we take part in all activities except in voting. Most of us do little talking.

"We still don't have a list of delegates, but they come from all over Africa. There have been excellent addresses on 'Working with Christ in the Cultural Revolution,' by William A. Eteki Mboumoua, president of the General Conference of UNESCO; 'Working with Christ in the Contemporary Social, Economic, and Political Situation,' by Mr. Jean Mark Ekoh, Minister of Agriculture, Republic of Gabon; and 'Working with Christ for the Renewal of the Church,' by the Rev. E. A. A. Adegbola, principal of Immanual Theological College, Ibadan, Nigeria. These were the keynote addresses on the theme, 'With Christ at Work in Africa Today.' Other addresses of interest were 'Fire on Every Horizon' by Aaron Tolen of the W.S.C.F. (World Student Christian Federation), and a greeting on behalf of the Roman Catholic observers by Archbishop Kojo Amissah of Cape Coast, Ghana. Particularly interesting was his plea to take up the study of intercommunion, as a contribution toward the renewal of 'all things in Christ in Africa.'

"There have been inspiring services of worship and Bible study. We are now divided into discussion groups, each dealing with one of the three major themes. Each in turn is divided into smaller groups. I am in Section I, on the contemporary social, economic and political situation, in a subsection on the Church's response to rural/urban relationships and problems of development. We have small transistor headphones and simultaneous translation is done into English and French.

"Last night Dr. Eugene Carson Blake, General Secretary, World Council of Churches, spoke on 'The Ecumenical Movement,' with special reference to Africa. Afterward I saw for the third time the film on the Upsala Assembly, 'Behold–All Things New.' I see more in it each time. Several African delegates shown in the film are present here. One evening we saw a play given by the World Student Christian Federation (Ivorian Branch), an original play written by a university student and based on an African folktale. The acting was very good, but I understood very little, since it was in French, and even the brief English explanations given were not very well understood because of the East African accent of the speaker

Delegates from Lesotho

Sierra Leoneans at the AACC

Loading the Bus

"Yesterday we divided into three groups to be taken on excursions outside Abidjan. I went with the group (two bus loads) which visited a pineapple plantation about sixty miles from Abidjan. There was some mix-up in arrangements, so we didn't get to the canning factory while the men were still working. (They stopped work at noon on Saturday.) But afterward we went to a village where the local Methodist Church people gave us a royal welcome and feast. They had obviously been preparing for our coming for days in advance. The buses stopped and we were greeted by the pastor and other officials, accompanied by a band and crowds of people, mostly women and children. We got out of the buses and were paraded through town (and march music becomes dancing music in Africa!) It was now 2:00 p.m. Almost the whole village followed us and the band. We finally came to a palm branch archway on which was a banner saying (in French, of course), 'The Protestant Methodist Church of Dabau welcomes you.'

Greeted by the Church at the Village

"We were introduced to various dignitaries–the President of the Methodist Church of Ivory Coast, a member of Parliament, the Prefect of the town, the village chief. We were then escorted to palm-leaf shelters, where tables were set for us. After we were seated we listened to a welcome speech by the pastor, had a Scripture and prayer, two or three numbers by the choir, and a welcome by the Prefect. Finally, at 3:00 p.m. we were invited to serve ourselves food. It was a feast–two or three kinds of rice, Couscous (made from rolled wheat flour, a food I first met in Algeria), foo-foo, yams, pumpkin, and several kinds of meat and soup (a sauce). We had soft drinks <u>with ice</u>, and lots of fresh pineapple and oranges for dessert. It was delicious.

Women Who Prepared Food

Children Eating Left-Overs

Dancing and Singing

187

"During the meal we had 'dinner music' by a band–all hymns played in a good marching rhythm and danced to by the crowds who weren't watching us eat. I've never seen people dance to 'Breathe on Me, Breath of God' before, but it was done with real joy, and I believe worship, there.

"We arrived home at about 6:30. Soon after I went out to the Beanlands', where I washed and dried my hair, and washed, dried and ironed my clothes. By 8:00 I was ready to eat a light meal. There were several Presbyterian executives there too and we had an informal evening until midnight.

"This morning we held an ecumenical service, open to the public, in the stadium. Pastor R. Andriamanjoto of Madagascar gave a challenging message in which he proclaimed that 'Christ is at work in Africa. He is at work here today, in spite of divisions, tribulations and trials of every sort, and He calls us to be with Him, that by His grace we may accomplish God's design for our continent.' The offering (which amounted to more than $1,000) for refugee work among the Sudanese was placed at the foot of the cross by the long line of robed ushers.

Marching to the Sunday Service

The Ecumenical Service

The Offering

Leaving the Service

"In a little while we go to a reception by the Methodist Church of Ivory Coast, who are the hosts of the Conference.

"One evening this week we attended a reception at the palace of President Houphouët-Boigney. He himself was not there, however, because of the O.A.U. (Organization of African Unity) meeting in Addis Ababa this week also. The building and grounds are fabulous.

"One can't help but be impressed by the apparent prosperity of the country. Buildings are going up everywhere. We were on paved roads on nearly the whole trip yesterday, and there was electricity in the village. Gayle Beanland says there is electricity almost everywhere. Africanization has proceeded rapidly in the years since independence, although there are still many Frenchmen in the country. They do have problems yet, of course.

"A home for refugee children from Biafra is near here. Ivory Coast is one of the four African countries which has recognized Biafra. Feelings on this issue are quite intense. Needless to say, there are no diplomatic relationships between Ivory Coast and Nigeria . . .

"I was grateful for this opportunity to increase my knowledge of and acquaintance with Christian leaders from many parts of Africa."

Love, Esther

[As of this writing in 2007, the situation in Ivory Coast (or Côte d'Ivoire) has been tragic in the last years, with a long civil war. Fighting has ceased at this time, but the country is divided into two, with rebels in control of part of it. A peace treaty is being negotiated.]

Information contained in a report to staff:

At this Second Assembly of the All Africa Conference of Churches there were five hundred fifty delegates, observers, consultants, visitors and staff members in attendance. The A.A.C.C. is made up of seventy-eight member churches (fifty-four English, twenty-four French speaking), eleven Christian Councils (three English, one French). Of these, nine are new members accepted at the opening session of the Conference. Among them were The United Methodist Church in Liberia, and for the first time, one of the independent churches, the Church of the Holy Spirit (a break-off from the Kimbanguists) from Congo-Kinshasha.

There were, no doubt, United Methodists whom I did not meet, but of those of whom I was aware there were three from Liberia (including Charles Minor, now working with S.C.M.s (Student Christian Movements) and the W.S.C.F., and Melvina Nagbe, who stayed only two days after the Women's Consultation. Shirley Mader attended the Women's Consultation, but left the day after. There were six from Sierra Leone, including two women who had attended the Women's Consultation, and Eustace Renner, now of the A.A.C.C. staff; two from Congo, including Bishop Shungu and a woman who attended the Consultation; Bishop Muzorewa of Rhodesia; Bishop Taylor; and Walter Cason, of the Theological Education Fund. G. M. Setiloane of South Africa, now on scholarship in England, was also present.

I did not stay for the business meetings, since I needed to be on my way to Nigeria, but some items of interest were:

(1) The proposal that there should be regional offices in both East and West Africa. This would cut down on individual staff travel and enable staff to give detailed attention to the areas covered.

(2) A United Methodist Woman, Mrs. Eugenia Simpson-Cooper of Liberia, was a newly elected member of the twenty member General Committee.

(3) Four new presidents of the A.A.C.C. elected at the Assembly were Dr. Jean Kotto, Cameroon; the Rev. Seth M. Mokitimi, South Africa; the Most Rev. Moses N.C.O. Scott, Archbishop of the Province of West Africa, from Sierra Leone; and His Beatitude Theophilos, Archbishop of Harrar, Ethiopia.

(4) The proposed 1970 budget called for $219,168, in contrast to actual expenditures in 1968 of $70, 534. The Assembly recommended that funds be raised through a new system of membership subscriptions, with each member church paying a minimum of four Central African francs per member in French-speaking countries, and two pence per member in English-speaking countries, on the basis of membership declared the previous years. Associate members (national councils) would continue to pay an annual assessment as before. A major share of the 1970 budget would provide for ten new staff members, raising the present staff of twenty-one to thirty-one. The Finance Committee also recommended a 10% increase in staff salaries. Among the new staff sought was a finance secretary who would assist in raising the increased budget.

PART II

GHANA – THE LAND OF GOLD

AFRICA

From p. 15, *Prayer Calendar 2007*, Daniel Licardo, ed. Women's Division, General Board of Global Ministries, The United Methodist Church, c.2006 by the General Board of Global Ministries. Used by permission. (Shading added.)

Introduction

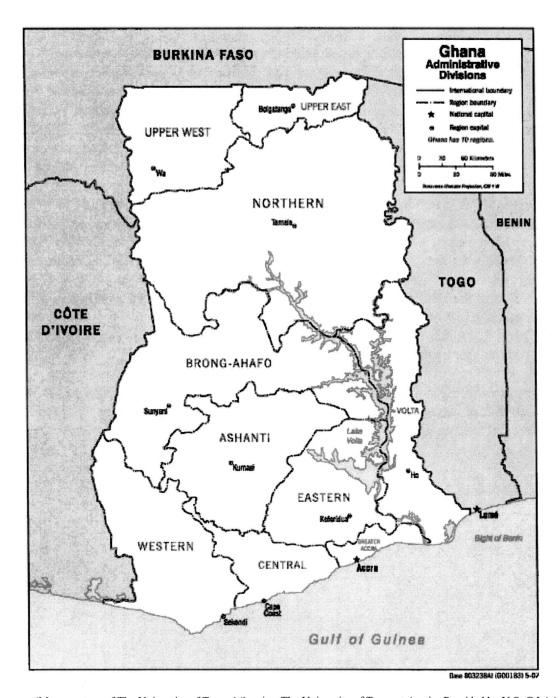

(Map courtesy of The University of Texas Libraries, The University of Texas at Austin. Provided by U.S. C.I.A.)

Ghana lies between latitudes 4° and 1 1 /2 ° north of the equator. It is not quite as large as the state of Oregon. The climate is tropical, with two seasons, the rainy or wet season, April to October, and the dry, November to late March.

The country is bound on the north by Burkina Faso, west by Côte d'Ivoire, east by Togo, and south by the Atlantic Ocean. It is divided into ten regions: Upper West, Upper East, Northern, Volta, Brong-Ahafo, Ashanti, Eastern, Western, Central and Greater Accra. The capital is Accra.

There are at least seventy-five tribes, distinguished by language, but of these only ten have significant numbers. English is the official language. Various figures have been given for the number in each religious group: from 60% to "nearly two-thirds," are Christian, one-sixth to 15% Muslim, and 25% to one-third who follow the traditional religions. The Christians are primarily Roman Catholic, Methodist and Presbyterian, with other smaller denominations, and several charismatic and "spiritual" churches.

Ghana is rich in natural resources, including cocoa, timber, aluminum and gold. The early European explorers named the area "Gold Coast." The British had extended their control to the northern territories by 1901, but on March 6, 1957, under the leadership of Kwame Nkrumah, Ghana became the first African nation to gain its independence. At that time the name of the country was changed from Gold Coast to Ghana, the name of an ancient kingdom which was powerful until the thirteenth century. However, that kingdom was in what is now southeast Mauritania and part of Mali, not in the area of present-day Ghana.

Ghana has a rich culture, expressed in festivals, arts and crafts, and customs which a foreigner can only begin to glimpse.

The above information has been obtained from the *Encyclopedia Britannica Almanac, 2005*; *A Glorious Age in Africa*, by Daniel Chu and Elliott Skinner, Doubleday & Co., 1965, and a booklet published by the Ghana Information Services, *Ghana Today No. 4, People of Ghana.*

Ghana National Anthem

1. God bless our homeland Ghana,
   And make our nation great and strong,
   Bold to defend forever
   The cause of Freedom and of Right;
   Fill our hearts with true humility,
   Make us cherish fearless honesty
   And help us to resist oppressor's rule
   With all our will and might forevermore.

2. Hail to thy name, O Ghana,
   To thee we make our solemn vow;
   Steadfast to build together
   A nation strong in Unity;
   With all our gifts of mind and strength
   Whether night or day, in mist or storm
   In every need what e'er the call may be,
   To serve thee, Ghana, now and evermore.

3. Raise high the flag of Ghana,
   And one with Africa advance;
   Black Star of hope and honour
   To all who thirst for liberty;
   Where the banner of Ghana freely flies;
   May the way to freedom truly lie.
   Arise, arise, O Sons of Ghanaland,
   And under God march on for evermore.

(This English translation submitted by the Rev. Samuel B. Essamuah)

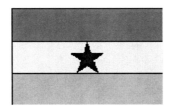

(Red at top, green at bottom, with black star on yellow)

Preface

When with restructure at the Board of Missions of The United Methodist Church I was no longer on the staff, I began to search for places in Africa where I might be able to use my doctorate in religious education. Because I had previously met Desmond Tutu (now Archbishop), who at that time was with the Theological Education Fund, I wrote to him and sent a résumé. He sent it to six different African countries. I heard from each of them, and all had something to offer. However, it was Trinity College in Ghana which sparked my interest, because they said they were interested in developing extension education. With approval and appointment by the World Division of the General Board of Global Ministries, The United Methodist Church, by the summer of 1973 I was preparing to leave for Ghana, while I waited for a visa. Finally, when no resident visa was forthcoming, the principal of the College told me to come ahead on a visitor's visa, and I would be able to get a resident visa when I arrived. I was going under the auspices of the Methodist Church of Ghana (related to the British Methodist Church, but autonomous), and was thus on the list of those allowed to enter and work in Ghana. The school term had already begun by the time I arrived in late September, and the house in which I was to live was not completed. So I settled in temporarily with the principal, Dr. Eugene Grau, and his wife, Dorothy. Trinity College, which was located in Legon, near the university, about ten miles from Accra, was a joint theological college for the Evangelical Presbyterian Church, the Presbyterian Church of Ghana, the Methodist Church, Ghana, and the Anglican Church. It was opened in 1943 in temporary buildings in Kumasi. Before that time ministers were trained along with other church workers at the various denominations. But from 1943 onwards the College, later named Trinity College, gave the normal preparation for ministers, at that time, of the two Presbyterian and the Methodist churches. The course of training was originally for three years, but by the time I arrived it had been extended to four.[1]

The story of my seven years in Ghana will be told by letters sent to my family and friends, by photographs, my memories and those of friends who took part in some of my experiences, and other sources.

---

[1]From the program for the opening ceremony of the new college buildings at Legon on January 23, 1965.

Chapter 1. Introduction to Trinity College
1973-74

As I entered the grounds of Trinity Theological College on that September day in 1973, I was impressed with the attractive, well-kept campus. There were the usual palm and frangipani trees, as well as other flowering plants and bushes. At the center of the campus was the Chapel, which also served as a community church for people in the nearby area. To the right was the two-story building, with outside steps, containing offices below and the classrooms above. On the left was the library on the second floor, and a room beneath that we later used for the Christian Education classes and the Sunday School. Farther on there were the dining room and the dormitory block for students. At various places around the campus were houses for staff. The house that I lived in (which was not finished when I arrived, but into which I later moved) was not actually on the campus, and was owned by one of the students. However, it was next to other staff housing so was very much a part of the campus.

View of the Campus

The Chapel

Christian Education Room and Library

Dining Room

Dormitory Block

Offices and Classrooms

My House

Some of the Staff

Eugene Grau, Principal

Rudolph Mack, Hebrew

Andrew Munro, Doctrine

Edmond Yeboah, Greek

Dieter Kemmler, New Testament

Sam Prempeh, Church History

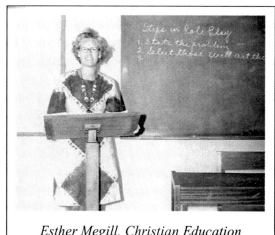

Esther Megill, Christian Education

At that time the principal was an American, Dr. Eugene Grau, a missionary of the United Church of Christ. Other staff members were Rudolf Mack (German), Old Testament and Hebrew tutor; J. deGraft Johnson (Ghanaian), Pastoral Counseling; Dieter Kemmler (Swiss), New Testament; Andrew Munro (Scots), Doctrine; Edmond Yeboah (Ghanaian), Greek & Biblical Interpretation, and Samuel Prempeh (Ghanaian), Church History. At times an outside teacher had taught some Christian Education. However, I was the first full-time, trained Christian educator.

I soon discovered that there were few suitable books on Christian education in the library, and I knew of no books written to teach Christian education (as we know it in the United States) in Africa. Therefore, while I started with the curriculum outline of the former teacher as a basis, I soon began to plan my own. Because I needed my books, I asked someone to open my crates that were in the unfinished house to which I would be moving, and found some that I needed. One afternoon as I was sitting there, looking over the books, I felt something run over my foot. Looking down, I saw a huge lizard! I called Matthew, who was working for me in the house and yard, who captured it. I took a photograph, and I am sure he had a good meal that night. As stated above, Trinity College was a cooperative school. Although it received some initial help from the Theological Education Fund, Trinity  was at that time supported entirely by the churches in Ghana, except for the salaries of expatriate staff. Some of the mission boards to which the churches were related gave scholarships which enabled the churches to send students.

In the 1973-74 school year there were seventy-seven students, which included not only those from the cooperating denominations, but also some other churches in Ghana, such as the Lutheran and African Methodist Episcopal. There was one student from Zambia, three from Liberia (one of whom was from The United Methodist Church), and two from Sierra Leone. I discovered that Edward Kargbo, one of the Sierra Leone students, had been in my children's

202

Esther Megill and Fourth Year Christian Education Class

church at Rotifunk in Sierra Leone, and later, when he became a teacher there, had carried it on. I also knew J. C. Humper, who later became bishop of The United Methodist Church there. It was now my privilege to be teaching them Christian Education.

That year I taught two classes in Christian Education, one to first year and one to fourth year students. When I began my first Christian education class (and to every new class thereafter) I explained first of all what was meant by "Christian education" in these courses. For churches established in the former British or European colonies, Christian education became the schools which were established by the churches. I had to explain that we would be learning about ways in which we teach the Christian faith to the members of all ages in our churches.

The Sunday School

Practical work for the first year students was in the Sunday School of the church which met on campus. There were unique problems one did not have in the United States. First, some of our classes met outside in the shade of trees. Fortunately, it seldom rained on Sunday morning, even in the rainy season (I don't know why) so we usually did not have to crowd inside the few buildings available to us. Another challenge was that I not only had to divide the children by age, but also by the language they spoke. That meant four different language groups–Ga, Ewe, Akan and English. The older students (equivalent to our Junior High) had learned English well enough in school that they could be taught in English. Then I had to match the Trinity students with the groups whose language they spoke. Each

Edward Kargbo, from Sierra Leone, Teaching the Youth Class in English

year I hoped that there would be more Ga speaking students, since that was the predominant language in the Accra area. The students from the North, who usually did not speak any of the languages in the South, and the foreign students, all had to teach the older classes, in English. We fortunately had copies of the old Africa Sunday School Curriculum, so I was able to adapt these to use, as well as later adding other materials which I wrote, often with the help of students. A great deal of my time was spent on the Sunday School.

Beginners (Kindergarten) Class

Coloring

Finger Painting

Football (Soccer)

Playing with Stones

204

Sand

Rhythmic Games

Christmas Party

205

Carrying Chairs to a Class Under the Trees

Sunday School Class

Leading Worship for Primaries and Juniors

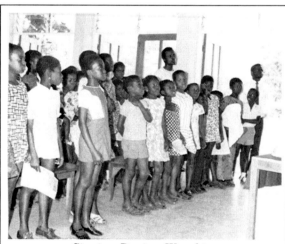

Singing During Worship

Primary Class–Puppets

Junior Class Making Puppets

Making Christmas Decorations

Making Christmas Decorations from Clay

Audiovisuals

I also taught a course in audiovisuals, divided into two groups because of the size of the class. We dealt only with those things that could be used in the churches–posters, puppets, dioramas, maps, flannel-boards, etc.–nothing which needed electricity.

A Frieze

Drawing Pictures for a Kamishibai

Maps

Models

Time Line

Making Puppets

I was asked by the principal to teach other courses for one semester–English reading and English comprehension. (As the principal said, I was the only native English speaker on the staff, other than the principal and the Scotsman, who both had full loads. I pointed out that I was an American English speaker.) I did not feel at all qualified to teach English comprehension or English as a second language. A reading specialist friend in Liberia sent me a book on teaching reading which helped. I later also taught a class in writing. One of my objectives was to teach them to write research papers and to use the proper format. Students complained, but later one who was able to enter the university told me that other students asked him where he had learned to write papers.

During one reading class period something came up about snakes. One student said, "There was a very poisonous snake below . . . and it especially likes white people!" I knew that they accepted me as a friend when they could tease me.

The students were all men, mature adults, who were preparing for the ministry. Most of them were married and had children, but their families did not come with them. The education given was on the post secondary level, probably equivalent to junior college work in the United States. Yet, we did use some textbooks that were used in seminaries in the United States and England. There was a wide variety of academic ability among the students. None had achieved the "A level" in their examinations, which in the British system would qualify them to enter the university. However, a number had additional work beyond secondary school in teacher training institutions. In addition to the four regular classes we had special two-year students who were not able to take the full course, but profited from the training we could give them. Those who attended for four years were aiming for the licentiate examination, set by the University of Ghana at Legon and our own school. A few of the students would go on to the B.D. work by correspondence, with tutoring by staff members, and each year a few were recommended to the churches for additional training overseas. A definite aim of the school was to select some of the best qualified students for further training to qualify them to return to Trinity as teachers. Many of our students of those years eventually earned PhDs, so they had the ability to learn when they were given the opportunity.

Worship

Every morning and every evening the drums called the students to worship. One of the students wrote the following for a class in writing:

The Talking Drums
Isaac K. Quansah

Obiri Addo on the Drums

"Holy God! Everlasting God! He who created all beings. You are fearful; you deserve praise and adoration. All of you come, come immediately and worship Him. Come! Come! Come! . . ." sounds the college drummer on two talking drums. Soon the Trinity Chapel is filled and worship begins. The pair of drums, male and female, are made of special wood. They are about three feet high with a diameter of about twelve inches at the top, hollowed out, and the surface skillfully covered with dry deer skin. The covering skin is tightened at the circumference by seven pegs slotted into holes and fastened with strings. The pegs help in tuning the sound. The base of both drums is smaller in diameter than the top. Supported by a drum-stand, the drums are placed in front of the chapel every morning and evening before worship. When beating the drums, the drummer stands behind. He uses two sticks especially designed for drumming, to sound the message of the call to worship. It may

seem easy when he is beating, yet it takes skill to be able to communicate a message on the drums. I regard them as being of great importance so far as the spiritual life of the college is concerned, for it is by this means we are assembled to worship both morning and evening. Because they are used in worship, the drums are found at the right on entering the chapel. They have replaced the old method of bell ringing, and it is good to let drumming have a place in worship so that African culture too may be used in our Christian religion.

By questioning the students I learned that while "talking drums" were much used in the past in parts of Africa to send messages, the custom was dying. I also learned that the drum beats were in different languages–they would be different from one language to the next. At the end of the school term I would begin to hear in the afternoon, after classes, the beating of the drum, and I knew that another student was being taught to beat the drums, to replace the one who was leaving.

Students and staff took turns in leading chapel. I learned toward the end of my time in Ghana that I was the first woman to preach from the pulpit. Once a month on Sunday there was a communion service at 6:00 a.m. The Methodist, Presbyterian or Anglican liturgies were used, depending upon which staff member was officiating.

Ghanaian Culture

I learned much about Ghanaian culture when I assigned the writing class to write descriptive essays. There were many descriptions of festivals and traditional beliefs. Because festivals are such an important part of the culture, I am including below another writing by Isaac Quansah.

The Traditional View of Festivals
Isaac Quansah

Once a year, in the life of every adult and responsible Ghanaian, there is a pilgrimage from one's place of work to one's hometown. People visit home with mixed feeling of happiness and sorrow. Why this exodus of people to tribal and ancestral homes? Often it is in response to age-long established festivals which are meaningful and influence the Ghanaians' moral, social and religious life. Christians have their festival of Easter to celebrate. So also Gas celebrate Homowo and Twis celebrate Odwira. The Fantes commemorate Bakatue, Ahobaa and Akomgo. The people of the Volta Region celebrate the Yam festival while the Dagaaba people of the Upper Region celebrate the Doro festival.

It is not accidental that a tribe or a community celebrates any of the named festivals. There are a variety of Ghanaian legends and myths designed to explain the origin and purpose of these festivals. For example, the Christian Festival of Easter has a biblical foundation. It is centered on the person, life and work of Jesus. God became man in Jesus. He redeems sinful mankind through His sacrificial death on the Cross. Easter which marks the resurrection of Jesus from His guarded tomb gives the militant Christian a hope. It is a hope of overcoming death as Jesus has removed the terror and fears of death.

211

The Homowo of the Gas, the Yam festival of the people of the Volta Region, the Bakatue festival of people of Elmina, and the Doro festival of Dagaare people of the Upper North, are connected with hunger at a particular period in the history of the tribe. To combat the severe hunger, the people of Ho in the Volta region found a species of an edible root, namely the yam. They planted the root and produced abundant food, which became their source of food supply. The people of the Ho area in turn paid tribute to the root with the celebration of the Yam festival.

Likewise, the Dagaaba of Lawra area in the Upper Region celebrate the Doro festival. This is associated with the harvesting of corn and groundnuts which once relieved the tribe of their severe hunger.

In the case of the Elmina people, Bakatue is of duel significance. Its celebration may bring either plentiful food production or bumper fishing during the year.

In contrast with views relating to the above-named festivals, the Ahobaa festival of the Fantes originated from an outbreak of an epidemic in Fanteland. The epidemic killed thousands of Fantes. No amount of medical treatment could control the indiscriminate killing of the people. Gods upon gods, priests upon priests, and medicine men of no mean reputation were consulted. Finally, it was revealed that the people could be saved from the epidemic only if one man voluntarily offered himself to be sacrificed to the arch-god of the Fantes at a shrine in Mankessim. A patriotic, humanitarian and selfless man among the elders called Ahor, feeling for his people, responded to their appeal. Ahor offered himself for sacrifice. As soon as he was killed and sacrificed to the gods the epidemic stopped. Ever since, the Fantes have honoured Ahor with this great Ahobaa festival, usually celebrated between the months of May and June.

With the foregoing, it is no wonder that Ghana is a country dominated by meaningful festivals. Christians mourn and make merry through religious hymns and songs during Easter Tide. Chiefs, elders, ritual specialists, young and old, welcome the celebration of Homo, Odwira, Yam, Doro, Bakatue and Ahobaa festivals with pomp and enthusiasm.

There is insistence on communal involvement and participation in these important traditional and religious festivals. People believe these festivals have double significance. They foster cohesion in the society. They bring prosperity and fertility to the tribes and people who observe them. In order not to forfeit the blessings that these festivals bring upon the participants, many Ghanaians travel home at least once a year to join in celebrating these festivals.

Government and Politics

After Ghana's gaining its independence in 1957 there were numerous political coups. In 1972 Colonel I. K. Acheampong overthrew the government of Busia, who had been elected with a multiparty system, and became the Chairman of the National Redemption Council. On January 14, 1974, the second anniversary of "The Thirteenth January Revolution," Trinity staff were invited to attend the Armed Forces and Police Parade at Independence Square in Accra. There was great pomp as the Chairman inspected the troops, bands played, there was a "trooping of the colors," the Chairman presented Redemption Day Medals, and then delivered an address.

212

Col. Achaempong

Women Police

Col. Achaempong

The Second Term

On January 27, 1974, I wrote to a friend:

"I am very busy these days, and feel rather settled into a routine, which is good after having so much 'unsettlement' for so long. I was glad to be able to start this quarter with more preparation done for classes than last term. Also, I am finally beginning on some of the writing which was one of the purposes for coming here. I am not doing programming at the moment, but am beginning to write a textbook to use in teaching Christian Education in Africa. It will be produced at least in a mimeographed form, and I hope to have part of it done to use experimentally in my teaching next year.

". . . This week we had a guest lecturer here who gave two lectures a day, so we had shortened class periods. He is a White Father, Dutch. I was invited to eat lunch with him at the home of one of the staff members, and enjoyed talking with him. He has been in Algeria and studied in Tunisia, so we had some things in common. (In 1976 I was asked to go to the Catholic Theological School in Tamale and give lectures on the use of audiovisuals. It was an interesting experience; I was told by one of the Sisters that it was the first time a woman had been invited to this exchange of lecturers.)

"Finally this week the carpenter finished a special cabinet for me to put my enlarger on and store photographic supplies in. So I unpacked and assembled my equipment, and now all I need is the time to print some pictures.

"We are working on the yard all the time. I'm having grass planted–you know what new building sites are like. The soil is very poor, of course, and it's the dry season, so we have to water all the time. I have a banana tree and two hibiscus bushes planted, and hope tomorrow to be able to buy some grafted mango trees to get started. I don't know whether I'll be around long enough to enjoy them, but someone will. Oh, yes, we have three guava trees planted too . . .

" I'm enjoying my contact with the students, and learning to know them. Some drop in quite often, either to bring papers, ask questions, or just to chat. I'm starting to have a group over for games once a week when the week isn't too busy–I'm going to make the rounds of the classes I teach."

During this term the Audio-Visual class had an exhibit of various types of A-V materials they had created. Other students, staff, and persons in the Community Church on campus were invited.

Demonstrating the Use of Flannelboards

Puppets

Shadow Puppets

Models

One of the interesting experiences during the term was attending with some students one of the "Spiritual" or Independent Churches, on a Friday evening. These churches, which are responsible for some of the rapid growth of Christianity in Africa, are interesting phenomenons. Churches independent of any mission body began to emerge several years before in South Africa, and multiplied greatly in sub-Saharan Africa. Dr. David Barrett, who was then secretary of research in an ecumenical unit based in Nairobi, several years before had written an article called: "A.D. 2000: 350 Million Christians in Africa." In 1982 the *Christian World Encyclopedia*, which he edited, was published. In it he not only spoke of the rapid growth of the churches originally established by missionaries, but also of the Independent Churches. He said, "They vary greatly, but include African indigenous culture within their rituals and beliefs. Many accept polygamy. They use drums and other African musical instruments and dancing in their worship. They emphasize the Holy Spirit and healing. Women often have important leadership positions. They base their beliefs on the Bible and are eager for more knowledge of the Scripture and the Christian faith."[2] There are many small sects, so there are differences and little unity among them.

We visited a service of the Aladura. Church. (These churches began in Nigeria.) It was long, but did not seem so because so much was happening. There was a mixture of the Anglican liturgy and African dancing and singing. While we may question how Christian some of the traditional beliefs are, we in the established churches should be able to learn something from their zeal, rapid growth, and self support. I discovered in Ghana that some members of the established churches also attended Independent Churches. It was obvious that their type of worship and beliefs appealed to many Ghanaians.

At the end of the school term in June we had farewell parties for the Graus, who were returning to the States. We had a school farewell, and the Evangelical Presbyterian Church (their sponsoring church) had a special farewell at Peki. I was able to go, along with others, to this important event. Gene preached a farewell sermon at that time.

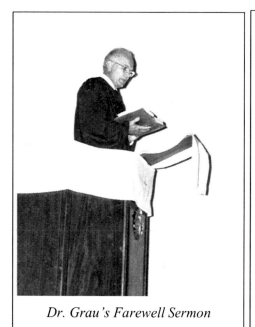

Dr. Grau's Farewell Sermon

Dr. Grau Shows a Gift from the School

---

[2] Barrett, David, "A.D. 2000: 350 Million Christians in Africa" in the *Christian World Encyclopedia.*

Dr. Mack Presents a Gift to Dorothy Grau at the Staff Farewell Party

A Farewell by the Tema Choir

*Trinity-Tema Choir,
Dr. Grau, Conductor
Dr. Grau served as a pastor
to an English language
church at Tema. The choir
from that church joined with
the Trinity Choir to form a
Trinity-Tema Choir.*

A Farewell to Eugene & Dorothy Grau by the Evangelical Presbyterian Church, at Peki

The "Long Vac"

During the long vacation period (summer for us in the northern hemisphere) I was busy holding three workshops, writing, and showing a stream of visitors around. I enjoyed having "old" friends, and making new ones. A vacation with three missionary friends from Liberia (Nancy Lightfoot, Hazel Tefft, and Lauren Spellman, whom I had not met before) took us to the north of Ghana. The villages in the north, with the round huts and thatched roofs, reminded me of those in Northern Nigeria. We stayed at the Mole Game Reserve, and visited the Akasombo Dam on the Volta River. This dam created the Volta Lake, one of the largest man-made lakes in the world. It produces electricity for Ghana and surrounding countries.

Nancy Lightfoot and Others at the Akasomba Dam

The "Akasomba Queen"

Then there were friends who attended the Faith and Order Conference of the World Council of Churches at the University nearby. I had known Jeanne Audrey Powers in New York (she was on the staff of the Division on Ecumenical and Interreligious affairs of the General Board of Global Ministries, The United Methodist Church), but met Sue Morrison for the first time. (She later was elected bishop, and retired in 2006.) I had corresponded with Jeanne Audrey, and told her that I was looking forward to meeting her when she was in Ghana. However, I would be holding a workshop on the weekend she arrived, so could not meet her at the airport, but would find her at the University when I returned to Legon.

When I met Jeanne Audrey, she was very glad to see me, but mainly, I think, because her suitcase had never arrived and she was in dire need of help. She had no means of transport, so I took her to Accra and we were able to find a few things. At that time in Ghana many items were becoming scarce, but we were able to get a toothbrush and toothpaste, soap, etc. However, there were no ready-made dresses, so I took her to a tailor, who measured her for two Ghanaian dresses. Because they would not be completed for close to a week, I took an American house dress which I had not yet worn out of my trunk. It was too large for her, but at least it covered her. Nancy Lightfoot was still with me, and she lent her some African clothes (which Nancy often wore). The suitcase was never recovered, including some family jewelry and her mailing list. At the time, however, her biggest concern was all the materials she had brought for the worship service which she was to lead at the Conference. She was able to phone New York and get copies sent with someone who came later–but had to stand before that assembly of mostly males, including heads of churches from different countries–to lead in worship in clothes that didn't fit.

A Naming Ceremony

During that July another very important event occurred–an "outdooring" or naming ceremony of a baby. K. A. Agyemang, one of my students, had asked if his niece could be named after me, and of course I felt honored. I knew that a name was very important in Ghana. People believed that a person would grow to be like the one for whom they were named. I invited Jeanne Audrey, Susan, and Hazel Tefft, who was still with me, to accompany me on the day of the ceremony to the village of Apinamang. I met Mary Kwakye, the mother, and many others there, including the pastor. The ceremony, they explained, was not like the traditional "outdooring" ceremony, but was a Christian one.

Early in the morning we gathered with the family in the hall of the house. The pastor then prayed, and we sang Christian songs to open the ceremony.

A man then brought the baby in front of the people and said, "We know why we have gathered here. We are going to name this baby girl."

He then introduced me to the people and told them the baby was going to be named after me. The people showed their happiness and welcomed me. The baby was then given to me and I was asked to give her the name, Esther Megill, which I did. All showed their happiness by clapping their hands.

The baby was then given a drop of gin on her tongue, by the elder who said, "Esther, if you see liquor, say it is liquor." This is done three times. He then put a drop of water on her tongue and said, "Esther, if you see water, say it is water," again three times. This is to enable her to be truthful and honest when she grows up, to distinguish between good and evil. I then gave her a gift, as others did also. The ceremony closed with prayer.

*Esther Megill and
Baby Esther*

*Owusu Asomaning,, Mary Kwakye
with Baby Esther, Esther Megill*

Owusu Asomaning, Father; Mary Kwakye, Mother; Baby, Esther Megill

Jeanne Audrey Powers, Susan Morrison

Jeanne Audrey Powers, K.A. Agymang with Baby Esther, Esther Megill, K.K.O. Asiedu-Asare (Trinity Student), Hazel Tefft, Susan Morrison

221

There was singing and dancing, especially by the children, and they fed us well. We went home with fruits from the farm--coconuts, pineapples and others.[3]

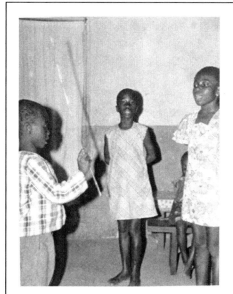

Children Singing

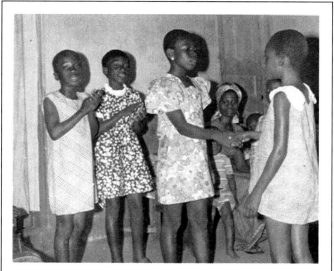

Children Playing Games

Gifts of Fruit

---

[3]

Mary Kwakye, Esther's mother, added to what I had remembered from the event; other information is from a description of an Akan Naming Ceremony, written by the Rev. Isaac K, Quansah, when he was a student at Trinity.

Workshops for Sunday School Teachers

As the first school year at Trinity drew to a close, I found that some of my students had become quite interested in Christian education. During the "long vac" the students were sent to various churches to work as interns with a pastor. Three of my students asked me whether I would go hold a workshop for Sunday School teachers in the churches to which they would be assigned. Of course I was glad to do so, although I told them I must have their help. So, I developed plans for a weekend workshop, and on three different weekends went to three places. As we were returning from the last one, one of the students said, "You should teach us how to hold these workshops." I answered, "I have been thinking of that, because you could do a better job than I–you speak the language and know the people. But I know how very busy you are, and if I give you training it would have to be in addition to your usual class work. I didn't know whether you would feel you could take the time for more study."

The student[4] answered, "I would," and others agreed.

Thus began a program of training selected students as workshop leaders. I chose those who had done well in the Christian Education classes, and from my observation of their teaching in Sunday School, I felt they had a good relationship with the children. Also, if they followed the lesson plans which I required them to turn in, they did a good job of teaching. Unfortunately, except in the English-language classes, I could not tell what they really taught.

As the years went by, I discovered that being selected for a workshop team was deemed a privilege, at least by some. One student, who had not done well academically, came to me and begged to be included. So, I let him in, since he was really interested.

Odumasi-Krobo

Esther Megill & L.K.Alorzukey, Trinity Student

Beginners – Wonder Box

---

[4]He was Kwaku Asamoah-Okyere, who eventually earned a Master's Degree in Religious Education and took my place at Trinity.

223

Using a Flannelboard

Scenes in and Around Odumasi-Krobo

Confirmation in a Presbyterian Church

Market Scene, Asesewa Krobo

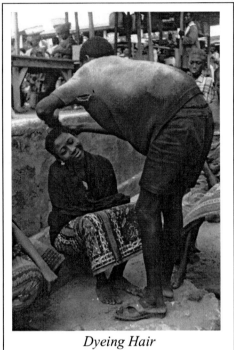

Dyeing Hair

Children in Market

Native Medicine Man and Herbs

225

Takaradi Workshop

Beginner's Class

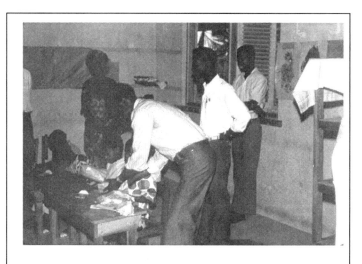

Primary Class, Making Puppets

Telling a Story with Puppets

Juniors–Litany

Accra Scenes

Kotoka International Airport

Major-General Emmanuel Kotoka was one of the co-conspirators behind the first bloody cou d'état in Ghana in 1966, when the regime of Dr. Kwame Nkrumah was overthrown. He is considered a national hero.

Kotoka Statue at Airport

Black Star Square

Memorial to the War Dead

The Lighthouse

The Castle

World Day of Prayer 1974

Fetish Priest   *Psychic and Traditional Healing*
Signs Showing the Influence of Traditional Religion

*View of Accra and the
Sea from the University*

Chapter 2. Workshop Teams, Christian Family Life Institute
1974-75

Metra Heisler–Picnic at Aburi Botanical Gardens

Helen & Stan Trebes

And so a busy and interesting vacation period ended, and a new school term began in September. I was pleased during that month to welcome Metra Heisler, a visitor from Sierra Leone. We had lived and worked together in Rotifunk. Also, Stan and Helen Trebes, whom I had known in Sierra Leone and in Nigeria, visited.

In December I wrote a letter to my friends and supporting churches which tells something about that first term.

Trinity College
P.O. Box 48
Legon, Ghana
December 18, 1974

Dear Friends Around the World,

"Time has moved at such a breathtaking pace this past year that it is difficult to believe that the Christmas season is here once again, except that the signs of Christmas are here in this warm country also. Christmas decorations have been up in the shops in Accra for some time, and our Christmas party for the Sunday School has come and gone. We always have to have it early, on the last Sunday the student teachers are with us before they go on holiday. (We continue the Sunday School, with the help of members of the campus church. I am even busier supervising during that time.)

"The children enjoyed making decorations for the assembly hall and their Christmas tree, a frangipani tree which grows near the assembly, and is conveniently in bloom at this season. This year because of the scarcity and cost of paper, we painted old newspapers and made chains from them; the kindergarten children used fingerpaint and sponges dipped in poster paint, and the older children used sponges and brushes. They all enjoyed it just as much as if it had been the smooth white paper or construction paper which would have been used in the United States. The young people made stars from small pieces of bamboo, and various other items usually discarded contributed to the variety of decorations.

"After the decorations were complete, on the day of the party we made a ring around the tree and sang carols. We learned new carols and enjoyed old ones, some in English and some in one of the Ghanaian languages. The children then marched into the hall, where the Christmas story was presented with shadow puppets, followed by worship. The lighting of the Advent Candles, new to people here, seems to be very impressive for the children. So the joy and wonder of Christmas are here also.

"An important part of the annual Christmas party–probably the most important for the children–are the refreshments we have. I try to find sweets (candy) for them, and we have bread and cocoa to drink.

"The kindergarten children and youth classes had separate celebrations.

"Last Sunday some of the children went with us to take the decorations to the children's ward of the hospital.

Decorating the Frangipani Tree

Singing Around the Christmas Tree

Lighting the Advent Candles

Shadow Puppets

"The first term of school has been extremely busy. Because of the shortage of staff, I have been teaching three classes in Church History in addition to my regular classes. (Sam Prempeh, the usual teacher, is studying in England.) I enjoy it, but it means new courses to prepare for again this year.

"An important event on October 27 was the induction of the Rev. I. K. A. Thompson, B.D., M.A., as principal of Trinity College–the first Ghanaian principal.

Induction of I.K.A. Thompson

Rev. I. K. A. Thompson, Principal

"Immediately after school was out on December 11, I held a two and one-half day workshop for a selected group of students, to teach them to hold workshops for lay people on how to organize and teach in a Sunday School. I hope to have five teams go out in April during the Easter vacation, and again next August. The men are doing this on a completely volunteer basis. The money for a set of materials for each team will come from special gifts some of you have made to Christian Education at Trinity College. We plan to have the project be self-supporting after the initial expense. Because of my experience holding three workshops this last vacation period I am sure we will have an eager response from the lay people of the churches. One thing one never lacks in Ghana is children. Often there will be as many as 400-500 children of all age groups with one or two teachers. (Many congregations have membership in the thousands–even as high as six or seven thousand; the pastor of such a church will also have responsibility for a number of smaller churches in the district; and he may have one assistant pastor and perhaps a few catechists or evangelists. Much responsibility is given to lay people also.) The problems are many, but if we can help with information and materials, I am sure more people will be willing to teach.

"I have succeeded in completing a manuscript for a book, *Education in the African Church*, and am using it, in mimeographed form, for my classes this year. It also will be used experimentally in the extension program of The United Methodist Church in Sierra Leone. Whether it will be possible to get the book published, is another question . . . "

During this time I took the class of students to Tema, the port city near to Accra. They saw there an example of urban ministry, ministry among people who had come from all over Ghana to work. We visited VALCO, the Volta Aluminium Company Ltd., with a smelter which produced ingots of aluminum from bauxite, with the use of electric power from the Volta Dam.

A pamphlet from VALCO stated that their smelter was one of the largest in the world outside of North America. At that time approximately 2,000 Ghanaians were employed in the round-the-clock operation of the smelter. Of this number nearly 300 had been elevated to supervisory positions. An active continuing training program was in force to train Ghanaians in supervisory and other skills.

The ingots which were produced were sent to customers all over the world. We saw a factory which made aluminum (aluminium to the British) items–cooking utensils, cups, etc. We were told that ingots shipped to Russia were processed, then the sheets sent back to Ghana to be made into items for use in Ghana.

The government was encouraging farmers to grow food for export, since foreign exchange was needed to pay the huge debt. This sometimes meant that there was not much encouragement to use the land to grow food needed locally. Signs along the road showed the emphasis on export. There were often long queues waiting to purchase food.

Once when I was shopping and saw a queue, I stepped into line and asked, "What are they selling today?"

The answer was, "I don't know, but it will be something I will need." And I, too, waited in line and was able to buy some canned evaporated milk.

We had eighty-seven students in 1974-75.

Queuing for Food

Trip to Togo

I was able to take a few days for some real vacation during December, when I had an opportunity to accompany the Mack family to Lomé, Togo. It was the first time I had been in that country, and it was interesting. We stayed in a hotel managed by a German Seaman's Mission, on the coast, and were able to see not only Lomé, but also Togoville, a town some distance away, which we reached by crossing a lake in a canoe. It was a typical African village. There was a Roman Catholic Church, but we particularly noticed the places of sacrifice with symbols of the gods which were worshiped.

Crossing the Lake to Togoville (Esther Megill)

Togoville from the Lake

Rudolph and Diehardt Mack

235

A god

Place of Sacrifice

Objects of Worship

Chapel in a Catholic Church

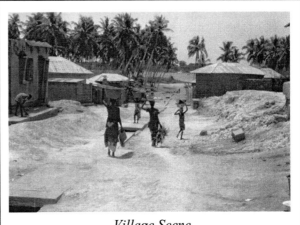

Village Scene

Rudolph & Waltroud Mack

237

Poling Across the Lake–
Return

Entering the Ferry at Atiteti (Ghana) on Return Journey

Ghanaian Fishing Boats

View of the Ocean from the Ferry

238

Although there are of course similarities, the differences between Togo and Ghana are in some ways marked also, as each is influenced by the colonial power which formerly governed it (England in Ghana, Germany and France in Togo). However, the eastern part of Ghana was at one time part of Togo. A plebiscite was held in 1956 under UN auspices to determine the future of the part of Togo under British trusteeship (formerly a German colony). The majority voted to become part of Ghana. This divided the Ewe people and the major church which had ministered to them–the Evangelical Presbyterian Church, established first by missionaries from Switzerland. I was told by one of the Ewe students that they still have their conferences together, when the Ewe language is used, so that the English/French languages do not divide them.

I had heard, of course, of the price rises in the United States, including the price of gasoline. The price of gas in Ghana was raised from about 56¢ to 86¢ per gallon. But in Togo it was about $7.00 per gallon; so perhaps those in the United States were not so hard up.

The Last Term, 1975

1975 Workshop Team

Back: Titus Pratt, E. D. Dennis, E. Kargbo, F. H. Gbowonyo, Sam Atiemo, K. Asamoah-Okyere
Middle/Front: A. Sunday Lana, I. Omaano-Gyampadu, Sam Ghartey, E. A. Arongo, Esther Megill, K.K.O. Asiedu-Asare, J. C. Humper, K. Asare-Bediako, E. A. Ashiety, L. K. Alorzukey

The last term continued to be busy, although I did not have quite as many classes to teach as I did for the first two quarters of the school year. A highlight was the three workshops for lay people to teach children in the church, held by three teams of the students whom I had especially trained during the Easter vacation. They brought back enthusiastic reports when they returned to school.

Another outstanding event was the Christian Family Life Institute held on a weekend for and by the fourth year students, as part of their learning in Christian Education. Their wives or fiancees attended also. The students' reports showed that they had gained a great deal, and were unanimous in urging that this become a yearly event.

Thompson Family Demonstrates Family Prayers

Panel Discussion

Role Play–Husband-Wife Relationships

240

The Place of the Pastor's Wife

Financial Planning–Rev. Thompson

Closing Service of Rededication, Communion

241

We rejoiced that all thirteen of the third year students passed their diploma examinations, thus receiving a Diploma in Theology. For the first time in history five of these passed with a B average, which would allow them to enter the university if they wished. (Even though their four years of training at Trinity was beyond secondary school, in the British system they were not eligible to enter the university at the time they entered Trinity.)

We were saddened to say "good-by" to the Mack family, as they returned to Germany.

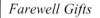

Farewell Gifts

The closing weeks were particularly busy for me, because I was leaving for a short furlough at the end of the school year. Trinity College had asked me to do so, during the long vacation period, rather than wait for the third year and a longer time off as was usual for United Methodist missionaries. I not only had to complete the school year, but also worked on materials to leave for the volunteer teachers who would carry on the Sunday School during the vacation period.

Three more workshops were held during this "long vacation" period.

Trinity College Scenes

1974-75 Staff
Munro, Megill, Mack,
Thompson (Principal),
Yeboah, Kemmler

Students in Different Types of Ghanaian Clothing

Adinkra Cloth

Cloth Prints

Kente Cloth

243

Chapter 3.
More Sunday School, Christian Education Classes, Visitors and Travel
1975-76

I returned from furlough on October 1 and was immediately plunged into another busy and interesting year at Trinity College. We welcomed three new staff members and their families-- Michael and Bronwen Thompson and children (England); Bruce and Ollie Gannaway and children (U.S.); and Wade Huie, Jr. and Vee and children, short term volunteers from the U.S. Ninety-four students were enrolled, including two more United Methodists from Sierra Leone – Daniel Mondeh and George Sandi. This year we also had two graduate students–students who were attending the university and studying religions. It was felt that they needed some instruction in practical subjects which would help them in their ministry, such as Christian education, worship, preaching, etc. There was a total of ninety-four students for the 1975-76 year.

The economic situation continued to worsen. It finally came to the place that Trinity College had to consider cutting the four-year curriculum to three. This meant many hours of work. Wade Huie, as an outsider, gave invaluable help with this project.

Christian Education Class: A Child Study

One of the assignments in the course on Christian Education of Children was for each student to do a child study. The following, written by one of the students, gives a glimpse of life in a village in Ghana.

The child is an eight-year-old boy, now in primary school. He is quite a buoyant and healthy-looking boy. I heard a friend of his parents advising them to get him a small cutlass suitable for his age. He gave this advice because whenever he visited their home he saw the boy actively using either a stick or an old piece of cutlass as his tool and was busy about his own work as a farmer.

His growth is steady, and as he is now in school he has continued his interest in doing something, especially manual work, quite seriously. I heard a remark his teacher made that he was very serious about his classroom work as well as ground work outside. The mother also once remarked that the boy seems to be more mature in his activities than his real age. When he was in P 1 (Primary 1) whenever older students were asked to get up very early and come to weed their school compound before school hours, he was among them, even though his class and other smaller children were not asked to come to work at that time.

He has made friends in school, and has had adventures with them, some of which were heartbreaking for his parents. On one occasion when the parents went to a funeral in a nearby village and he was left with his grandmother, he went out into the bush with his friends, and the grandmother became embarrassed. She did not know when he went out. She said the boy disappeared not long after the parents had left home. She expected him to turn up for lunch, but he never came. The old lady was afraid and sent to the parents to inquire whether the boy had followed them into the next village. The parents were perplexed and immediately returned home to look for him. It was late in the afternoon when he returned home with his friends. He had seen them going to their father's cottage, and simply followed them as an adventure. They did their own cooking and had a meal; he therefore did not need to depend on his granny's lunch.

He is now able to prepare his own meal at lunch time when he comes from school and the parents are out on the farm. This shows some independence. He already makes a little farm of his own because the teachers have told everybody to have a farm to meet the demands of "Operation Feed Yourself" [a government campaign]. *Last year the mother sold two cedis worth of cassava for him.*

His inner control over choices of right and wrong is what I think he needs to develop. For him adventure with his peer group has landed him in trouble when pilfering some folks' vegetables.

He is aggressive against his elder sister as well as the younger one born after him, especially when he is provoked or taunted by them or his parents. On other occasions he may weep, owing to some emotional strain, but when questioned he will not speak.

In the home he is found to be more dutiful in helping his mother in the household duties even more than his sister. He had another boy in his home, and when it comes to telling tales and riddles, he and the other boy form a group to oppose the girls' group.

The boy lives with the father and mother and I consider him to be having traditional upbringing and vocation. He is seen at times very early in the morning following the father to the farm. He is quite cooperative in his household duties. He sweeps the parents' bedroom every day. He carries the little water gourd as he accompanies the father to the farm on Saturdays and holidays.

I think he is loved, but this is not so pronounced and I am not quite sure whether he is aware of being loved or not. He is well fed and looked after. He always has what he needs for school, and the parents are not too harsh with him, so I consider him loved. He was asked on one occasion to give some of his old clothing that was too small for him to a younger cousin who was an orphan. He is at times taken to the grandmother's and grandfather's farm by the parents to work for the old man. I consider such actions opportunities for his expression of love. I consider his physical environment and home as well as the family a trustworthy surrounding for his development. He is often commended for his dutifulness and I consider him well accepted both in the home and in school. His belonging to a family group and a peer group is assured.

His farm produce was sold and money also from his poultry has been used this school season to buy a school uniform and footwear for him. He excels on the farm among his sisters and cousins in the home, and he is commended for it always. He therefore has his work occasionally approved by others. One of his school teachers by chance came across his farm and was pleased, and later praised him for it. He has much opportunity for self-respect and his uniqueness is seen by all members of the family, but his parents see some of his ways to be leading to naughtiness, and they bring pressure to bear upon him.

The best opportunities for his religious development are not ample, as I see them in his present environment. He and other children go together to the adult worship service where they stay throughout without any meaningful message suitable for their age. I think the church should provide the opportunity for Christian education in his own age group. Although he has some Christian teaching in school, I think the church of his village has got something to do about getting Sunday School teachers for such work. The church should provide the child with ample opportunity to learn through experiences suitable to his own age and development, joining others in worship, discussing and finding answers to religious problems, working with others to worthwhile ends, feeling a sense of sharing with Christian adults–the only one I think has been fulfilled is by worshiping with the adults always, but they are also thrown out on festival days.

–O. K. Klu, 1975

A Christian Naming Ceremony at Trinity

On November 8 Edmond Yeboah and his family had a naming ceremony at the chapel for their new baby, Perpetua. He followed much of the traditional format, including the pouring of an oblation. [Traditionally, the oblation was gin offered to a god.] This ceremony was followed by baptism of the baby. Edmond told me that he wanted to show that some African tradition can still be used, in a somewhat different format, by Christians. He said that ancestors were not worshiped in this ceremony, but simply remembered and honored. One of his students later told him that he almost lost his faith when he had the ceremony. There is a struggle between wanting to keep their own culture and yet to be Christian. This was shown also in the program we had one year on the question of polygamy, and another on using drums in worship.

*Edmond and Marie Yeboah,
Baby Perpetua*

Pouring Oblation

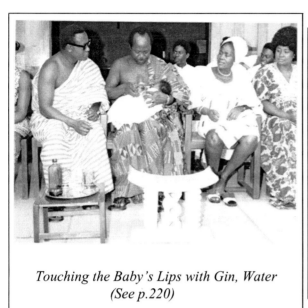

Touching the Baby's Lips with Gin, Water
(See p.220)

Baptism

Ceremony at House–Pouring Oblation

Marie and Edmond Yeboah

My letter to friends and supporting churches in January of 1976 described life at Trinity at that time.

January 1976

Dear Friends Everywhere,

"I had intended that this be my annual Christmas letter; but it will now have to go simply with my deep appreciation for Christmas cards and letters which have finally arrived here after long delays (one airmail letter took six weeks to reach me), and for the interest and concern even by many of you whom I do not know personally.

"As usual, my life has been extremely busy ever since I arrived in Ghana from furlough on October 1, after a brief but pleasant stop with friends in Liberia. In addition to my classes in Christian Education and Church History I am spending, along with other staff members, a great deal of time on a complete revision of the curriculum for the school, which must be ready to present to the Board on March 12.

"In December after the end of the term I had a two and one-half day training session for selected students, as I did last year, to teach them to hold lay training workshops in the local churches. It is always a pleasure to teach adults who want to learn. Fourteen have volunteered to give their time and energy for this. We were all very tired, but because they were interested we were able to accomplish a good deal. It is now a tradition that we make a hand freezer of ice cream on the last meeting. With the shortage and expense of sugar and milk, it is an even greater treat these days. [When I was planning for this I asked my neighbors who had refrigerators, and some, freezers, to make ice cubes on several days and save them for me.]

"One of my vacation jobs was writing and sending out letters to churches about a workshop for workers with children in the church to be held here on March 13, and another offering teams for other workshops the end of March.

"During the vacation period I also attended a meeting of the Ghana Theological Association at Cape Coast. We met (and stayed) in a Roman Catholic seminary. The papers on African traditional ethics and Christianity were stimulating.

"Prices are continuing to rise here. The cost of gasoline is now the equivalent of $1.12 per American gallon. Even locally grown food has increased so much–some as much as 30% or more during the three months I was gone. Shortages continue, and there will be no improvement so long as there is the lack of foreign exchange. For example, we cannot get flashlight batteries–made in Ghana (especially important for radios), evaporated milk, toothpaste, sugar and many other things, except rarely. They did have sugar before Christmas, at $1.30 per pound. I hear that toilet paper has disappeared from the shops. Many of these things can be found in the market, sold above the controlled price. But I refuse to pay $3.48 for a small tube of toothpaste! However, it is much easier for me than for the ordinary working man or woman in Ghana. Life is increasingly difficult for them.

"Work with the Sunday School continues to occupy much of my time, even more than usual during the Christmas (and other) holidays when students are gone and I depend upon local church members. The children enjoyed making Christmas decorations and decorating the frangipani tree outside the Assembly, as usual. The decorations were then taken to the children's ward at the hospital. This year we also had a program for the church after the students left, with the assistance of the local people.

248

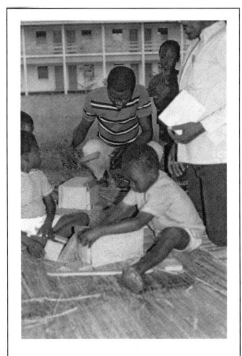

Beginners Enjoy Blocks

Créche

J.K. Atto-Brown, Stories With Children

Rhythm Instruments

Primary Dramatization–"Playing a Story"

Christmas Worship–Primary

Nativity Scene at Church

Planning With Local Teachers

251

"Although it now seems long ago, I have warm memories of many pleasant experiences during my three months of traveling around the U.S., speaking and attending conferences, and visiting my family and friends. Thank you to all who shared in making my furlough so wonderful!"

Sincerely,
Esther Megill

We frequently had weddings during the vacation period, for which I became the unofficial photographer. I developed the photos in my bathroom darkroom.

In December Kwaku Asamoah-Okyere was married to Agnes Sarpong. [He took my place at Trinity.] Also, I attended the ordination services of some of the graduates.

Ordination of
L.K. Alorzukey

In February I wrote a personal friend:

". . . That December 'vacation' went by with half of the things on my list not done. And we've spent hours on the new curriculum since then. We're ready to present it to the whole staff on Monday. If the Board accepts our recommendations, we'll have a better school. We're recommending longer terms and shorter vacation periods to help make up for some of the time lost by cutting to three years. I'll be eager to know the Board's decision . . . It means cutting of some of my courses, but perhaps later there will be opportunity for continuing education for ministers and lay persons. I'd like so much to do individualized instruction here – but it is almost impossible because of the system into which I have to fit. It can be very frustrating . . ."

In February there were some special events. I went to the International Trade Fair in Accra with some of the students. Very interesting–especially the Chinese Pavilion.

U.S. Pavilion

Tanzania Pavilion

China Pavilion

The Garden Party

"On the 28th Trinity hosted the community 'Garden Party,' which I later learned was an annual event, and was a source of income for the College. There were much drumming, dancing and singing."

Yeboah & Children

Students Counting Money

For my class in Christian Education for Youth I invited Mr. D. A. Quarcoo, the International Commissioner of the Ghana Boy Scouts Association, to speak to our class about scouting. I particularly remember the story he told of how the official Boy Scout left-handed handshake developed:

> The Boy Scouts were started in England by Lord Baden-Powell, who had been in the British army during the Ashanti Wars in 1875. Quarcoo said that Baden-Powell had gained some of the inspiration for scouting from the youth groups in the Ashanti culture. [This is not mentioned by Baden-Powell in his account of how Boys Scouts started.] When the British, with their superior weapons, had won the war, a chief of the Ashanti people offered his left hand to Baden-Powell, saying, "In my country the bravest of the brave shake with the left hand."[5] What Baden-Powell did not know was that to shake with the left hand is an insult not only in the Ashanti, but many African, cultures!

Trinity College
Legon, Ghana
August 1976

Dear Friends:

"Another school year is past at Trinity College. Important events in addition to teaching regular classes in Christian Education and Church History have been–
"–Long hours spent with other staff members in designing a new curriculum for Trinity College. Our former four-year course has been reduced to three (although with longer terms), due to financial problems of the supporting churches.
"–A special intensive course at the end of the first term to train fourteen selected students in holding lay education institutes for workers with children in the church.
"–A workshop with the aid of volunteer students, for lay persons from the Accra area. The photos show:
Helping leaders to plan a Sunday School syllabus for a year. (Photo #1)
Using puppets with kindergarten children–a demonstration class. (#2)
Those in attendance making puppets. (#3)
Demonstrating the proper use of pictures (#4)

---

[5] See *Historical Perspectives on Scouting*, "BSA Hand Clasp," "The History of the Left-Hand Handshake Comes from Africa." (On the Internet)

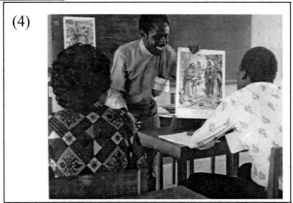

–"A first" for Trinity United Church (the church that meets in the chapel)–the youth
in charge of the Sunday morning service. Theme: 'Let Justice Roll Down Like Waters.'
The pictures show a dramatization of injustice in present day Ghanian life, developed by
the young people.

"–Planning and preparing materials and holding extra sessions with students to prepare them
to hold follow-up workshops in areas where a team has previously been.

"–Revising and retyping the manuscript of *Education in the African Church*, a textbook
I have written for teaching Christian Education in theological schools in Africa–now
at the press for printing.

"These and many other activities have kept me busy during the year. I continue to be grateful
for financial support from many of you through the United Methodist Board of Global
Ministries, gifts of teaching pictures and used Christmas cards, and support by your interest and
prayers. I pray that these may be used to help strengthen the church of Ghana as we seek through
Trinity College to serve in Christ's name."

Sincerely,
Esther Megill

I did not mention in the letter that we held another successful Christian Family Life Institute
to which wives of final year students were invited. As usual, the students had helped to plan the
Institute as part of their class work on adult Christian education.

Some of the Participants

Role Play

Panel–Rights and Responsibilities of the Pastor's Wife– Moderated by Dr. Huie

Closing Service

259

On July 3 (a Saturday, when people were not working) I attended the Annual Independence Day Picnic held by the American Embassy. This was the 200th Anniversary of Independence. The program began with a flag raising ceremony by the Marines. (They had trouble getting the flag to go up–I heard someone say, "We can't even get a flag raised right in Ghana.")

There were remarks by Ambassador Shirley Temple Black (which of course brought back the memory of many Shirley Temple films). Among other things she expressed appreciation for the Peace Corps and for missionaries who knew the people of Ghana in a way that government officials did not.

We then had cokes, hot dogs, and ice cream–all very special, for these were scarce or unobtainable in Ghana. They tasted good even to me, although I seldom drank cokes or ate hot dogs when I was in the U.S.

We of course all joined in singing the national anthem.

Ambassador Shirley Temple Black

I also attended a production of a famous South African play, "Sizwe Bansi Is Dead," by the drama department of the nearby Achimota College. At one time the Vice Principal of this college was the famous "Aggrey of Africa," James E. K. Aggrey. Born in the then Gold Coast (1875), he received his university education in the U.S. In 1920 and 1924 he traveled on educational missions to Africa with the Phelps-Stokes Fund. He was then appointed Vice Principal of the Prince of Wales College at Achimota (called Achimota College when I was there). For its shield he designed a symbolic piano keyboard. It was the emblem of his statement that blacks and whites were like a piano keyboard–neither the white nor the black keys alone make good music; it is necessary to play them both together.[6]

At the end of the term we had a farewell party for the Huie family.

Back: Wade Huie III, Vee, David, Ollie
Gannaway
Front: John Huie, Shealagh Munro, Ian Munro

The Huie Family

Travel North with Friends

In July and August of 1976 I enjoyed the visit of Verna McLain, a longtime friend, and her two children, David, age eleven and Sylvia, eight. We saw some of the sights in and near Accra–the large outdoor Makola Market where I went each week to buy my vegetables and fruits; a picnic, including the Gannaway children, at Ridge Park; a visit to Aburi Gardens where we saw the lines of Royal Palms and the orchids and other flowers in the botanical garden.

---

[6]See "Aggrey, James Emman Kwegyir," in *Columbia Encyclopedia*, Sixth Ed., 2001-2005. Found on the internet.

*Picnic at Aburi Gardens, with Gannaway
Children: David, Bill, Sylvia;
Grace Gannaway, Verna in background*

*Aburi Gardens:
David & Sylvia McLain*

Royal Palms, Aburi

*Ridge Park:
Sylvia, Verna McLain; Grace, Bill Gannaway;
David McLain*

Ridge Park:
  Esther, David, Sylvia, Verna
  in "Ananse" Clothes

R idge Park: :
  Traveler Palm

(Ananse, or Spider, is the mischievous character in many West African fables.)

Then began our adventure along the coast. As we traveled along the Cape Coast Road we saw fishermen mending nets, and canoes, often with elaborate decoration.

263

Sunset at Elmina Motel	*Elmina Wharf*

We first went to Elmina, eight miles west of Cape Coast, and stayed in a motel there. In this area we saw sites important in the history of Ghana. The first visit was to Elmina Castle. In 1471 the Portuguese had discovered the place, with its vast amounts of gold, ivory and slaves for trade. In 1482 they built St. George's Castle at Elmina, and it became their headquarters on the (then) Gold Coast until the Dutch, after repeated attacks, captured it in 1637. This was an important trading center for centuries. In 1872 the Dutch sold the Castle to the British.[7]

Elmina Castle–In Distance and Close-Up

---

[7]See "Elmina Castle in Ghana" on the internet.

264

We took a guided tour through the huge ancient structure, and saw the slave dungeons where Africans were held until they could be loaded on to slave ships. There was the Prempeh I room, where after capturing him in 1896, the British held the Asantahene, King Prempeh I, a prisoner. They were worried that the Ashantis might want to revive their former empire.[8] In the courtyard we saw a compass which it was said Columbus had used to set his own compass before sailing on next day to [what became] America. There were male and female slave yards, and the Governor's quarters within the latter had a secret passage to his room.

Oldest Part of the Castle

Prempeh I Room

Slave Dungeons

The Compass

We also visited a second castle, the Cape Coast Castle. It was originally built by the Portuguese as a small trading lodge, but became a fortification. In 1637 it was occupied by the Dutch, then captured by the Swedes in 1652. They named it Ft. Carolsburg. In 1664 the British fought for and captured it, and renamed it the Cape Coast Castle. It was the seat of the British

---

[8]"Ghana: The Prempeh Room," by Mark Moxon, on the internet.

administration of the Gold Coast until they moved to Christianborg Castle in Accra in 1877. This castle also played a significant role in the gold and slave trades.[9]

In this castle we saw a chapel, the dungeon and magazine, the three rooms at the main beach entrance, formerly used for holding slaves; the 1861 clock, which was still working; the artificial harbor made during the 18th century; the entrance through which the slaves were passed to the beach to be loaded on the boats; and the former quarters for the army garrison which were presently being used by the Prison Department.[10]

View Through Grated Window

View of Elmina from the Castle

We stopped at the Wesley Methodist Church, the oldest Methodist Church in Ghana. In the church was a plaque commemorating the early missionaries.

---

[9]"Forts and Castles of Ghana," on the internet.

[10]Some of this information was in a paper given to visitors at the castles.

From Cape Coast we headed north on the Kumasi Road. Along the way we saw cocoa trees, for we were entering the area where much cocoa was grown, and stopped to have a picnic lunch on the wayside.

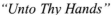
"Unto Thy Hands"

Verna was interested in the sayings on the "tro-tros" or lorries (trucks which carried passengers and loads), so wrote them down as she saw them. A few were, "Cry your own cry," "Waste no time," "Oh God help me," "Man proposes, God disposes," "God will provide," "Love is strange," "God never sleeps," "The evil that men do," "Sew [sic] in tears," "Money rules all," "Free woman," "Suffer to gain," "It's too late," "No man is free," "Be content with your lot."

We went on to Obuasi. Kwaku Asamoah-Okyere had asked his father, a Methodist minister, to make arrangements for us to visit the Ashanti Gold Mine. Visitors were not usually allowed in, so we appreciated the privilege given us. We went deep down into the mine in an elevator, saw the men drilling for gold, the process of pouring molten gold to make bars, and then weighing them.

Preparing to Enter

Drilling

Pouring Molten Gold

Pounding the Gold Bar

Weighing the Bar

268

From Obuasi we went on to Lake Bosumtwi, a crater lake formed either by the impact of a meteorite centuries ago, or perhaps the site of an extinct volcano. "Bosumtwi is a sacred lake to the Ashanti. According to traditional beliefs, the souls of the dead come here to bid farewell to their god Twi. Because of this, they only considered it permissible to fish in the lake from wooden planks, rather than the usual traditional canoes."[12] We were fascinated to see the fishermen, even at the time we visited, lying on the planks and paddling with their hands.

We then headed about nineteen miles northwest to Kumasi, the capital city of the Ashanti Region, and very important in the history and culture of the people. At the heart of the city, in front of the Ashanti Regional Hospital, the Komfo Anokye Teaching Hospital, we saw the statue of Okomfo Anokye. According to the Asante legend, Okomfo Anokye was a seventeenth century priest who summoned the Golden Stool from the heavens to land in front of Osei Tutu, who was to become the first Asante king or Asantehene. The statue shows a man holding high a stool. It was believed that if the Golden Stool were captured, the Asante state would lose its power and disintegrate.

There were several interesting places to visit in Kumasi. We went first to the zoo, where we saw a puff adder, an extremely poisonous snake, and crocodiles, among other animals.

---

12 "Lake Bosumtwi," in *Wikipedia, the Free Encyclopedia,* on the Internet.

The Cultural Centre was out next stop. There we saw weavers weaving the strips of Kente, the traditional cloth of the Ghanaians. The colors and patterns all have special meaning. Equally interesting was the demonstration of embroidering, then printing, an Adinkra cloth. Symbols were carved from a guard, pressed in ink, then on the cloth. The symbols each had a particular meaning. We were interested also in the wood carvers and the pottery makers.

Weaving Kente Cloth

Embroidering Adinkra

Printing Adinkra

Potters at Work

Wood Carvers

Boabeng

Fetish House

Children's See-Saw

After spending some time in Kumasi we were on the road again, heading north, toward the Boabeng-Fiema Sanctuary, where there are many monkeys. We were still in the tropical rain forest area of Ghana. That night we slept in a guest house, made in the traditional fashion of mud and wattle, with a palm roof. After we arrived, the caretaker asked me what we would prefer to eat–chicken or fish. I chose fish, because it would take less time, and a woman started to cook our food–rice with a stew made from fish. When we were served, we discovered that the fish still had heads, considered a delicacy by many Africans. At first the children did not want to eat anything, but hunger finally gave in and they did eat–not the fish head, I am sure.

Preparing Food

We were up early the next morning, the best time to see the monkeys. It had been suggested that we bring bananas with us, to entice the monkeys, which we did. We followed the guide on the path through the forest until we came to a place he indicated. We put out our bananas, and waited. We saw a few monkeys, but were disappointed that we did not see many. According to the description there were many monkeys in this reserve.

The Forest Path

We bumped along the narrow, rutted road out of the Sanctuary, and found our way to the paved road leading to the north. After going a few miles we stopped to get petrol, and the man in charge checked the oil. I was astonished when he informed me that we had no oil! I had added oil before I left Accra. Therefore, I bought some oil, including some extra cans to take with us. We began to watch the oil gauge, and soon discovered that we obviously had a leak. Periodically we would stop and add oil. We were now in the north of Ghana, grasslands with fewer towns or villages. We looked at the map and decided to go until we reached the town that had the largest dot. Later we found that was no indication of its having the resources we needed.

Finally we stopped when I saw a man at the roadside as we were entering a village. I was able to make him understand that I needed a "fitter" (British for "mechanic.") He was able to direct us to a house where there was a young man who spoke English, and said, indeed that he was a fitter. I explained our problem, and he examined the car. After his examination he announced that we had punctured the "pan," or oil filter, which was causing the oil to leak. (Obviously, this had happened when we drove over the rough road out of the monkey reserve.) He told us, however, that he did not have a replacement. He might be able to repair it by welding, but the welder was not then in the village. So, he would have to go find the part (back to a town we had passed through). I asked him to get some oil, too, since he had none.

As this conversation was going on, the curious inhabitants of the village were surrounding us. I suspected they may have never seen white children in this rather remote area of Ghana. Since the fitter was the only one who spoke English, I asked where there was a latrine. He said, "You can go into the bush." I replied, "With all these curious people around us?"

He then said that if we followed the road up a short way we would find a school, and there was a latrine there. So, as he found a lorry (truck) driver to take him to the town where he could find what he needed for us, we made our way up to the school. There was indeed a latrine–with several seats in one building, and some of them broken. But, we did manage to take care of our needs.

We then went back to wait for our rescuer to return. We didn't like to eat with the audience around us, but we did have a little lunch and drank some water. We were sorry we hadn't filled both thermoses with water, instead of coffee in one.

As the people gathered closer, Verna got up, drew a large circle around us with a stick, and said, "If you go past this line I will put a hex on you!" (I detected some Tennessee mountain heritage.)

I am sure the people did not understand the words, but they knew what she meant, and drew back beyond the line.

As time went by, we tried to play some games with the children. Becoming worried, Sylvia said, "Where are we going to sleep tonight?"

Her mother replied, "I don't know, but we will just have to have faith."

"But I don't have faith," said Sylvia.

"Then Esther and I will have to have faith for all of us," answered Verna.

I had not told Verna that I had originally reserved a place at the motel at the game reserve for Sunday, until I discovered that the stations were not open on Sunday because of the shortage of petrol. I had written again asking for rooms for Saturday night but had not received a reply. I just hoped they were expecting us.

As evening approached, the fitter finally returned, with what he needed to repair our car. Needless to say, we paid not only for the cost of the parts and the lorry, but a generous "dash" (tip) also.

Thus, we were finally on our way north again. In Africa near the equator there is no long dusk. When the sun goes down over the horizon (at about 6:00 p.m., year around) it is dark. So it was not long before we were driving along an unfamiliar African road in the dark. At one place a soldier flagged us down and asked for a ride. In Ghana one did not dispute a soldier, so he got in the car with us. Actually, he was helpful in our finding the Mole Game Reserve.

It was after midnight when we drew up to the gate of the Reserve. How thankful we were to find a watchman, who took us to a room prepared for us in one of the villas, and we gratefully crawled into our beds.

We enjoyed our stay in the Reserve, and saw birds, monkeys, antelopes, and a crocodile, although we did not see many large animals. Each morning we went out to buy bread. Verna had brought along peanut butter for the children. We also ate meals in the small dining room at the Reserve.

Mole Game Reserve; Chalets in Distance

David and Verna McLain

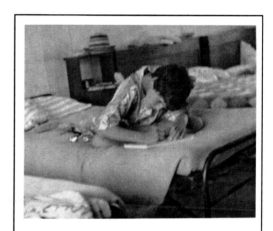

David Writing in his Journal

David and Sylvia with Guide

A Village in the North

On our homeward journey we stopped for the night in Tamale, the third largest city in Ghana. There we stayed in a guest house of the Wycliffe Bible Translators.

Early the next morning we drove south, wanting to get to the ferry over the Volta River before it closed. There were few road signs, but we left town on the only road going out. After traveling for nearly one hundred miles, we came to a sign that said "Upper Volta." I, with my faulty sense of direction, had gone the wrong direction on the road! David was upset, and said, "We're lost!" I answered, "No, we're not lost–we are on the only road–we just came the wrong direction."

So, around we turned, and traveled what was now a long distance to the ferry. We did arrive before it closed, and took out place in the waiting line of cars and lorries. As we were sitting there, some young men in a nearby lorry ("motor boys" who assisted the driver with passengers), called to me and pointed to the tire–it was flat!

We had had tire trouble earlier in the trip, and were using our spare. Tires were difficult to get in Ghana. What were we to do?? The helpful men told me there was a place the tire could be repaired, took it off, and rolled it back along the road a short distance where two men were working under the shelter of a shed, with a fire. They were able to repair the tire. It was amazing what people could do with very little equipment and materials. Our friendly helpers put the tire back on the car, and we were ready to drive on the ferry when our turn came. The rest of the journey was uneventful.

To Apinamang

On August 3, Verna and I went on a trip to Apinamang, the village in which my namesake lived. Mrs. Gannaway offered to keep the children, so Verna decided to leave them. The two of us then drove to the village to visit Esther and Mary Kwakye (her mother) and the family. We spent the night, and then returned the next day, as was usual on such trips, loaded with coconuts, bananas, pineapples and other fruits. We did visit the chief's "palace" and saw and heard his drummers, and as we walked through the village saw men playing the game of "Oware," a game popular in other countries of Africa and elsewhere (though with different names).

Esther (rt) and Cousins

Playing Oware

The Chief

Drummers in the Chief's Palace

A few days later I saw Verna and the children off to the States.

Other August Events

On August 11 I went with others to Cape Coast to attend a "Service of Commissioning, Dedication and Holy Communion" at Wesley Chapel. This was a service of dedication by the Methodist Church of Ghana of expatriate missionaries (from the Methodist Church in England), and some of their own pastors who were being sent as missionaries to other countries.

The **big** event was my trip to Alavanyo-Agome in the Volta Region to speak at the Thanksgiving service for the recent ordination as a pastor in the Evangelical Presbyterian Church of Y.K. Buasilenu, who had just graduated from Trinity College. On the way there on August 21 I passed near the Alavanyo-Agome waterfalls and took photos. When I arrived, Rev. Buasilenu met me and took me to his house. In the Ghanaian fashion, he offered me water to drink–as he said, in an African cup (a gourd). I hesitated to drink the water, but decided that he knew that we expatriates needed to be careful to drink boiled water, so, not wanting to insult him, I drank it. (I suffered from that for a day or two after I returned home. I mentioned this to one of our Ghanaian staff, and he told me he did not drink water in the villages either–that if I had taken a sip it would have been adequate–but I did not know that.)

Buasilenu then took me to the government rest house which they had prepared for me to stay, and where they did provide me with boiled or perhaps filtered water, and with food.

The next morning as I drove to his home in the village I saw streams of people walking, all coming to attend the service. As I was waiting at his house I asked a foolish question–after all the years I had spent in Africa I should have known the answer–I said, "When does the service start?"

The answer: "When they all get here."

Finally the time came when the crowd walked to the place that had been prepared, with rows of benches and seats under a shed made of sticks and a palm branch roof. Soon the Queen Mother appeared, followed by her attendants, one of whom held a large umbrella over her.

The Queen Mother plays an important part for the Ewe people and other ethnic groups in Ghana. "The Queen Mother is not necessarily the mother of the Chief. Though she is related to the Chief in some complex way, there are different lines of relatives in the clans associated with the Chief's line, from which the Queen Mother is chosen in some alternating fashion. The attendants to the Queen Mother are usually very close blood relations like nieces, daughters or sometimes descendants of people who served the chieftaincy system as slaves or merely maid servants whom the Queen Mother has adopted as her children."[13]

The program was made up of hymns, Scripture readings, songs sung by several different choirs and "singing groups," an offering, and three addresses in addition to my sermon. After a closing hymn the entire group processed to the Buasilenu house.

There followed much singing, dancing, drumming and playing of other instruments. One which was new to me was the bamboo band. The young boys had various lengths of bamboo, and pounded them up and down on the ground in rhythm.

---

[13]Information from the Rev. Sam Atiemo, a former student and presently pastor of a Ghanaian Presbyterian Church in Brooklyn.

Rev. Buasilenu interpreted for me the songs the girls and others were singing–praise for their teacher who was now a pastor.

There was of course also food. The celebration was long, but impressive.

Boys in Alavanyo, Volta Region

Rev. and Mrs. Y. K. Buasilenu

Esther Megill and Y. K. Buasilenu

Pastors Who Took Part

A Singing Band

The Bamboo Bands

Traditional Dancing

The Drums

Chapter 4.

Cooperation with Roman Catholics; More Workshops
1976-77

Trinity's 1976-77 school year began with one hundred and one students. This meant 30-40 in a class, and the classrooms were becoming very crowded. The year was difficult for all staff members because we were phasing out the four-year program and starting a three-year program with a new curriculum. With everyone on the new curriculum the next year, it would be easier.

This year Edmond Yeboah and I began co-teaching a new course in liturgics. Teaching new courses in addition to my usual ones in Christian Education meant that I had not been able to do much in lay training and continuing education of pastors, which all agreed was needed.

During the "long vac," teams once again went to various towns to hold workshops for children's workers.

We began this year with a week of debriefing from field education experiences during the long vacation period. This was one of the innovations in the new curriculum. Although there were some problems, on the whole it was quite successful. It was a good experience to share in a small way in some of the difficulties and joys of being a pastor in Ghana.

How many of you would walk fourteen miles each way to visit a small church? What would you do if you found village church after village church which had not had a visit from a pastor for a year, and thus had no communion or guidance? Or if you discovered that there was not one Bible or hymnal available in the church?

How does one face the problem of being a pastor of a large church (some have as many as 2,000 members), with possibly one or two young pastors to assist you, but with thirty or forty out-stations for which you are responsible? In addition, you have no transportation, except that you are able to get by taxi or the "tro-tro" (a small covered truck, with rows of seats or benches), or by walking. Is it any wonder that some stations see a minister only once or twice a year, at which time he will question those who have supposedly been prepared for baptism by a catechist or elder, baptize, and confirm candidates, then give communion, all in one day?

Our students saw tremendous needs for better education of people who joined the church, and of lay leaders who took so much responsibility. One student, for example, spoke of how he saw people being confirmed and accepted into the church who had little understanding. Some said they were coming to church because fetish worship gave them no gain; some wanted safety from evil spirits; but no one said he wanted to follow Christ. The question of healing is very important in African traditional "spiritual" or independent churches. "Spiritual" churches offer protection from unseen forces and have regular healing services. These all pose questions for young men preparing for ministry, who are themselves caught in a fast-changing culture, and are learning new concepts which sometimes conflict with life as they have experienced it.

Workshops and Other Concerns

In September a few students and I met with Roman Catholics in an Audiovisual Production Workshop in Nsawam to work on audiovisual materials for churches and in the new religious classes in the schools. The government had approved the project, and we were hopeful that they would pay to produce the pictures. A student and I worked on an outline of lesson materials to be printed on the back of the large pictures. Others who had artistic ability worked on the drawing. Because this was an ecumenical project we were able to obtain some funds, which continued for several years. I enjoyed working with Sister Mary Ann, who was in charge of Christian education for the Catholic Church in Ghana.

Mary Kwakye and Esther visited me also in September. From the picture it seems that Esther was not too happy. However, she looked a little happier, though solemn in December.

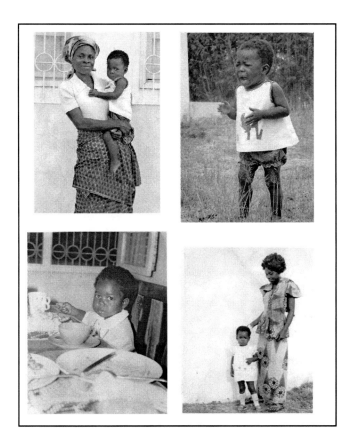

We had another workshop for children's workers in the Accra area in December, with the usual big attendance and many of the students busy in teaching. Children were there also, as students taught for observation by the workshop participants.

J. K. Otoo

Choral Reading–Sandi & Asare-Bediako

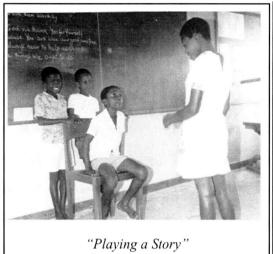

"Playing a Story"

Rhythmic Movement E. Martey

Planning Worship–E.A. Arongo

Planning a Syllabus–K. Asamoah-Okyere

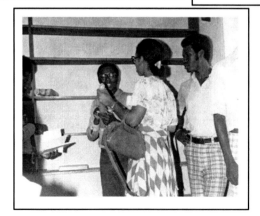

Sale of Materials–
I. Omaano-Gyampadu

284

In March for the first time we had a workshop for youth workers in the church

Teaching Rhythmic Movement

Role Play

We held our third annual Christian Family Life Institute with the final year students and their wives in April.

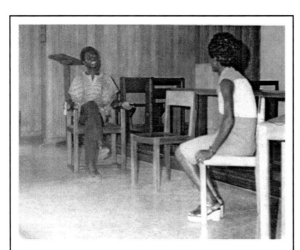

*Role Play–K. Asamoah-Okyere &
Mrs. Kumasa*

Recreation–Table Games

More Recreation

Closing Communion

The Sunday School

The Sunday School continued, taking a great deal of my time. The following photos show some of the events of the 1976-77 school year.

Youth Putting Up
Christmas Decorations
They Had Made
(Grace Gannaway was
part of the class)

Youth Christmas Party (Daniel Mondeh)

Rhythmic Movement–"O Come, All Ye Faithful"

The Primary Class Visits the Church

An interesting, though sad, event occurred during one Sunday School period. As was my custom, I was walking around the various classes to observe the students as they taught. One morning I saw a small boy sitting on a bench outside the classroom. (We used the College classrooms for some of our Sunday School classes). He was crying, but could not understand English well, so I called one of the students teachers out of the classroom and asked him to find out what was wrong with the child. The boy told us that his friend had died of malaria during the week. (The child had been in Sunday School the Sunday before.) They had had an earlier argument, and there was bad feeling between them. The boy said that the other children were accusing him of having caused the death of the child, by putting a "swear" on him. He may have thought himself that he had.

I had the student interpret for me as I talked to the crying boy, and then told him to go back to the classroom, and tell the student who was then teaching that before the class ended they should deal with something more important than the lesson of the day. The children should understand that although we are sorry when we have had an argument or a fight with a friend, especially if the friend dies soon after, that was not the fault of the child. We cannot cause the death of another person by wishing it on him, and surely the boy did not wish his friend to die. God forgives us when we have done wrong, and can comfort us when we lose a friend.

The students reported how they had dealt with the problem. The child was back in class the next Sunday.

The Textbook

The textbook, *Education in the African Church*, went to the press in July but was still not available in quantity by Easter of 1977. In a letter at that time I wrote, "I hope to collect all the books next week. First there was a breakdown of the press, and someone had to come from Norway to repair it; then a long delay in obtaining paper, and when it arrived, to get it out of the harbor. The press had to do a backlog of work, their own denomination's (Assembly of God) of course taking precedence; then my book went to press in January. However, after it was all printed, a belt broke in the folding machine, and it took a long time to find parts. So they folded fifty copies by hand, and I had books for my first year class by the middle of the term. I had been able to send copies by persons traveling to four other countries in Africa, and someone was to take twenty-five to Kenya if I could get them by the next week. Three hundred seventy-five out of the one thousand I had printed (with grant money from the Women's Division of the Board of Global Ministries, The United Methodist Church) were already committed for sale. So, I was encouraged. The plan was that if they sold well (at just a little above cost, to allow for complementary copies), the money would be used to reprint.

Responsibility with the Methodist Church

The Methodist Conference officers asked me to help them reorganize their Christian Education program. At the time of my letter at Easter 1977 we had had only one meeting, but it had been an encouraging beginning. One of our emphases would be to inform pastors and catechists of what Trinity College was offering for lay training, and about some new concepts of Christian Education in the local church. Therefore, I was scheduled hold an all-day session the next week at Kumasi for catechists who would be gathered for a week's course. I had not planned to ask any of my students to help, because they have such a short vacation period. However, some heard of it, and three who would be spending their vacation in or near Kumasi offered to help. That made it much easier for me.

Life in Ghana

Life was becoming increasingly difficult for people in Ghana, with a soaring inflation (at least 60%), and many shortages, with many food and other items nonexistent. Bread cost 90¢ a loaf; rice $2.70 a pound; a large yam about $3.50 to $4.00; a chicken (when available, and small) $12.00-$15.00; eggs $3.00 or more a dozen. And yet the minimum wage for a laborer was $1.80 per day. A pastor, in addition to his house, got $50.00-$100.00 per month. The clerical garb his church required him to have cost at least $150.00. Yet, we had more students who passed the entrance exam than the churches could afford to send to Trinity College, so that many had to be turned away.

Furlough

I had a short furlough in the United States which was planned to be from about July 5 to the middle of September. But plans changed suddenly when the principal announced that the college had gone so far over the budget for food that there was no money left, and that it was getting extremely difficult to buy food for one hundred people. So, we closed school on June 10, with ceremonies on the 12th, and I left Ghana on the 19th.

As usual my furlough was spent in having medical exams, attending a missionary conference, in speaking engagements, visiting family and friends, shopping and packing supplies for Ghana. The women of the Knoxville District, Holston Conference (Tennessee) gave me a shower. So I had many wonderful items to ship to Ghana.

My brothers, parents and I went to Utah to be with my brother Rex and sister-in-law Abbie to celebrate our parents' 55th wedding anniversary on August 15. Unfortunately, mother had a heart attack just before that time (a second for her) and was hospitalized. However, the doctor did allow her to come home, especially since our brother Don, a doctor, had arrived and was there to look after her. She was able to return to Santa Fe where she and our father lived in a retirement home. She later had another heart attack and had to stay in the health unit for a time.

I did have some good news during this time, when I learned that scholarships had been obtained for Kwaku Asamoah-Okyere and his wife Agnes to study in the U.S. He would work for an M.A. in Religious Education at Scarritt College in Nashville, Tennessee, and his wife on a master's in Home Economics at Peabody Teacher's College. He was being prepared to take my place at Trinity College. So, when I returned to Ghana on September 17, it was to stay three years until he could replace me.

Chapter 5.

Trouble in Ghana; The Good News Institute, and Other Experiences
1977-1978

I arrived in Ghana about an hour late on the morning of September 17. One thing I noticed immediately was a sign at the airport exit saying, "Be a good citizen and vote," and "Register to vote now." This was a new thing in a country with a military government. The registration was for the purpose of voting the next year on whether to accept a so-called "Union" or "National" Government. This was an attempt to work out an African approach to government, basically by consensus, and without political parties, which they had experienced in the past as bringing dissension and bloodshed. There was still a question of whether, or how much, the police and army would be involved in the new government. However, at least the people were being given a chance to vote on it.

The rest of the day was spent trying to sleep and catch up on the jet lag. Then on Monday morning I went to town to get some food. Prices were higher than when I left, and there were more shortages. For the first time in my twenty-five years of missionary service I was bringing food to Africa.

Monday afternoon there was a staff meeting, and on Tuesday we began our four days of debriefing field work experiences and orientation for new students. I also spent time getting the Sunday School reorganized, and checked on supplies and money from sales and travel accounts from the workshops held by the teams during the vacation period. There was also preparation for a series of Saturday training sessions for a new workshop team. So, life continued to be busy, but I did not feel the pressure as I had the previous year.

My freight arrived in Legon just before Christmas, and it was like Christmas to open all my cases of riches–many of them given by United Methodist Women of the Knoxville District. I shared some with my neighbors, mostly other staff members, who were very grateful. I gave more to the Africans than the expatriates, since the former weren't able to get these expensive or nonexistent items. I began to eat steadily from the canned meat. Unfortunately, the freeze-dried food which didn't get to New York in time and which I asked to have sent by mail, hadn't been heard from by the middle of January. A dock strike in the U.S. delayed it, but it should have arrived by then. I had a paper saying I could get five parcels in duty free, but I was concerned that if it took too long to get to Ghana after my arrival it would no longer be good.

Everything arrived safely, because it was in a container, not opened until I was there. There was only one problem–or two. Apparently the company from which I had ordered a spirit duplicator and supplies didn't get the correction pencils in the order; and the Board didn't send on the spirit, which was inflammable, and had to be on deck. I didn't see the bill of lading because it had been lost. But when I realized that the spirit wasn't in the order I made a special trip to Tema, the harbor town, sixteen miles away, to see the copy the shipping company had. It said the spirit "will be sent later," but didn't say when. In the meantime I was fortunate to find some in Accra–the first they had had in four years, but it cost about $30.00 a gallon. However, I really appreciated having the duplicator, bought with gift money which had been promised but had not yet arrived. There were so many things which didn't seem to merit expensive stencils and ink, but took a lot of time to do by carbon. The new duplicator saved time and made some things possible which weren't before. Of course, I didn't expect to import supplies always, but we often could not get things, and when we did they were very expensive. There was always hope that some day conditions would improve.

The School Year

We began the first year of our new three-year curriculum with eighty-two students. It was easier than the previous year. We were glad to have three additional Ghanaian staff members, one of whom had returned from Scotland with a PhD, and another, a former student, after completing his studies in the U.S. We now had five out of eight staff members who were Ghanaian.

Although I had a lighter class load, I was busy with a special training course for the new workshop team, a Youth Workers' Institute for people in the Accra area, and the annual Christian Family Life institute for our final year students and their wives, held in December rather than April as before.

Training Workshop Teams

L.E.K. Adzu and S. K. Ablorh–
Tests and Games

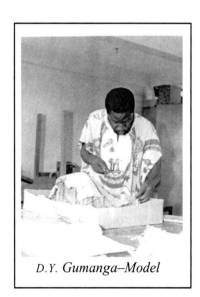

D.Y. Gumanga–Model

C.N. Oppong–Worship

Kofi Martin–Frieze

1977-78 Workshop Team

Front	*Middle*	*Back*
S.K. Ablorh	J.A.Y. Adubah	K. Martin
E.F. Nyarko	C. Gyang-Duah	D.Y. Gumanga
C.N. Oppong	S.A. Alondo	T.H. Smith
L.E.K. Adzaku		

The Final Ice Cream Party: Gumanga,
Adubah, Ablorh, Gyang-Duah

Christmas in the Sunday School

We celebrated Christmas in our Sunday School in the usual way. For several weeks the children worked on Christmas decorations for our party, using old Christmas cards and materials available in Ghana. On December 11, the last Sunday when our student teachers were there, we had a party, for a total of three hundred and eight children. This was an all-time high. The Sunday School had grown slowly but steadily, and we particularly saw the difference in our larger youth group.

A Puppet Story for the Children

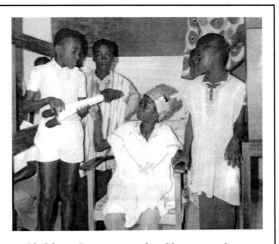

Children Dramatize the Christmas Story

293

Youth Make Christmas Decorations

Youth Dramatization

On Christmas Day I was invited, for the first time since the first year when the Graus were there, to eat Christmas dinner with one of the families. On Boxing Day (December 26) I had the two Sierra Leone students (who of course had to stay on campus during the vacation period), and two Ghanaian young men who teach in the Sunday School during vacations, for Jollof rice and games.

I was also working on a Self-study Guide to accompany my textbook. We tried for weeks to get duplicating paper, then a typist, and then our mimeograph broke down. I finally managed to get the essential pages for the new class, but we had to wait for the mimeograph to be repaired to finish it. Finally in December, the office clerk was able to begin mimeographing it. The textbook seemed to be selling well in Ghana, but I had only one small order from outside Ghana. However, the Nigerian who wrote seemed to feel the book would be helpful for them. One problem was that all the African countries were having financial difficulties, and it took foreign exchange to get the book.

We began an A-V lending library. Since the purchase of the light plastic projectors for filmstrips, which were run on batteries, we were accumulating a number of filmstrips.

Another step had been taken toward expanding our services to the churches, in the official establishment of a Department of Church Leadership, of which I was the director. I began planning for a week during the long vacation period when we would offer three courses for pastors and lay persons.

In January I again visited Esther and her family in Apinamang.

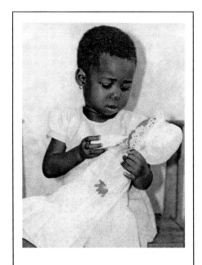

Rev. Kwakye (Mary's father),
Mary with a new baby boy,
Owusu Asomaning,
Esther and her Doll

Esther with her doll
(brought from the States)

In February we took the youth Sunday School class to visit the Madonna in the Cathedral in Accra. The Madonna is dressed in a Kente cloth.

The Children's Workers Workshop
February

Making Puppets

Flannelboard

Writing Stories for Beginners

Planning a Lesson

On March 19 we celebrated Palm Sunday in our Sunday School as usual, with the children marching around the campus, and in the surrounding village, waving palm branches and singing. They often braided the palm leaves and added flowers.

A New House for the Principal

There was an official presentation of the new principal's house, a bus, a tennis court, and an improved road into the college, all given by the S.M.C. (Supreme Military Council), the ruling government, on March 17

The Presentation

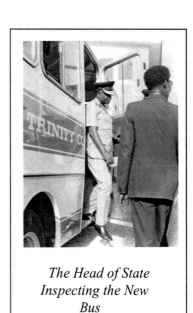

The Head of State Inspecting the New Bus

The New House

Inspecting the House

Rev. I.K.A. Thompson,
Principal

A Youth Workers Institute was also held on the campus in March

298

Tribute by a Visitor

In February I hosted two Americans, Rosaland Smith and her son Bob, for a short time. After they left I received an article which Rosaland had written and sent to the *Response* editor, hoping it would be published. It was not, but I am including it here–with some hesitation because of her too lavish praise of me–but because it does describe my life in Ghana. I have made some factual corrections.

Christian Education Tested in Ghana
by Rosaland W. Smith

Dr. Esther Megill, who teaches Christian Education at Trinity Theological College in Legon, Ghana, and is the only person under the Board of Global ministries now in Ghana, works against odds that would be intolerable anywhere in the United States.

Let me describe one of her days. She gets up at 5:30, gets breakfast of grapefruit or an orange, bread, and coffee with canned milk (if there is any available) and goes to the chapel for service at 6:40, and then to class at 7:15 or back home to get ready for classes later, which meet from 7:15 to 1:10 (although Esther does not teach all periods). From lunch she takes from her wonderful 220/50 cycle refrigerator brought from New York, some bread (kept there to keep the tiny ants out of it), a precious piece of cheese, an orange and a banana. After lunch, during the hottest part of the day, she rests and reads the latest Christian education journals she's received. [I have to confess it was usually the current paperback mystery, or *Time* magazine to catch up with U.S. news.]

She then types stencils for materials to be used in a forthcoming Christian education workshop for Accra area churches. She has to make the arrangements for meals and housing for those who will attend. Frequent trips by car are necessary to see people who can't be reached by phone, since the phone seldom works. Her car has no spare. It took five months and countless trips to a dealer in Accra to get a recap, and then she found that someone who had sold her a worthless tube had removed the valve, which meant three more trips. Prices have more than doubled since last year because of inflation.

When the mail comes, she checks it through, glad to see letters from home. Requests for the "Ghana Journal of Theology," for which she is the treasurer, can't be met because of printers' delays of three years, due to paper shortages and press breakdowns. Payment by check means a visit to two banks (opened different hours) to accomplish complicated, time-consuming, frustrating cashing and deposit procedures. While she is reading the mail, a student is likely to knock at the door–or while she is resting or eating–to ask about an assignment or explain an absence.

In further preparation for the weekend she bakes cookies with precious products given her at a shower by a United Methodist Women's society in Tennessee, brought back from the States. The only ingredient procured locally was eggs. Then she fixes supper– a salad of tomatoes, peppers and lettuce (soaked in disinfectant water), an omelet, a banana and a slice of fresh pineapple.

Esther knows where to find the juiciest pineapples and oranges in the market. The morning I went with her to the Makola II market in Accra, where a white face is rare, she made her way through the maze way back to a pile of beautiful pineapples which she was lucky to get for ¢1.20 (one cedi, 20 pesewas)

We had parked across the street in the hot February sun at the Methodist Book Depot, where she knows the man who watches the cars. A smiling ten-year-old girl appeared as we drove in, offering to carry her basket for four shillings (the old designation for money). A woman who is shopping is not expected to carry what she buys, but Esther often does. Into the basket and on to the little girl's head went three pineapples, four oranges (one cedi), six lemons (one cedi), four grapefruit (one cedi), a hand of bananas (¢1.20), and about a pound of pear tomatoes (¢2.00). Then we walked over rough ground through the narrow paths between stalls piled with dishpans full of dried beans, whole corn to be taken to the mill for grinding to make "kenkay" (a fermented, solid food steamed in a corn or palm leaf and eaten warm or cool), dried, hot peppers, smaller pans of unfamiliar spices, stewing beef (uncovered in the heat, and attracting flies), cheap jewelry on racks and one stall with eggs. But nowhere did we find cabbage or margarine, matches, flour or sugar. Esther made her way to one stall where she could buy lettuce–three small bunches for a cedi. By bargaining she often reduced the price asked. When we got to the car Esther gave the girl fifty instead of forty pesowas.

After supper she goes to the classroom building to meet with her selected team of second or third year students who are to conduct the workshops. During the term she spends seven Saturday mornings training them to teach Sunday School teachers, having them practice what is to be done, including cutting out pictures (a process with which many are unfamiliar), pasting, and making simple puppets of the tubes from toilet rolls and scraps of cloth to illustrate the Bible stories. Because of ordering difficulties, she prepares many of her own materials.

The evening I was with her a young Anglican pastor who had been on her team the year before came to ask the help of a current team member for his twenty-four churches during the summer. To get to one church he had to walk fifteen miles. Six miles, he says, is nothing. Visual aid materials must be light enough to be carried by one person that distance. Since transportation is difficult and the crowded "bus" or "mammy wagon" or "tro-tro" may charge as much for the box as for a passenger, he urged Dr. Megill to limit the supples she sends to one box.

By ten o'clock she is ready for bed, a day well spent. She has been at Trinity for four years and intends to stay two and a half more until her former student completes his training at Scarritt and returns to continue the work she has well underway. She is planning two courses for lay people, catechists and evangelists, on worship and a survey of the Bible; a course in pastoral counseling for twenty-five pastors; and two more advanced Writers' Workshops, in cooperation with the Catholic Education Office. One is to be held at Abetifi, sixty miles north of Accra, for southern Ghana, and one in Kumasi, for the Ashanti region and the north. Invitations to register have been sent to selected persons with a view toward training in preparation of materials for children, youth and adults.

In spite of staggering difficulties, Esther Megill's spirit remains joyful. She refuses to be destroyed by them. Her Christian commitment is strong and sound.

[This was entirely too flattering of me. I am afraid she hadn't seen the many times I became impatient with the students, or was to the point that I didn't think I could take any more frustrations–I was not always joyous and easy to get along with. But it does give the insight of an outsider on life in Ghana, and so I have included it.]

Trouble in Ghana

National Redemption Day, the celebration of six years of the present military government, was celebrated with a holiday on January 13. Some of the students at the nearby university were in Legon village and on the main road into Accra, handing out papers urging people <u>not</u> to vote for the proposed "Union Government" in the March referendum, when the police began to beat them. Some were chased to their dormitories, where some jumped out of windows in an attempt to escape and ended in the hospital with broken bones. The Head of State had said people were free to speak their minds on the proposed Union government, but these events indicated otherwise. The students had to take their examinations for the last year at the beginning of the 1977 term because of strikes and the closing of the university the previous year.

The referendum was held on March 30. The day in general passed with quiet voting. Then an announcement was made on the radio that the police were to collect the ballot boxes and take them for counting. The Electoral Commissioner protested that the counting was to be done on the spot, with observers from both sides present. There were protests in some areas. There was much confusion over the results, and we did not hear the final results until Sunday morning (after the voting on Thursday). They said 56% were for Union Government, 46% against. Only about half the people who registered voted. They were very slow about publishing results from Accra and Kumasi–both votes went against the government. We weren't sure they ever did publish the Legon results. Someone said it was one thousand plus against, three for! Where the government side won (if in fact they did) was in the rural areas where the people were illiterate. Many were convinced the results were rigged. There were certainly many irregularities. In the North, where people always follow their chiefs, it was said that the latter were paid money to vote for the Union Government. Scarce items like milk were handed out in the villages the day before the Referendum by the military. In some villages there were no "No" (red) ballets available; in others, illiterate people were told to put the blue ballots (Yes) in one container and the red (No) in another. The latter contained acid to destroy the ballots, but illiterate people didn't realize that in that way they were voting "Yes" instead of "No." Almost all the regional capitals, where there was a higher percentage of educated people, voted "No." These people distrusted the proposal for a no-party government, in which it appeared that the police and military might still have a part. There was a lot of intimidation of those who spoke against the proposal, but there was no violence, except that the Electoral Commissioner had disappeared. It is said that Thursday evening the military surrounded his office. However, someone told him he should not drive away in his car. So he got in a taxi, and his driver and car went ahead. An army car crashed into his car, wounded the driver, who was then beaten and died in the hospital. They thought it was the Commissioner. No one knew where he was. The government announced that he was fired because he left his job, and appointed someone in his place.

The Catholic Secretariat and Christian Council sent a letter to the churches, and the Catholic bishops another letter to their people, which was read on Palm Sunday. They deplored the lack of freedom of dissent and violation of human rights, and urged all Christians to vote according to their conscience. The government-controlled papers refused to print them, but for a week or more the papers were filled with distortions of what had been said. Only the Catholic paper had the courage to publish consistently both sides of the story.

The Constitutional Committee was being formed and both the Christian Council and Catholic Secretariat were to be represented. People were waiting to see what would become of it.

There had been very few classes at the university for a year because of student strikes in protest of government actions and the whole economic situation. [Because the government supported the university and paid for all students, they could close it whenever they wanted.] After the Referendum the government admitted to imprisoning thirty-five of those who campaigned against the Union Government. One student who was able to leave the country said there were three hundred. (This may have been an exaggeration.) Amnesty International registered a protest. We got the truth only from BBC. Of course, the government paper kept accusing them of telling lies.

Because student leaders were arrested university students continued on strike, and teachers also went on strike because some of them had been imprisoned. A Trinity student told me that the head of the University Student Council and some teachers had been released, so the teachers were considering when to go back to work.

In the meantime the economic situation continued to deteriorate. We all wondered how long the country could survive

Workshop for Christian Writers

Sr. Mary Ann and I cooperated in holding a workshop for Christian writers April 3-8 at the Ramseyer Training Centre, a Presbyterian center in Abetifi. This was made possible by a grant from the World Division of the Board of Missions of The United Methodist Church and other grants, including some from Catholic sources. We had hoped to have a second session in Kumasi in July, meant primarily for those from the north, but reluctantly decided that because of the gas shortage and the scarcity and cost of food, we would postpone it. We planned these because there was great need for Christian education materials for all age groups. We had a group of twenty who worked hard learning skills in writing, and some useful materials for Christian education were produced. We hoped that some would continue to write. Several Trinity College students were among those who attended.

Students Hard at Work

While we were at the Ramseyer Centre we learned something about the history of the Presbyterian Church in Ghana, as we visited the first classroom in which Rev. Ramseyer taught. We also saw a fetish house, and the house of the High Priestess. The sign at the entrance said, "No entry if you are undergoing menstruation." [I have learned since that in traditional religion menstruating women were considered unclean and could not go near sacred places. I understood then why one of my students questioned how a woman could be ordained and thus give communion. How could she give communion when menstruating? This reminds us, of course, of some of the Old Testament restrictions.]

The First Classroom Where Rev. Ramseyer Taught   *Inside the First Classroom*

Fetish Room

We observed the "outdooring" of a priestess who had completed her study with the Chief Priestess. The priestess, and sometimes the Chief Priestess, danced and twirled to the rhythm of the drum. Eventually the novice priestess appeared to be "possessed" of a spirit, according to the people's belief.

The House of the High Priestess

High Priestess Dancing

The New Priestess

The Priestess "Possessed"

The Good News Institute

In the second term I began a new venture. Erma Grove, a Mennonite missionary, asked whether I would be willing to teach at the Good News Institute twice a week. This was a lay training center for members of the Independent or "Spiritual" churches, which had been established with the help of the Mennonites.

At the Institute I taught a course on how to teach the Bible to adults. There were two different small groups–mostly women on Wednesday morning, and men on Thursday evening. These adults had a primary or perhaps junior high educational equivalence, so I taught on a different level than the courses at Trinity.

A Change in Government

On July 5 a simple announcement was made over the radio that General Achaempong, who for the previous six years had been Head of State and Chairman of the Supreme Military Council which ruled Ghana, had stepped down as Head of State and resigned from the army. This was done, it was stated, for the sake of "unity and stability of the nation." Lt. Gen. Akuffo took his place, and the S.M.C. remained the same except for the addition of one new army officer. The British Broadcasting Company termed it a "bloodless coup." It was very low key in Ghana.

No statement was made of the policies of the new government. All those imprisoned because they were against Union Government were released, and the results of the March Referendum were challenged. Whether there were thirty detainees as Gen. Achaempong admitted, or three hundred as some members of the opposition who had left the country maintained, we did not know. The new government did promise a return to civilian rule by the next July. They had not yet said (by August) what they were going to do about Union Government. People had a "wait and see" attitude.

The Economic Situation

The economic situation continued to worsen. B.B.C. gave varying figures of 150 to 200% inflation. There was scarcity of everything. I did not know how the ordinary person survived. One small yam (these are the large yams which taste something like potatoes, not the ones like sweet potatoes) cost more than the minimum daily wage of the laborer. Yet there were many with money, as evidenced by the Mercedes-Benz cars and expensive buildings going up. Corruption and bribery were the order of the day. At the end of June there was a crisis when there was no oil, because Ghana had not been able to pay for the oil it had imported. The whole country was about to grind to a halt; some oil arrived in the nick of time. With no oil for gasoline, goods produced in the interior could not be transported to the cities. The big Makola market was nearly bare. The currency was being allowed to "float," so each day there was further devaluation. It would have to go a long way, however, to match the black market rate. All imported items, which included paper and books, now cost a great deal more. However, this was a step long overdue.

Rumors (heard through my British friends) were that new money was being printed, and when it was out we would have to exchange five cedis for one. I had been careful for some time not to keep too many cedis on hand, but I did have quite a lot for our Christian education program which I wanted to use, and then credit my U.S. bank account before a more radical devaluation occurred.

In my letter of July 5 I said that "It is frustrating and time-consuming just to survive here, but we really experience so little of what the Ghanians do. Many of our students are concerned because of the widespread corruption and materialism which are so dominant. Pray for the people of Ghana, and especially for those who are trying to live honest and fruitful lives in a very difficult situation."

The School Year Completed

We completed another school year in June, with recognition of achievements in certain fields, photographs of the student body, various individuals, denominational groups, and installation of new officers for the Methodist Students' Union. We had to close five days early, however, in order to allow students to go home, because it was thought that there might be no gasoline to enable transport to operate.

We had few workshops during this year, partly because of the difficult financial situation. However, the second and third year teams had one workshop each after January, and we held one at Trinity College for the Accra area.

During this school year the Department of Church Leadership had been formally established. We had our first residential courses for pastors, catechists, deaconesses, evangelists and lay persons. We were disappointed at the small attendance–we had hoped for seventy-five, the maximum we felt we could take–but there were only eighteen. They were unanimous in approval of the courses and program, however, and felt they had learned a great deal. (Although some who had a limited education didn't show it.) I always enjoyed teaching people who were eager to learn. Probably the expense and difficulty of travel were reasons for the low attendance, although perhaps some of the churches did not distribute the material I had given them.

We also offered a correspondence course, and I tentatively offered an extension course in Christian education. We had to wait to see how many would respond, and in what places, before we could definitely plan for it.

I had nearly completed a Self-Study Guide, which I was mimeographing, that I hoped some would use to accompany my textbook, *Education in the African Church.* I hoped to complete a Teacher's Guide for the Self-Study Guide and textbook, for use either in a classroom situation or for extension education.

In August I drove to Kumasi, and arrived on a Monday morning at the Methodist Church. In the afternoon I made a presentation on our Leadership Education program and Field Education for pastors–the purpose of my going. While there, I enjoyed talking with several former students. I stayed in the home of a well-to-do Ghanaian family. There were so many people living in the large houses that there was noise everywhere until late at night and early in the morning. They gave me good food, things I could not afford to buy, and some that were hard to get unless one had the right connections and/or paid an exorbitant price. They fed me *obroni* (white person) food and the pastor and his wife Ghanaian food. I would have been quite willing to eat the same.

On Tuesday evening I attended one of the three mission evenings they had. A pastor who was in charge of an "Opportunity Centre" in Takoradi spoke. (A former student sitting next to me interpreted.) One of the things he did was to give vocational training to prostitutes and help to rehabilitate them. He hoped to be able to enlarge the Centre so the judges would send them more prostitutes who were arrested instead of sending them to prison. Also, a Methodist missionary nurse from Lake Basumptwi spoke. The offering that night amounted to more than ¢4000. It is true that the Asantahene (Paramount Chief) gave ¢1500 and his wife ¢500, and another man gave ¢1000, but only about four hundred people were there, and that was very good considering the financial situation.

On Wednesday morning I went to a Laymen's meeting, honoring the British delegate and his wife. There were women there, but everyone was addressed as "brethren," and always it was laymen. For the first time the Methodist Church voted to allow women to elect their own Secretary of the Women's Fellowship without approval of the Conference. (Yet there were some well-educated women in Ghana.)

The Conference also finally voted for church union, after having turned it down twice previously.

I started back at 2:30, but by the time I stopped to buy food and take the two men home who came with me, it was 8:30.

Time for a Vacation

At the end of July I went to Liberia for a restful vacation, and also to talk with the people who were involved in a new church school curriculum, which I was hoping we could use in Ghana, and perhaps have some Ghanaians take part in the writing.

After five days in Liberia I went on to Sierra Leone, to visit with friends there, both missionaries and Sierra Leoneans. I felt that it might be the last time I would visit these countries, since I hoped to travel elsewhere when I left Ghana in two years' time.

While in Sierra Leone I purchased two tires, since they were unavailable in Ghana. After I returned to Ghana I spent practically a whole day getting my tires out of customs and having them put on my car. They made it incredibly complicated, so that one was forced to hire an agency to do it–which cost ¢35.00. I stayed with them for two hours until after I paid the duty–and then discovered they had to get eleven more signatures. At that point I went home. The agent told me to come back at 2:30. I arrived at 3:00, and they still had two signatures to go. The agent told me if I would give them a cedi to give to the man to sign it, it would be done more freely. I refused, but the agent gave it anyway. It is all done quite openly. I spoke my disapproval out loud. I was really upset that day with all the corruption and inefficiency–but instead of being quiet about it, I let them know it–which of course did no good at all and left me feeling unhappy. I was so glad that I knew other Ghanaians who were helpful, hospitable, and honest. It was very difficult, I am sure, to be honest in a society which was riddled with dishonesty and corruption. The small tires in the end cost me $70.00 each, but I was grateful for them.

The Musama Disco Cristo Peace Festival Celebration

On August 26 I was up at 5:00, and at 6:30 was on my way on another trip with Erma Grove, my Mennonite missionary friend, a Ghanaian, retired from the Language Centre at the university, and a young American woman who was doing research on the healing of mental diseases. We traveled about sixty-three miles to Mozano, the church headquarters. The town was made up only of members of the church. This was a celebration of the Musama Disco Cristo Church, part of a ten-day celebration. This church was the oldest "Spiritual" or Independent Church in Ghana, established in 1919. It was founded by a former Methodist catechist. It combined African tradition with Christian beliefs and practices, and laid great stress on healing. They had a Prophet at the head–an hereditary position–who was treated like a chief. They had prophets, priests, healers. The circuits were headed by lay elders, and these, too, were "chiefs"–with "linguists" and all the traditional honor and ritual. What we saw on Saturday was a *durbar*. This in the traditional society is a gathering of chiefs for fellowship and in honor of a visiting Asantehene (Paramount Chief) or other person of importance. There was always a *durbar* when the Head of State visited any place. So it was a regular *durbar,* except that the Prophet (Head of the Church) was the Asantahene, and the elders who were heads of church circuits were the chiefs. People were there from many places in Ghana, and also Ivory Coast, Liberia, Nigeria and London. There was a great deal of traditional dancing and singing in both the traditional and modern African style, but with religious words. (See the photos below.)

We met some of the dignitaries, and finally the prophet Maritaiah Jonah Jehu-Appiah, Akoboha III. He was a young man, not yet married, a trained teacher who spoke both English and French. We were then given coffee and sandwiches and afterward one of the prophets took us around the town, where we saw the Temple, still under construction; the House of Prayer; a shrine where the two former Akobohas were buried (father and grandfather of the present one); a Healing House; and a place where mentally ill people were brought for healing.

| The House of Prayer (Holy Place) | Shrine (Burial Ground) |

At about 11:00 the "chiefs" began to arrive with all their retinues and dancers. Then, a parade began through Mozano and two other villages close by. A student from the Good News Institute took us to the platform which had been prepared for the ceremonies, where we could watch them as they passed by. The Prophet was carried in a palanquin, an elaborately decorated portable hammock, borne on the men's shoulders, and covered by a huge umbrella, as was the custom for chiefs at various festivals and events. [This was an ancient custom, adopted from the East.] At about 3:00 everyone was gathered at the back of the platform (we sat there with important people), and the long ceremonies began, with singing, dancing and speeches.

The Prophet Arrives

The Prophet

The organization was persecuted when it began, sometimes by the Methodist Church itself. In his short English speech, the Prophet spoke of how early missionaries thought all of their customs were bad, and people were taught to disregard them all–but the Musama Disco Christo Church has shown how their tradition could be taken and sifted, changed where necessary, and used as an expression of their Christian faith. Now they were a light to others who were seeking to find their roots. People were even coming to learn from them.

I took many pictures and recordings. It was a very interesting experience.

At 5:00, after the Prophet had spoken, we asked permission to leave. They gave us food already prepared. It was 8:45 when I arrived home.

311

Chapter 6. A Troubled Time in Ghana
1978-1979

The 1978-79 school term began with eighty-eight students enrolled. This included an Anglican student from Uganda as well as the usual other mixture: eleven from the Evangelical Presbyterian Church (found in the Ewe area of Ghana and Togo); twenty-six from the Presbyterian Church of Ghana[1]; thirty-three, Methodist Church–Ghana; one from the Lutheran Church; fourteen from the Anglican; one from the A.M.E. Zion; and one from the Mennonite Church.

Music Workshop

On September 14 I held a music workshop to translate good children's hymns into three vernacular languages–Ga, Ewe, and one of the Akan languages (Twi, Ashanti, or Fante). I also

E.A. Ashiety (Ga),
Rev. S. B.Essamuah (Akan)

hoped to have some created in the African style that would be useful for children. I was working, with the help of students and others, on a hymn book to be published for English-speaking Africa, with a vernacular edition of words only for Ghana.

Translating hymns is not an easy task. One must not only know music, but also both English and the vernacular well. Some present and past students, two other pastors and one lay person worked on the project for several months. One of our former students, Rev. E. K. Ansah, wrote the notes in *solfa*, which many adults could read, although they could read, although they could not read musical notes.

---

[1]

The Germans from the Bremen Mission and the Basel (Switzerland) missionaries , both from Reformed churches, began the work in Ghana. When the first World War began the Germans had to go, and the United Free Church of Scotland was asked by the government to fill the gap. The Scottish missionaries organized the work of the Basel Mission in the Presbyterian Church of the Gold Coast, and that part of the Bremen mission work which was in British territory into the Ewe Presbyterian Church (later named Evangelical Presbyterian). (F. D. Harker, *The Church Is There (In Ghana)*. Church of Scotland Foreign Mission Committee, Edinburgh, 1964, p, 10). Later the Presbyterian Church and United Church of Christ in the United States contributed missionaries and funds.

*Rev. Essamuah, T.W. Kwami,
Rev. F. M. Akyea (Ewe)*

Rev. E. K. Ansah writes Solfa

(Rev. Ansah joined the Army as a Chaplain, and sadly, died of a heart attack while drilling, still a young man.)

On October 13 I went with some students to visit the High Priestess Nana Okomfohene Oparabea, at Larteh. Recently I have discovered that she was a very famous person, known for her spiritual and psychic healing.

In October I also offered the staff a course in writing for individualized instruction. Livingston Buama (a former student, then on staff), Maclean Kumi and Michael Thompson took part.

Livingston Buama,
Michael Thompson, Maclean Kumi

There was also the usual workshop team training.

G.R. Ahorble, J. Ayanwale, C.F. Kakotse,
S.E. Frempong

J. Ayanwale, J. Baffour-Awuah,
Mark Dadzie

Ayanwale with Hand Puppet

Workshop Team 1978-79
Back: M.K. Forson, E.A. Ashietey, S.N. Agye-Mensah,
S.E. Frempong, G. Mensah, J. Ayanwale, W.G.K. Klu (Dei)
Front: G.R. Ahorble, J. Abbour-Awuah, E. Okyere-Twum, C.F.
Kakotse, G.A. Dadzaa, D. Y. Sarfo, M. A. Dadzie

Good News Institute

From September to December I taught another course at the Good News Institute, one on "Using Drama in Christian Education." I had long since learned that both children and adults in Africa love drama, and are good at putting a story into dramatic form. (I did not try to get them to memorize lines of already produced plays.) At an open house on December 9 the class performed a drama based on the parable of the Prodigal Son, and another which had the same message, but in a Ghanaian setting. I learned that when one wants to beg forgiveness in Ghana he kneels on the floor, with head hanging low, before the person he has wronged. If the person touches him on the shoulder, he is forgiven. (As we were working on the play some of the students didn't want the father to forgive the son, but I reminded them that the Bible story shows how God forgives those who seeks it.)

The Prodigal Son

Father Gives Money to His Son

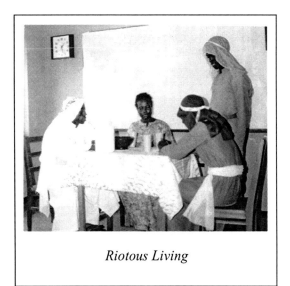

Riotous Living

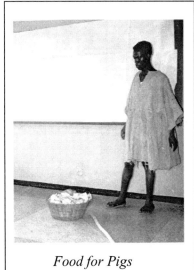

Food for Pigs

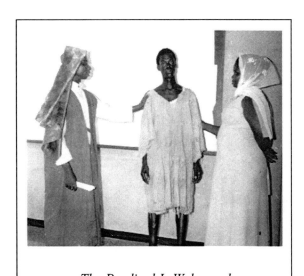

The Prodigal Is Welcomed

Working in Accra

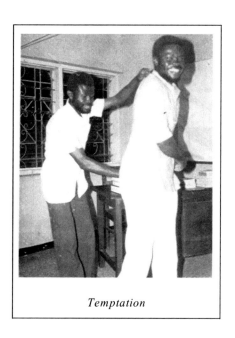

Temptation

Job Hunting After Prison

Destitute–The Prodigal

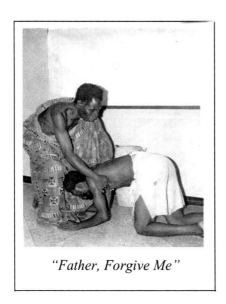
"Father, Forgive Me"

Welcome Home

More Trouble in Ghana

A letter written to my family on November 5 describes problems we were having at the time:

"There is no use in my mailing a letter for another ten days, because the airport is closed and no mail is going in or out of the country. But I decided to write my usual letter, only on ordinary paper, and I will add to it next week.

"This has been quite a week. At 11:00 a.m. on Friday the electricity went off. This is certainly not unusual, but when I went into town to shop I discovered that it was off all over Accra also–no street lights, no elevators running, cars lined up for gas, but no electricity to pump it with. Then at about 8:30 yesterday morning my water stopped completely. Again, this is not unusual–but I discovered that it was off all over Accra. (In fact, I am always the lucky one on campus–I have water longer than anyone else, because my house is a little lower. Other staff members have had none since about 4:00 p.m. Friday.) By that time we were discovering that this was not just a breakdown which so often occurs, but a strike. Rumor had it that it was going to extend all over Ghana; that workers at both light and water supplies, and all the civil servants were striking. This is not only for higher wages, but to demand that the military get out of government completely, and hand over to a temporary civilian committee until elections can be held. The radical devaluation of 140% is increasingly making itself felt, and added to the already high rate of inflation, is making life unbearable for many people. The government seems to be investigating some of the corruption, but people are still skeptical–it's still the military, and it is suspected that they all have their foreign bank accounts. A lot is being published these days about corruption being uncovered in high places, but it is so endemic–from top to bottom–that I really don't know what can be done about it.

319

"However, our electricity came on last night at 10:30. I was asleep, but woke up when the light went on. I got up immediately, cleaned out the melting ice from the freezer section of my refrigerator, and started it. I was very grateful, for it was just in time to keep food from spoiling. However, there is no water yet in Legon. We have some storage tanks on the campus, but with nearly one hundred students and eight staff families, they are not going to last long. In addition, the whole village behind us gets water from Trinity. There is an intermittent battle to get them to connect to water for themselves, but people, even when told not to, still get some water from the tanks. I had company yesterday–some Americans from the E.P. training center in the Volta Region who are attending my workshops to see what I do. So my sink is piled high with dirty dishes. Fortunately, I still have some to eat out of. I have a pan of water Matthew [the young man who worked for me part time] carried over for me yesterday, and it is amazing how little one can get along with. We just keep hoping that the water will come back on soon. It is on in at least some parts of Accra, but I talked to a friend by phone this morning and her electricity isn't on yet, but her water is.

"One of the students says that they announced on the radio that there was a general shortage, but they were working to get it available to everyone again. Of course, that is not the whole truth. They apparently said nothing about the strike."

[Later, after this letter was written, it was discovered that one large pipe that brought water into the city was clogged; they had to get people from Israel, who had originally put the pipe in, to come repair it. Fortunately, another pipe carried water to the far side of the city. I got out my empty 44 gallon drum, and large pans were gathered. The students then went in the van to collect water thirteen miles away for the staff members and students. They brought me a big pan of water.]

"I think I wrote you last week about my shock when I received word that the twenty small flashlight-battery powered projectors which I had ordered from Guatemala had arrived at the airport. I had written in all three letters I had sent to the elderly priest about this order that it should go to the Christian Service Committee of the Christian Council. They can get things in duty free, and are set up to clear all the things they receive. I have spent, in the last ten days, a total of twelve hours (divided into four different days), five trips to the government ministry offices, and three trips to the airport. This was at least one hundred twenty miles of travel, and gas is in very short supply. Finally I got them in duty free as religious education equipment. But then I had to pay a large sum to get someone to clear them. He refused to give me a receipt, and admitted he had to pay quite a lot in bribes. The customs department is so corrupt–no one will do their job without being paid extra. I am sure the young man who cleared it probably turned in only part or none of what I paid to the company he represents. I am going to write them, I think. I was utterly fed up with the whole thing. And, to make matters worse, though I said we must have the cases for the projectors so that the men could carry them back to the village, they were sent without the cases–to save me the cost of freight! Of course, I told the man in Guatemala to send them by parcel post or ocean freight–not by air. Now if we ask him to send the cases, it will add a good deal to the price, because the cost of handling, etc. will all have to be paid for again. I have to see what the students who paid for the projectors want to do. Of course, anything they pay for now costs them 140% more than it did a few months ago because of the devaluation. It is a mess. I haven't even received a bill. The man writes me all those super-friendly letters, and apparently has no business sense at all, and doesn't even look back at letters. He wrote me in June they were all ready to go, and when I finally wrote him last month, he replied that he didn't know what happened–he just forgot he hadn't sent them. Then the same time I got the letter, here they appeared by air.

"I have been tired all week, but still have so much to do that I have to keep working at top speed. Today I gave Sunday School materials to the lay teachers to teach next Sunday, because we have a midterm break. It really won't be much of a break for me–I have no classes on Fridays and Mondays anyway, except for a pastoral group meeting on Friday mornings; and I will still have responsibility for the Sunday School.

"Well, I will stop for now, and continue the letter next week."

November 12

"What a week! Our water finally came on Sunday night–mine at least started running into the toilet at 9:30, and so I flushed the toilet, filled up the bottles of drinking water, and then washed my stack of dishes. Then on Wednesday our lights went off again, at about 4:00 p.m. This time it was a fault in the lines, not a strike. But it took them until the middle of the afternoon on Friday to get our particular line on. Again, it was just in time to save things in the large freezer (which belongs to my neighbor), but I am trying to eat the meat I have had in my own freezer. I don't like to risk meat that has thawed or begun to thaw twice. I am so grateful to have electricity again. The fan feels good, too–this is coming into our hottest season now, and I often go to sleep with the fan on, as well as use it in my office as I am now.

"Although the government managed to get the electricity and water workers back on the job, many of the junior civil servants did not return to work, even when they were told they would be sacked (fired) if they didn't. I believe it is about 2,000 workers who have lost their jobs. The government has set up hiring offices, and thousands of people have flocked in to apply for the vacancies. On Monday night the Head of State (General Akuffo) announced a state of emergency. This was never done, even in Achaempong's time. It has made no difference to our life here, but it means that anything which disrupts the economy is considered a crime against the State, and there can be immediate arrests (leaders of the strikers have been arrested), and trials will be by military tribunal. I know that the economic situation is desperate for people–but I imagine they do have to stick to the devaluation, increased taxes on petrol, liquor (the latter I have no objection to at all!), and a drastically reduced budget. But when a laborer still earns ¢4.00 a day, and a pound of meat is ¢7.00 (when sold legally–actually, it is apparently being sold for ¢12.00 in some of the markets)–what can one do?

"Incidentally, there were many losses when the lights were off. The main hospital, where the one blood bank is, has no auxiliary lighting system. Several hundred pints of blood had to be thrown away; patients could not be admitted; bodies in the mortuary waiting for autopsies began to decompose. Cold stores began to sell their meat, fish and other supplies at half price, but lost a lot. The stores were mostly closed and Accra looked like Sunday on Saturday morning last week.

"This week I have worked very hard on getting materials started for my extension course. I am going to write letters today to those in Accra who plan to take it that we will meet on Friday evening, the 24th, to start the class. I am still trying to make arrangements for a tutor and place to meet for another group in Cape Coast.

"This weekend is the midterm break. I have kept very busy, and had to spend more hours than usual on the Sunday School because I had to arrange the classrooms this morning. Things went well, however.

"I have received word from Cassell (Geoffrey Chapman) in London that they are very favorable to reprinting my book, and if I can get a grant in hard currency, they can keep the cost down for Ghana. Since I have saved the money I have received for sales, I can do that. (I will write the Board, but I see no problem.) This will mean reducing the cost of the book here from ¢20.00 to ¢5.00, if I can give £900–which is about $2000 now. I have already told them any royalties I get could be used to subsidize the Ghana sales, and they have agreed. So I am going to send them the original photographs and two more copies of the book soon, since I hope the airport will be opening this coming week . . .

"Needless to say, I am eager for airmail to come again. This week I received two letters sent by surface mail, one exactly a year ago, and another fourteen months ago. Maybe the post office is working on part of its backlog since they don't have airmail to deal with. I hope they soon find some of our long delayed textbook orders."

Love,
Esther

December 3, 1978

"I am tired this evening. It is after 6:00 and I am just now getting around to letter writing. Yesterday we had a Youth Workers' Institute, with sixty-nine in attendance. I taught a class in 'Youth and Worship,' with student help, and I assigned the class on 'Planning and Leading Bible Study for Youth' to a group of students. We all worked very hard, but it seemed to be successful.

Games

Rhythmic Movement

Sale of Materials

"Then this morning was a special day at Sunday School, and I was on my feet from 7:00-12:00. For the first time this year we celebrated the annual 'Harvest Sunday' along with the adults. On any day there would not be room for all our Sunday School children in the church (chapel), and certainly not on this special day. Anyway, the service is too long for them. But we had our own celebration of thanksgiving, with various activities. The primary and junior children made a mural, had rhythmic movement, dramatized a Temple celebration in the worship service–and used local instruments, including drums, for their singing (as people did in Old Testament times). We could tell that they really enjoyed that. They brought gifts of both money and fruits, vegetables, etc. These were taken to the adult service, with a group we made into a choir following. They presented the offerings, and then sang two songs, using the instruments. It was all very hectic, but things came out all right in the end, and I think the children enjoyed it. Now in two more Sundays we have our big Christmas party. I don't know how I can get sugar and milk for their cocoa this year–I guess I will have to bring some from Lomé when I go with Erma on the 15th.

"Now this week we have to finalize plans for our Christian Family Life Institute for third year students and their wives, which we have the last few days of school. We close school on December 20. . . .

"I just received yesterday some letters mailed from New York on October 27 and 31. They must be some that were held up during the closure of the airport–though obviously they came through. I seem to have received yours fairly regularly. . . .

"Last night when we had figured the money for our sales, and put things away, I discovered four of the students who were working hadn't been at the dining room in time to eat supper, and someone had eaten it–probably the kitchen staff. So I brought them over, and opened a #10 can of goulash, given me from the 'Food for the Hungry' materials (which I felt bad about receiving). Anyway, it fed the hungry last night and we–mostly they–consumed all the goulash and two loaves of bread. They liked it, and thought it was a party. I even had margarine for the bread, which they hadn't had for a long time.

"The Ghana government has now announced that they will have political parties to elect the new civilian government. That's what many people have wanted all along, but the S.M.C. kept insisting on a 'National Government' (a no-party government), so that it is surprising to have them change their minds. There was recently a local government election for the first time in years, and people were plainly elected along old party lines, even though officially there were no parties. So I guess they decided to give in.

"They are making raids against hoarders and smugglers, and investigating some of the big government corporations–the whole thing is scandalous.

"I must close this and get on to other things."

Love,
Esther

December 10, 1978

"It's another Sunday afternoon, and I am very tired. Yesterday I spent from 11:00 to 6:00 (counting travel) at the Good News Institute. We had an open house, and my two classes gave the plays they had created. They are very good at drama, and people enjoy it as much as children at home. We are too sophisticated and have too many "things" for adults to enjoy such simple things in the United States. They did well. It was a small group in addition to the eighteen in the two classes–some former graduates, a few board members and the staff–all of us part-time and teaching without pay. It was a good experience.

Extension Students

"On Friday evening I taught the second of my extension classes in 'Ministry with Children in the Church.'

"I have spent time this week driving around trying to get people to take part (as leaders) in our Christian Family Life Institute we're having next weekend. Students had seen about several of them, but we had to get substitutes, and it's easier for me to use my own car than to try to get the use of a school car.

"I went to collect my passport yesterday; it has been at immigration for weeks to get my residence permit renewed. I had also asked the Methodist Church office to get me a multiple re-entry visa, so that I can go to Lomé and get back. I had expected to get my passport. However, I found that the residence permit had not yet been given, and therefore they couldn't get me a re-entry visa. With the change in government, they are apparently investigating all expatriates–hence the delay. So I guess I'm in the country illegally, except that since the application was made before it expired, they can't do anything about it until they make a decision. Anyway, the man finally said if I would bring another letter from the Methodist Church asking for a single re-entry visa, he would get me one tomorrow. So it means more hours spent when I had hoped to have a day to work tomorrow. One spends so many endless hours here in order to get anything done. But I really want to go to Lomé and get some things for Christmas. I can't even get milk and sugar to make cocoa for our children's Christmas party next Sunday here, and plan to bring some back. . . ."

Trip to Lomé

On December 15, as stated above, I went to Lomé, Togo with Erma Grove. She had suggested that we deposit checks in dollars in a bank in Lomé; then on our next trip we could withdraw money in the Togo currency. Going to Togo, although not a long trip, took a good deal of preparation. We had to have an international driver's licence, and also a tag on the car that allowed us to drive in another country. Besides having to get our return visas, we had to go to the bank to insure the car for international travel, and certify that if anything happened to the car in Togo we could pay in dollars. (I never did understand this, but it necessitated a trip to the bank each time we went.)

We always enjoyed being able to eat in a restaurant and order chicken and other food that was hard to get in Ghana–even ice cream. I will never forget, however, that on one trip we were eating ice cream outside, sitting under a large umbrella, when a woman with a baby came up to beg for food. She was only one of many who had escaped from the drought in the Sahel. We knew that if we gave to one we would be swamped by others–so we just left. We never ate outside again in Lomé.

We had to check through customs going out of Togo–it took some fast talking to persuade them to let me take the evaporated milk (which included what I needed for the party), and other items. (I had purchased some cutlery for the college, which to be honest, just got buried under a lot of other things, so the customs people never did see it.) Then after we passed through the first check, as is so often true, we were stopped farther on our way. We managed to get by that without giving a bribe.

Then, of course, we had to get back into Ghana–so wherever we went it was a problem. However, we always enjoyed our trips, and in the last years in Ghana went every few months.

December & January Events

In addition to our big annual Christmas party for the Sunday School, I invited the staff children over for a party on December 16, and on the 29th Mary Kwakye and Esther came to visit. I took the Prempeh and Kumi children and Esther (who was too young to really enjoy it) to the zoo. We also went to the airport so they could see the planes.

Christmas Party for Staff Children

*A Trip to the Zoo–Mary Kwakye &
Baby,Esther and Prempeh and
Kumi Children*

*At the Airport–There is more than one way to
see the planes!*

Christian Writers Workshop

On January 3-8 Sister Mary Ann and I were able to hold the Christian Writers' Workshop we had postponed. We met at St. Louis Teachers' Training College in Kumasi. It was another busy and fruitful time.

Mrs. Sowah, One of the Instructors

Students Writing

Titus Awatwi Pratt

Cecilia Edu & Asante-Frempong

Dining Room

January 21, 1979

"I have some good news this week. A representative of Cassell Ltd. (a subsidiary of Collier-Macmillan) from London was here to see me. They are definitely going to publish my book. Now I have the job of doing the revision I want to do and get it to them by the end of February. It will take about a year to get it out. He would have brought the contract, but the severe winter weather they have been having in England delayed getting them before he left. The New York office which gave me the grant for the book in the first place has agreed that I can use the $2,000 I now have replaced to help depreciate the cost for Ghana. With the devaluation of the cedi, the book will now cost ¢21.00. In dollar terms it is not unreasonable for a limited edition book in these days, but that is five days' wages for a laborer here. In fact, I really don't see how people are going to survive as the effect of the devaluation is more fully felt. Yet devaluation seems to have been absolutely necessary, and in fact, may be necessary again. Anyway–to continue about the book. I am also giving whatever royalties I get to the fund to subsidize the Ghana sales. So, the book can probably sell at ¢8.00 here instead of ¢21.00.

"Something further on devaluation–an officer from the banks spoke to the students last term. He told them that Acheampong had printed lots of money to hand out to people to get them to vote for the Union Government, and it had no backing. Someone else who seems to know says that one-third of the budget for the country was made up of money printed with nothing to back it. So some people have thousands of cedis, and will pay anything to get the scarce items–and almost everything is scarce. One tire they tell me now sells at ¢700 (seven months' salary for some of our pastors). Just after devaluation the black market exchange rate was almost the same as the legal rate. Now it is up again–I have heard figures of from ¢15.00 to ¢20.00 per dollar, as compared to the legal rate of ¢2.75.

"I have organized four different groups from the workshop team to hold four workshops this term. One will be here in Accra on February 17. Another will be at Tema (sixteen miles away) on the 10th. I still have to get the dates set for one at the spiritual church where we attended the durbar, and one for the leaders of the Methodist Girls' Fellowship here in Accra. Of course, I have to get the materials ready, and work with students individually or in small groups on these.

"I finally yesterday got back to writing materials for the extension course I am teaching–I have to have it ready before we finish what I have done already. I also must work on correspondence courses for the two Methodist probationers who are in process.

"On Thursday night I will give a lecture on writing for juveniles at the Bible School in Accra. I can use the material I have used for our Workshops for Christian Writers.

"I have started the M 1 (freshman) class in Sunday School and Christian Education now. This always makes the second term busier in some respects. The class in liturgics (which we did not teach last year because we changed it from the second to the third year) is going well. Our only problem is that only half the books–ordered in October 1977 and mailed in the U.S. on December 22, 1977–are here. So, students are sharing books at the moment . . . "

January 28, 1979

"I have just a few minutes to start this letter, but will at least begin before I go over to see about Sunday School. . . . I have already been to a 6:00 a.m. communion service, and have a busy day before me. I have decided that to show you something of the life I lead I would tell you how I spent yesterday. It was a day in which I had hoped to be able to be quietly at home and get some steady work done on the extension course I wanted to finish writing and cutting stencils for. It was unusual in that I slept until 7:30, since Matthew cleaned the house and washed the clothes on Friday (to suit his shift in work at the university). I got breakfast and washed and set my hair. I then took some information about workshops over to students at the dorms, and came back to settle down to work–by then it was 9:00. Sammy came to wash and check the car. [Sammy was a grammar school student who did part time work for me in the yard.] I managed to work rather steadily until 11:30–wrote a final exam for the course and started cutting stencils. Then I started to get lunch–but before I could eat Mr. Frempong, a student from the Good News Institute who is very anxious to learn to write, came for the help I had promised. He left at 2:00, and I ate lunch. He brought some information about a workshop they have requested for their church (a spiritual church), and that meant I had to go give another message to some students. I rested about half an hour, then started to work again. Managed to get some typing done. But at 5:00 Matthew came to iron. He couldn't do it on Friday because the electricity went off just when he was ready to do it. I had to get out some things I wanted him to press in addition to those washed. I had started to work when a student came–he asked for help with materials for his services at the Accra Girls' Secondary School where he had been assigned for his Field Education experience. That took thirty or forty-five minutes. Before he left another student came–request for some materials for the Sunday School of a church where he had been assigned. I went back to work. Very soon a Methodist pastor who had applied to some U.S. schools came to see me for information. The Crusade Scholarship Committee secretary of the Board told him I was their representative and he could get application forms from me–they have never sent me any. I talked to him about the need for undergraduate work first, etc. I went back to work. By this time Matthew had finished, and so at 6:30 I got supper, and listened to a radio drama while I prepared it, ate, and washed dishes Finally at 7:30 I was back to work, and typed steadily until after 10:00. And this is the usual story for my 'uninterrupted day'! I was also invited to a dinner and celebration by Mr. Frempong–a personal invitation from the Prophet–but declined with regret. If I had gone there at 4:00 I would have achieved nothing. I still have quite a lot of typing to do on the extension course.

"We're wondering why we haven't heard when our librarian who's coming for a year is arriving.[2] She was to come in January or February, and it's almost February. I'm glad that at least we know that the new equipment and materials for the library have now been shipped from England. If they are not held up too long in the port, she may have something to work with when she arrives."

February 4, 1979

"Yesterday I buried myself–as much as that is possible–and spent the whole day except for washing my hair and eating some quick meals on revising my book for publication. I have to try to find some up-to-date statistics on two subjects, if possible, and then type it. I hope that by the end of the week I can mail it to England.

"In the meantime I had two sets of papers to grade, which I have just ignored. I also am in the midst of preparing students for workshops, and spent two afternoons during the week meeting with small groups. There will be more of such work this coming week. One team has a workshop next weekend, and we have ours here on the 17th.

"We've had more water problems this week. The water supply has been intermittent for some time, and especially marked the last three weeks. As is frequently true there is water here when there is none over at the school or at some of the staff houses. However, I also was completely without water from Wednesday afternoon until Friday morning, when water came on at my place–not at the school (pressure too low). So students helped to carry water to the kitchen so they could have food. Yesterday the 'matron' (the term for the woman in charge of the dining room) was with other women carrying water for the kitchen. I overheard one of the students talking to her. He was joking when he said, "But that is your work–to carry water. If you were in a village, you would have to carry water [being a woman]." She answered, "That's why I didn't stay in the village!"

"The water problem is due to a combination of reasons: there hasn't been enough rain for about three years, and the reservoirs are low; there are just too many people in Accra, and I am sure the number continues to grow–at least, houses keep multiplying, in spite of the economic situation (those people who have money by bribery and corruption invest in real estate.) Also, everything is breaking down in Ghana. There are not adequate spare parts for anything, including

---

[2]We had a good library, [at least for Africa] but much in need of organization, classification, etc. I had suggested that our Board might send someone for a year if we requested it. They had found someone, and we were eagerly awaiting her arrival.

pumps for the water. I am sure I can list general lack of management and inefficiency as another reason.

"It's amazing how little water one can get along with when one has to, even in a hot climate. I didn't wash my dishes for two days (it would be much more difficult for a family). The toilet was just not flushed; my bath was taken with half a bucket of water, and I used what was left to wash my face in the morning.

"I note that the cedi has been devaluated again, a small amount. Paper is now costing ¢30.00 a ream (which isn't a full ream). Imagine what is happening to school budgets–including our own. "

Our Accra Workshop (at Trinity College)

Greeting Arriving Participants

Registration

A Class

And We Still Had Sunday School!
Photos Taken in March
Beginners

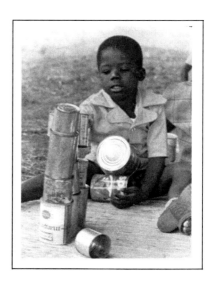

A Nurse (Vida Kumi) Visits

332

Primary Classes

A Mother and Baby Visit

Playing Synagogue School

March 15, 1979

" I am sure there is no use in my mailing letters for some days, for all borders are closed and no one is going in or out legally. But I will take a little time tonight to write you the news to date, and continue it later.

"I wonder if there has been any information about Ghana's change in currency and the borders closing in the U.S. news. Some people began to suspect that something was going to happen–in fact, Bronwen Thompson (Michael Thompson's wife), told me Friday morning that the borders were definitely going to close as well as the airport, and that there was to be new currency. Even though the old currency is still supposed to be legal tender until after the 26th, no one will accept it. For five days now all the major stores and most of the smaller shops have been closed, and even the market women are not selling. For several days you couldn't get petrol, unless you paid exorbitant prices. Fortunately, I didn't need any.

" People are standing in line at the banks all day and still not getting money. Some of our own students slept in line at the bank all night last night, in order to get some money changed–one who was there all night got back at 10:30 this morning. Others who went at 4:30 this morning came back in the late afternoon with nothing. At first we were supposed to be able to change up to ¢5,000 (for 70% of the value), and those with over ¢5,000 could also change, but get only 50% of the value in new currency. But they cut this amount down to ¢500 per person officially, and, in fact, some give even less. This means that people will have to stand in line again for long hours to get some more. The bursar of our college is having great problems–next week he needs ¢12,000 to pay the students' travel and allowances. He can't get to the bank, and in fact, they aren't letting people take out such quantities. He doesn't even have money for food. At the University it is worse–one of our students said another student lent a cedi to a friend at the University who hadn't had anything to eat for a long time because he can't get any money changed–and apparently the University cafeterias are not taking the old money either. There have almost been riots in some places. I have heard that some people have died of heat exhaustion after standing in the hot sun for hours; at one place a man was killed by a policeman because he (the policeman) claimed he tried to push ahead in the queue.

"Bronwen told me an American friend of hers told her she took a student from the Bible College where she teaches with her to stand in line, as protection. Some people had been waiting all night at the bank, and when by 10:00 the bank was still not open, they started to throw rocks and break the windows. Then the policemen came in with their clubs and started beating the people. The American said to her student, 'If he hits me, I am going to report to my Embassy. And if anything happens that I am knocked down, you go immediately to the American Embassy and report it!'

"But the student took hold of her arm and said, 'We're going! We're not going to stay here!'–and so they left.

"I also heard that some students discovered a man went into the back door of the bank and came back out with money. They pushed his car into the pond at the University.

"What this is attempting to do is to get some of the vast amounts of money that have been accumulated illegally, and are contributing to the runaway inflation. That is why the borders are sealed, so that some of the people who were hoarding cedis can't get into the country to change them. There are stories of traders and market women and others bringing in suitcases and cocoa bags (large gunny sacks) full of notes–not only thousands, but millions! They say one woman who stood in line at Tema with a cocoa bag full became so frustrated that she began to tear up the money; another started scattering it to anyone who wanted it. Certainly these people will have to account for this. I wouldn't be surprised but what they will catch some for income tax. They have now asked for the list of all persons who deposited large sums of money for the few days leading up to Friday night, because money which is already in the bank is not discounted. Obviously some heard about the currency exchange ahead of time.

"Unfortunately, the ¢8,000 cedis from the recent Garden Party money had not been deposited–that means that the College has lost 30% of it. One can't really blame the bursar, however, since he knew that this next week he would need ¢12,000. I hadn't realized that if money was deposited it wouldn't be discounted. I didn't have much, but I do have other funds, some from materials I sold recently at the workshop–so with my own money and the various funds I have I had ¢582.00 in all. I did go to town on Friday and bought some books to sell at the workshop this week-end, and thus saved some money. I also bought stacks of bread, both to save the money and because there is going to be another shortage of bread–there is no wheat in Ghana at the moment. I freeze it in my neighbor's freezer, which I brought him from the U.S.

"There are some sad things, too. One of our older students told me today that just last month he got an advance on what amounts to a pension fund (for teaching). It was for ¢3,000, and he left it with his wife so that they could try to get some spare parts and get his car running so that it could be used as a taxi to earn money. Then on Friday–the last day before the announcement was made–he checked out ¢2,000 more. This means that he will lose ¢1,500, which he can little afford. The students aren't getting much done in class or school, with having to go home or stand in lines at banks to try to get what money they have changed.

"I don't know what I would do if it weren't for the students. They took five hundred of the cedis I had, along with some from Thompsons and from what the students had collected. They are trying to get ours changed along with theirs–though only some had any luck today, after being in line all night or since early this morning. (They went to different banks.) Then yesterday a student came to tell me he had been able to change some money, and wondered whether I needed some. He gave me ¢100 as a loan. Another student came this evening and offered some. Then this morning on my way to town I stopped to pick up a young woman who teaches in the Sunday School during vacation periods. She works at the military base, and apparently doesn't have trouble getting money, for she offered to change what old money I had with me in the car, which was ¢80.00. I am overwhelmed with what people do for me at times.

" I do have a real problem. Late Friday afternoon I broke the frame on my glasses. So I am very anxious to get money to buy new frames, if they are available. But I went in to town this morning (fortunately we had changed one of my classes for another reason), but I could find none of the four places open where I might get my glasses fixed. I have an old pair, but they really bother me, for they don't fit my eyes, nor are they comfortable on my nose. But I will just have to put up with it, and hope that on Monday, when I don't have classes, the stores will be open. I just hope they have the size I need.

"My friend Sister Mary Ann and I had an appointment to work on the Writers' Workshop for most of the time on Monday. I knew she was going to Lomé for the weekend, so I was not surprised that she didn't come. I checked this morning at her office, and it is as I suspected–the border closed after they were in Lomé, and she won't be able to get back until March 26. Also, a group of Methodist pastors have been in Israel, and can't get home. One of them is an important person in the hymn translation workshop I am planning for the 30th. I don't know whether he can come now or not, even if he is back in the country. I have heard of a British woman who came to be with her daughter when the baby was born. When they heard the airport was closing, they changed her reservation back home, and got her on Ghana Airways on Thursday night–or thought they had, for she had a reservation. But as so often happens, she was bumped. (Someone else no doubt paid a bribe to the ticket sellers.) So her son-in-law took her to Lomé to get on a flight there. But the border closed, and he is in Lomé, while his wife is here with the new baby and two other children.

"Our lights went out (as they do several times a week), but didn't come back on after a few hours as they often do. After being out since 11:00 a.m. on Tuesday, the principal went on Wednesday to the headquarters of the light company. (Our phone hasn't worked for weeks, so it is impossible to phone). There wasn't anyone in the office to receive his complaint–everyone was out trying to change money. It happened that he knew that the man at the top is a Methodist. He went to Methodist Headquarters and got his address, and went to see him at his house in the evening. He explained our problem, and the man picked up the phone and ordered someone to see about repairing our lights. So we were all pleasantly surprised when they came on again at 8:00 p.m. Wednesday evening (last night). It was just in time to save food from starting to spoil. This is the hottest time of the year–it's 88-89 degrees in the house most of the time (it's 88 now at 9:00 p.m.) So a refrigerator is not a luxury–it is a necessity.

"And to top it off–we have just heard that all our new library equipment and supplies which the librarian who is supposed to be coming at any time was to use has burned in the shed at the harbor. When we saw in the newspaper about the fire in the shed, we said we hoped our shipment wasn't in Shed 8, but I guess none of us really wanted to believe it might happen. Usually insurance is good only until the shipment reaches the country. This, and the fact that we have no import permit (but it was a gift from the Methodist Church in England) may mean that there is no compensation. So–what now? If we can even get another gift of $3,000 or $4,000, it will take several months to get here.

"Bronwen said when she was talking with some of the women yesterday, one of them looked at her watch and said, 'Take courage! It may be another forty-eighty hours before we have another crisis!'

"It's one thing after another–one wonders sometimes how one can keep going. But we who are foreigners can leave–the Ghanaians are here. It is very hard for some of them, especially those who have lived in the U.S. or Europe or the U.K. for a time."

Sunday, March 18

"The situation has continued to be tense. Our students have finally managed to change the money students and staff had here. Some are almost ill from being pushed and shoved and standing for hours in the hot sun with no food or water; some have been bruised by policemen hitting them. Many are concerned about their wives and families in the villages, where there are few banks. Along the border they have closed all banks, because it is easy for people to come over from other countries to change cedis which have been hoarded there illegally. One student has a wife near the border who is pregnant and has a small child. Friday morning someone came to tell him his wife had no food and couldn't get her money changed. He had stayed all night two nights before to get his money changed, and so he left immediately to take some to her, and bring back the money she had to try to change it here.

"In spite of all this, on Friday afternoon I went with a team of four to a town about sixty miles away where they will hold a workshop for one of the spiritual churches–the same one where I attended the festival in October. They wanted very much for me to go, so I went with the bus and then came back in the evening. Many of their pastors weren't able to come because they didn't have any new money and couldn't get transport, but a remarkable number were there. We will send a team in August. The prophet expects about one hundred fifty pastors and lay leaders, with about one hundred young people working in a work camp, with whom they could meet at night. I really don't know how I am going to handle it.

"We discovered after we reached Mozano that we had brought a wrong box and left an important box of supplies behind. So I had to lend the school driver my car and pay him extra to have him take the correct box to them yesterday. The team returns this evening . . ."

From a general letter written in April:

"The immediate result [of the currency exchange] was to increase prices again, especially at first when there was little available to buy. The shops in town were closed for a week; even the market women didn't have food because they didn't have new money to pay for it. Those in the rural areas, where there are very few banks, and along the borders, where the government closed the banks, were hardest hit. I asked one farmer friend what he did. He said someone came around and offered them 50% to change it for them, so he gave it to them. People who wanted to go change their money couldn't get transportation because they had no money to pay for travel, and the bus, 'tro-tro' and lorry (truck) drivers wouldn't take the old. It was only toward the end of the time that the government finally sent vans out to the rural areas to change the money."

Mary Boatswain Arrives

On April 1 our long looked-for librarian arrived. She was Mary Boatswain, who had taken a leave of absence from her job as a librarian with the army to help us. When I went to the airport to meet her, I saw no one whom I thought could be she. When it seemed all the passengers had come into the main room, I asked whether she had been on the plane. They said "Yes," and that she was waiting for me inside the waiting room. I was not supposed to go there, but they let me, and there I saw a lone woman–an African-American, whom I had not expected.

*Mary Boatswain &
Esther Megill
(Graduation Day)*

She stayed with me for a time, then settled into one of the staff houses, and I began to orient her to the college and Ghana. Mary and I became good friends, and after we both returned home, for many years we talked on the telephone nearly once a month. I went to visit her in Boston, and she visited me in Mississippi. When I returned to Africa in 1989, she met me in Sierra Leone and then went on to Ghana with me. Then I did not hear from her for some time, and was quite sad to learn that she had Alzheimer's, and later that she had died.

Esther

*Esther and Her Father,
Owusu Asomaning*

Children Carrying Water

"It's the end of another busy week–or the beginning of another, whichever way one wants to count it . . . This week I had my usual classes with my students here, which really aren't so many–four classes with the first year, four periods a week (two courses, two periods each) with the third year. But of course I am now teaching two hours a week at the Good News Institute–one on Tuesday morning, one Thursday evening. The travel time totals about an hour each time. For that course I am writing a textbook–or what I hope may be a little booklet–as I go along, so that always takes some time. Then this week I had the two-hour class for the extension course on Friday evening. I am also still helping Mr. Frempong, who is attending the Good News Institute, with writing about once a week for a couple of hours.

"This last week I was able to spend several hours again on writing material for the Holiday Church School. (We use the term "holiday" instead of "vacation," as the British do.) There is still a long way to go. . . .

"Tomorrow we have an all-day committee meeting here of the Catholic Education Office–Trinity College Christian Education, to do further planning for the picture sets we have been trying to get done for ages. Whenever Mary Boatswain's things come, there will be materials to finish some of the paintings for printing. I am glad we have been able to resuscitate the committee. Of course I can make no contributions to the art, but I can to the educational aspects. I have made arrangements for lunch to be supplied by the College. I will set up the room and have bought fruit to go along with it, and Sister Rose, the chairperson, and I will supply coffee and tea. In case we should go on into the evening I have bought a supply of bread and will use some of my food here . . .

"Some good news–I have received $2,000 from the Women's Division (of the General Board of Global Ministries) toward the children's hymnal. It isn't enough, but if gifts continue to come in as they have lately in supplementary gifts and Advance Specials, I may have some more to add to it. Anyway, I am continuing to work on it."

"Yesterday I was busy all day, but didn't get to any of my school work. I had a steady stream of people from 9:00 to 12:30, including the man I am helping with writing. There was a former student from the north who came to return a book and report about some workshops he's been leading. I am very pleased to see my efforts multiplied in the form of pastors who are beginning to take Christian education seriously. I also had a visit from a Catholic priest and a catechist who want to attend the residential courses in July. And the Prophet of the spiritual church, the Musama Disco Christo, wants to send seventy of his pastors! I told him I couldn't possibly take that many, because I have to give preference to churches which support Trinity College. However, I gave him forms for fifteen, and promised more if I should see that the orthodox churches are not responding. Now one of the Catholic sisters, also engaged in Christian education in the Accra district, has asked if I could take five, and the Father who came makes six. So I have responses from these, but none yet from the churches who support the College. But if they don't respond, we will fill our space and take all we can of the others. We are offering four courses, and I'd like to have twenty-five people in each course. That is all we have room for in the dormitories and about the most a classroom will hold.

"An order for library supplies to replace those burned was sent to England after Mary came. Since it was so close to the time of her coming, it was decided that we should wait and let her say what she would need. There are some coming in her things, but she was late getting her personal effects to the Board, and the shipment hadn't been sent when she left. We still haven't heard whether it's on its way. It always takes a minimum of three months for a shipment to arrive.

"A very sad event occurred last weekend. Some university students had been in town, engaging in a cleanup campaign around the railroad station. When they finished, a bus came to take some students back to the university, and the rest waited for it to return. They started singing, and I suppose were rather boisterous, as a crowd of students can be. Then a policeman came up and threatened to arrest them for disturbing the peace. One of the students talked back to him, and so the policeman grabbed hold of him to arrest him. There were two or three policemen, all with their rifles that they always carry with them. There was a scuffle, and the policeman shot the student who had protested, and there were more shots in which two more were injured. The policemen left–the wounded and everyone.

"The students managed to find transport for the wounded and took them to the large teaching hospital, but the doctors are on a 'work-to-rule' strike, and there were no doctors to attend them; so they were sent away. Then they went to the Police Hospital, which refused to take them. On their way to the Military Hospital the first student died. Needless to say, the students are up in arms again. They are boycotting classes. The government has appointed a committee to investigate, but so often we never hear a report on what these investigating committees do. On Friday bus loads of students and some relatives of the deceased went by bus to the eastern part of the country where the burial was to be. A bus load of policemen was also going, supposedly to show their sympathy, and weren't all like the one who killed the students. We haven't heard what happened, but the students were saying they wanted no policemen around, and were going to stage demonstrations. There is real antagonism toward both the police and the military, who are so arbitrary in what they do. We've heard nothing of the investigation of the soldier who shot a man in the back during the currency exchange because he (the soldier) said the man was trying to get ahead of someone else in line. I have heard of other people who were killed, and many were beaten, by soldiers during that exercise. One wonders whether the civilian government which is supposed to take over July 1 can reduce the power of the military and the police. . . .

"Last Monday I was hostess to the audiovisual committee which is working on the teaching pictures. The lack of materials has slowed it down, and in the meantime people who started the project have left. On Tuesday I attended the first part of the Education Committee meeting of the Christian Council, and then went on to teach at the Good News Institute. And so, life has been busy, as always."

"It's a rainy Sunday morning. I wouldn't mind at all, except that this is the Sunday the youth classes are in charge of the church service. They have been working hard, and it would be too bad if there is poor attendance, as usually happens when it rains.

"I have been working hard on the Holiday Church School material this week. I don't know whether I am going to be able to finish it all before school is out so that I can give it to the students before they go. I am hoping that I can at least get the children's material finished; then perhaps I can get the material for youth and adult classes to the smaller number of teachers after they leave. The problem is that the postal system is so slow that one wonders whether they would even get it.

"I also have to work soon on materials for the long vacation period for the Sunday School, and will have to have some training classes for the teachers. I am going to turn it over to the local teachers a week earlier than I had planned. Although the principal hasn't said what he is going to do about letting students off so that they can travel back to their home towns to vote on June 18, I am sure a number will go, and I'd rather not worry about having teachers for all the classes on the 17th.

"The last day of the school year is on the 28th. They are going to try to have a school dinner this year for the first time in three years.

"There was excitement this week–an attempted military coup. A group of air force officers attempted to take over from the present Supreme Military Council. They had planned to take the two top men into custody and kill the other five members of the S.M.C. Apparently they wanted to stop the turnover to civilian government. I heard about it when I went to the Good News Institute on Tuesday morning. One of the students had come from work, where some of the women were wives of military men. They were very upset–said there was shooting at Burma Camp. When the news got to central Accra everyone started running–market women left their goods–everyone ran, trying to get away from the center of the city. The rumors were that the army and police were coming, and were shooting everyone in the way. It was true that there was a skirmish at the Military Hospital, but the rest were false alarms. Everything was back to normal on Wednesday morning. The men who attempted the coup are in custody, except for one who was killed.

"People in Ghana are fed up with military government, and they certainly wouldn't take kindly to another coup which would prevent a return to civilian government. However, they so seldom resist that I wonder what would have happened if the coup had succeeded. Certainly that is the last thing we need now . . .

"The university students have still refused to go back to classes. They say they won't until the commission that is investigating the students' deaths gives its report. However, the university authorities have said that examinations will be given on schedule. Under this system examinations count for everything–it's not what you do day by day in a course, but how you do in final comprehensive exams that determine whether you get a degree or not. All schools (except for Trinity) will be closed this Friday for a memorial service for the dead students."

341

"As I sit here tonight I occasionally hear the sound of gunfire, and I am listening to the Ghana Broadcasting Corporation, with its music, occasionally interrupted by a broadcast. We are in the midst of a coup. I had planned to go to town the middle of the morning, make some phone calls, go on some important errands, and buy some food. It was 8:00 when I discovered that there had been a coup. Needless to say, we all stayed in today. It is interesting that the B.B.C. has kept up with the news almost as well as we have. I understand that the Voice of America has broadcast too. This means that someone is keeping telex and/or phone lines open to the outside world . . .

"Some time during the night apparently a fellow army officer let Flight Lt. Rawlings, who is under court martial for an attempted coup two weeks ago, out of prison. His forces (the 'Revolutionary Forces') now claim to be in charge of Ghana (as stated above). At 10:00 this morning I heard the Chief of Staff of the Ghana Armed Forces claim that a coup had been put down. Then about noon came an announcement by an unidentified person saying that the revolutionary forces had taken control, as follows:

Officers and the men of the Ghana Armed Forces yesterday successfully overthrew the last vestiges of the S.M.C. regime. We, the junior officers, and the other ranks wish to assure the nation that we are firmly in control of the situation. And in the meantime, an Armed Forces Revolutionary Council, comprising of junior officers and the other ranks, has been set up. Countrymen! I do not wish to recount here the mal-administration of the S.M.C. government and the shambles in which this government has thrown our economy . . .

"However, there has been the sound of large guns (it sounds like canon) and rifle fire intermittently throughout the day, from various places in and around Accra. This evening there was a lot of noise from the university, and it sounded like gun fire–I was afraid a massacre was going on. However, Michael Thompson thinks it was fire crackers. The university students seem to be in favor of the coup. To me it doesn't make sense that a group takes over power for a month, and then will turn over to civilian government. However, they are announcing that elections will go on as planned. They say it is for the sake of the country, and the working-man who has been oppressed for so long. There was just a repeat of the announcement that they have taken over all centers of power–all of Burma Camp, the army headquarters, the airport. They are calling for all members of the Achaempong-Akuffo regimes (the NRC and SCM) from 1972-1976 to give themselves up at the airport police station. If they don't, they will suffer the consequences. A curfew has been imposed from 8:00 p.m. to 6:00 a.m., although essential services should continue. They have called for a number of people to report at the airport station–various army officers, and some civilians, including a well-known Catholic bishop and an Archbishop. In spite of all this, I hear the boom of a gun occasionally.

"To complicate all this, we are without electricity and water again. Of course no one is working on anything today. But it seems the water situation may be widespread and as serious as it was before when we were without water for two weeks. The tanks on the campus are nearly empty, and there are one hundred or more people here. No one can go out to see where in the city water might be. Fortunately we had a downpour of rain this afternoon. I was able to flush my toilet, which needed it badly, fill up the tank again, and wash a stack of dirty dishes with rain water, and still fill up every available container. This will last me for three or four days if necessary . . .

"I still have a little coolness in the freezer section of my refrigerator, but I am sure the chicken in my neighbor's freezer is thawed out. I am eating today some meat that thawed last week. There is more in my freezer. I don't want it to go to waste, but it is so expensive that I hate just to give it away.

"I don't know when I can get to the airport to mail letters, or when the airport will be open to take them anywhere. But when I do, I'll include this letter, and add more tomorrow."

Wednesday Evening

"Well, the country seems to be slowly getting back to normal, with a new government in power. The airport reopened today, so I will try to get these letters in the mail tomorrow. Yesterday morning I went into town to see if the students had come to class at the Good News Institute–they hadn't. I was stopped by soldiers twice. They said they are looking for army officers who were members of the SMC which had ruled the country. One asked me for money–he stressed he wasn't forcing me–to buy bread. He said they would have to stay there until 6:00. I did feel a little sorry for them–they were in pouring rain with no raincoats or protection against the rain, and apparently no food either, and probably had not been paid for some time. I gave them some money, then went back home, and was glad to stay in.

The Ghana News tonight said the airport is open, the curfew is lifted, most businesses and banks were open today in town. There is still confusion at the two big markets down town. (One is where I always go to buy my fruit and vegetables.) There was a lot of looting on Monday, and they are trying to sort things out. Soldiers are surrounding the markets, but are now called back to barracks otherwise. They said on the radio that the food situation is better, with food coming into Accra. I guess I will be able to go on Friday and get some food. I have been eating so much meat, trying to eat it before it spoils. I gave some away.

"The new government is now a ten-man 'Armed Forces Revolutionary Council,' headed by Flight Lt. Rawlings. It is made up of men of lower officer ranks, even some privates. This is a revolt of the lower ranks against the upper, and women they accuse of having grown rich off the poor man. They say they are determined to bring justice, and want it all cleaned up before turning over to civilian rule. They have given strict instruction that commodities are not to be sold over controlled price. We heard that some soldiers shot some Makola market women, I suppose for that offence. They have announced that any looters will face the firing squad. So they are going to be ruthless, it seems, to keep law and order.

"A young man who lives next door, who used to work for Trinity and is now working at the university, told me Rawlings came to the university yesterday. He really has the students behind him. He said the students told him we had been without light and water here since Saturday, and Rawlings said he would do something about it. This afternoon our lights came on! I am so grateful. Of course, it has meant taking several hours cleaning my refrigerator, and trying to salvage some of the food. Bread got wet, so I put some in the oven and dried it out. Several of my cake mixes are soaked, so I am making cakes tonight and will freeze them. I roasted beef and a chicken this morning, and gave half of it to Mary . . .

"It's been raining most of the time for three days, so we're managing for water. Perhaps what the water supply needs is electricity to pump it into tanks. Someone said it is flowing at the university now, and so we should be getting it by morning, at least at this end of the campus . . . ."

June 10, 1979

"It's a beautiful, sunny morning, after having rain most of the week–and today is my last day in Sunday School for three months, for which I am grateful. I do have a lot of work to do yet to turn it over to the Trinity Church teachers, however. Yesterday I met with the Junior teachers–the half who came. I hope to make arrangements today for three more meetings before next Sunday. I am still working on syllabuses and suggestions for the teachers.

"Life has returned to normal in Accra. Mary and I went into town on Friday. As usual, I spent most of the time seeing people about various things (a telephone could save much of this), but we did do some shopping. The big market where I buy fruits and vegetables was in business, and the large department stores. However, according to the paper, the other market was closed. This is where they usually sell 'essential commodities' like milk, toothpaste, soap, mackerel, margarine, sugar, etc.–all at exorbitant prices. Since the government has put out the decree that goods must be sold at controlled prices, these things have now disappeared from the market, as everyone expected–they are just hoarding until things settle down again. However, some shops were selling them, and for the first time in at least two years I saw long lines of people standing in line to try to get some. It is difficult for the working person to do so (of course, some people just take off from work–which is one of the problems), but at least some people are able to get items at a reasonable price. Some raids have been made on hoarders also.

"Now the talk is that the elections will proceed as planned on the 18th, but there will be a delay of three months to turn over to civilian rule, to allow the army to 'clean up' the corruption. I couldn't believe that they would go to all this bloodshed to hold power for six weeks. We will see whether they really will do any cleaning up. They do seem to have good intentions . . . High officers have been taken out of government positions; civilians who were in government offices have been reappointed and some of them put in charge, at least for the present. Consultations have been held with all political candidates, and also with church leaders, leaders of the National Union of Ghana Students, etc. They do seem to be seeking advice, and have the common people in mind, as they claim.   But it is too bad that there had to be so much bloodshed. I have heard there were fifty deaths (which is probably a more reliable figure), but I have also heard that there were as many as two hundred, most of these soldiers. Some civilians were killed for looting. But I heard of one market woman, with a baby on her back, who was gathering a load of things she was taking home and was shot with no question as to whether they were her own things or not.

"Soldiers collected a lot of money from people who tried to travel on Tuesday, so those fighting corruption are still engaged in it. They are really out to get the Lebanese and Indians, who own many of the shops and businesses, and whom they blame for many of the economic problems in the country. It is true that they have made a great deal of money off the country, but of course they are not the sole cause of the sorry state of the economy, and it is not justice to

344

attack every Lebanese without question. Apparently in some cases Lebanese who were driving cars were told to get out and the soldiers drove the cars off. Sr. Mary Ann told me she worked in her office in town on Monday and Tuesday, and bullets were flying all around. They were firing at the house next door where some Lebanese lived. Bronwen Thompson said when they took the children to the International School on Wednesday some of the mothers were remarking that nearly half the children had not come–and then they realized that they were the Lebanese and Indian children. They probably will be driven out of the country. One Ghanaian said yesterday that they would just go to nearby countries for a time, and then come back. I am sure that Lebanon wouldn't hold all the Lebanese around the world, even if they weren't having a civil war there.

"The second and third year students have been studying for their diploma exams this week, and will take them this coming week.[3] With fewer classes I have a little more time for other work, but I still don't see how I am going to get all the Holiday Church School and workshop material ready for students before they go . . . "

[The rest of the letter dealt with arrangements my mother was making for me to have people in the U.S. help set up the children's hymnal for offset printing, and about funding.]

June 17, 1979

"On Wednesday morning I picked up the *Daily Graphic*, the local newspaper, and was reading the front page as I walked on home. It had a picture of some people inspecting the firing range where sand bags had been piled in preparation for execution by firing squad of all enemies of the State convicted of smuggling, stealing, hoarding, etc. Just then I heard a volley of shots from the direction of the firing range over by the sea. It really made me feel terrible. A military court had just been set up, and they were already executing people–or so I thought. As it turned out, it was just practice on Wednesday. But yesterday morning two people were executed. One was General Achaempong, the former head of the Supreme Military Council for six years, who had a lot of responsibility for bringing the country to the economic chaos it is now in. The other was the former head of the Boarder Guards, who was no doubt involved in getting rich through smuggling goods across the border which he was supposed to be guarding. Although both these men were undoubtedly guilty, I still feel that execution by firing squad after a short 'trial' by an army group, headed by the man who less than three weeks ago was himself on trial by a similar group (but with a lawyer to defend him) is a travesty of justice. In the first place, I don't believe in capital punishment. Secondly, any person has the right to a fair trial, and you don't get this in two or three days without a lawyer to defend one. There are fifty people in detention, so I fear this is the beginning–or continuing–of a bloodbath. Likely to be one of the next is Lt. Gen. Akuffo,

---

[3] With the change of our curriculum and new staff members, the university was approached to ask that our students who made at least a "B" on their exams (given by the University) would be allowed to enter. This was agreed –for the first time–but they could take classes only in the religion department. We also persuaded the University to "set" an exam for the "practical" courses, such as Religious Education, Preaching, Liturgics, Counseling. This was agreed, and now the students felt it important to study for these subjects as well as the traditional diploma subjects. Actually, we at Trinity wrote and graded the exams. They had to be approved by the University staff, however.

who was deposed two weeks ago by a group of junior officers led by Flight-Lt Jerry Rawlings, who is carrying on the executions. They say Akuffo is hardly recognizable—the implication being that he has been beaten and tortured since he gave himself up last week. The irony of it is that he is the one who started the cleanup and opened the way to civilian government.

"Elections are going ahead as planned tomorrow; but the new Armed Forces Revolutionary Council has said that turning over to civilian rule will be delayed to October 1, instead of July 1 as was originally planned.

"Matthew came in yesterday with some cloth for pants and a shirt which he had been able to buy in town at controlled price. But he said the soldiers are beating the traders. It seems that the army is forcing people by gunpoint to sell. Apparently they tell them what price to sell for, and this extends even to things that have had no price control. Someone said that Kingsway (one of the main department stores) has very little left to buy. Unfortunately soldiers are using their power to extort money from people too. This whole exercise is such a mixture. The people are fed-up with the situation, and there has been such widespread corruption that many have become wealthy, while life is almost unbearable for the common person. But to commit injustice in the name of justice doesn't always solve the problem. In the question of execution one wonders who can throw the first stone. There would be few people left in Ghana if they killed off everyone involved in profiteering and smuggling, etc. At least they seem not to have stopped with the small trader as has been true in the past. They have in detention some of the top military people and also managers of some of the stores.

"Indians and Lebanese are apparently being harassed. BBC said that Indians had appealed to their embassy for protection and help in getting their women and children out of the country.

"Representatives of the Christian Council and of the Catholic Church have been called in for consultation. I wonder what their reaction has been to the executions.

Bronwen, Rachel, Rebecca,
Michael Thompson
(1976)

"Yesterday morning at 5:30 I went, along with Mary and some of the students, to see the Michael Thompsons off to England. I will really miss them. I couldn't help but think that in thirteen-fourteen months I will be the one to leave. A whole bus load of students came to see them off, and the vice principal and his wife and one other staff member. The principal didn't bother to show up. When I leave there will be few students around because I cannot possibly be ready to leave until at least two weeks after the end of the term. I have to do the teaching plus all the errands for final documents. All the packing and everything–I have to be both wife and staff member. Also, I want to have a chance to turn responsibilities over to Kwaku. I hope he can be here by July 1.

"I have finally turned the Sunday School over to the Trinity Church teachers, and this morning I will go to Ridge Church, the one English-language church in town, to worship. I spent almost all day yesterday on the Sunday School–gathering final materials and having training classes with two groups of teachers. It always takes me a while to feel detached. That is one of the reasons I don't want to go to church here. The other is that part of the service is in Akan.

"I have allowed my M1 students some class time to do some written assignments, so have had only two classes this week. But I have finished the little booklet (which I hope it will someday be) for my class at the Good News Institute. I was able to get a copy of my textbook off to the publishers in London with the Thompsons. By terms of my contract with them I have to give them first chance at anything I write, and I also have to have their permission to print this anywhere else if they don't want it. That is because I used some material from my book, and also because it covers some of the same material. However, I do not feel that it interferes with the sale of the other book in any way. This is meant for a different target group. In fact, sale of the first book might stimulate sales of this for use by teachers in teaching lay people or those with a lower educational level.

"I also had a farewell party for the children on the campus. We simply weren't able to find time when people involved in staff could get together for a staff farewell. We could have done it last week, but without water or electricity it would have been difficult.

"Diploma exams were this week. Now tomorrow I have to grade my part of them. There are some arrangements I must make for courses and workshops to follow soon after school is out. Then I simply have to work at high speed to see how much I can get done on the Holiday Church School materials before I meet with students the week after. I had a two-hour meeting on Friday regarding the curriculum workshop we are planning for August. Of course, I taught at the Good News Institute twice during the week, and had to spend nearly a whole day in town on errands and to buy food . . .

"We are losing three staff members at the end of this year, two Ghanaians and the Thompsons, who have already left. At the moment there is no one in sight to replace them. We will have a new principal beginning September 1, the present vice principal (the churches take turns having one of their members as principal)."

June 26, 1979

"It's Tuesday, and I haven't had time to write letters or do anything else for several days. I have worked eighteen or nineteen hours a day, stopping only to eat quickly, for three or four days. I now have the materials ready for all children's classes and the adult classes for the Holiday Church School–written, run off on the spirit duplicator, and assembled. I have the youth course outlined, but could not complete it. Needless to say, I am exhausted, but I still have some more work to do on the Workshop for Youth and Youth Leaders. I meet with the students who will be the Holiday Church School team this afternoon, and with those for the Youth Workshop tomorrow afternoon. Then on Thursday we have the closing graduation ceremonies, and this year a school lunch. They leave on Friday.

"I hope on Friday, with the help of the student who will be the superintendent, to get most of the materials packed for the Holiday Church School–there will be a little time later, but he won't be here to help. (The school is the last week in July to the first of August.)

"I teach at the Good News Institute today. The extension class is supposed to meet Friday night, but I am not sure whether anyone will come. With no phones I've had a difficult time contacting anyone. Even the army people have had transport problems. It's a wonder we are able to do any profitable study and work here, with the constant problems in the country.

S. A. Alondo, E.O. Dakwa, Kofi Martin, E. F. Nyarko

"On Saturday I begin a week's intensive workshop on Individualized Instruction, writing for correspondence courses. I expect nine or ten people–all but two are students just graduating or former students.

"I have had to make three trips last week and this to apply for renewal of registration of my car for international travel and an international driver's license. It's incredible how much time it takes–so much inefficiency. I still have to make another trip to collect them, and to get insurance for the car for Lomé. Then on the 9th I must go to Lomé to shop–I have only three days until I start the Residential Course. In the meantime I have to grade all my final papers, get grades in, and plan for that course–and also finish the Holiday Church School youth course.

"I'm not sure whether Mary will be able to go with me to Lomé. She still doesn't have her residential visa, which means she probably can't get a re-entry visa to return to Ghana. They finally discovered that she had to produce certification of her educational attainment. The principal couldn't find the papers originally sent him, so they had to send back to New York. They just came.

"The situation is tense in Accra. In one way, it has been good, temporarily–for the first time ordinary people are able to buy some essential goods at fairly reasonable prices, if they have time to stand in line for hours. But the soldiers have ordered goods sold at gunpoint in some places, at times pricing things at ridiculously low prices (for example, refrigerators, air conditioners, etc.) The shopkeepers are not likely to restock even if they can, if that is going to happen. Now it is beginning–most of the food has been sold, and there is nothing. Food is not being brought into Accra because people are afraid of being molested by the soldiers. Because I have the 'camp' (freeze dried) food and some canned food, I can get along. But it is really beginning to affect most people. The paper appeals (the Armed Forces Revolutionary Council, that is) to people to bring their goods to the market, and assures them soldiers are there to help. But that is not the way people feel. They can be brutal. In town the other afternoon we saw a soldier attacking a young man, probably caught pickpocketing or something. He hit him hard, knocked him down, and stamped hard on his stomach with his heavy boots. We also saw armed soldiers going into a shop.

"So far the former head of state, Acheampong, and the head of the Border Guards have been executed by firing squad. Firing ranges have been set up in Kumasi and Tamale also. Many people have been arrested, and trials are going on by a military court. There is no appeal. Those convicted of embezzlement, hoarding, profiteering, etc., will be shot, they say. Those with lesser crimes will be sent to prison . . .

"In the meantime, elections were held and a party which is really a reincarnation of Kwame Nkrumah's old party has won. There must be a runoff election for the president, however. The present government has promised to turn over to civilian rule by October 1 . . .

"I must get on my way to my class in town."

Ramseyer Training Centre
Abetifi via Kwahu
July 24, 1979

"I am so sorry that I did not get a letter written last week. That is especially bad since mother's last letter said you had not heard for a month, and you were concerned because of the news about the students tearing down an American flag. I did not write you that because I didn't want to worry you. However, I have written every week except the last . . . I don't know why the letters don't go through when I mail them right at the airport, but that's Ghana. My last one was mailed from Togo. I hope you have received it before now.

"Last week we had our Residential Course for lay persons and pastors. In spite of the severe petrol shortage, more came than had signed up. I believe we had fifty-six in the end. They consisted mostly of members of the spiritual churches and Catholics–the orthodox churches which support the College had a very poor representation. However, the response of the participants was good, and we had some good teachers. Mac Kumi taught a course on 'Planning and Preaching Sermons.' It was the most popular, for catechists, evangelists and lay preachers. There was a course on 'Basic Evangelism and Follow-up,' taught by an American who is here with the Navigators, an evangelistic group that seems to be more sensible than some. James Sarpei, another Ghanaian, taught a very good course on 'Urban Ministry,' and opened our eyes to the condition in parts of Accra. He is a good example of a balance between social action and evangelistic emphasis. Then I taught a course on 'Ministry with Adults in the Church.' I had ten, which was a good sized class to work with. Unfortunately, I caught a cold and had laryngitis. For the last two days I barely managed to talk enough to finish my classes.

"We finished the course last Wednesday, and in the early afternoon on Thursday I started toward Abetifi, with one passenger. I picked up another along the way, a former student. We arrived here at about 5:30.

"Although there were transport difficulties–one man from the north was on his way three days and nights–we had fifteen participants, all but four of those we expected. Sister Mary Ann and another Sister, Sister Joan, and I were the staff. This was the last of our series of Workshops for Christian Writers. Some really good material has been written. I am hopeful we will be able to get some published. These have been made possible by grants from the World Division (United Methodist) and Catholic sources, although we have some local support.

Dontaus Homeni, S. A. Alando,
I. Quansah

Workshop Group, with Sr. Joan (Left);
Sr. Mary Ann, (Rt.); Esther Megill (middle)

"This morning I got up at 2:30, after having slept only two hours, and loaded my car with baggage for those leaving. It had poured rain for hours, but had slackened off. I could not use petrol to make repeated trips to the place where they would wait for the bus, so most walked. However, it was not far. They were there before 3:00 to get a bus that is scheduled to leave at 6:00, but would leave whenever it was full–and often people are left who cannot get on. I finally managed to sleep a little, but not much. Fortunately, I have almost recovered from my cold, although I have had a sore throat and a lot of coughing during the week. I had no medicine and no way to get any, but gargling with salt water and drinking water with lemon juice helped.

"Tonight we are supposed to start our Curriculum Workshop, to work on revision of the Liberian Lutheran-United Methodist Sunday Church School Curriculum, and to start on a Kindergarten Curriculum which they have not done. We are writing our own materials because it is impossible for us to order materials from outside the country due to the lack of foreign exchange. Also, the first books were quite disappointing, and need a lot of improvement. It looks as if the second year's books will be better. Also, some things need to be changed to be better suited for Ghana. We need Sunday School materials desperately, and I just pray there will be a way to get them printed here. This is all a venture in faith, because I have no money to publish material, though some promise of support from the Presbyterian Church. There is no press which has the supplies to print, and we don't even have final permission from the committee in Liberia yet. Anyway, I am expecting thirteen people. One stayed over from the last workshop. Two were here, but had to go to Accra for meetings or personal affairs, and were to return today. Three are residents here. So far only two have come, in addition to the four here. So I will not start tonight. I ordinarily would not anyway, but had hoped to get some introductory information given tonight. I will spend all day tomorrow giving lectures, then will drive back to Accra tomorrow afternoon.

.

E. K. Ansah, Cecilia Edu (unknown names)

J.K. Baiden, D. S. A. Allotey, E. Martey

I have just enough petrol to get there, and have some which I bought in Lomé to fill up again to return. I will spend all day Friday in intensive preparation of the Holiday Church School team. Then I return here on Saturday. I just pray that all sixteen students who are teaching in the Holiday Church School can reach Accra, that they were able to buy a spare tire for our bus, and that the driver, who has been ill, is well enough to drive. It seems that we never know what is going to happen from one day to the next. But we just keep going, and somehow God has enabled some things to be accomplished.

"The petrol situation is bad. We are allowed two gallons three days a week, if we can wait in line for hours to get it. Some public transport still keeps going, because there are no restrictions on them. But in some places there is just no petrol. I am sure that is why more people haven't reached here yet.

351

"Now I'll tell you about the student demonstration. As Mary and I started to town a couple of weeks ago we noticed a lorry full of students at the entrance to the university, with big signs protesting Nigeria's criticism of the execution of the former head of state in Ghana (also by England and the U.S.). Others were gathering. Later, as we were trying to return home, we were caught in the traffic jam caused by hundreds of marching students. They were waving branches from trees. As they marched past us they threw leaves and branches through our open window, and shouted, 'C.I.A.! Imperialists! We'll kill who [sic] we want! Go home! You're part of the problem!' Mary said, 'Here I thought that since I was black they would accept me.' I answered, 'Mary, you are still an American and that is what they think is important.' But she has a good sense of humor, and laughed about it.

"From there they went to the Nigerian embassy, and then to the British and American embassies, where they tore down the flags. They were protesting these countries' protest of the executions. It is the most anti-American feeling I have ever personally encountered in Africa. However, it is not universal. I am sure that many of the 'students' were not even university students–some looked too young, and I am sure many of the drifters who have no job and manage to survive by pickpocketing, etc. joined them. Actually, only a small percentage of the thousands of university students demonstrated. Classes continued as usual.

"I do not believe there is any danger for us. It is true the American embassy has asked all Americans to report, and for the first time in six years I have registered with them. But as long as I go about my business there will be no problem. Ghana has recently deported about twenty-five Lebanese, Indians, and Europeans, but these were business people.

"The food shortage is becoming acute because the farmers are refusing to take it into the cities to sell, for fear of the soldiers. The word is that an oil tanker has arrived in port. Perhaps in another week at least this present crisis will be over.

"I am no longer planning a vacation to the north, because of the petrol crisis. Now if it gets better, I will have no chance to contact people. But we will see. I know I must take some vacation somehow, and it is difficult to really relax at home when there is so much work to do.

"Mary's granddaughter, about nine years old, I believe, was to have arrived on Monday. I hope that she arrived all right, and that someone had enough petrol to take Mary to the airport to meet her. . . .

"It is past 8:00, and no more people have come. So I'm not having any meeting tonight. I must close now, and try to get a good night's sleep, to be able to make a good start tomorrow. I will mail these letters in Accra on Friday."

Ramseyer Training Centre
Abitifi via Kwahu
July 29, 1979

"It is a cool day, as is usual in the high hills of Abetifi. We are in the midst of our workshop for revising the Liberia-Sierra Leone United Methodist Sunday School Curriculum. We have only nine of the thirteen people I had hoped for, because of transportation difficulties. However, I am grateful for those who are here. They are working very hard. Six are graduates of Trinity, two of them also of the university. There are two women and one male who are teachers.

"As I said in my last letter, this is very much a venture in faith. . . .

Loading the Bus to Go to Apinamang

"I made a trip back to Accra on Thursday afternoon, and worked from the time I arrived at 5:30 until 2:00 a.m. on Saturday to get the team ready for the Holiday Church School in Apinamang. I am grateful that in spite of the transport difficulties because of the severe petrol shortage[4] all sixteen people were there. As usual, I found that the school had not done much to help me. They were still hunting for another tire for the bus–they were running with one of a double tire flat, and there is no spare. (Of course, I would have started hunting for a spare two years ago when they got the bus–but this is Ghana!)

At least the bus driver was well after having been in the hospital. They had made no contacts with a nearby Presbyterian Secondary School to see if they would lend their bus if we couldn't take ours. So I used precious petrol and time making two trips back and forth to see the headmaster. Fortunately, our driver came back at noon saying he had a tire (no spare, but at least all are fairly good now.) So I could tell Presbyterian Secondary that we didn't need their offer of the loan of their spare tire. Then I spent an hour and a half and more petrol trying to find kerosene to take to the village. The classes for youth and adults will be at night, after they return from their farms, and they must have kerosene for lights. I could find none, and could send only the little I had, also my pressure lantern. I hope they were able to find some on the way to Apinamang.

"I met with different groups of students all day, and then at night two students and I finished packing all the materials.

"I left yesterday morning at 7:30. The students were eating breakfast and were ready to load the many boxes of material on the bus. I am hopeful that this first Holiday Church School will be successful, and that we can pay for it, although I doubt that their offering at the end of the school will pay nearly all the cost. I had to pay transportation for the students to and from Trinity, and for their meals, in addition to lesson materials and some other supplies. I will go with the driver to Apinamang next Thursday, stay overnight, and return with the group the next day. Thus I will see the closing program, and visit with my namesake and her family.

"The next day after I return I will be giving last-minute training to the team to go for the Workshop for Youth and Youth Leaders. When this is over my engagements for the "long vac" will be finished. I hope that before then I can finish grading my papers. I have been able to do a few here, and hope to do more before I leave. There is writing I will have to do, but I won't feel under such pressure as I have the last months.

---

[4]The shortage at this time was due to the fact that Nigeria had stopped shipment of oil after Achaempong was executed. He was a friend of the Nigeria head of state. It was some time before they relented and sent more tankers. Also, there may have been a problem in Ghana's not paying its bills.

"Fortunately, some oil arrived in the country this week, and the refinery started work again on Wednesday. So by the end of next week the situation should be eased, at least for the present. . . .

"The food situation is becoming acute in the country. For one thing it is just before harvest in some areas. But the main thing is that people are refusing to sell at the price the government has set. Also, the lack of petrol has cut down on transportation of foodstuffs to the cities. People are queuing for staples such as rice. But in some places the soldiers have beat people standing in line, calling them lazy and accusing them of trying to buy and then sell at higher prices. In one place they forced a whole lot of women to lie on their backs in the square and stare at the sun. They have attacked women wearing pantsuits. Women as well as some men have been stripped naked and paraded, shaved and beaten. (They did this to the head of the Army's chaplains' corp.) The fact is that this has been a revolt of the lower ranks against the officers in the armed services, and discipline has broken down. So many officers have been arrested or flogged, etc., that they hardly dare to order the men to do anything.

"They have served good food here, although I get tired of having Ghanaian food three times a day for two weeks, but it is a struggle for them. Every day they have to hunt for food to keep us supplied.

"I met Mary Boatswain's granddaughter briefly. She is eleven instead of nine as I said previously. She told Mary that she heard a man on the plane say that a relative of his told him that when the mail stacked up because of the two border closings they burnt some of it so they could catch up. This may not be true, but certainly something has happened to our mail. . . .

"When I think of all that has been accomplished in the month since the school term ended, I am grateful and amazed that in spite of so many problems we have been able to achieve so much. I am grateful that God has given me the strength and so many fine people with whom to work. It is these I remember, and not the ones who threw leaves and branches at me and called me an imperialist!

"I am sorry that you were worried, mother . . . I hope Pat Rothrock called you with assurance that so far as I know there has been no violence against any Americans. About two dozen Lebanese, Indians, and a few Europeans were given twenty-four hours notice to leave, but these were people with businesses. The state is taking over a whole group of formerly Lebanese companies. If it is the same as all the other state corporations, they will soon be in the red.

"People have been warned to pay back taxes, and millions of cedis have been paid. Mercedes Benz cars have been taken back from various people who bribed to get import licenses or were given 'gifts.' Some good things have happened, but unfortunately there are the other things, too.

"The President and Vice President elect have moved into their offices, and are apparently beginning to plan. There is talk of bringing back state farms and the youth brigade that Nkrumah had (this party is the old Nkrumah party with a new name.) One of the men here said they had better stop first to evaluate what happened last time with these things. . . .

"I shall close now and get on to other letters."

"At last I am home, and glad that I don't have to go anywhere for a while. Yesterday I completed my last main responsibility before school starts. Now I can get on to all the work which needs to be done in my office, including grading papers from last term. Usually I have these finished and my grades in by the end of the first week after school is out, but this year it was impossible.

"I do have an all-day committee meeting (the Catholic-Trinity College committee on audio-visuals), but it will require no preparation by me, except to plan to feed five or six people. If it were Americans, we would each bring a sandwich, I would furnish coffee and fruit, and that would be it. But the Ghanaians don't like that kind of food, so I will open a big can of goulash which was given me, which I discovered my students like.

"On Tuesday we returned to Trinity with no problem. I got lunch for myself and the three people with me, put some more petrol in my tank, and delivered people to town where they were staying, or where they could get transport out of Accra. Transportation is so difficult now that it would have been cruel not to take them. I also did one or two errands for myself, making use of my trip to town.

"On Wednesday I had to go to the police licensing station to get a statement of ownership of my car so that I can get it valued. Like everything else in Ghana it took me a considerable amount of time. I wouldn't have gotten it at all if a man behind me hadn't made a big fuss because of the slowness with which people were taken care of (that was his second day in line) and accused them of taking people who approach them privately, of course with some money. This is true–it always is–but it is an interesting sign of the times that several policemen gathered round, trying to placate him and others who also began shouting, and some even started to help find the files of some of the people waiting. Previously, it would have meant only that the person didn't get waited on for sure, but there has been so much done to people who have taken bribes that people in authority now have some fear. Anyway, I was one of the last served. Then in the afternoon I had to make a trip out to a place where I hoped to get my car appraised. They did nothing but look at the tires, including the spare, and take my original customs papers. I don't see how they can know anything about the condition of a car without looking at the motor and testing it. Anyway, it was forty minutes to closing time, and the excuse was there wasn't time to take the fee to the office and get a receipt, so of course I have to use precious petrol and time to make another trip. The amount of time one uses to get anything done is incredible.

"I was lucky on Wednesday, and happened on a station which had only three cars in line. It was one of the days I could buy gas, according to my number. I also learned that the rule had been changed so that one can get six gallons each week, instead of having to sit in line on three different days to get two gallons a day. That in itself has meant some decrease in lines. So I got a full tank. Unfortunately, I had just put in one of the precious gallons I had saved, and couldn't take all the six. They are refining oil again, but Lt. Rawlings has warned that difficult days are not over. Apparently they have to hunt for the next oil from somewhere else.

"On Thursday I went with the bus to Apinamang, to be there for the last evening and to bring the students back on Friday. The last four miles of road into the village were very bad. This is the height of the rainy season, and there has been an unusual amount of rain this year, too much for

355

some of the crops. By the time we got to Apinamang one tire was flat. I have never discovered just what we did. Apparently we went with only one tire on the double tires–back to the main road (six or seven miles) the next day, when we got the tire repaired. But it was flat again by the time we got home.

"However, I was able to attend one of the last adult classes, and the closing program. The amount of noise can drive one crazy, but one has to accept this in Africa. The small church was packed with people, including many children, sitting on the floor and in every available place. There was hardly room for the performers. Of course, we had only lantern light. However, on the whole things went well. The people are very grateful.

"As I was walking back to his house afterward with Esther's father, on a dark night, the path lighted with a lantern light, he told me several times how much they appreciated what had been done. (He and his wife did much of the work, and contributed a good deal financially.) He said, 'We meet and read from the Bible, and sing, and go out, but we don't understand what we have read. Now we have learned many things. I know now what the "Kingdom of God" means! This will help us to be better Christians.'

And they do meet–every morning at 5:30 for prayers. I attended, with the students (who had taken turns being in charge during the week they were there) on Friday morning. This goes on in many villages–people meeting for prayer early in the morning, before they start the working day with daylight (6:00 a.m.).

"The problem is that the village could not begin to pay all the expenses of the School. The biggest cost is to pay the students' transport to Trinity and back home, and to feed them when they were here for their final briefing. The village fed them well there; that took a lot for sixteen people, but at least they had some food grown on the farms. They also gave me ¢100. But the cost will probably be more like ¢500 or ¢600 when I get it all counted. It will have to come out of funds given by the students from the Garden Party, although I feel it is a good project for some of my tithe also. Materials have now been prepared which, with an addition of translations of the hymns into other languages, can be used many times. But I don't know when the churches will be able to afford to use them.

"–which reminds me of the Curriculum Workshop. A lot of good work was done, and will continue. We have people with more education and better background (theological, biblical and educational) than the teams who wrote the material originally in Sierra Leone and Liberia. I was pleased that some of my former students saw the shallowness and errors in biblical and theological interpretation in some cases, and want to rewrite it. They are convinced of the need for this material for our churches in Ghana. But with the churches, and everyone else, struggling to survive economically, I don't know whether we can begin to convince them of the need for a large sum of money to print the materials here. We are going to try–but ¢90,000 for 3,000 copies of each of the four books for the first year, to be repeated two more years, is a lot to ask, even if we could get all the denominations together. But we cannot depend too much on outside resources. They have to find most of the resources within Ghana itself. Otherwise, work will not continue when the money is gone.

"On Friday evening and Saturday morning my six students who are leaving today for a week's workshop for workers with youth arrived (actually three were at Apinamang also). Again, we were fortunate that everyone was able to get here, in spite of transportation difficulties, although two were a little late. We spent all day yesterday going over the materials and study to prepare them for the week. Last evening we packed the materials. They will leave by bus at 10:00 a.m. today, and will return next Saturday, although they will get off in Accra to go on to other places, and I will not see them until school reopens.

"Now I feel that I can slow down a little, though there are endless things to be done just to finish the events of the last month. It will take me a long time to straighten out all the financial accounts, for example. Also, I still have to check and put away things which were used for the Holiday Church School. And, of course, there are my other uncompleted writing jobs and grading of papers. But now I don't feel under so much pressure. I had hoped to take two weeks for a vacation and go to the north, but this is impossible now. Perhaps Mary and her granddaughter, Mia, would like to go with me for a weekend at a Botanical Garden twenty miles from here. They have rooms for rent and a restaurant. For that distance I could get petrol. Otherwise, I am going to cut down to eight or nine hours of work a day, and spend the evenings on more relaxing pursuits . . ."

August 12, 1979

"This week has been less hectic, although I have of course been busy. I have spent several days just trying to figure out the finances for all my workshops and courses. Wednesday was spent

in town doing business and shopping. Mary and Mia went along. We took our lunch and stopped in at a friend's, and then continued on into the afternoon. I have also finished typing stencils for a project I've been working on for over a year–a series of worship services for a year, to use with children. Now it will have to be put together (100 copies) and I will have to take it to a press to staple it.

"Yesterday I spent in a committee meeting with the Catholics on producing the picture series we have been working on. This has been going on intermittently for three years. Everything goes so slowly because of lack of materials. Now we are handicapped by transport problems.

"I still haven't graded the last set of papers, and I must get on to that on Monday. I really dislike that kind of work, and I will be glad to finish it. Then I can start planning for a new term, which is only five weeks away . . .

"The petrol situation is no better. Although some oil has come into the country, apparently they are not sure of further supplies, and so are continuing rationing. Apparently in the Upper Region of the north the situation is really bad. There is no petrol and no kerosene, which is the only thing people have for lights, and some for refrigeration and cooking.

357

"This week all non-African immigrants had to report to immigration with all our documents and more photos for registration. No re-entry visas are being given, and one has to obtain permission at the army camp even to leave the country. Unless this is changed by the first of September there will be no chance for me to go to Lomé for a little vacation or for necessary shopping before school starts. Perhaps they are trying to discover the many people who left the country after the coup–?? They are out for the business people, but the rest of us have to suffer.

"I am still using petrol I brought back from Lomé, which has been added to somewhat since then, but I don't have much left. They no longer allow us to get it at the university. In town there are long lines. Many people leave their cars overnight and then go early in the morning to sit until they can get petrol. But we are five miles away from the nearest station since the university is closed to us, so that isn't practical. I am just going to have to resign myself to sitting in line most of the day before long if I am to get more . . .

"I hope you finally received my letters, and know that I am fine. There continue to be a lot of frustrations, but I am in no danger. . . ."

August 19, 1979

"It's a rainy Sunday morning. It rains almost every night during the rainy season, and it may clear later, but for now I am canceling a proposed trip to the beach after church. I had promised to take Mia and Mary, but it may have to wait for another day. We shall see.

"The petrol situation is getting worse instead of better. I am still getting along for the little driving I do on what is left of what I brought from Lomé. The lines are very long, and so far I have not wanted to take a day to sit in line. Some people have sat in line for hours and still not been able to get any. I will have to do it one of these days, however.

"I received a letter some time ago from a United Methodist who had planned to be in Ghana this week, and implied that he would like me to help him get around. He is doing some preliminary exploration of a study he wants to do of black American churches in Africa. I did not try to meet the plane he said he would be coming in on, as he said the travel agent was making a hotel reservation for him. First, I don't feel I can use the petrol; second, I wonder if he was even allowed in the country. Since they have canceled all re-entry visas, I suspect they may have canceled other visas also. I am still wondering about a friend who was in Nigeria on vacation when this ruling went in. She was supposed to return yesterday. . . .

"On Thursday I received a cable from Pat Rothrock [Area Secretary], sent exactly twenty-one days before! It had been received in Accra, they said, on August 8–I got it in Legon on the 16th. I can't imagine what they do with them--or why it should take thirteen days to get from New York to Accra, either. Anyway, apparently you have been worried, mother and contacted her, although this was not said. Pat said she is worried about my health and wanted to know whether I wanted a vacation outside the country. I replied that my health is good and that I can't leave the country because no re-entry visas are allowed. I do hope you will not worry about me. It is true that I have been very tired, and wanted to take a vacation. But, although I am still working, I am under no tension at this time, and am trying to take some time just to relax. Mary and Mia have helped me some evenings to sort a stack of Standard Publishing Company materials which some church spent a lot of money to send to me (very poor educational materials and narrow theology). That has been

358

rather fun. We celebrate with popcorn or a drink and cookies after a job. On two evenings I went to bed with a book at 6:30 or 7:00, and I sleep until I wake up, which is always early.

"For the last three days I have been working on grading final papers and notebooks, and am almost finished with my grades for last term, which is a job I will be very glad to have out of the way.

"I received a letter from the publisher of my book asking me to send autobiographical information for the cover as soon as possible, which I did.

"On Wednesday the school V-W bus took us to town, and I left my car to have new upholstery put on the two front seats. I saw two people on business, and we managed to do some shopping. It always seems to take a full day to get everything done–more business than buying. The big market is really scarce on food, compared to what it has always been. I am so grateful for the food I brought. I only hope we're going to be able to get to Lomé again before school starts. . . ."

September 9, 1979

"This has been another not particularly eventful week. We've been without water for a day, but it came on again at night. I've had electricity all week, but part of the houses on the campus, on a different line, have such low voltage that the refrigerators and stoves won't work. I took my car to town this week because Mary and I were invited out for dinner, but I still have no more gasoline. (Mia returned to the U.S. on Monday.)

"I have been working this week on plans for my classes for the new term. I'm trying to teach in a different way and see if I can have more success in getting the students themselves to work instead of depending on me to spoon feed them all the time. I am going to use a 'Skill Training Tape' I have from the Board of Discipleship on 'Teaching the Bible to Adults' for my class in adult ministry. In both classes I am dividing them into study/discussion groups; we will meet as a class only a few times during the term.

"I also finally have about one hundred thirty copies of a booklet, 'Let Us Worship God,' put together, and will take it this week to a press to get it stapled. This is a series of worship services for a year to use with children. It is always a lot of work to get these materials out. I do everything but actually run the mimeograph.

"I have taken time, however, for some relaxation. We enjoyed our 'night out' at our friend Erma Grove's home. She had two other Mennonite missionaries, so there were five of us single women. It was good food and we played games afterward. Then Friday night Mary came over and we played games again, and had popcorn, some that was still left from what I had bought in Liberia a year ago. Last night I started to work on my photograph albums with which I haven't done anything for three years.

"I have one more week before school begins. I want to get some odds and ends cleared up, get Spirit masters cut and run off, start on another series of worship services which we will use in the Sunday School this year and then will put into a book, and hopefully start on typing the revision of the Liberia-Sierra Leone Sunday Church School Curriculum.

"I am so pleased–Liberia has agreed for us to use the material, and has even asked us to do the Kindergarten material. This means more work for me, but I feel it is a contribution Ghana can make. Also, one of my former students who is working on the revision told me that he and another

member of the committee presented the project at their Anglican synod, and they have agreed to put in a good deal of money. If I can get the Sunday Church School curriculum well on its way before I leave, I feel I will have done something with really lasting benefit . . .

"The AFRC (Armed Forces Revolutionary Council) have announced that they will turn over to civilian rule on September 24 rather than October 1. Plans are being made for gradual turnover already in some areas . . .

"I will be speaking at the Women's Fellowship in the church here on campus this morning; it meets after the church service . . . "

And so ended my sixth year at Trinity College.

Chapter 7. Farewell
1979-1980

The 1979-1980 year, my last at Trinity, began with eighty-nine students including two women. Finally, one church–the Presbyterian–had decided to ordain women. Unfortunately, there was no place for them in the college dormitories, and they had difficulty finding a place to stay. But it was a first step.

Margaret (Maggie) Boama-Secu
& Mercy Adu

When students returned, I heard reports of their experiences during the long vacation period, including in the workshops. In Apinimang they now have a Sunday School as a result of our Holiday Church School there. The men who went to the Musama Disco Christo center to hold a workshop for youth and their leaders had a good experience. Before they went we listed a number of topics in which youth would be interested, and I provided some material the students could use to develop the course. They said everything went fine, except that they could not teach the section about marriage because the church believed in polygamy.

Some correspondence courses were being used, and more were being written. On October 16

we had our usual final party for the 1978-79 workshop team, complete with ice cream made in the freezer.

1978-79 Workshop Team

Back: C.W. Ackeifi, D. E. John-Teye, J. B. Impraim, D. F.
Gyan, G. B. Boateng, B. Ntreh
Middle: A. A. Adjei, A. Abraham, E. Appiah, S. R.   Bosomtwi-
Ayensee, M.Y. Adom, G. R. Akorli,
A. Owusu- Achaempong
Front: R. Addo, G. A. Ampiah-Bonney, E. E. Walters
Not Present: E. J. O. Quaye

We welcomed Father Mark Garrison, an Episcopal priest from the United States, as an addition to our faculty.

Civilian Government

On September 24, as promised, the AFRC (Armed Forces Revolutionary Council) turned power over to a civilian government. So, for the first time in years Ghana had a parliament and a president, Hilla Limann. There was freedom of the press, some of the "house cleaning" continued, and soldiers were removed from many of the positions they held under the military government. However, the economic situation was so bad that one wondered how much the government could do to help. We still had gasoline rationing, but the allotment was raised from six to eight gallons a week, to be bought on specific days and available only in certain places. This was more than I needed for Accra, but it was impossible to travel far. Just before Christmas the government subsidy was removed, and the price more than doubled. We then paid the equivalent of $3.25 for an American gallon. That was more than the minimum daily wage for a laborer.

A letter to my parents reports on events in October:

October 21, 1979

"It's early morning, after a downpour of rain which started in the middle of the afternoon yesterday and lasted on into the night. The croaking of the frogs mingles with the usual sound of insects, and it is cool. Since our weather is steadily becoming hotter, it is a welcome break.

"This week as usual has been busy. I have spent a good deal of time grading papers. There was our usual trip to town. We are collecting all the papers necessary for our trip to Lomé in two weeks. It all takes so much time. We still have to apply for and pick up our Togo visa; and we don't know whether we still have to obtain exit permits from the army, but will have to go see.

"I spent many hours this week writing my report for the Department of Church Leadership for the last year. When I look back over it, I marvel that we have been able to do as much as we have, with all the difficulties. It is true that a lot of time has gone into some things with small return in the number of people reached, but we continue with the hope that this number will grow.

"One example is the small extension class I started last year, with the hope that I might get at least one other center started. This was not possible. I had eleven sign up here, but only four are finishing–and even two of these missed on Saturday. We had to stop the classes last May because of transportation and other problems. I am making weekly trips out to a suburb in an effort to finish. I had hoped that could be next week, but we decided on Saturday that we would have to continue it one more week.

"I had a long and useful session with the workshop team in training on Friday afternoon. The last hour was spent in showing them how to use the projectors.

"I had a visit from a Ghanaian Anglican Sister who has been put in charge of Christian education for the diocese. She came to ask for my advice and help.

"I also spent some time working on suggestions for using some of the pictures in a set our Ecumenical Audiovisual Committee is still working on producing. We have been working on this project for four years, and no pictures printed yet. We have another all-day meeting on Monday. I hope they will report that the press has started printing the completed set.

"I have finally hired a former College office clerk, who lives next to me, to type some stencils for me and run them off. I can't keep up with all the typing I want done, and the office can't get them all run off. Now I have started a search for duplicating paper. The Ghana Publishing Company, where I have obtained supplies in the past, on the basis of being an educational institution, has nothing–no duplicating paper, no stencils, no ink, no chalk, no lined notebook paper.

"The situation is the same in the stores. I went into one of the big grocery stores this week just to see if they had anything. All there was were a few plastic buckets and other containers; a quantity of baking powder, not available for months (but there is no flour, so I can see why people aren't buying it); a little scouring powder; a few bottles of catsup. No meat or dairy products of any kind; no vegetables; no bread; <u>nothing</u>! This is the story all over. (There were still clerks in the store, with little to do; because the store is owned by the government, they still hire people.) One can buy fresh fruits and vegetables at the market; there is some fish; meat, especially beef, is rarely available. Bread was short for a while, but there is apparently a new supply of flour because we were able to get some at the bakery this week, and some women were selling it along the road again. A Mennonite friend was asked to check prices on some basic items, to help them judge whether their missionaries should have a cost of living increase. She said she hunted for basic furniture–couldn't find any; tried to find a chicken–impossible. In fact, she wrote her Board that she couldn't find most of what was on the list to price them! The fact is that we expatriates live off what we brought with us or what we get in Lomé, except for some fresh fruits and some vegetables. And to the cost of food in Lomé must be added the cost of getting all the papers necessary and the trip there. . . ."

Induction of a New Principal

On October 26 we had the induction of Dr. Sam Prempeh as Principal. He was Presbyterian, and took the place of the Rev. I. K. A. Thompson, Methodist, who had been our first Ghanaian principal. Dr. Prempeh had taught church history before going to England to continue his studies.

"I have good news this week! Pat Rothrock wrote that I have been given a grant of $10,000 for the Children's Hymnal, and $2,000 for producing worship materials for children. This should supply my needs quite adequately for the rest of my time here, in addition to the Advance Special funds which are being used to buy some necessary supplies and equipment (including audiovisual materials) for Kwaku to have to continue the program . . ."

[There was some discussion about the continuing effort to get someone to do some preparation for printing the hymnal, and to find where it might be printed in the U. S., since it was impossible to get anything printed in Ghana at that time.]

"There is a young man who is going to stop here for three weeks in December, on his way back from a conference in Nairobi, to work with Mary in the library. Pat Rothrock has told him to bring along his own food and toilet articles.

"The situation seems to get worse every day so far as basic supplies are concerned. There has been no fresh meat for a long time. Now there seems to be a shortage of flour again, for the bakery we usually go to didn't have bread on Thursday because they had no flour, and of course this is affecting other people who usually sell bread. The stores are nearly bare. We can still get a good supply of fruits and some vegetables which are grown locally. I am grateful for the 'camp foods' I have been using, though pretty tired of them. They all taste much alike. Also, some are spoiling. Apparently the heat spoils them even when they are vacuum packed.

"Incidentally–I say there has been no <u>fresh</u> meat, but there hasn't been any canned meat for years, except rarely, corned beef. There is fish, but it is high in price and I don't care much for it. It is a staple for the Ghanaians. I just don't know how people continue to survive.

"Government offices and schools are almost grinding to a halt because there are no ballpoint pens, even though some were manufactured in Ghana previously. And of course paper is not only extremely costly, but in very short supply. I may need to find a place from which we can import paper. We don't have an import license at Trinity College, but can import through the Christian Service Committee of the Christian Council.

"I had my last extension course yesterday, and the last full session of workshop training on Friday. Next Friday I will have an hour's session, and then have a party.

"I have been able to spend some time on the revision of the Sunday Church School Curriculum this week, and hope to be able to do more this next week.

"Last night Mary, Mark Garrison and I played bridge, as we have been doing for some time. (They had to teach me how to play it!), but I can see how it becomes an obsession with some people. We originally said we would play for an hour once a week–last night we played for three hours, and finally gave up with no one winning a game. But it is nice to have some recreation. . . ."

"Another Sunday, and a very busy one–I started work at 7:00 getting materials ready for the primary children of the Sunday School, who are working on Christmas decorations. Then I went to help put costumes on the junior children, who gave a play as part of their Sunday morning church service. Things went quite well–I'm the only person who is bothered if an 'Egyptian soldier' insists on wearing his cap, and some of the characters don't have costumes at all, or if there is a long pause between scenes–so I don't let it bother me too much. On the whole, however, things went well, and I hope it was a good experience for the children as a climax to their unit of study. Afterward they joined the primary children for a "Praise Parade," which was a climax of a series of worship services.

"I am going over to get the youth groups started with the materials they need for making gifts and Christmas decorations. The student teachers take charge, but I just need to get some things out for them. Later I will observe one of them teaching.

"On Friday twelve of us Americans, and one Ghanaian who is married to an American, celebrated Thanksgiving. Thursday was just too busy a day to do it. We all met at my house, and everyone contributed. I still had some cranberry sauce which I brought with me; we bought chickens in Lomé, and also some mincemeat; someone made pumpkin pies from local squash; we had candied sweet potatoes from a can, with marshmallows the U.S. AID people bought at the P.X.; someone contributed a can of American corn and beets; and we had salad. So it was a sumptuous meal, although the only turkey was the picture on the paper table cloth which I bought on sale the summer of 1975 when I was in the U.S. It was a nice time. We remembered our fellow Americans being held hostage in the embassy in Iran, however.

Mary Boatswain, Erma Grove, Sr. Rose, awson Adzaku, Mark Garrison

Anna Kurtz, Vi Adzaku, Martins

Anna Kurtz & Vi Adzaku

"We are in the midst of planning for our Christian Family Life Institute now, and also for the Youth Workers' Institute on December 8. Again I didn't spend as much time as I would have liked on the revision of the Sunday Church School Curriculum. There always seem to be other more pressing matters to take care of.

"It's getting hotter now, as it always does this time of year, but we are still having rains occasionally. We are having an unusual amount of rain this year. This should be the dry season.

"I am expecting little Esther and her father, mother and baby brother on the 22nd to spend Christmas and Boxing Day here. I have not yet told them that I am leaving Ghana in July for good, but must do so this time. I also expect to have Arba Herr, who was with the Board of Christian Education in Nashville, I believe, but has been working on a special assignment in Liberia, working on the Sunday Church School Curriculum (the one we are revising for publishing here.) . . . .

"We finally got one correspondence course out, and another is on its way. Two who are working on one on church history have shown me what they have done, and they are making good progress. The problem is in getting people to know about them. The church headquarters are doing very little. I paid a lot of money to advertize in the paper, and have had two replies this week. Others may come, but the mail is so slow that it will take time. . . ."

Events in December
Christmas Party December 14, 1979

On December 14 Mary and I joined with our Mennonite friends for a Christmas party in their home in Amasaman; we had our Christian Family Life Institute the following weekend, and of course before the students left for their Christmas holiday, our usual Christmas parties for the Sunday School.

Mary Boatswain

Lydia Burkhart

Youth Christmas Party

Christian Family Life Institute
December 17

Staff Children's Christmas Party

Margaret (Esther's Cousin) & Esther, rt.

Margaret and Esther

*Boxing Day Ice Cream–Mark Garrison
& Mary Boatswain*

Trip to Cape Coast

Some of Mary Boatswain's family visited her at the end of December and in January, and so on January 1 we, with Araba Herr, made a trip to Cape Coast. We stayed in the Elmina Hotel, and visited the sights there, including the Wesley Methodist Church, and of course, the two castles where Africans were once kept until they could be put on to ships and sent as slaves to the New World. This was most meaningful to them.

Lunch by the Roadside

*Albertha Sistrunk, Mary Boatswain,
Cyril Shepard, Arba Herr*

371

Breakfast at Elmina Motel

January and February 1980

In a letter sent to my mailing list after I returned to the U.S. I outlined some events of these months:

"The months since I last wrote were more than full, as I worked to try to complete some of the many projects in which I was engaged. Classes continued as usual, and much time was spent in writing and planning. In January a small group met for a week to plan and begin writing a two-year cycle for kindergarten children for the 'Food for Christian Growth' Sunday Church School Curriculum, which was being produced by churches in Liberia and Sierra Leone. They accepted our offer to contribute by writing the kindergarten lessons, and several writers are continuing to work on the first year materials. Also, revision and editorial work on a Ghana edition of the Primary I book has continued. Several correspondence courses for pastors and lay persons are in process. Many hours were spent on the children's hymnal, which will be produced in English, and we hope eventually in three Ghanaian languages. All of these yet remain to be edited, and I hope to be able to finish some of them from here.

Charles Ackeifi–Use of Pictures

"Our annual Accra workshop for teachers of children in the church had the largest attendance ever–178. As much as I regretted it, I had to turn people away because we simply had no more room for them. We had several interest centers on 'How to Teach

Bible Stories to Children,' led by Trinity College students who were members of the workshop team.

Elizabeth Aggrey and
E. Walters–Game

G. A. Ampiah-Bouney–
Costumed Story Teller

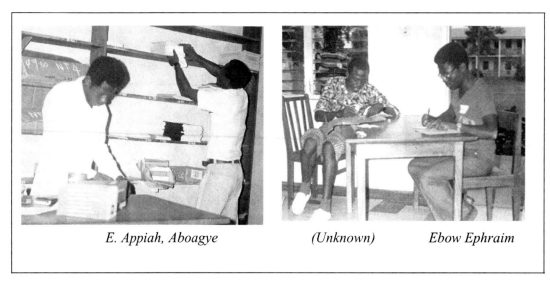

E. Appiah, Aboagye   *(Unknown)*   *Ebow Ephraim*

"Additional time was spent in extra training in youth work for workshop team members, and to give help to two students who were to spend a month of concentrated work in leadership education for their long vacation field education assignment.

"Plans were nearly complete for the one-week residential course for pastors and lay persons when I left. That was held in the first week of August. . . ."

Farewell to My Mother

In March I received a delayed cable from my brother telling of our mothers' serious illness and urging me to return home. I did not know whether she was still alive by the time I received the cable. We had no functioning telephone, so I tried two different missions who had ham radio contact with the States. However, one said that the missionary who had the license to use it was on furlough, and another that the equipment was rusted so much, due to its nearness to the sea, that they could only contact someone on a Saturday at a certain time who would be listening for their message. Then I finally thought of the U.S. Embassy (which I should have thought of before, but I had had no time for making contacts with other Americans who were not on the Trinity staff). They were able to get a cable through to my brother, although with the time difference it still took until the next day to get an answer.

The Embassy then delivered the following messages, as they arrived:

DEPCFF called Megill residence and spoke to Mr. Keith Megill's wife. Mrs. Megill said that her mother-in-law, Mrs. Pearl Megill, is still hospitalized and being treated for congestive heart failure and cardiac arrest. She is currently in the coronary care unit at the hospital. Although she has improved somewhat from last week, her condition is still very serious and due to her age (82) doctors are not sure of the prognosis. Family considers it very important for Ms. Esther Megill make arrangements to return home ASAP. Mrs. Megill said she should have sufficient funds but family willing to assist if necessary.

Department has been in contact with Keith Megill who advised that attending physicians stated that mother is doing better, but that if at all possible Ms. Megill should try to come home. Brother, Keith, advised that he is willing to offer any financial assistance needed.

I therefore immediately returned to the United States, and had two weeks with my mother, whom they moved from the hospital to the nursing section of the retirement home in which my parents lived. I also used the time to get some necessary dental work, and to make contact with companies and persons I had been trying to get information from for the children's hymnal. Two of my other brothers also came, and we had some time together as a family, and I had time with mother.

Two weeks after I returned to Ghana, I received a message from the Embassy telling of my mother's death on April 10. The students and faculty of the school were very sympathetic, and planned a memorial and thanksgiving service for her which was held in the College chapel.

More Farewells

On April 14 the whole school had a farewell party for Mary Boatswain, who had done so much for us in the library.

Mary Boatswain

Mrs. Prempeh, Mary Boatswain, A. A. Akrong,
A.A. Otoo, C.R. Ahorble

A.A. Akrong and Mary Boatswain

*Student President C. K. Ahorble Presents
a Gift*

Trinity Staff 1979-80

Back: A.A. Akrong, L. K. Buama,
Mark Garrison
Front: Maclean Kumi, Esther Megill,
S. Prempeh (Principal)

In June there were the closing graduation ceremonies.

Closing Ceremonies

Dr. Esther Megill

Before the students left there were farewells for me. The students delivered some glowing statements (greatly exaggerated), as seen on the following pages. They and the college also gave me gifts. The students gave me a carved ebony lamp stand, of a woman nursing her baby. The college Student President said this was because they honored me as their mother. Others gave a strip of Kente cloth which had designs they felt significant and books with words of appreciation written in them.

Farewell Luncheon

DR.   ESTHER   MEGILL-

AFRICA   IS   GRATEFUL

TO   YOU

****

1. The love for the LORD's work was burning within her,
   Yet she would not say this with words,
   But to demonstrate her zeal with works.
   She left her American home for Africa in 1951,
   And her works continue to live in the
   Medical Technological History of Sierra Leone.
   How can the Missionary annals of Liberia and
   Nigeria be ungrateful to her name?
   And how can Algeria and Tunisia
   Forget about her deeds?

2. Thou who entered the power house of Ghana,
   Full of zeal and full of spirit.
   The older she grew, the brighter the
   Fire in her glowed.
   She was more a Pastor than a theological tutor,
   And we saw a male soldier at work
   But not the picture of a female civilian.
   A living testimony to ministerial students
   That the Christian is a soldier of Christ,
   Alas! It is such a Mother who leaves Trinity soon.

3. As the Aircraft shoots into the Air,
   How can we help gazing into the sky
   With grief and pain in our hearts?
   Our eyes shall desire to follow
   The craft till it lands her at home,
   And our ears shall strain to hear
   The booming noise to the journey's end.
   But yiee the limited faculties of men.
   Moments later, and we are cut off from
   The sight and sound in pain.

4. Yet when wishes have failed
   And we stand gazing into empty air,
   She won't like us continue bearing the pangs in pain
   But to take solace from our Spiritual Union with her,
   And live with the precious knowledge and
   Literature she has bequethed to Africa.
   Yes, she is a great Mother whose children
   Inherit the treasure which endures to eternity.
   Nothing can our best parting gift be
   Than to keep the flames of her fire ever glowing.
   Trinity College leads Africa to say:
   BRAVO! Thou Lovely and dutiful Mother.

N.B. This poem was written and read by Alexander Akwasi
      Amankwaa (Secretary to the S.R.C.) on the occasion
      of Dr. Esther Megill's departure from Trinity College,
      Legon to America in June, 1980. Dr. Esther Megill
      had been a Lecturer and the Head of the Christian
      Education, Psychology, Audio-Visual and Liturgics
      departments since 1973.

Farewell Gift from College Board

The Farewell Poem & Gift from Students

379

–And a Gift from the Staff
MacLean Kumi, Vida Kumi

The Sunday School also gave me a party, with the children and the teachers, including the lay teachers from the church who always took over in vacation periods. The children sang some of the songs we had taught them, and danced.

S.S. Teachers--Kwaku Asamoah-Okyere on my right

What the children liked most!

Prophet Mills, Faith Brotherhood Praying Circle

The Communion Service

On my last Sunday I attended the service of the Faith Brotherhood Praying Circle, one of the spiritual churches which had sent many people to my workshop. I met the Prophet before the service and told him I would be leaving Ghana on Thursday. I also asked to take some photographs of the service. He said he would ask the people, and reported that they agreed. So I was able to take some photos of their communion service and other activities. [Ghanaians did not mind having photos taken during a service or marriage ceremony–but wanted to know how the photographer use them.]

Before the service was over Prophet Mills told the congregation that I would be leaving, and expressed appreciation for being able to share in some of the learning events. He also said, "If I had known you were leaving, we would have had a gift ready for you. But if you will go [to a room behind], Sister____ will measure you, and we will have something for you at the airport."

Of course they did – another gown. I had to carry it on the plane, but I appreciated their gift very much.

The Final Days

After the College closed there was a flurry of work, as I packed, disposed of unwanted accumulations and prepared to turn things over to Kwaku Asamoah-Okyere, who returned to Ghana two weeks before I left, after receiving his MA in Religious Education at Scarritt College in Nashville, TN. We worked many hours, and I knew that I was leaving my work at Trinity College in good hands.

When I left Ghana on July 12 several students in the Accra area came to see me off, and I received the parcel from the representative of the Faith Brotherhood Praying Circle. I was very tired, and was sad to leave after seven years of work and learning to know so many students and others in Ghana. However, I looked forward to meeting a friend in Amsterdam, and we had a great time visiting England, Scotland, Holland, Switzerland and Germany. I visited friends, several of whom had taught previously at Trinity College, and of course went sightseeing. The climax was the Passion Play at Oberammergau on August 8. I arrived in the United States on August 10, ready to start a new chapter in my life.

Ghana 1980-1989

The new civilian government was not able to solve the economic stagnation of Ghana. During 1980 Jerry Rawlings gained more and more popularity as he continued to demand an end to corruption. Internal conflicts finally broke up the ruling party, and on Dec. 31, 1981, Rawlings took power again in a military coup. According to an article in *The Knoxville* [Tennessee] *News-Sentinel*, January 1, 1982:

"Rawlings announced on the radio the establishment of a Provisional Military Council, and he said Thursday's takeover was 'not directed against officers of the armed forces,' although its backing apparently came from junior military men. He said a 'people's defense organization'–apparently a militia–would be set up alongside the existing military establishment.

"In the broadcast, Rawlings appealed to Ghanaians not to harm Limann, a 51-year-old doctor and former diplomat. Rawlings asked Limann to remain in his presidential quarters.

"'I am prepared at this moment to face a firing squad if what I've tried to do for the second time in my life does not meet with the approval of Ghanaians,' he said."

An article in the January 3 issue of the same paper stated that "Ghana's new rulers, who seized power by force, on Saturday dismissed Parliament, suspended the constitution and banned political parties. Rawlings lashed out at the 'greed and corruption' of politicians and bureaucrats, saying they 'have turned our hospitals into graveyards and clinics into death transit camps because of lack of medicine and supplies.'"

A *New York Times* article of January 5, 1982, reported that "President Hilla Limann of Ghana, who was overthrown last week in a military coup, was arrested this morning as he was apparently trying to flee the country, the Accra radio announced today. . . . The state-run radio station . . . also said that all personal and business assets of the deposed president, his Cabinet and the 140 members of the dissolved Parliament had been 'frozen' by the new Government . . . In the capital itself, hundreds of demonstrators took to the streets shouting slogans in praise of Mr. Rawling's coup. 'Jerry, our Savior!' they cried."

The New Mexico Daily Lobo, May 5, 1982, printed a letter written by Elisa Poulsen, a Peace Corps volunteer in Ghana. She wrote, ". . . There is absolutely nothing in the markets now except produce–tomatoes, onion, pepper, etc. . . . No one will sell anything at the enforced low prices for fear of the soldiers. All commodities are supposedly distributed and sold at control prices . . . I still haven't seen them, and don't expect to. I'm sure black marketing and selling things out the back door continues, but very quietly. People are very afraid. Many market places and kiosks have been burned; market women have been beaten for overpricing . . . [She continues with the difficulty of transportation because of the lack of petrol.] There was evidence of the support by Libya, and an anti-American attitude which had not been there before. Soldiers, carrying arms, were much in evidence, many showing their power in frightening ways." She reported an event in Kumasi, saying "A soldier was killed in a church by the congregation–supposedly he was waving his gun around, telling the people to get out and fill potholes; the minister told him to leave, and the soldier took aim. A police woman in the congregation knocked him down and the congregation beat him (to death). When the news got out, soldiers seized the minister and beat him to death; they drove the body around Kumasi on the front of a truck and forced people to spit and urinate on the body Then the body was burned in the main circle.'"

In an August 3, 1982 personal letter from England by Stephen Dawes, a Methodist minister who had been teaching at Trinity College and was preparing to return to Ghana after a brief furlough, wrote:

"The situation in Ghana is bad . . . We heard from friends at the University last week, saying that garden lizards are now for sale as meat; such is the shortage, and the customary June-August lean time for local produce began this year in March . . . . It is almost impossible to sum up the situation since the coup, except to say that tiny superficial improvements in the economy which we were seeing under the Limann government have ceased entirely and the economy just seems to have stopped; the mood of the people is moving towards despair. High Commission friends say that it is only a matter of time before there is another coup but after that it's anyone's guess. However, the College and church are prospering despite the setbacks; and we have no hesitation in returning."

During 1982-83 there were several coup attempts by dissatisfied parts of the army. However, by 1984 the economy finally showed signs of improvement, and Ghana was able to obtain loans from the IMF, and development agencies in the West began to pour vast sums into the country. President Kaunda of Zambia declared that "Ghana is our Mecca." Ghana in those years had the highest growth rate in Africa. It was touted as a showcase of Third World development and a bright light for Africa. By 1985, however, the prisons were crowded with political prisoners.[5]

The Rev. Kwaku Asamoah-Okyere continued the work in Christian education, and was given other responsibilities by the college and the Church.

In December of 1986 as I was on the way to a special event in Sierra Leone I stopped in Ghana for a short visit. I visited the Sunday School party, the Christian Family Life Institute (now a week long and held during the December vacation), and was introduced to a class which was using my book. Kwaku took me to the fish pond he had started, and also the pig project and the college farm. All these things helped to feed the students. (Kwaku had been given this responsibility, and others, in addition to his work in Christian Education.)

Mary Kwakye and Esther came to see me and I visited Sister Mary Ann. It was good to see all that had happened since I had left Ghana in 1980–this in spite of the political and economic problems.

5

"Ghana–Timeline," *The Crawford.dk Home Page* and "Ghana on a Road to Freer Economy," *Insight*, Sept. 12, 1988, Vol. 4, No. 37.

Kwaku Asamoah-Okyere

The Fish Pond

The Ewe Children–Dancing and Drumming

The Drama

387

Lighting the Advent Candles

Reading the Scripture in Twi, Ga, and Ewe

Refreshments

388

Christian Family Life Institute

Meeting Old Friends

With Sister Mary Ann (on right)
(and another Sister, name unknown)

Mary Kwakye, Esther,
Esther Megill

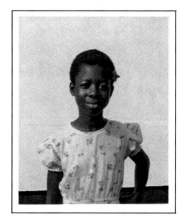

Part III

African Odyssey
1989-1990

Introduction

In 1989 I retired from my position with the North Mississippi Conference of The United Methodist Church, and Wood Junior College in Mathiston, Mississippi. I had planned for some time to return to Africa for a year of volunteer work after my retirement, inspired by my desire to complete some of the work I had left unfinished in Ghana. I had extensive correspondence with Kwaku Asamoah-Okyere in Ghana and the heads of various African churches and others, so I felt I could contribute something to the churches. I began my "Odyssey" September 27, 1989, when I left for Sierra Leone, my first appointment. On December 10 I flew to Ghana, and stayed there until December 30, when I left for Nigeria. After two and a half months in that country, I went on to Zambia (March 17, 1990), on July 1 to Kenya, and then, on my trip home (when I went around the world), a stop in Egypt as a tourist before going on to Israel/Palestine and the Philippines. The following information is taken from a journal I kept during that time, and photographs and scrapbooks.

AFRICA

From p. 15, *Prayer Calendar 2007*, Daniel Licardo, ed. Women's Division, General Board of Global Ministries, The United Methodist Church, c. 2006 by the General Board of Global Ministries. Used by permission. (Shading added.)

Chapter 1. Sierra Leone

I arrived in Sierra Leone on the night of September 28, and was met by the Rev. Francis Tommy, from the United Methodist office in Freetown. Even before we met, however, I was greeted by one of the men in customs who said, "Are you Miss Megill? I was with Morlai Turay [my laboratory assistant] in Rotifunk." He must have been in my Children's Church. I was let through customs with no problem. Rev. Tommy was just outside and gave me a hug in greeting. (He told me later that he had spoken with the customs people; that explained my easy pass through.) So I felt the warmth with which I was received.

I also met Angie Myles, the coordinator of the Medical Center program. Rev. Tommy had come in the car with her and others were there to meet Mike Cunningham, a doctor who had come to work in the eye clinic for a month. Some of my loads were left at the clinic, and Rev. Tommy took me in his V.W. "Bug" with two suitcases to the house near Congo Cross where I would be staying. It was rented by the Conference for missionaries and short-term volunteers. The house smelled musty and stale since no one had been in it for some time, but I opened windows and made a bed with sheets which were there, and boiled some water to drink. It was good to have a shower, even with cold water and in the dark, since the lights weren't working in the bathroom, and then go to bed. It had been a long trip from New York.

The Guest House – the Conference Rented the Lower Floor

The Scene Across the Street

On the next day, Friday, I woke up with the alarm clock, ate a breakfast of instant oatmeal which I had brought with me, and did some unpacking before Rev. Tommy came for me. He took me to the office, where I met the principal of the Theological Hall where I would be teaching–Rev. Dr. Markwei, and the Director of Studies, John Mills, from Britain. I was told that I would teach the third year, two hours on Monday and one on Tuesday.

Rev. Tommy then took me to the Paramount Hotel for a good lunch. He was to send someone in his car to drive for me, but he couldn't get anyone, so took me himself to do some necessary shopping. I bought fruits, vegetables and rice from the market women along the road, and some supplies at Choitram's, a department store. At about 4:30 he took me home. Lights were out, and thus the refrigerator. (I soon learned to expect this frequently.) I ate some bread and jam, coffee and an orange for supper, and one piece of Swiss chocolate I had bought in holland. I had a stove with an oven (of sorts) run on bottled gas, and a refrigerator which was cold some of the time, when the electricity was on long enough. So, in the days that followed I managed to cook some meals for myself, and even have guests occasionally. It was a good thing I was used to stying alone, for I knew there would be long days and nights of being alone. But I enjoyed my tape player, and reading in my spare time.

The next day I cleaned bathrooms and cupboards, and unpacked my things after Rev. Tommy brought the rest of the baggage. Then it was time to begin work on lesson plans.

I woke up with the rain the next morning, and Rev. Tommy picked me up for church at King Memorial, the largest and oldest United Methodist Church in Freetown. It was World Communion Sunday. There I saw several people whom I knew, and others introduced themselves. Daniel Mondeh, one of my former students in Ghana, was an associate minister. He greeted me with an African hug, and introduced me during the sermon. Nancy and David Forrest, missionaries, and their children were there, and she invited me home for a chili dinner. We then went to meet Stuart and Janet Clarke, British missionaries. The rest of the day was spent in napping, writing letters, and doing more preparation for teaching.

David Forrest arrived at 8:00 a.m. on Monday morning to take me first to his house, and then to the Theological Hall, where I taught my first classes, which went well. I then went to town in a taxi, ate, and went to the Conference office. In my wandering around town I met another former Trinity College student, Edward Kargbo, and Van Jollie, a United Methodist Committee on Relief (UMCOR) missionary, who was stationed at Yonibana and was digging wells. I needed some money, and discovered that the only way I could get it was to go with Van to a Lebanese merchant, who gave me leones (the local currency) for a check payable to his son in the U.S. The conference treasurer did not want to cash my check because he would have trouble getting cash from the bank for it. So, from then on I dealt, reluctantly, in the black market, as did everyone else who lived in Sierra Leone.

Sunset at Lumley Beach

That evening Van took me out to eat at a restaurant on Lumley Beach. There was a lovely sunset and the view of the ocean at night as I ate a salad and chicken kabob.

I was grateful to Van, who would take me to eat, and to other places when he was in town on business.   My second class was on Tuesday, and I enjoyed it, as I had the first. One of the students, James Boy Caulker, told me that his father was Julius, who had worked in the laboratory at the hospital in Rotifunk when I was there, and that he had been in my Children's Church.   The next day, after a quiet morning of reading, writing letters, and sorting my materials, David Forrest took me to the Clarkes for lunch, along with the Forrests and a doctor who had been there for three months. We each contributed something; I had some Dutch spice cake I had bought in Amsterdam. We enjoyed the conversation. The doctor said there was much malnutrition and extreme poverty in the villages, but that the upper-class Sierra Leoneans had little understanding of the conditions under which many of the people lived.

Dinner at the Clarkes'

Stuart and Janet Clarke, at the Aqua Club

The Clarkes frequently took me places, such as the British Council or the Aqua Club, where we would have a good meal and sometimes watch a video on T.V. The Forrests also invited me to their home, or we went out to eat, and perhaps to the beach to swim. Also, people who were visiting or had come from upcountry would be at the guest house. One was a young mission intern who was making her way around Africa. An Operation Classroom work team stayed overnight before going upcountry. Lennie (Arlene) Hache from Taiama and Pat Bowers, Manjama-Bo, both nurses, also were in town. Other missionaries came at intervals. When they and others were in town with a car, they would take me with them to eat or to the beach. We often played games when there were visitors. Since the lights were frequently off, it was at times by lantern or candlelight. Several times I invited some of these friends for a meal, or we shared food and ate together when there were others staying in the house. On one Thursday when Van and I were eating a lunch of bread, peanut butter and jelly, cheese, cucumbers, tangerines and bananas, I suddenly remembered that it was Thanksgiving!

At times I just listened as the missionaries talked about their many frustrations. Some were not well. One was very depressed. I sympathized with them at times, but also felt that they were not always right. I began to wonder whether all missionaries shouldn't be withdrawn until the church could sort out what they wanted.

UMC Misionaries at Lakka Beach

Playing Rook: M. Schultz, B. Walter, N. Forrest, E. Megill

When I was returning from teaching at the Theological Hall, I often stopped to eat in a restaurant in town. Francis Tommy provided help as needed. He offered me a car, but after seeing the traffic in Freetown, I declined. This meant I rode by taxi or bus and did a lot of walking. At times I was picked up by former students at Harford School, someone who had been in my Children's Church in Rotifunk, or a missionary who was staying at the guest house. Almost everywhere I went, I saw people who had known me–adults who had been children in the Sunday School at Rotifunk; former students whom I had taught for a short time at Harford School for Girls, Moyamba; and others I had known as Area Secretary. I stayed in the homes of some, was given rides by others in Freetown, and everywhere was greeted as if I had returned home. The Conference driver, Abdulai Jalloh, took me to the places where I held workshops.

Since I had been in Sierra Leone as Area Secretary (1972), the Sierra Leone United Methodist Church had become autonomous on February 13, 1973, with the Rev. B. A. Carew as its first bishop. However, when a new bishop (the Rev. Thomas Bangura) was elected, the decision had been made to become a Central Conference of The United Methodist Church. It was October 9 before I was able to greet the bishop. (I had known him as an evangelist in Moyamba.)

On October 11 I was invited to attend part of the plenary session of the Conference Programming Boards, where I was greeted royally by a number of people whom I had known in other years–Eustace Renner, George Sandi (student in Ghana), Alice Fitzjohn, Ada Bailor, Etta Nichol, and others. I also met members of the Operation Classroom work team who were there. At the Christian Education meeting I was given a schedule of workshops which I would hold.

When I returned home, I thought of the contrast between the cordial welcome I had received and the bad feelings which had been expressed between Conference members and missionaries.

I continued to enjoy meeting missionaries, which included those from Germany and Sweden, and Sierra Leonean friends. My namesake, Esther Bailor Momoh (Paramount Chief Madame Honore Bailor-Caulker's daughter), came to visit me with her sons, Nyakɛ and Dieter, and Honoria brought gifts.

I was invited by Alice Fitzjohn to the 74th birthday party for her husband Willie on November 5. There was rice with meat and fish stew, Jollof rice, salad, sweet potatoes, punch and ginger beer, pumpkin pie (she had learned to make that in the U.S.), birthday cake, banana bread and rice bread. As I arrived, Shirley McCauley was leaving. She had been in my biology class at Harford School years ago, and met me joyfully. The next morning as I was trying to get a taxi to the Theological Hall, Shirley stopped and picked me up. I discovered that she was the head of personnel at the Bank of Sierra Leone. She had the driver take me on to the Hall, so I arrived in a large, air-conditioned car. On other days other persons whom I had known from previous years stopped to pick me up. A ride, as always, was welcome, for it was often difficult to get a taxi or bus.

The Sierra Leone Theological Hall and Church Training Centre

Teaching two classes a week in Christian education at the Theological Hall and Church Training Centre was rewarding. The theological hall had been started in 1975, largely through the efforts of an Anglican Church Missionary Society couple, Rev. Philip and Mrs. Betty Ross.[1] Another Anglican couple, Rev. Stuart and Mrs. Margaret Baxter, also worked there in the early days, as did Rev. Hugh Thomas, a British Methodist who had been a missionary in Ghana and also the Africa area secretary of the British Methodist Church. (I had met and consulted with Mr. Thomas in that capacity when I was the Africa Secretary for The United Methodist Church). In 1980 Monica Humble, a Methodist missionary, set up the Extension Department of the Hall (Theological Education by Extension).

The Theological Hall started at the United Methodist Church's Albert Academy, a secondary school for boys, from 1975-1983, then moved to the Anglican Old Bishop's Court in the summer of 1983. It was there when I arrived, but a cotton tree had fallen on it during a storm

The Theological Hall

The Building to Which They Moved

[1]The United Methodist Church had begun plans for a theological school during the last year I was the Area Secretary.

in the early hours of May 28, 1987. We had no electricity most of the time. The secretary had an office upstairs. The stairs were in such bad condition that they did not encourage anyone else to go up there. I wondered how he could see. It was difficult for the students also; and I was there in the dry season, when the sun was shining all day. Shortly after I left, early in 1990, the school moved to the former Methodist Boys' High School building.

The principals after Philip Ross were all West Africans. At the time I was there the principal was Dr. Matei Markwei from Ghana. All principles since then have been Sierra Leoneans.[2] The Hall remained a cooperative project of the Anglicans, Methodists and United Methodists, although students from other denominations, including some of the independent or "Spiritual" churches, attended. Two of my students had been in my Children's Church at Rotifunk when they were small children. I was in Sierra Leone long enough to teach an entire term, and was able to use the textbook, *Education in the African Church*, which I had written and used in Ghana.

A Classroom on the Veranda

Youth/Adult Ministry Class

James Boye Caulker

David Forrest Serving Communion

---

[2]Much of this information was obtained from the Rev. Stuart Clarke, who was head of the TEE program at the Hall when I was there, and who consulted with others in England who had served there to obtain information.

During my time at the Hall during the three hours a week I taught I gave intensive courses in teaching and learning, and on ministry with children, youth and adults. I also made assignments and graded papers for the extension course on Christian Education. Some students did well, but others did not. Several were disappointed with the grades, but I could not pass anyone who had not done the work, or give a good grade if they had not done it well. Before I left, I worked out a suggested curriculum for the Hall, and presented it to the principal and the Director of Studies. They seemed receptive to the suggestions, but I do not know whether they were actually followed.

Before I left, I was able to see the building to which the Theological Hall would be moved. It was a great improvement.

The graduation ceremonies were held at a secondary school on the afternoon of November 18. Those of us in the staff sat on the platform. I was asked to announce a hymn. Classes continued, however. I had my last one on December 5. Mary Boatswain and I attended the communion service. The Principal said some meaningful farewell words. In closing they sang "God Be With You 'Til We Meet Again," and we shook hands all around.

Before that time Ted and Rosemary Townsend had arrived. They were to teach at the Theological Hall. Shortly after, on November 30, the Clarkes left. They took me to the Aqua Club, and were my guests for a farewell luncheon.

Workshops

I enjoyed holding four workshops for Sunday School teachers in different places–Freetown, Yengema, Bo and Moyamba–and one with a small group in Freetown whom I helped to get started in writing materials for their youth camps. I had brought quite a few handouts (most of it excess baggage), and otherwise used only a few things which could be easily gathered. I did not want to suggest anything that people couldn't get, because I wanted them to feel that they could improve their Sunday Schools. Also, I tried to help them learn how to develop a lesson for children using a Bible passage, since that was usually all they had.

Freetown

The first workshop was held at King Memorial in Freetown, on a Friday afternoon and Saturday. Alice Fitzjohn had prepared the room before I arrived. Sixteen persons attended on Friday, and there were eighteen before we finished on Saturday. Everyone seemed to appreciate it.

Playing a Bible Game

Yengema

*Abdulai Jalloh,
the Conference Driver*

My most memorable journey was to Yengema, in the Kono area, known for its diamonds. Since the years I lived in Sierra Leone the railroad had been taken out, and many more roads built. However, these were in bad condition in 1989. Also, it was difficult to get parts for the car, including tires, and petrol was scarce. I had hoped to leave early, but it was 3:30 before we were on our way. The first twenty-five miles to Waterloo were on good hardtop road–then the potholes began. About thirty miles out of Lunsar a tire went flat. The driver and the "motor boy" who was with us put on the spare tire, but it was late in the afternoon then, and would soon be dark. I told the driver that we would have to spend the night in Makeni. Fortunately, I knew the Rev. Mary Johnson, who was District Superintendent. I had in fact met her the day before in Freetown. When I found her house, I discovered that she had not yet returned, but I persuaded the young girl in charge of the house that I knew Mary, and I was sure she would allow me to stay. She offered to prepare food for me, but I had bought bread and fruit along the way, and had a few items with me. (I am sure she was

surprised to have a white woman coming to her door and asking for a place to sleep.) Mary arrived at about 8:30. In my journal I wrote: "I feel so at home here–although there is no electricity, and thus no running water." Mary said that in Makeni the electricity was on, and therefore the water pumped, from Fridays to Sundays–and they had flush toilets. She had big barrels which she filled with water when it was on. I told Mary about our tire problem–we now had no spare, and I was expected in Yengema by ten a.m. People would already be traveling to the workshop. So she offered me her district van, and because of her influence was able to find a tire for us fro the Conference car while we were in Yengema, so we could return. [During the night at Makeni there was another flat tire.] Later, in a speech I gave after my return to the U.S., I described the last part of our trip and the workshop:

There was the faint beginning of dawn; palm trees marched up the dark bulk of the hills, silhouetted against the pink blush of the sky. Goats' eyes shined green from the grass along the roadside. We climbed the hills through the fog, over bone-shaking potholes. Then, suddenly, the blazing orb of the sun rose in the African sky.

I was on my way to a diamond mining town in Sierra Leone. I had been expected the day before, so that I would be prepared to start a workshop for Sunday School teachers at 10:00 that morning. But, a late start and two flat tires had delayed me. I had to stay overnight in a town along the way. Now, through the kindness of the District Superintendent (the first woman D.S., a longtime friend), I was traveling in the district van to Yengema.

How glad they were to see me! The (Yengema) District Superintendent, the Rev. David Bockarie and his wife, Lerina,[3] had been concerned for me, and there were no telephones or radios by which we could communicate. People were already arriving for the workshop. Twenty-five came, some from a long distance. Some had paid their own way, although a number were school teachers who had not been paid any salary for three or four months. I was so glad that through the kindness of friends I had been able to arrive in time to begin as we had planned. They were eager to learn and quite receptive to what I had to offer. [The workshop was held on Thursday and part of Friday.]

Puppets

Rhythm "Instruments"

[3]Lerina was one of the many who died as the result of the civil war.

Operation Classroom Workshop Team

While in Yengama a VIM (Volunteer in Mission) work team from Indiana was in nearby Koidu working on the school buildings, and David took me over. We had supper and fellowship with them.

The next evening David took me to the home of Dr. Turay (a Muslim) and his wife, Laura Caulker, whom I had known as a child in Shenge and as a student at Harford School.[4] We, along with the team, were invited for a delicious buffet meal: rice, Jollof rice, fish and beef soup (stew), cassava, plantain, couscous, banana fritters, doughnuts, small meat pies, lettuce and tomatoes, canned vegetable salad and baked beans, bread, oranges, tangerines and bananas, along with soft drink.

A Meal with the VIM Team

Dinner with Dr. & Mrs. Turay

---

[4]Laura also was killed during the war.

On the way, because we were early and David needed to see him, we stopped at the home of the S.D.O. (Senior District Officer). We chatted about the area. I learned that the National Diamond Trust had reduced mining–only about 3,000 of the original 8,000 people were working. The supply of alluvial diamonds was coming to an end, so it was necessary to dig deeper. Therefore, more capital was needed. The Sunshine Corporation, based in the U.S., was negotiating investment. Retrenchment ("redundancy") was part of the provision. There were other legal companies besides the national one, but there was much smuggling. Lebanese especially would go to Brussels for "medical treatment" to get rid of the diamonds. The government had put pressure on the Sierra Leone Diamond Mine Trust to release land to others, so there were many individual miners. Koidu and Kono could be compared to the gold rush days in the United States. There were many Sierra Leone tribes and other Africans there. David Bockarie said before he became the pastor, emphasis in the church had been on miners. But he said, "You can't build a church on foreigners."

We were up early on Saturday in order to try to get petrol (no luck) and do errands for David. We then went to the UMC church at Motema for a meeting of the Koidu Christian Council, where I had been asked to speak on Christian education. I discovered that very few churches had Christian education for <u>any</u> age group.

Lerina brought food: rice and okra soup, oranges and bananas. The Bokaris gave me a piece of gara cloth (cloth dyed with a dark blue dye from local plants) as a farewell gift. We left at 12:30, and fortunately were able to get three gallons of petrol, at an inflated price, beyond Makeni. Leonard, Lerina's nephew, rode with us. I taught him Rook as we traveled–which he won. When we reached Freetown we took him to Mr. Auriel, on the other side of Fourah Bay College, another long, rough ride. We barely had enough petrol to take the car to the Bishop's house. I was in bed by 9:00 and asleep soon after.

<u>Bo</u>

On the weekend when I was to travel to Bo it was uncertain until the last minute whether there would be any petrol to make the trip. Finally, we left at 11:40 on Friday morning. It was a good, fast trip. We arrived at 3:40. Rev. Donald Wonnie met me and said that the workshop would be the next day, beginning at 9:30. Pat Bowers was expecting me, and I stayed with her. Rev. Lamboi came to greet me. Pat and I and some others ate a chicken dinner at the Black & White Restaurant.

I was at the Bo Training Institute by 9:00, and set up for the workshop. Thirteen people attended, two of whom were women. They represented four churches. Rice and stew were served at noon. We finished at 4:15. It had been a good day.

A Bible Game

On Sunday there was a Women's Day service at the Centenary Church. There were many singing groups–Krio, English, Mendi, often with drums and *segbula* ("shake-shake"). Elizabeth Sankoh was the speaker. She told me that she was in a class at Harford when I taught there. After the service Mary Tholley introduced herself. She told me she was in the children's choir at Rotifunk and remembered the "robes" and the Christmas programs when the children sang. She said I taught her to sing (much more credit that I deserved).

I was given the honor of crowning the Woman of the Day. After church I changed clothes and packed the car. Then Pat and I ate with a work team which had arrived the previous day. We enjoyed the conversation. The driver and I left Bo at about 2:00, and arrived home just before dark. The car stopped four times with clogged gas lines because of dirty petrol. We were able to buy two gallons at a steep price.

After the weekend in Mendi country I discovered that I was recognizing some phrases and words, but remembered little of the Mendi I had struggled with years before.

Writer's Workshop, Freetown

After some confusion as to where and when the workshop would be, I began the workshop on a Friday evening with four persons who were interested in writing materials for youth camps: Alice Fitzjohn, Emerson Grovie, Tamba Edward Saffia from Jaiama, and the president of the Conference Youth Fellowship. We resumed the next day,

Emerson Gorvie

with a stop to eat sweet potato chips and fish which Alice had prepared, and cucumbers and bread. I provided pineapple, oranges and soft drinks. We did some serious work, and those present did well.

Moyamba

Mile 91, Road to Moyamba–Drying Rice on the Road

The Forrests allowed us to get some petrol from them so that I was able to go to Moyamba for their workshop. We arrived at Harford School a little after 3:00. I stayed with Etta Nichol, the principal.

We started the workshop at 4:30. Rev. J. K. Yambasu, Harford Chaplain and Sunday School teacher at Trinity Church, took the lead in organizing it. The room was packed–twenty-seven people, including two men from Rotifunk, and many Harford School students. We continued the next morning, and finished in three hours. At that time we had twenty-four people. Rev. Young from Rotifunk came into the class. I thought it went well.

After eating plantain and broiled chicken, and resting for a time, I went with Etta to see the library extension that was being built, the poultry shed and piggery, and then the site of the June Hartranft[5]

Harford Girls at the Well

Cement Blocks for the Library Extension

[5]June Hartranft was principal of Harford for a time when I lived in Sierra Leone. She had to return to the U.S. when she discovered she had cancer, and died some months later. The new school was in her memory.

On Sunday I ate lunch immediately after the service, and then we were on our way to Freetown. I had left Van in Freetown, and discovered he was at the beach. After he came home, we played several games of Rook.

Other Visits

Mary Boatswain arrived on November 30, and with Van's help I was able to meet her at the Helliport. (The helicopter from the airport was a new addition since I had been in Sierra Leone previously.) She had never been in Sierra Leone, and was looking forward to our going on to Ghana.

Mary went with me to the Theological Hall for my final classes, and we had to walk back to the center of town because we couldn't find a taxi. Once when we were in town, we went to the old Mission House, long since turned over to the government. It was sad to see what had happened to it. I had spent many nights and days there during my twelve years in Sierra Leone. We also went to the wharf, and to Victoria Park.

On Sunday we went to Price Memorial Church where Alice Fitzjohn was pastor. It was a two and a half hour service, with much singing. We at the noon meal at the Forresters, along with the Townsends and Van.

Rev. Alice Fitzjohn

Pa Lokko

Together we visited other places of interest. We went one day to Pa Lokko, where the Swedish United Methodists had established a Children's Village and a school for children with handicapping conditions. Eva Ogren, the missionary, showed us around. We saw the carpenter shop, where young people were learning a trade, and the clinic, as well as the homes where they lived.

While we were there, we met Honoria (P.C. Honoria Bailor-Caulker). She was president of WAND (Women's Association for National Development), which was meeting there. She introduced us to the group.

Eva Ogren, Swedish Missionary with Children

408

The School

The Clinic

Staff Houses Made from Shipping Containers

Urban Ministry

The Kissy Eye Hospital and Urban Ministry, which had just started during my last year as Area Secretary, was of special interest. Dr. Lowell Gess, who had been a doctor at Rotifunk during the time I lived there, had started an eye clinic in Kissy, a suburb of Freetown. By 1989 the eye hospital was supplied with doctors who came as volunteers from the States, and of course, African staff. A baby clinic and prenatal clinic were also there. At the time we were there Dr. Russel Boehlke and his wife Donna were there as Volunteers in Mission.

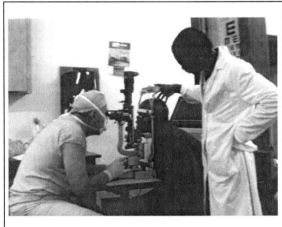

Dr. Boehlke

Donna Boehlke

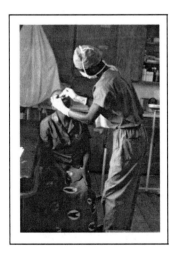

Mohammed Rogers, Nurse

Shenge

I could not leave Sierra Leone without a visit to Shenge, the home of my African "sister," and now a Paramount Chief, Madam Honoria Bailor-Caulker.[6] Van Jollie volunteered to take us to Shenge in his four-wheel drive vehicle, so off we went for the weekend at this place of which I had so many pleasant memories. Honoria went with us. We left Freetown at about 2:30. We stopped at Yonibana, where Van was stationed, for an hour, and arrived in Moyamba at about 8:30. We stayed overnight with Virginia Pickarts.

We were up by daylight. Van went at 8:00 to take Honoria to the District Officer, and I took Mary around the campus and to meet Etta Nichol. Kara, a Peace Corps worker, joined us, and she and Van worked at tying her bike on top of the van. We left Moyamba at 10:15, after picking up Honoria and a policeman, and were on our way to Shenge.

The roads were very bad when I was there in 1986, and the years since had not improved them. Madam Honoria had hopes that the International Labor Organization (ILO) would at last work on an improved road to Shenge after the first of the year. She had been working on that project for fifteen years. [They eventually did build the road, which greatly improved transportation of people and goods to and from Shenge. Unfortunately, this was all undone in the civil war which began in 1991.]

It was a rough trip. We arrived at about 2:30, and stayed at Zainabu's Rest House, new since I had been there. They cooked cassava and fish for us, and then we went to swim. I found it very difficult this time to get down to the beach at the former Mission House (now used as a home for the Shenge pastor), because of erosion. After bathing and changing to a lappa and docket (Sierra Leone clothing), Mary and I went to see Honoria. We gave her our gifts and had a good visit. She then presented us with a great, a great honor. I asked her to have it cooked for us, and of course it was shared with others.

We had only one day and two nights in Shenge, but it gave time to visit friends from former days, and to swim twice at the "mission beach." But it was cloudy and rainy all day, most unusual for December in Sierra Leone, and we were not able to get a boat to go out to Plantain Island as I had hoped to do. There we would have seen the remains of the slave pen John Newton had built to hold the captured people until they could be loaded on a ship bound for the Americas.

Mervin, Honoria's son and the chief at Plantain Island, was not able to come because he could not get transport from Moyamba. He arrived just before we left, and I saw him briefly, and was able to give him a calculator.

Madam Honoria's projects to improve the welfare of her people were impressive. The Rural Fishing Villages Project was one, as well as her hope for the improved road.

On the last evening Mary and I went over to see Honoria again, and I gave her a check for the church and some money for her mother's memorial service. Several of the women came to sing for us.

---

[6]In 1986 I visited Sierra Leone, along with friends who had taught at Harford School, Elaine Gasser and Florence Barnhart, and a friend of Elaine's, Joyce Anderegg, to attend the 25th anniversary celebration of her chieftancy.

Fishermen and Boats

Buildings for Fishing Villages Project

412

Zainabu's Rest House
(Pineapple Growing in Front)

P.C. Madam Honoria
Bailor-Caulker

Back: Van Jollie, Esther Megill
Front: Mary Boatswain, P.C. Bailor-Caulker,
Chief Mervin Bailor

On Friday, December 8, we returned to Freetown, taking Honoria with us for about twenty miles. She had interrupted her tour of the chieftaincy for our visit, and she was now to continue it. We were sorry that we were not able to wait to see the people gathering, and hear the blowing of a horn announcing her coming. They would then carry her by hammock to the next destination.

We arrived at Moyamba at about noon, ate some more goat meat, which had been sent with us, and rested a bit, and then were on our way to Yonibana. We took pictures of the Betty Carew Centre, and the Community Development sign. Betty was the wife of the former Bishop Carew, and had been very active in women's work. She had been killed in an automobile accident some years before, and the Centre was named in her honor. I also saw Edward Kargbo again. We left at about 5:30 and arrived home at 9:00.

Yonibana

Betty Carew Women's Training Centre

A New Well

Leaving Sierra Leone – Once Again

On our last night in Sierra Leone we went to a farewell dinner at the Paramount Hotel, hosted by Francis Tommy. His wife, Esther, was also there, as well as Mary and Van. Francis introduced us to President Momoh, who was there for a special dinner. He and Francis had been fellow army officers, and had been in prison together. I was given a farewell gift of a tie-dye dress with the "jaromie" stitching.[7]

Van Jollie, Francis Tommy, Esther Tommy,
Mary Boatswain, Esther Megill

Mary and I were up at 5:30 on Sunday morning, struggling to close suitcases and get ready to go. We got on the ferry just before 8:30, and arrived at the Lungi airport at 10:15. It was a madhouse! Without Francis Tommy we would never have gotten through customs and on the plane in time. As it was, we barely made it. There was a stop at Robert's Field in Liberia and in Abidjan, Ivory Coast, although we could not get out of the plane. We arrived at Accra at 3:20–and were returning home again!

---

[7]This stitching was done by men on a (treadle) sewing machine, without a pattern.

A Nation That Was Bankrupt

And now for the other side – I was saddened to see the way Sierra Leone had deteriorated. An inept and corrupt government had brought the country to the brink of ruin. The entire infrastructure had nearly broken down. Roads were terrible; gasolene, kerosene (so essential for light for many people), and bottled gas were in constant short supply. At that time it was acute. Gasoline, when you could find it, was sold on the black market, and one gallon for nearly ten times the usual cost, more than many people earned in a month. This was a great hardship, and increased the cost of food in the city. In towns where there was once running water and electricity they now were nonexistent or very erratic. In Freetown I could count six or eight large firms (selling dry goods, groceries, etc.) which had been there when I lived in Sierra Leone but were now closed.

Teachers had not been paid for three months; some had just quit teaching. As one teacher said to me, "It is difficult to teach when you are hungry." The same was true of other government employees; postal clerks slowed down their work; people did not report to offices; the garbage collectors were on strike. The result was that there were a few wealthy people and many, many in poverty. Many children were dying before the age of five, more than 300 in 1,000 in Sierra Leone. (It ranked second only to Afghanistan, where there had been war for years.) Nurses reported many, many children too ill from malnourishment to save. What they needed was food, and the nurses could do little about it–just give a few selected infants powdered milk.

One day when I rode by taxi to the Theological Hall (along with the usual three or four other passengers), they were speaking in Krio, probably not thinking that I might understand them, and complaining bitterly because the taxi driver had increased the fare. He said he had to increase it, because it cost him more. (There was also the problem that the drivers had to give bribes to the police. If they didn't, they would be called in for some technicality. There was even a place in Freetown, I was told, where the taxis lined up early every morning, and made a one-time payment so they wouldn't be bothered the rest of the day.) One of the passengers said it was all the fault of Momoh [head of the military government], and others agreed. One woman said, "In any other country, there would have been a revolution before this, but we in Sierra Leone don't do anything."[8]

The military government ruled with an iron hand. Since I had been there, eight people had been hanged, accused of attempting a coup the year before. So often the people said, "God will rescue us." I had no idea at the time what the result would be, and did not know how most people survived. If they were asked, they usually said, "Now God" or "God dey" (meaning that God is there, and it was only through God's help that they managed from day to day.)

The result was that there was much crime. Robbery and thieving were very common. There was corruption from top to bottom. One had to give extra money to get almost anything done.

-----

[8] I am sure that if she had foreseen the years of violent civil war ahead, she would not have wished for it.

People frankly said that they had not been paid, or that what they were paid was not nearly enough to take care of their family.

The banking system was also in shambles. They did not have enough cash. Even if one put dollars in the bank you would stand in line for hours to get some leones. Sometimes people who waited at the bank would be given only Le250, which was about $2.50 (black market rate). The result was that most businesses wanted at least half of their payment in cash; sometimes they would accept no checks. So, another banking system developed. As has been seen previously, people with foreign currency gave their dollars or other money to the traders, mostly Lebanese, who then paid a black market price in leones. It was very difficult to get money if one did not do that.

Sadly, many suspected that there was also corruption in the church. In a culture which was so full of it, it would be very easy to be part of the system.

Those were difficult day to be missionaries in Sierra Leone, very different from when I was there. I was disturbed at some of the things I saw, and blamed both the church and the missionaries in some cases. There was a great deal of sickness among the missionaries also. So many had severe cases of malaria. It was obvious that the malaria organism had become resistant to many of the drugs used for treatment, which had served us well when I lived there.

There were, however, many Christians who continued to serve with integrity, against great odds. I was grateful for the opportunity to be in Sierra Leone once again, although I did look forward to having a little easier time in other countries. I carried with me many warm thoughts of my friends, yet sadness for what had happened to the country that had played such a large part in my life.

Sierra Leone Since 1989

A little over a year after I left Sierra Leone in 1989, civil war did indeed break out. In March of 1991 a small band of men, calling themselves the Revolutionary United Front (RUF), under the leadership of Foday Sankoh, began attacking villages near the Liberian border. Before long they had control of the diamond mines in the Kono area. It has been proven that Charles Taylor, who led a long civil war in Liberia, was involved in starting the war in Sierra Leone. Many of the diamonds which were mined were funneled to him, and he used them to buy arms.

In 1992 Capt. Valentine Strasser, in a military coup, took over the government from Major General Saidu Momoh, who was exiled. Strasser then formed the NPRC (National Provisional Ruling Council). More and more of the country, however, was taken over by the RUF. They killed, pillaged, and maimed by cutting off arms, legs, ears–even of infants. Many children were kidnaped and forced to be sex slaves or child soldiers.

Because Strasser and his government had not been able to combat the RUF succesfully, there was increased demand for elections and a return to civilian government. In 1996 Ahmad Tejan Kabbah, who had been a diplomat in the UN for twenty years, won the election. He was able to get a peace accord signed with the RUF in Abidjan, Côte d'Ivoire, on November 30, 1996. However, Major Johnny Paul Koroma overthrew Kabbah in May of 1997. A U.S. newspaper clipping from June 4 reported that U.S. marines had rescued 1,200 foreigners, the third evacuation since the May 25 bloody coup.

Koroma was eventually ousted by the Nigerian-led ECOMOG (a multilateral armed force established by ECOWAS, the Economic Community of West African States). Kabbah was re-instated in 1998.

Then in 1999 The RUF once again tried to regain the country, and reached Freetown. Thousands were killed and wounded in the fighting which ensued. Finally, the UN Mission to Sierra Leone was sent, and the UN remained in Sierra Leone until August 31, 2005, when it was substituted for by a 300-strong UN Integrated Office in Sierra Leone (UNIOSIL).[9]

Even after the UN forces were sent, the RUF violated the agreement once again, held hostages, and killed some people. Foday Sankoh was arrested. The British sent troops to evacuate foreign nationals and established order. Fighting continued in some places, however.

By May of 2002 Kabbah and his party (SLPP–the Sierra Leone People's Party) were re-elected, and the UN began gradually to withdraw troops.

At that time the Sierra Leone government asked the UN to assist in setting up a Special Court, and a Truth and Reconciliation Commission, modeled after that in South Africa, was established. Bishop J. C. Humper of The United Methodist Church (who was one of my students

---

[9]UN Resolution 1620 (August 31, 2005). (From the Internet.)

at Trinity College in Ghana) was the Chairman of the Commission. Both began operating in the summer of 2002. Foday Sankoh was indicted for war crimes, as were several others. Sankoh died in prison of a heart attack in 2003.[10]

Charles Taylor, who by an agreement as the Liberia civil war was settled was allowed to go into exile in Nigeria, at the insistence of Sierra Leone, was sent to the Hague to be tried. At the time of writing (summer of 2007) he is being tried.

"The Final Report of the Truth & Reconciliation Commission of Sierra Leone" may be downloaded from the Internet.[11] There is also an edition for senior schools and a children's version. The report "calls for introspection and a retrospective examination of the political, historical, economical, social and moral activities of both the state and the nation. While particular attention has been paid to the plight of victims, the motives and perspectives of those who committed terrible atrocities were intensively explored . . . Our ultimate goal of peace and reconciliation will be reached if all living within its borders sincerely respect the human rights of all, without exception . . . Reconciliation is strengthened through acknowledgment and forgiveness . . . Learning to forgive those who have wronged us is the first step we can take towards healing our traumatised nation."

Thus, after many years of civil war, Sierra Leone by 2007 was gradually beginning to repair the extensive damages to infrastructures, and to deal with the many problems the war had caused. One was that thousands of young people had known nothing but war–many had participated in the killing themselves, and all had seen killing and atrocities. They had no education, and knew only how to fight. Many people cannot work because they have lost limbs.

On August 11, 2007 elections were held. Although the Sierra Leone National Elections Watch (a coalition of more than one hundred local civic and non-governmental groups) pronounced the results were "peaceful, fair and credible" and Seth Obeng, heading the observer mission of ECOWAS, said "the voting process . . . was adequately free, peaceful, and credible," rioting broke out when the results were announced on September 3. Ernest Bai Koroma of the All People's Congress (APC) had won with 44% of the votes, while the SLPP candidate, Vice President Solomon Brewa, had 38%. A runoff vote was held on September 8.[12] On September 17 Koroma was sworn in as Sierra Leone's president.[13]

---

[10]Much of this information was obtained from *Wickipedia, the Free Encyclopedia*, found on the Internet.

[11]May be found at http://www.trcsierraleone.org/drwegsite/publish/indexshtml or just Google "Truth and Reconciliation Commission, Sierra Leone."

[12]"Votes Counted in Sierra Leone Elections,." ABC News (Australia), August 13 and "Election Violence Grips Sierra Leone Capital," Sept. 2. Internet.

[13]*The Epoch Times*, Reuters, September 17, 2007. On the Internet.

The United Methodist Church is one of the churches which is doing a great deal to assist the Sierra Leoneans. Through Operation Classroom[14] not only have schools and medical facilities been repaired and supplies provided, but training courses are assisting both the educational and medical work. Persons have been sent to help train pastors and teachers how to counsel young people and others suffering from trauma.

Many volunteer teams from United Methodist churches in the United States and also from Norway have assisted in a remarkable renovation of some of the buildings and renewal of former institutions and programs, as well as staring new ones to meet new needs. The following information was received from Bishop J. C. Humper, Dr. Lowell Gess and Rev. Joe Wagner of Operation Classroom:

Medical Work

In Rotifunk, where it is reported three hundred houses were burned and the hospital nearly destroyed, a great deal of work has been done. Extensive repairs have been made on the hospital and are continuing. The outpatient rooms and maternity block and outside barrie have been beautifully renewed. The surgical ward is completed and ready to be used; the doctor's guest house has been rehabilitated and almost completed; work on the men's and women's wards was in progress in May of 2007, and were expected to be completed by the end of the year. Doctors from Norway were to begin work at the hospital before the end of the year.

Facilities have been repaired and clinics are open, under the direction of Sierra Leone nurses, in Taiama, Jaiama, and Manjama, with a new one in Makeni. There is an active program in Manjama addressing the HIV/AIDS situation. Julius Caulker, whom I trained in Rotifunk, is the dependable laboratory technician. In Jaiama the clinic now has the capability of conducting eye care outreach with a slit lamp and operating equipment. Many of the houses in Jaiama were bare walls as recently as 2006.

The Kissy Eye Hospital is now a department of a new Kissy General Hospital, where there is a surgical ward in use and x-ray installed. The main Urban Centre building will be used to make room for emergency wards and diagnostic equipment. There is also an active HIV/AIDS program. The work of the hospital is exploding.

Dr. Dennis H. Marke, a Sierra Leonean, is the Chief Medical Officer at the Hospital. Dr. Eugene Muembo, a Congolese, works with him, and has been appointed a missionary by the General Board of Global Ministries. Dr. Ainor Fergusson is in charge of the Eye Hospital. (He was trained in eye surgery by Dr. Gess.) The hospital has impressive new buildings: a new surgery, outpatient department, and hostel in which families can stay while members are under treatment.

The main building of what was the Bo Bible Training Institute has been converted to a hospital called the Mercy Hospital. It was to be opened at the beginning of October in 2001. A full time doctor and business manager had been employed, equipment was expected to arrive in

---

[14]Headquarters address: Operation Classroom, PO Box 246, Colfax, IN 46035.

Freetown soon, and a laboratory building was in progress. By the end of 2008 the former dining hall and classroom building were to be rehabilitated with a surgery constructed and wards established to become a full hospital.

Child Rescue Centre

A new child rescue center works with orphaned children, and an impressive new complex has been built behind the old BTI buildings, now a hospital. A new building to be called the "Missionary Training Centre" was also under construction. Provision was made for work teams and medical doctors who come on a short term basis.

Education

All the schools in Taiama, Jaiama, Bo and Moyamba are open and functioning, with enrollment increasing annually. Harford School for Girls has returned to Moyamba, after being forced into exile in Freetown as a result of the rebel war which ravaged the school compound. However, a new United Methodist Secondary School for Girls continues in Freetown, situated in the former Conference Office building which was used by Harford School. They now have 1,300 students. Another Girl's Secondary School was established at Tankoro, Kono in 2004.

Plans were under way to construct both an elementary school and a clinic at Kabala, where for years children of United Methodist missionaries attended school.

Bishop Humper reported that the 127th Session of Annual Conference met in February 2007 for the first time in history at Weaver Memorial Church in Bonthe Sherbo, with host District Superintendent Rev. George S. Sandi. The theme was "You are the light of the world." (Matthew 5:14). Well over six hundred people attended the Conference. And so, the church continues in strength in Sierra Leone.

Chapter 2. Ghana
1989

Mary Boatswain and I were almost the last ones to get off the plane in Accra, and the last in line at Immigration. But what a contrast to Sierra Leone! I had heard that Ghana had made remarkable economic progress since the difficult times when I left in 1980. This was apparent as soon as we entered the well-organized, clean and attractive airport. The streets in the city were good. There were many shops, and so many cars that the traffic congestion was terrible. However, in talking with a Ghanaian friend I was reminded that I must not forget that there was still much poverty, that the conditions, especially in the villages, were often not good. Although goods were now plentiful, many people of modest income could not afford to buy them. However, Ghana was being held up as an example of an African country which had been able to lift itself out of economic collapse.

We were met at the airport by the Rev. Kwaku Asamoah-Okyere, my "son" and former student whom we prepared by the aid of scholarships to take my place at Trinity College. He was not only Christian Education teacher and Director of the Department of Church Leadership, but was Vice-Principal, was in charge of development and the farm program which he had started, and also Council Director of all the newly-reorganized boards of the Methodist Church (an organization for which he was largely responsible.)

Mary and I stayed in the house in which she had lived. Livingston Buama and his family had moved out, since he had just been made principal. [We discovered later that there were still problems with the water, and there were times when there was none. When that happened Agnes and the children carried buckets of water from the tank for us. Before I left, I learned that Trinity owed the university money for water, so they cut it off periodically until they were paid.] After we arrived, we went over to Kwaku's and Agnes served us a good meal. We visited for a while, then came back to the house for a bath and bed.

The Library/Christian Education Building–with walls!

Livingston Buama and Family

Student Dormitories

The theological school was full to overflowing; they had decided not to take so many students another year, for they simply did not have dormitory facilities or classroom space for so many. A women's hostel was an urgent need. There were now a few women students, but they had no satisfactory place to stay. Kwaku was working hard to upgrade the facilities to make it more suitable for international meetings, and had received a grant to help with some of the needed renovation. The college in recent years had added a B.D. program, in cooperation with the nearby University of Ghana.

With the help of Kwaku and the school bus we were able to get into Accra to buy food, take care of immigration matters and confirm our flights from Ghana. I learned that I would have to leave for Nigeria on Dec. 30 instead of January 1, so sent a cable to tell the people there of the change. I also applied for a visa to Nigeria. All this, as is usual in Africa, took several trips and sometimes long waits until we could see the proper officials. But we settled into the house and were ready for work.

Livingston Buama took me to the college the first morning, to talk informally to the class on Youth Ministry, and on other days I went to the classes on Ministry to Children and Ministry with Adults. The students asked for my book to be published again so that they could get copies.

On December 13 we went to a three-hour carol service. Kwaku introduced us, and they asked me to give greetings. We had been in town most of the day and had not changed clothes, and they put us up on the stage on the front row. On Sunday we went to the community church service in the chapel. They combined singing and dancing and used a keyboard, along with the usual British-style liturgy. There were two offerings. One was given as they danced to the front. Mary and I were introduced and welcomed. Some were arriving to take part in the curriculum writing. One was Maggie Boama-Secu, who was one of the first two women students at Trinity, whom I taught the last year I was at Trinity. She had been to the States and completed a M.A. in Religious Education. She had worked for a long time on a food preservation project. and was very frustrated with all that prevented her from doing what she had planned, but she truly had commitment and tenacity. I also met another member of the team, Dinah, who had just returned to Ghana with a M.A. in Religious Education from Princeton.

The Children's Hymnal

I went to Ghana to complete, or at least restart, two projects which I had begun more than ten years before. One was the vernacular translations of songs in the children's hymnal, *Come, Let Us Sing*. When we were settled, I asked Kwaku about the manuscripts for the translations into the three Ghanaian languages. Kwaku at first said that he could not find them, and thought they had been eaten by termites. I was depressed, for that meant hundreds of hours of work from many people lost, which could not be reclaimed. How glad I was when Agnes appeared the next morning with the manuscripts which had been found! I spent time checking these and editing these, and with Kwaku's help was able to contact some hymn translators who I hoped would be able to finish the translations that remained, and check the others. Two came to Trinity and worked on the Ewe translations for a time. We went to see Mr. Abbie, who had translated the Ga hymns, at the Bureau of Languages. He promised to help us, and to get estimates for the cost of typing and printing. Then Kwaku and I worked to make an estimate of the cost for completing and producing the books. The next problem would be to find the money.

The Kindergarten Curriculum

The second project was to complete, if possible the two-year curriculum for Kindergarten children. (Actually, we changed it to preschool, and also gave suggestions for use with a younger group.) Kwaku had arranged before hand for a select group of persons to meet at Trinity while I was there for a writer's workshop. Our purpose was to complete at least the first year of the Kindergarten Sunday School Curriculum, and to make a beginning on the second year. There was only one person there who had been on the original committee–Cecilia Edu (Evangelical Methodist), who had a nursery school and had been in our writers' workshop during the time I was in Ghana. There were Maggie Buama-Secu, and Dinah Abbey-Mensah (both Presbyterian), who had master's degrees in religious education; Eric Anum (Presbyterian); David Nartey (Roman Catholic, in charge of education; Sr. Mary Jo (Roman Catholic, American). Some were not there all the time, but they did some

Cecilia Edu and David Nartey

Eric Anum and Margaret Boama-Secu

productive work. I left with almost all the materials for the first year, which I edited later, and an outline for the second year, with lessons for that section divided among the team members. We met December 18-21, with some working longer.

Kwaku was able to get a typewriter for me so that I began work on editing and putting together the kindergarten materials. While I was busy with the curriculum writers, Mary Boatswain was helping Faustina Frempong, the new full-time librarian. Mary had reorganized the library when she was in Ghana in 1979-80. The young librarian was very glad to have her help in organizing the library again.

Faustina Frempong, left, Mary Boatswain, right

Christmas Decorations

We also had time for relaxation and fun. Sr. Mary Ann, with whom I had worked in previous years on writers' and picture projects, and Sr. Mary Jo joined us for dinner and to play Rook one evening. Mary and I put up sparse Christmas decorations in the house in which we were staying (a string of red bells Mary had brought and my three Christmas cards). There was a three-hour church service on the 24th, "Nine Lessons and Carols."

It was a warm, sunny Christmas day in Ghana, as it always is, and we attended a three-hour church service conducted by the youth. There were many songs in Twi and in English, and dancing and clapping, as some waved white handkerchiefs. This was mixed with staid 18th and 19th century British songs. The youth gave a drama, in Twi. There was a sermon in English and Twi, emphasizing Mary's quiet time of meditating on the meaning of the birth (Luke 2:19), and our need for quiet in the midst of the noise of celebration. Late in the afternoon we had ten children from the Asamoah-Okyere and Buama families, and the son of one of the women students over. Agnes and Kwaku, and eventually, Maggie also came. We fed them popcorn (brought from the U.S.), drinks, and cookies, and gave each a piece of candy. The children played games, and the adults played Rook. It was a good Christmas.

Children Playing Games and Eating

Mary Boatswain, Sr. Mary Ann, Sr. Mary Jo

Mary and I also did a little shopping, especially at the Cultural Centre, which was much larger and improved since we lived in Ghana. There were booths with many African artifacts. Mary bought a number of things for gifts to take home, and I bought a few. On the 28th I was able to get a permanent at a hotel.

On my last day people came in and out all day. My namesake, Esther Megill Owusu, and her mother, Mary Kwakye, came for a brief visit. They brought fruits for me and I gave Esther a set of towels and some money. Mary enjoyed seeing some of her friends from previous years during the time she was there.

Esther Owusu and her Mother, Mary Kwakye

Then, once again we said goodby to Ghana–Mary left for the States on December 31, and I for Nigeria on the 30th.

Ghana Since 1989

An article in *Africa News*, April 17, 1989, "Government Wins Vote of Confidence," describes an election which was held for district representatives. The last time the people of Ghana had voted for district representatives, in 1978, only 18% of the country's eligible voters came out. Now, in 1989, almost 60% had voted. Many Ghanaians were talking about how to proceed with national elections, a step the government had not yet scheduled. "The rulers of Ghana–having declared their intention to create a grassroots democracy–have apparently succeeded in getting to the grassroots."

The writer continues to say that "Ten years ago, Ghana was foundering on the brink of economic collapse . . . . " Since Rawlings overthrew the elected government in 1981, "under his leadership, Ghana has enjoyed a dramatic economic resurgence. Rawlings' policies have earned praise from Western lenders, who have pledged more than $4 billion to support the country's structural adjustment program. In 1987, Ghana initiated a supplementary program–Program of Action to Mitigate the Social Costs of Development (PAMSCAD)–that aims to lift the burden of adjustment off the shoulders of the poor, who are hardest hit when social programs are sacrificed to pay off foreign debts."   In November of 1992 multiparty elections were held. Rawlings won the presidential election with nearly 60% of the votes. In 1996 he was reelected with 56% of the votes. In December of 2000 a new president was elected, since the Constitution allows only two terms for a president. The winner, John Kufour, was from a new opposition party, the New Patriotic Party.[15]

In an article on the Internet[16] the issue of corruption is discussed at some length. It was stated that "corruption has been a major impediment to the socioeconomic and political advancement of Ghana since independence. Its pervading influence on public decision-making processes has been a cause and consequence of the structural and economic decay. A recent diagnostic study of the problem showed a veritable culture of graft and rot in several governmental institutions. Some of the institutions which rated low in terms of honesty and integrity were the Police, Government Ministers, Political Parties, the Customs, Excise and Preventive Services (CEPS), the Judiciary, and the Ministry of Finance and Lands Commission. In response to the public outcry that met the publication of this report, the Vice President Alhaji Aliu Mahama promised the establishment of a code of conduct and an office of accountability in the President's office to combat corruption."

In addition, there had been mixed results of the Structural Adjustment Program, and there were still many economic problems.

---

[15]See *The Crawfurd.dk Homepage,* "Ghana Time Line–The Gold Coast."

[16] "Ghana–History and Politics," on the Internet.

429

Kufour was reelected in 2004, but will not be able to stand in 2008.

Kwaku Asamoah-Okyere, in a letter written March 1, 2006, wrote:

> *Politically, as you may be aware, Ghana is now a democracy and very peaceful, with the economy picking up steadily. The latest issue that has been hotly debated is the Representation of the People's Amendment Bill, popularly known as ROPAB, which seeks to allow Ghanaians everywhere, including those overseas, to vote. The opposition (minority) members of Parliament allege that the government wants to rig future elections with the passage of the bill and boycotted parliamentary sittings. The government, of course, has denied this and the majority members have gone ahead to debate the bill and passed it into law. It is now left to the independent Electoral Commission to work out the modalities and determine whether the law could be put into effect at the next General Elections in 2008.*

The election of Kofi Annan as General Secretary of the United Nations was of great pride to the Ghanaians. He was welcomed home as a hero when he returned in 2007 at the end of his term.

Trinity College is now Trinity Theological Seminary, and in connection with the University of Ghana gives a Bachelor of Divinity Degree. There is also now a women's hostel, which was officially named the "Megill Giagge Hall," in my honor and that of Annie Giagge, a famous Ghanaian Judge of the Supreme Court of Ghana.

Chapter 3. Nigeria
1990

On December 30 I was up at 4:00 a.m., ate breakfast, and finished packing. Kwaku and I were in line at the airport at 5:45, and I had to wait until 6:00. Then at the last minute I had to pay for the excess baggage, and found that the cashier wasn't there to receive dollars. So Kwaku finally paid in cedis and I gave him $40.00. I didn't even get to say goodby to him. Cecile, Maggie and Mary came to see me off.

The plane did not leave until 8:00, an hour late, and arrived in Lagos at about 10:15. I went through immigration and customs fairly easily, then took an expensive taxi ride to the domestic airport to take a plane to Jos. I paid a man to get my ticket and take care of the excess baggage. It took a long time, and I paid $80.00 for the excess to Jos, which had cost only $40.00 from Accra. I discovered that this was an "Environmental Day." This was true the last Saturday of each month. No one was to leave home and no one was to travel until 10:00. Everyone was supposed to clean up around the home. That meant the plane didn't leave on schedule, and apparently there was technical trouble also. It was a long wait, with not much to eat, but I was glad I did not have to stay in Lagos overnight. When I arrived in Jos and got my baggage it was 5:15, and there was no one to meet me! (The cable had apparently not been received..) I was able to get a taxi to "Sprite Lodge,"[17] the United Methodist guest house, but found the gate locked and no one there. The taxi man took the watchman with us to find the caretaker, Jojo Bentel. He wasn't at home, but a man living with him was able to take us to find him. The taxi driver and the others were so helpful. I discovered that Jojo

Sprite Lodge

and his house mate were both Ghanaians. All the missionary staff was gone. However, Jojo

---

17

I was able to arrange for the purchase of this building when I was Area Secretary. When they debated on a name, someone suggested "Sprite Lodge," since there was a sign advertizing Sprite on the road nearby.

Ethel Johnson and Ann Kemper Getting Water

was able to let me in, and told me where I could find a place to eat, so I was able to stay there. I walked to the Yahu Restaurant nearby and had Jollof rice, then home, had a warm bath, and a long night's sleep.

The next day Ann Kemper, with whom I would be staying, and Ahmadu Maidoki, Conference Youth Director with whom I had been corresponding, arrived, along with Ayuba Ndule, principal of Banyam Theological Seminary. Ethel Johnson, whom I had known at Hartford School of Religious Education (Hartford, CT)

arrived on January 1, with the pilot, Jim Keech. Thad McGinnes and Leah (his young daughter) also arrived. We did some shopping, ate at various restaurants, and talked–and played Rook. Ahmadu Maidoki and I planned for three workshops. Again–no water! There was a broken water main in town. Fortunately, there was a well, but water had to be pulled up in buckets.

Doris Horn arrived after returning from Germany, where she had taken her co-worker home, who had leukemia. One evening we all went to Thad and Jeannie McGinness' and played Rook. I

Loading the Pick-up

worked on curriculum materials from Sierra Leone during those days also.

On January 5 my passport was ready, with my visa extended to January 30. I tried to take it, my application for a Zambia visa, and my tickets to a travel agent, but she wasn't in the office and had moved outside the city. I left it with Jojo and Teri Erbele, the mission treasurer. That evening a number of us went to a Chinese restaurant.

Ahmadu Maidoki and Esther Megill

432

On January 6 we were up at 6:00, Ahmadu Maidoki and Ayuba Ndule loaded the pickup, and afterward we went to the TEKAN headquarters and guest house to eat breakfast. We ate bread, jam and coffee with them. Then Ahmadu, Ann and I left for the long trip by road to Bambur (nearly 300 miles). We stopped at a supermarket in Bauchi, bought a few things, and Ann and I ate a little while we waited. We arrived at Bambur at about 7:00, very hot and dusty. I met Ilse Bertsch, the nurse at Wurum (nearby), and she went with us to Keeches' for a chili supper and ice cream.

On Sunday we went to church at Bangai, a section of Bambur. The church was full by the time the service was over. Men sat on one side, women on the other. There was a choir, and women played traditional instruments. Pastor Para's sermon was quite dramatic. He remembered me from the time I was Area Secretary–also Adamu Biyam, the literacy worker who used to work with Heidy Dennis.

Ahmadu came with some rice to help with my food. It was very dry and hot.

The next day Ann went to the Theological Seminary, where she taught. I worked on curriculum most of that morning and in the following days. News came that day that the Conference treasurer had been killed in an automobile accident, and one of the teachers at Banyam seriously hurt. Naturally many people were very upset.

Karim Village

On January 10 Ayuba Ndule came for me in the pick-up–already with a lot of passengers (and more were added as we went along), to take me to Lankaviri, the Conference Office, where I could greet General Superintendent Peter Dabale, and wait for the *Magalissa* (annual conference). He stopped at Karim, a small typical Northern Nigeria village, to see the widow of the Conference treasurer.

In my journal I wrote some impressions of that long, hot journey:

–Nomads passing with their herds of large, thin, humped cattle, with long horns. The government has designated paths for them to take, where people are not to farm (otherwise, the farmers would be suing for them for spoiling crops). They pay ₦10 (ten naira) per head of cattle as tax. Ayuba says that they get nothing from the government, and are considering setting up mobile schools. They are migrating to the Benue plain where there is more grass

-- The women do all the work. They make their little round grass huts, cook, care for children, milk the cows, and sell it. The men just drive the cattle to pasture. I saw some girls and young boys also helping with the herding.

– Men, women and children carrying guinea corn on their heads. It is harvest time.

–Conversation with Ayuba about his and his wife's problems. With a good education, the church won't hire them because they say they can't pay them. Finally, he's been appointed to the Theological School, but not his wife. But the church needs educated people. The UMC is losing educated lay people.

Stopping for Prayer

It was a hot and bumpy ride. The General Superintendent had sent a driver to pick me up at Newman, since the pastors were going on to Yola for a meeting, but somehow we missed him, so I finally took a taxi. The driver stopped for prayer at a Muslim prayer site at about 2:15. All the passengers, except for a woman, got out to pray. They poured a little water in a milk tin (can) for ablutions, and washed their face, head, mouth, hands, arms and feet.

We arrived in Lankaviri at about 3:00. I was welcomed, and moved in with Ethel Johnson. Work on the curriculum continued, but now with a newer typewriter ribbon which Ethel had. We ate dinner with the General Superintendent – pounded yam, chicken soup, greens, a banana. Ethel and I played Rook that night.

Ethel went to Bambur for a meeting and was gone a day and a half, and had work to do when she was at home. However, I kept busy working on the Sunday School materials. Also, people came to see me: John Dandazo,

General Superintendent Peter Dabale

the Director of the Council on Ministries; James Yakaka, secretary to the General Superintendent; the General Superintendent, to take me around the compound; the McGinnis family, whom Ethel invited to stay for supper (they lived nearby in Jalingo), and later, Roberta Ellis, who taught at Hillcrest, the school for missionary children. (We remembered that we had seen each other at the Ghana airport.) When Bishop Bangura came to conduct the *Magalissa* (annual conference) we chatted for a time. On many nights Ethel and I played games, frequently Rook–and sometimes by candlelight, after the generator was turned off.

On Sunday we of course went to church. We had to walk a considerable distance, which was painful for me, because I had developed arthritic spurs in my heels after the extensive walking in Sierra Leone. However, it was an interesting experience. We sat on narrow, plaster-covered mud block seats, with no backs. There were so many men and young people that they had to bring in benches to seat everyone. I noticed the wide-eyed, smiling babies. Mothers nursed their babies, and got up and went out at times. Through the open door I could see the compound next door, and women pounding yams.

The service, which of course was in Hausa, began at 10:00 and lasted for two and one-half hours. There were several choir numbers, some by the women's choir, who used traditional instruments.

The choir officers were introduced, and those of the district evangelists, who had met the previous day. Two offerings were taken, the second for the evangelists. The men went up first to take their offerings, and the women last. Afterward a clay tea pot was auctioned off. It sold for ₦11.00 (less than $1.50), and a razor blade, for ₦1.00.

The Iowa Conference Presents a Banner Signifying Their Partnership with the Nigeria Conference

The sermon began at 12:00–not by the pastor, since he was seldom there. The speaker dealt a good deal with how women should stay with their husbands and not be concerned about material things. He also spoke about love–"we say *lafyia*[18], but don't mean it. (Romans 12:9ff). (This was Ethel's synopsis.)

The *Magalissa* started in the Jalingo church on Wednesday, January 17. The seats were hard, but I was fortunate to sit next to the wall so I could have support for my back. There was translation between English and Hausa, and lots of arguing and confusion. Roberta and I went home for lunch, and had expected to go back

18

Meaning "fine" or "well"– a response to the standard greeting meaning "How are you?" –Dean Gilliland

that night, but Ethel sent word that she would not be coming home until that night. Ann Kemper was staying at Ethel's also. We left at 8:15 the next morning. Again, there was a lot of wasted time, wrangling and disorganization. We missionaries ate at the hotel. A group from Iowa who had brought information about a project they were supporting came as we were leaving. I was able to talk to Ahmadu, Jollie, and briefly to the two Bible School principals about what I would be doing. We came home for the evening. The General Superintendent came in as we were eating, and joined us. Ann and I did not go back for the evening session.

Ordination of Deacons
Rev. Ayuba Ndule and Bishop Bangura

Several of us went shopping the next morning. I was trying to find a place to photocopy the unit I had completed writing, but no place had enough paper. We had another long, tiresome day at the conference. In the evening there was a drama, which depicted a traditional wedding, with dancing.

The conference session continued the next day, with some committee meetings, including one with the missionary maintenance committee. In the ordination service that evening, five deacons and nine elders were ordained. The Secretary of the German Mission Board, Bodo Schwabe, and Gesila Hensler, a Board member and head of United Methodist Women in the German church, arrived that evening.

The final session of the conference was the Sunday morning communion service. When the General Superintendent read the appointments for fifteen districts, I noted that there were, in addition to the District Superintendents, only one to five ordained ministers in each district. In the Conference there were now sixty-four ordained elders, some deacons, and at least six hundred evangelists.

Bodo Schwabe preached in the morning service. He spoke very forcefully about the need for different tribes to get along, as the first step in the Kingdom, when they will come "from East and West, North and South," bearing gifts (Rev. 21).

On Monday I went shopping with Norma Seaman, and after trying a number of places we finally found one that could do decent photocopies. Norma had some done, and I had copies made of the Sunday School lessons I had prepared. I then sent copies to Sierra Leone and Ghana.

On Tuesday I flew to Bambur, and prepared to stay there with Ann Kemper for most of the rest of my time in Nigeria.

In the letter I wrote near the end of my time in Nigeria to many on my mailing list I described some of the changes in Nigeria since my time there as Area Secretary 1968-72. I wrote:

"There is a vast difference between this part of Northern Nigeria and Accra and Freetown. It was less than twenty years ago, when I was one of the Area secretaries for the World Division, that we started the first secondary school in this area. In fact, it is only a little more than sixty years ago that mission work of any kind started here. Now there is a rapidly growing church of more than 300,000. For this number of members there are only fifty-four ordained ministers, many of whom have limited education. There are many evangelists, who take care of the village churches. The conference is divided into fifteen districts. In one district, at least, there are only three ordained ministers, one of whom is also the District Superintendent.

"The United Methodist Church in Nigeria is a Provisional Annual Conference. This means that they are attempting to meet the requirements to become a UMC, and hope to elect their own bishop in 1992. In the meantime Bishop T. S. Bangura of Sierra Leone is the presiding bishop.

"As is usually true of new churches, there are many "growing pains." One can read the epistles of Paul to the early Gentile churches, and feel that he was writing the churches in Nigeria. They have so many of the same problems. Ethel Johnson, retired from teaching at METHESCO in Ohio, has been working with them for some time as a consultant in administration. She has been here for about five months this time and will stay for another year. She and I were classmates in graduate school in Hartford, Connecticut. I have spent a good deal of time with her here, and we have enjoyed renewing our friendship. We have played many a game of Rook, often by candlelight.

"Both English and Hausa are official languages in this part of Nigeria. The Bible and hymn book have been translated into Hausa, and it is used in the churches. Children study Hausa when they go to school. However, there are other local languages which are also used in the churches at times.

"The federal government of Nigeria took over all schools (including the new secondary school) and the hospital some years ago. The church has a good health program, with village dispensaries in many areas.

"There are agricultural development and village well programs.

"Most of the people in this area live in round mud huts, two or more in a compound, surrounded by a fence made of woven grass or corn stalks. The staple food is guinea corn, but rice and yams are also eaten. At present it is the dry season, and it is very dry and hot. Someone with a thermometer said it was 105 degrees the other day. It is getting hotter as the harmattan begins to recede. The 'harmattan' is a dust-laden wind which blows off the Sahara Desert. At times it is so thick that even the domestic Nigeria Airways planes cannot fly. There is, of course, dust everywhere. The only advantage is that it blocks some of the rays of the sun, so it is not so hot. Fortunately, in most places it becomes cooler during the night, and in the early morning, before sunrise, it is quite pleasant.

"The church area is divided into two parts, one on the north and one on the south side of the Benue River. Transportation is quite difficult, especially during the rainy season. A mission plane is essential. Everyone appreciates the "Bishara," ("Good News") and the pilot, Jim Keech. In addition to the transport, it brings the mail when it goes to Jos on a trip, and that is always welcome.

"Many of you will be interested in the Women's Fellowship (*Zumuntar Mata*), which is becoming United Methodist Women. I recall how impressed I was when I attended their annual meeting years ago. I was not able to go this time, but heard the reports. There were more than 6,000 women gathered in a village. Shelters (for shade) were made; they sat on limbs which had been cut from trees, knots and all. Each woman had to bring her own cooking pots, food and water, and many had babies on their backs. At night many simply spread the cloth which was part of their clothing on the ground and slept on it. One of the husbands told a missionary that the women really didn't want to leave their families to go to the meeting; they were lonesome for their husbands and children. But what a different story the women tell! They love being away, and dance and sing and talk for hours, day and night. They took an offering which amounted to the equivalent of $2,500. This is a great deal, because salaries even for pastors are only about $40-$50 a month. I can't help but contrast this with places in the U.S. where members of the U.M.W. will not bother to attend an annual meeting when it is in their own town or even their church.

"Water is often a problem during the dry season, as is true in so many parts of Africa. One learns to get along on very little–I have washed my hair, taken a sponge bath, and poured what was left into the toilet–with half a bucket of water."

My Work in Nigeria
Bambur

Soon after my arrival in Bambur I met Doris Horn and Ilsa Bertsch, both missionaries from Germany. Ann invited them and Bodo Schwabe and Gesila Hensler for a meal in her home, and we had a good time visiting. On another evening we all went to the home of Saratu, a Nigerian woman who made peanut butter for the missionaries. It was interesting to see the inside of a round hut. There were posters and family photos on the walls, a refrigerator, chairs, a single bed, a couch, and a coffee table. We moved the table and chairs outside and sat there to eat the pounded yam and soup. It was a pleasant time visiting, in three languages. On Sunday I went with Ann to the church service at Bambur. Bodo preached, using the story of Mary and Martha. He stressed that men must share home responsibilities with women, so that women, too, might worship and join in church activities.

Women's Christian Training Centre

That evening we attended a dinner at the Women's Training Centre, which the church had planned to greet the two German mission officials. The women served a good meal of rice, beans, greens and beef soup. When they had us women go first to serve ourselves, we insisted that the Nigerian women should go too. They were reluctant, but some obviously enjoyed it. (However, some served the men and then ate.) Afterward they sang for us and played their traditional instruments.

The guests were each asked to speak, and then others were given a chance to talk. Two of the women expressed special appreciation for the sermon that morning, and voiced the hope that men and women could begin to share in work and fellowship. They sang a song that said that though we leave, we will all be joined in Spirit, through Christ. Ann brought a carload of women home with us. As we passed men walking, Ann remarked that the men were walking and women riding. One of the women said that it was good for them for a change, and the others laughed.

Christiana Sonti, Acting Director, WCTC

Dinner Group

Women Playng Instruments

Also, in Bambur, I enjoyed a meal in the home of Ahmadu Maidoki and his wife, Garba Ahmadu. They were building a new house, so he told me that if I would come back to Nigeria I would stay with them.

Ahmadu Maidoki

Lami, Garba, and Ahmadu Maidoki

Dinner with Ahmadu Maidoki and Wife, and Guest

The Keeches shared their videotapes with us at various times, and invited us all to a Valentine Day dinner.

The Bishara, Jim Keech (pilot), with Seamons and Others

441

Banyam Seminary

Now to my work–with a rapidly growing church and a pastorate with little training, the need for all kinds of Christian education was pressing. Ann had asked whether I would be interested in teaching seven hours at Banyam. This was the first year of the "seminary"–not at all on the level of our seminaries. (It was the first year of the English post secondary theological school.) I had given copies of my book on Christian education to the seminary, but the students there were limited in education and I am afraid did not learn very much from my time with them.

I was asked to help organize a Sunday School for the children of the students, and did so. I typed a list of items that missionaries might be able to collect for them to use, and visited their first classes.

Junior Sunday School Class

Primary Class

Workshops for Sunday School Teachers and District Youth Workers

Puppets

Malam (teacher) Ahmadu Maidoki, the conference youth coordinator, and I spent a good deal of time together. (When they said "youth" it included children in Sunday School, youth, and young adults.) He was a very dedicated person, well organized, and worked hard. I held two workshops for Sunday School teachers, one on each side of the river. The first was at Bambur. We started late, and some left before it was over. I realized that what I had planned (in consultation with Ahmadu) was too concentrated for them, and talked with Ahmadu about possible changes for Zing.

442

Ahmadu & Esther Ready for a Journey

The workshop at Zing, on the other side of the river, was held the next weekend. Things went well (I had shortened it), and response was good. Eighteen people began, and another woman came on Friday evening. We finished at 12:45 on Saturday, and then had a lunch of rice, beans and palm oil soup with a few greens. I think I got the piece of ham bone and the meat on it which was used to flavor the dish.

Part of the Group at Zing

The Cooks

Eating Breakfast

We had another workshop for the District Coordinators of Youth Work at Bambur, on "Planning and Leading Bible Study." There was a good response, and most seemed to have gained something from it.

District Youth Leaders–Workshop

Using a Time-Line in Teaching

Ahmadu Maidoki

New Bicycles for District Youth Coordinators

Kikulu Bible Institute

Kikulu Bible Institute

445

I had expected to fly on February 5 to Zing to take part in a workshop at the Kikulu Bible Institute, and then to hold one at Zing for Sunday School teachers. However, there was a very heavy harmattan, and the plane could not fly. So Ahmadu Maidoki sent his pickup for me, with the Women's Training Centre driver. We picked up a pastor's family, and left at 8:30, arriving at Zing at 1:15–dusty, and needing water to drink. Word was sent to Rev. Jolly Nyame that I had arrived, and after a quick lunch with Alan Seaman I took a bath and then went out to the Bible School.

Hassan Bandre Leading Bible Study

For the first session of the workshop on "Planning and Leading Bible Study" I gave a survey of Bible history and what the Bible is. This raised many questions for some, and they asked questions and had a discussion for an hour afterward.

I ate with Rev. Jolly and then his driver took me to a house near the Seamans where I was staying. The next afternoon Rev. Jolly came for me, and we picked up Mrs. Ndule, who gave a lecture on women's place in development. She received many questions and feedback. I wished I could have understood it all. It was late before I had my part, so I had two hours instead of the three for which I had planned. Many did not understand, but some did. They were assigned Bible studies, so I would see the next day how much they had understood. Those done in Hausa were translated for me, and I spent the next morning checking them. In the afternoon the Bible study went pretty well. There were several responses on the evaluation, showing some did learn from this intensive experience. It inspired Jolly Nyame to get a group together to write some Bible studies. I offered to help them get started if they wished. Later I wrote an outline of suggestions for getting organized for writing Bible studies, and met with Ahmadu and Pastor Jolly and his assistant in Zing to discuss it.

Writing and Typing

During my time in Nigeria I worked on putting together and typing the first year of the Kindergarten Sunday School curriculum for which materials were written in Ghana. Also, as the result of work done at the Theological Hall in Sierra Leone, I completed a ten-lesson unit for children. Fortunately, I was able to borrow a typewriter in each place, and after a search found a ribbon to replace the well-used one in one of them.

During the last part of my time in Nigeria I stayed in Lankaviri with Ethel Johnson. When she could spare the time (she was far busier than I), we played Rook. One of the things I remember from Lankaviri was my visit to the women's choir practice, using the traditional instruments. They obviously enjoyed it very much, and seemed pleased that I was taking photographs.

Lankaviri, Conference Office

Children on the Compound

Esther Megill & Ethel Johnson, Playing Rook

447

Women's Fellowship Choir, Lankaviri

"Boom-Boom" (Bass)

"Boom-Boom" (Kata-Ko), Soprano

*"Hingwa" and
"Kocha-Kocha"*

"Sound"

Musical Instruments

When I was at Lankaviri I became aware again that women in Nigeria were truly oppressed, and many were beginning to recognize it. They worked very hard. It took hours to buy and prepare food. They often walked for miles; were responsible for all child care, except for the help of the older children, and carried water. Most were expected to have babies at frequent, regular intervals. Women had no rights under Nigerian law. According to traditional custom, at least in that part of Nigeria, all that the couple had, and the children, belonged to the man's family. There was the tragic case of the young widow of the conference treasurer, who had three young children, the youngest about a year old. The church had no pension system for conference staff; she had little education. The husband's family had taken the house which he had built in their village. They had saved some money and had bought some things to make life easier for them. But she could not live in the house, unless she married the husband's brother. They came and took away everything except the personal clothing for her and the children. They even emptied her son's clothes out of a little suitcase the father had bought him, and took it. They were insisting that she should go live with them in the village. She didn't want to go; she said they were "not nice" to her. (She was of a different tribe.) But if she didn't go, they could take the children. And this case was multiplied many times over.

[I learned later that General Superintendent Dabale prevailed upon the family to allow the children to stay with the mother in Lankaviri. Later she was able to get a job in a new nursery school the Iowa Conference of the UMC established in Jalingo.]

The Garba Cedi Church

One of the interesting events was attending the commissioning of a new district superintendent and district officers. The Garba Cedi church was packed, with as many people outside the church as in. The service began at 10:00 and lasted until 2:30. Ethel and I were given "choice" seats–on the platform, facing the congregation. Twelve choirs sang. The history of each charge was read, and officers were commissioned for every charge. There were six, each with many village churches attached. For these there were three ordained ministers, one of whom was the district superintendent. Each village church had an evangelist. These were trained at Dadango and Kikulu Bible Schools (formerly at Banyam).

Commissioning of Superintendents and Officers

The Offering

A woman took Ethel and me afterward and fed us, rice and yams with palm oil soup and a little meat. We went to the General Superintendent and discovered he had not been fed. They finally brought him food. We left at about 4:00 and arrived home at 5:00.

A Visit to Zing

I also visited Zing, where I stayed with Doris Horn, who was a nurse, and I was especially interested in the health clinic. I took pictures of the Child Health Clinic, and of a man who had come from Jalingo by taxi to be fitted with glasses. While I was at Zing I met Dee Ann Dejong, who also worked in the clinic, and visited with Norma and Alan Seaman. I borrowed some paperbacks from the "Station Library," and relaxed by reading. When it was time to return to Lankaviri I was able to go by taxi, after a long wait.

*Dee Ann Dejong
Weighing a Baby*

Doris Horn Fitting Glasses

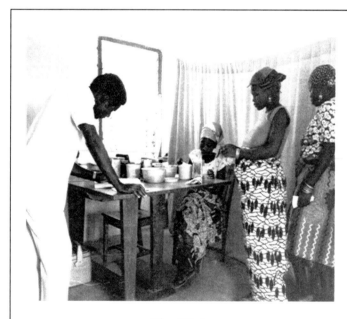

The Clinic

Zinna Peak, a Landmark

To Jos, and the Missionary Retreat

On March 7 Ethel and I left for Zing, where she had a meeting. Norma Seaman gave me a permanent, with a boxed one I had brought with me, then gave us a quick lunch. We went to the airfield, but it was nearly an hour before we took off for Jos. The harmattan was quite bad, but we did make it. Ethel and I ate at the Yahu that evening and the next noon. Doris and Dee Ann were at Sprite Lodge also. We all had breakfast together, then went shopping until time to leave for Miango for the missionary retreat. It was a beautiful, restful place, owned by the Sudan Interior Mission (SIM). We arrived at about 4:30, had supper, and attended a meeting that night.

Ann had asked if I would have something for the older children during the business meetings, and I was glad to do so. I told a Bible story, and then the children made puppets and practiced dramatizing it. They took part in the talent show that evening, and did well. It was a big event for them.

Andrew & Anna Erbele Making Puppets

Bob Fletcher, the Area Secretary from the Board of Global Ministries was there, so I met him and we had some discussions together.

452

The Children's Puppet Show

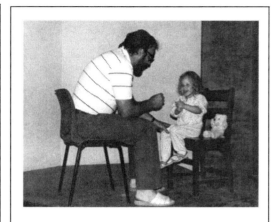

Thad and Leah McGinnis

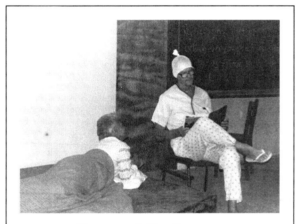

Norma and Alan Seamans

Jojo Bentel

Ilsa Bertsch, Syle Show

Traditional Indian Dancing

Bob Fletcher, Area Secretary; Roberta Ellis

Before I left Nigeria I received the letter on the following page.

United Methodist Church in Nigeria

Nigeria Provisional Annual Conference

Youth Division

P.O. Box 659, Jos-Nigeria

Director–Ahmadu Maidoki   **Date** 8th March, 1990

Dear Dr. Esther Megill,

Greetings to you in the name of the Lord Christ Jesus whom we are serving.

On behalf of the Youth Program of the United Methodist Church in Nigeria, I am writing to register my sincere thanks and gratitude for the help you have offered during the three sessions of the courses done this year. Many letters came to my office from the Sunday School teachers and the District Youth Coordinators asking and requesting you to come back again in 1991 or 1992. This is really a testimony of the job well done by you. You are really a Christian Educator. "A GOOD CHRISTIAN EDUCATOR MUST HAVE NOT ONLY THE KNOWLEDGE OF THE BIBLE, BUT ALSO PATIENCE, UNDERSTANDING, AND ABOVE ALL A MOTHERLY FEELING, A GENUINE DESIRE TO HELP. SUCH PERSONS ARE RARE, BUT DR. E. MEGILL IS ONE. SHE IS ALSO A HELPER AND A FRIEND EVER READY TO GUIDE YOUR ENDEAVOURS."

Thank you for your guidance and tremendous concern that you have in Youth Program and the desire and initiative created in promoting Christian Education in Nigeria.

You are always fresh in the memories of the Sunday School teachers, the District Youth Coordinators, and the entire congregation of the United Methodist Church in Nigeria.

May the Lord bless and guide you as you travel round the Continent of Africa. Amen.

Yours in Christ Jesus,

(Signed)

(AHMADU MAIDOKI)

YOUTH DIRECTOR

cc. General Superintendent

Director, COM

Dr. Ethel Johnson

March 12 was a busy day as I packed and re-packed, got a cholera shot, finally was able to get a hotel reservation in Lagos, etc. On the 13th I was up at 5:30 and ready for Jim who took me to the airport. There I discovered that the <u>private</u> airline left early, but that Nigeria Airways not until 12:30. A book helped me pass the time, and I finally arrived in Lagos (an hour's flight), and at the hotel. I had to stay in Lagos for a few days in order to obtain a visa for Zambia.

Formation of the Nigerian Conference (UMCN)
1991- 2007

We have been calling attention to the period of education and training required for the eventual formation of the new Nigeria Conference of The United Methodist Church. The late 1980s and early 90s was a period of growth, anticipation and especially, education for leadership. Bishop Arthur Kulah of Liberia continued to oversee the Provisional Annual Conference that was formed in 1984. He took initiatives in several ways to bridge the old Nigeria Muri Church with the fledgling United Methodist Church (Nigeria). Bishop Kulah sent one of his own Liberian leaders, Jefferson Labada, to the Nigeria church leaders as an educator, introducing them to the organizational structure and the *Discipline* of the denomination, especially as these apply to the African Central Conference. Labada and his wife resided in Nigeria from 1985-1987 to carry our this training task. In this way, together with the work of Ethel Johnson, things began to take shape as the time for full conference status drew closer. Bishop Kulah ended his episcopal supervision of the Nigerian Church in 1990 and was succeed by Bishop Bangura of the Sierra Leone Conference who served until 1992

Meanwhile, Done P. Dabale, the General Secretary of the Provisional Annual Conference, had been moving forward in the establishing of new local churches (charges) and expanding the districts of the church. This was a period of remarkable growth in membership and in expansion of the borders of the church as churches were started in places as far away as Jos, Bauchi, Gombe and Abuja. By 1990 the number of charges had more than doubled from fifty to one hundred twenty.. Dabale purchased a site for the church headquarters in Jalingo while he was treasurer for the church. This land, just six miles from Jalingo, the capital city of Taraba state, would provide high visibility for the church and room to expand. Additional building was done on the former mission station of Lankaviri, looking forward to the residence for and offices of the first bishop.

It was a momentous occasion when The United Methodist General Conference voted to grant Nigeria the right to become a full conference in 1992. Subsequently, in the same year, when the West Africa Central Conference was held in Sierra Leone, The Rev. Done P. Dabale was elected as the first Bishop of The United Methodist Church in Nigeria (UMCN).

As General Superintendent Bishop Dabale had already put changes in place that would help facilitate the start-up of the new conference. The transition to a self-governing conference continued in incremental steps as the new bishop began his work.. Both the growth in membership and the new structures called for greater diversity and enlargement of the training institutions. The number of districts had now risen to fifteen. Each needed a superintendent and had to train leaders to fill the positions that the new organization required.

The decade of the nineties will be remembered for progress on all fronts. as the new conference took up its work. New projects were laid out to give incentive and a sense of progress as Bishop Dabale settled into leadership. The programs which we shall mention briefly also provided links with conferences in the U.S.A. as they became a means of support and the building of relationships between Nigeria and churches in the United States.

Evangelism was always a priority. This was the first commitment of Bishop Dabale and the intention in the conference was that all projects undertaken would foster and build up the church. Church growth continued until the districts increased from fifteen to twenty-one in number. By 2000 there were well over 220,000 members in the UMCN (United Methodist Church of Nigeria). Rural health became a major area of work in all districts. The health program was centered at Zing, where a small but fully operative hospital was built, along with an eye clinic, while a busy maternity clinic was located at Bambur. The agricultural program became very important across the conference, with training in farming, dry season gardening, raising and marketing poultry, and cooperation in the Heifer Project. The "Bishop's Appeal for the Children of Africa," coming from the U.S.A., generated interest in caring for children who had been orphaned by HIV/AIDS. An orphanage was constructed with U.S. funds. In education, progress was made at both primary and secondary levels. These schools, located in Jalingo, were maintained by the church, as all former mission/church schools had been take over by the government. The former Muri Christian Training School was up-graded and became a fully recognized seminary, while "junior" seminaries were operated in two separate locations.

Bishop Dabale, who was very supportive of women, developed two centers to carry out Women's Leadership Training. These centers focused on helping women to become self-sufficient in domestic work and in business ventures. Of course, mention needs to be made of the youth programs and the well-digging projects carried out all over the Conference and which became a major means for churches in the U.S.A. to link up with the UMCN.

In 1997 a very adequate office building for the new conference was built and dedicated at Jalingo, the church headquarters, and at the same time a new library at the Banyam Seminary was opened.

Early in 2000, however, tensions arose in the church around the leadership of Bishop Dabale. Five districts located on the north side of the Benue River felt the bishop's leadership was unacceptable and that certain inequities were being developed by his policies. The historical and ethnic issues that accounted for some of the unrest cannot be dealt with here. Suffice it to say that this situation created a very difficult time for the church. A counter movement developed among five districts that was aligned against the Bishop. The difficulty continued throughout most of 2003 through 2006. Ultimately, this problem led to the Council of Bishops granting Bishop Dabale a leave of absence while the leadership of the West African conferences attempted a settlement. Much of the progress of the UMCN was on hold during these negotiations. Bishop Dabale was reinstated in March of 2005, only to be cut off from further leadership by his unexpected death in August of 2006. His dedicated service as first bishop of the UMCN was lovingly celebrated on August 26, 2006 with a memorial service at the Cathedral Church in Jalingo.

At this writing it can be reported that the successor to Bishop Dabale was elected on March 3, 2007 in Liberia at the West Africa Central Conference. He is The Rev. Kefas Mavula, who had previously been the assistant to Bishop Dabale. Our prayers are with The United Methodist Church of Nigeria as they take up anew their sacred task. [Word was received in January 2008 that Bishop Mavula had died suddenly.]

–Dr. Dean Gilliland

Chapter 4. Zambia

Zambia is a landlocked, tropical country located in southeast Africa, 10-18 degrees south of the Equator. Thus, the seasons are reversed from those in the United States, with summer from October to March and winter from May to August. The rainy season occurs between November and March, but even then the sun shines an average of four hours a day. Temperature may vary from 80-90 degrees Fahrenheit, dropping in the evening as low as 57 degrees. It is on a high plateau, about 4, 265 feet above sea level, with some mountains and hills, and is somewhat larger than Texas.

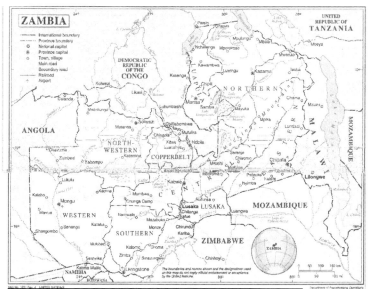

(Map courtesy of the University of Texas Libraries The University of Texas at Austin. Provided by US CIA)

The population is made up of mixed races and religions. English is the official language, but seventy-eight different languages are spoken. There are a number of other races–British and Indian being the most common. Christianity is the dominant and official religion, but traditional religion blends with Christianity in many syncretistic churches. Islam is present, particularly in urban areas. There are also a few Jews and Hindus.

Main places of interest are the Victoria Falls, the Livingstone Museum and Game Park, the mines in the Copperbelt, and other game parks. Mining and refining of copper is vital to the economy. Agricultural products include cattle and goats.

Zambia is a republic and contains three branches of government: the executive, the legislative and the judicial. It was formerly a British colony, called Northern Rhodesia. After a two-stage series of elections, in October of 1964 it became the independent Republic of Zambia. The capital is Lusaka.[19]

HIV/AIDS was becoming a serious problem in Zambia by 1990.

---

[19]From *NDEKE Tales,* published for Zambia Airways, 1990; *Wikepedia Free Encyclopedia*, Zambia.

A Sojourn in Lagos

Although I traveled to Lagos on March 13 and planned to arrive in Lusaka on March 17, it did not happen that way. The first night I stayed in the Bristol Hotel where I had managed to get a reservation by phone, but it was expensive for the type of hotel, and the surroundings were unpleasant. The next day I took my passport and visa application to the Zambian High Commission, and was told I could pick them up on Friday. Someone had told me that the American Embassy had a guest house where it might be possible to stay, so I went to the Embassy, and they called the guest house. Fortunately, I was able to reserve a room for only $35.00 a night. From there I went in search of British Airways. The taxi driver couldn't find them, but I finally did after a lot of walking. They referred me to the Ethiopian Airways. I went to the Bristol, checked out, and took a taxi to the American Embassy. On the way I stopped at Ethiopian Airways and was able to change my reservation to Ndola in Zambia to allow for a stop in Lusaka.

I was living in luxury. It was like an American motel, and I could even have a salad, apple pie, and iced tea for lunch, and a pizza for supper. The next morning a breakfast of orange juice, a cinnamon roll and coffee were brought to my room at 7:30. At 8:00 I got a taxi and went to NITEL, where I was able to phone to B.S. Chuba in Lusaka. He said he wanted me to go to Ndola on Monday. He would be going to a meeting there on Tuesday. I tried unsuccessfully to reach Jim Gulley (whom I had known as a missionary in Liberia) in Ibadan (Nigeria). I was hoping to speak to him about possible assistance at the airport on Saturday.

In between making travel arrangements I read, played solitaire, wrote letters, and enjoyed the American food. On Friday I was able to pick up my passport and visa at the Zambian Embassy with no problem. The next day, the 17th, I packed and was moved out of the room before lunch, but did not head for the airport until 6:20. I waited for two hours at Ethiopian Airways, and then they announced that the flight was cancelled because of technical difficulties, with no promises of when I could get another. I was devastated, because I didn't know where to go. I sat with all my extensive luggage in the airport, wondering what to do, when a UN airport representative offered to help, and took me back to the Embassy Guest House, where I was able to get a room again. The next day was spent in reading, playing solitaire, and eating. I tried repeatedly to call the airport hotel to leave a message for the representative from the Clarke-Prescott travel agency who was to pick up my ticket, but either the line was busy or they didn't answer.

The next day I partially packed, in case it would be possible to leave, and was able, with some difficulty, to find the Clarke-Prescott Travel Agency. A young man went with me to Ethiopian Airlines. We got there at 9:00 a.m. and left at 4:00. Computers were down part of the time, but finally I got a reservation to Zambia for 2:30 a.m. Wednesday, with a two-days layover in Nairobi. It was too late by that time to call Lusaka. I headed for the motel, and discovered in the taxi that my envelope with $300 was missing! The outside telephone line was not working, so I took a taxi again to the travel agent–and found they had saved it for me.

The next morning I went again to NITEL, and made a call to Lusaka. I talked to Chuba's secretary. Needless to say, they were wondering where I was. Again, I moved out of the room by 12:00, and spent the rest of the day in the lobby. At 8:00 p.m., with the help of several people, I got a taxi and went to the airport. Mr. Uche, the representative from Clarke-Prescott, was there, as was also Mr. M. Musa, who was in the office. He came just because of concern for me–it was not his job at all. I had found so many helpful people! (I wrote a letter from Zambia to the people at the travel agency to thank them, and received one in return.) It took until 1:00 a.m. to work out all the details and get me to the gate for the flight.

I was reminded of snatches of conversation I had overheard at the Embassy Guest House. Many there seemed to have only contempt for anything Nigerian, including the people. They were preoccupied with making a "little America" and complained when it didn't come up to American standards. I thought–I'd hate to live in Africa and be so unhappy.

On to Zambia

The Ethiopian Airlines plane was late, and it was after 3:00 a.m. before we finally took off. We arrived in Addis Ababa at about 12:00 their time (two hours ahead of Nigeria time). There was more checking of tickets and waiting for the plane to Nairobi. In Nairobi I had to get a transit visa and the baggage, and caught the Ethiopian Airlines bus just as it was leaving for the "680 Hotel," where I had a good night's sleep before having to arrange for the flight to Lusaka, and found that the first would be the next afternoon. While in the hotel I was able to contact the bishop's office, and the conference secretary, Dr. Nthamduri, came to see me. I was relieved to be

Queen Sendoya and Noreen Mapala

able to talk with someone from the Kenya church, since I had had little information from the bishop.

It was Friday, March 24, before I finally arrived in Lusaka, where I was met by a man from the UCZ office, Queen Sendoya, and Noreen Mapala, the Administrative Secretary of the synod. I had come to Zambia to work with the United Church, the largest Protestant church in Zambia. It is the result of union of Methodist (British), Congregationalist, Presbyterian and Reformed Churches, which grew out of the work of various missionary societies: London Missionary Society, Church of Scotland (Presbyterian), Paris Evangelical Missionary Society, and the Methodist Missionary Society (England). When I was there in 1990, they celebrated the 25th anniversary of the formation of the church. They had about 150,000 adult members. I had contact with the church through the General Secretary, the Rev. B. S. Chuba, who had been one

*Wendy Kilworth-Mason &
Helen Johnstone*

of my students at Trinity College in Ghana. He had previously taught at the theological school where I would be staying, and had introduced my text book there.

I took a plane to Ndola and arrived at a crowded airport at 6:30, where I was met by Graham Shaw, English pastor of St. Andrew's Church, who took me to his home. I met his wife, Sandy, and two children. We ate supper and visited, and then I was glad to go to bed for a good night's sleep. The next day Abdul, a driver from Mindola, came for me. An hour's ride took me to Kitwe, and then to the Mindolo Ecumenical Foundation. There the Rev. Helen Johnstone shared her home with me until I could move into the guest flat (apartment) at the Theological College. Helen, who taught at the Theological College, was an ordained minister of the Church of Scotland. Wendy Kilworth-Mason, English, was Dean of the College, and lived next door, and joined us for lunch. Alan Greig, the principal with whom I had been corresponding, came over later. They would be leaving soon. I enjoyed talking with him, and he gave me some information about what was expected. I was invited to his home for coffee after church and then lunch. The next day we went to the Catholic mass in the Mindolo Ecumenical Foundation Chapel–a thoroughly enjoyable experience. We were welcome to take communion with them.

There were beautiful murals in the chapel, no doubt painted by students or graduates of the Africa Literature Centre, where such art was also taught.

After the service I went to the Greigs (Alan and Ruth, and children), and after lunch Alan took me to see the guest flats where I would be staying. They were skimpy, but adequate. I moved in

*Mindolo Chapel & Women's Training
Centre*

on March 26. I was grateful to be able to be independent, but was glad for being taken to the bank to get some money, and then to shop for food. On that day I attended chapel at the college, and was introduced to students and staff, including Father Charles Helms, the acting principal (taking Greig's place).

On other Sundays I attended with Ruth Greig the St. Margaret U.C.Z. Church in Kitwe. There I met Arnold Thompson and his wife, Rachel, from Sierra Leone. He was the chaplain at the Mindolo Ecumenical Foundation. I also met Murial Sanderson, financial comptroller. Helen and I went with her to the big market to buy food. At another time she stopped by with Larry Hills, a United Methodist missionary in Zaire, whom I had met in Zambia years before. He had to come to Mindolo from the Congo in order to make a phone call. That evening we had dinner with Murial, and pleasant conversation. At another time I met Rose Aminarh from Ghana, who preached and led the service. She was taking a course at Mindolo. Later I discovered that she had attended Trinity, and used my textbook. I also met a woman from our church in Nigeria, Elsie Bellow, who was attending a course at Mindolo. We talked about problems of the church in Nigeria–I listened with a sympathetic ear.

Murial was able to get an appointment for me with a doctor, an Indian woman, at the Mines Clinic. X-rays showed spurs on both heels, and she gave me some pills and later referred me to a surgeon, who gave me cortisone injections, which helped my walking a good deal. Paul Bwalya, the Moderator of the Copperbelt Presbytery, took me to the hospital to have that done, and helped in many other ways during my stay there.

Paul Bwalya

After the heat and dryness of northern Nigeria, it was a welcome change to arrive in Zambia near the end of the rainy season. I enjoyed the temperate climate, and the grass and flowers everywhere. It was in the center of the Copperbelt. Work went on around the clock in the nearby copper mines, and I heard the sirens which signaled the changing of shifts. This was the biggest industrial area in Black Africa, the fifth largest producer of copper in the world. Unfortunately, the market price of copper had halved in real terms since Zambia's independence in 1963. This had severe effects on the economy. Like so many countries in Africa, they were too dependent on one source of income. An economic system established by colonial powers is hard to break away from, but in recent years Zambia has tried to diversify its sources of income.

My Work in Zambia

The Theological College

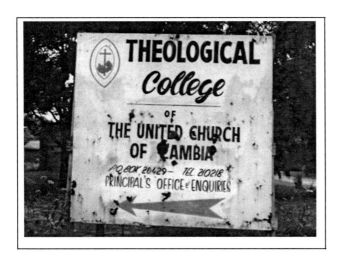

On Wednesday, March 28, I attended the chapel service, and then began a six-day seminar with the students. This had been arranged ahead of time by the principal. They had all studied the textbook I had written for teaching Christian Education in theological schools in Africa. There were thirty-five students to begin, and three men from the UCZ Church offices, Andrew Muwowo, Synod Director of Youth Work; John Ng'Andu, Synod Sunday School Coordinator, and Clement Chimese, Youth Convener of the Kitwe Consistory. Also, for the first

College Campus. Chapel at Left.

half, John Burgess, English, from TEEZ (Theological Education by Extension in Zambia) attended the sessions. There was a lot of sharing and discussion as we dealt with age-level characteristics, human development, and teaching and learning. The next day the emphasis was on methods, and the Synod Youth Director taught a Zambian musical song/game, with drums and marching. As the drums played and we marched, children began to gather. After break I began with planning a lesson and gave assignments.

Time was also spent on cutting stencils, planning lessons, and checking the written assignments. I led chapel one morning. The next week we worked with writing Bible studies for adults, with suggestions for adaptation for youth. At one point there was a rather heated discussion about theology–especially the interpretation of the Temptation story. However, I was pleased with the response to the Bible studies which were presented. I asked for volunteers to write more lessons of each–children and adult Bible studies. I also handed out hymnals *(Come, Let Us Sing,* which I had edited and compiled in Ghana for use with children) to those who would translate some of the songs or get others to do so. These

Student David Sampa and Esther Megill

could then be used in the children's lessons. The material the students wrote became part of the manuscripts which were completed after I returned to the States and settled in a retirement home.

At the close of the final session the students gave me "a vote of thanks."

The next day there was the final communion service of the year, and good-byes were said to Alan and Ruth Greig, who left for leave in Scotland.

Workshops & Other Educational Programs

Workshops

During the time I was teaching in the Theological School I was able to meet with the three men from the UCZ offices to begin plans for workshops for Sunday School teachers. We had very profitable discussions. Three workshops were planned: in Lusaka, The Copperbelt Presbytery, and Kabwe.

Lusaka

I flew to Lusaka on April 27 to hold the first workshop. Noreen Mapala took me to the YWCA, where I would stay, and helped me get some stencils run and materials gathered. I visited with B.S. Chuba, and had tea with him.

The next day the workshop began, with thirty-two people in attendance, eleven of them women. We stopped for lunch, but continued until it was nearly dark. We moved to the sanctuary of the church for the evening session, but there were no lights in that area of town. After supper we met again, with the participants divided into groups, each to work on an assigned lesson for a specific age group.

Singing

Planning a Lesson in Small Groups

I was taken to the pastor's house (Rev. Musonda Bwalya) for lunch and supper. In the evening his wife had to find charcoal and cook on that, since the electricity was off. She served me with rice, chicken, and cabbage. I discovered that Zambian women traditionally curtseyed–or nearly knelt on one knee-when offering something to a guest. This the pastor's wife did as she informed me that the meal was ready.

On Sunday morning Noreen took me to Matero, and we attended the early service. We were introduced and I was asked to give the benediction. We sat in front, facing the congregation, on a six-inch bench. At least we could lean against the wall! The service was an hour and a half long, in Bemba. There was a visiting choir, very good, which used drums. As is so often true in Africa, the service was lay led, with the congregation's secretary having a prominent role, and a visiting layman preaching. The workshop participants surprised me by singing "Thank the Lord" (a song from Ghana, which I had taught them), in both English and Bemba.

We went into the workshop immediately after the service. Reports were given on the group work, and lesson plans evaluated. They had worked hard, but I saw again how difficult it is to introduce new ideas; much more time was needed. But they expressed appreciation, and I had a list of some who would be interested in writing if it was possible for me to get a writer's workshop organized. They were also interested in publishing the hymnal, but that did not happen. The problem was no doubt the lack of money.

There were closing speeches and photos, and then I was off to the airport. There was no one at the Ndola airport to meet me, but after about half an hour the pastor arrived and took me to his house. He had a two-hour meeting, so I read and slept until he came with the layman who had the car, and they took me to Kitwe.

Musical Games

On May 18 Paul Bwalya picked me up to take me to the workshop in Kitwe. It was held in the Muchunga Family Centre, which was part of the church. We began at 6:45. Before the evening was over there were nineteen people, including two women and two Theological College students. The next day was a full one. My part was finished by 5:00, and I assigned them work for the evening. They served me rice at noon, and the rest had *nshima*, a thick corn mush, the basic food in

Zambia. I asked to taste some, and found it quite good. I told them to tell the women I would be glad to eat that; they need not prepare special food for me.

The next day the moderator began with a short devotional service, and the workshop continued. Mr. Muwowo was there, and told me that the Synod had agreed for a writers' workshop if the congregations would pay expenses for their delegates.

Singing

Report of Group Work

467

Kabwe Workshop

At 2:00 p.m. on Friday, June 8, I left on a bus for a three-hour trip to Kabwe. It was interesting to see something of the Zambian countryside–tall grass, with some trees. There were occasional villages, with small square mud and wattle thatched houses. There was always a round hut, a roof over poles, with seats. (This was called a "palaver   Leone.) Occasionally there were rectangular, whitewashed schools. Sometimes women were selling fruits and vegetables along the road.

I was met at the bus station by three young men, Hezron Chilanga, the Presbytery youth coordinator, and two others. Rev. Mwansa, the moderator of the Central Presbytery, arrived, and we went to the Uhuru Secondary School (a private school owned by an Indian), where we were met by Patricia Chunda, the Consistory Youth Secretary. They all took me to the Pan-African Institute for Development guest house. People from East, Central and Southern Africa stayed there when they were taking various courses. I had a comfortable room, but it was in the men's section because they thought I must be a man since I was a "Doctor."Saturday was a full day of conducting the workshop. Fourteen attended (three women)–but they had expected forty or fifty. However, it was a good group and the small group made it possible to finish in one day.

That evening was "Africa Night" at the Institute, when the students cooked food typical of

their countries. I had to eat earlier than they in order to get back to the church, but the party was still in full swing with loud music when I returned at 10:30, and continued until after 12:00.

I had a very warm feeling of friendship after the strenuous time in the workshop.

I copied this from a chart in a minister's office:

Principles of Zambian Humanism

1. Man at the centre.
2. The dignity of man.
3. Non-exploitation of man.

468

4. Equal opportunities for all.
5. Hard work and self-reliance
6. Working together
7. The extended family
8. Loyalty and patriotism

The next morning, Sunday, the moderator picked me up at about 9:00, and I was taken to the church. We went into a little room with the leaders. Choirs were singing. At about 9:45 we went into the sanctuary, all sitting on the platform. Mr. Muwowo sat next to me and interpreted the Bemba. There was much singing of songs composed especially for the occasion, the induction of Hezron S. Chilanga as Central Presbytery Youth Coordinator. Mr. Chilanga and his wife sat in chairs facing the congregation, and then facing the moderator as he preached and gave words of advice to them. A special offering was taken for him.

The service was not quite over when the moderator left with me at 1:00. He took me to the guest house. Patricia Chunda went with us, and we ate lunch before going to the Elephant Head Hotel, where the driver from Kitwe was to meet me. He came after a time, and I said goodby to the people who had become my friends. Some of them I expected to see at the weekend workshop for writers.

Workshops for "Women Aglow"

When I had been in Kitwe for a short time, I met a young woman who became a good friend, Frances Sombé, was a Nigerian, married to a Zambian. She asked whether I would teach a group of professional and business women how to plan and lead Bible studies. She invited me to speak at their fellowship meeting of members of "Women Aglow," a conservative organization from the States, of which I had not heard before. So, on a Saturday in April Frances and her husband Rogers picked me up to take me to the meeting. It was quite an experience–being part of a Pentecostal meeting. My talk on "Women: Witnesses, Receivers, Messengers" was received well, however. There were fourteen present, including a young girl and one man, who was in Christian radio, and asked to interview me later.

We arranged for a series of noon meetings at the YMCA, with lunch, which the women (mainly Frances) brought. Six women met weekly for nine weeks. We had planned for ten sessions, but had to cancel the last one, as described later. The women were quite open to new ideas, and did good work. I included a few of their Bible studies in the collection I was making from different countries, which eventually became a manuscript. At our last session we met in the home of one of the women for a farewell luncheon. There was delicious food, including the *nshima* I had requested, and good conversation. They presented me with a copper plate. It has a raised figure of Jesus praying, and my name and "Lunch Time Bible Study 1990" engraved on it. It is a gift which I treasure.

Noon Luncheon Meetings. Frances Sombé in Center

Farewell Luncheon

Christian Education for Pre-School Children

Frances Sombé also asked if I could give a course on Christian education for pre-school children. She arranged with the Mindolo Ecumenical Foundation for us to meet at the Africa Literature Centre, and to observe the nursery school. Nine persons (two of them women) attended some or all of the course from June 11-15. At one session they wrote stories to use with young children. One of the Theological College students came to help teach some Bemba songs. The last session was observation of the nursery school, and evaluation, although few participants of the workshop were there. Frances served refreshments.

Slides and Swings

Blowing Bubbles

Mother and Baby Are Guests

"Together Time"

Observers

Writers' Workshop

Another very fruitful workshop was with a selected group of persons to help them write stories for children for use in Christian education. There were difficulties in making arrangements, both with the UCZ Synod and the Theological College. However, the college agreed to allow us to meet there and use the resources of the library. In the end we had eighteen persons. Four were college students, and two were young women who were attending a course at Mindolo; Ellen Moore was from The Gambia, and Rose Aminarh from Ghana.

Working in the Library

Writing Stories for Children

Mr. Muwowo, Director of Youth Work of the the United Church of Zambia, arranged for the workshop:

472

The United Church of Zambia
Synod Headquarters

14th May, 1990

Dr. Esther Megill
UCZ Theological College
P.O. Box 20429
KITWE

Dear Dr. Megill,

Thank you very much for your letter dated 3rd May, 1990 concerning some matters which have arisen from the Sunday School seminar you held in Lusaka during the weekend 27-29 April, 1990.

In the first place, we would like to thank you most sincerely for a commendable job you are doing of training our Sunday School teachers. We feel greatly honoured to be with you in our church to carry out this important task. The participants you have trained have appreciated highly your workshops whose results are quite fruitful. We pray that the Lord continues to bless you and guide you in all your plans concerning Christian Education.

As regards the writers' workshops to be held in Kitwe, so that the library resources could be easily utilised, the idea of holding the intensive weekend courses for seven people is a good one.

Due to financial constraints faced by our Synod Headquarters at the moment, we shall request the participants' Congregations or Consistories to sponsor them. To do this administratively, more time will be needed for the appropriate authorities to consider your request. In this case 15-17 June would be suitable. But 25-26 May is too late for such congregations to consider. I therefore suggest that this be substituted by 22-24 June. Please let us know what you think about this.

Concerning my trip to Namibia, it was pleasant and our Conference was quite successful. It is rather unfortunate that I missed the workshop you conducted in Lusaka.

With kind regards.

Yours Sincerely,
(Signed) A. Muwowo, DIRECTOR OF YOUTH WORK
United Church of Zambia,
Synod Headquarters,
P.O. Box 50122,
LUSAKA.

473

To: Consistory Chairmen,
   Chelstone, Kafue and Matero Consistories,
   United Church of Zambia, <u>LUSAKA</u>

Dear Ministers,

SUNDAY SCHOOL WRITERS' WORKSHOP.

I wish to inform you that there will be a Writers' Workshop at the UCZ Theological College, Kitwe from 15th to 17th June, 1990. The workshop will be conducted by Dr. Esther Megill.

The delegates should arrive in Kitwe on Thursday, 14th June at 1800 hours. They should carry with them bedding, towel, soap, plate, cup, spoon and Good News Bibles.

Due to financial constraints faced by our church, Synod is unable to sponsor the delegates concerned. We would be grateful if your consistory or congregations could sponsor them. Those who have expressed their willingness to attend this workshop are as follows:

[Names listed]

Some useful material was produced by those who attended the writers' workshop. It was a new idea for them that one could teach religion by using stories other than Bible stories. I explained that they could use Bible <u>ideas</u>, but have stories related to children's lives. I gave some lectures, they wrote stories, and then we evaluated them. I worked with small groups at times. On the last day, Sunday, Helen Johnstone led a meaningful worship service for us to begin the day. Paul Bwalya gave a talk at noon.. We worked until 3:45, and then quit. I led a short brief service–they gave a "vote of thanks"–I took a photograph–and it was over.

Through my classes at the Theological College and the Writers' Workshop I came to know some of the students fairly well, and considered them to be friends. One student said to me, "God has sent you to help us know better how to teach."

Other Engagements

In addition to the scheduled classes and workshops and the talk to the "Women Aglow" group. I was asked to take part in some other events. On one Saturday I gave a presentation on "Planning and Leading Bible Study" to a Consistory (District) Seminar. It was interpreted into Bemba for the sake of the women present. Twenty-four persons attended, in addition to Margaret Miller, a staff member at the Theological College, who took me there.

During the time I was in Zambia I continued to work on curriculum and Bible studies, compiling and editing materials which had been written in each country. I also had to cut stencils and type materials for the programs and workshops in Zambia. Fortunately, I was able to borrow a typewriter.

| *View of the Campus* | *A Fountain at Reception* |

The U.C.Z. Theological College was on the campus of the Mindolo Ecumenical Foundation. Although this was described in Part I, Chapter 5, more information is included here.

The Foundation was established in 1958 by churches as a center of study, worship and consultation. It coordinates, arranges and facilitates a wide variety of courses for the churches, church-related organizations, and non-governmental organizations, and also participates in community-based programs. It is governed by a pan-African Board which included (in 1990, and possibly still) representatives from the All Africa Conference of Churches, the Christian Council of Zambia, the Zambia Episcopal Conference, the National Assembly, Copperbelt University, and other related institutions. While Mindolo was striving for economic self sufficiency, it depended (and still does) on gifts from overseas partners. Various courses were held, some short term, most from one to three years. There were courses in Ecumenical Church Ministries, Women's Training Programme, Youth Leadership Programme, Pre-School Teachers and Trainers Programme, Industry and Commerce Programme, Community Development Programme, and a Youth Development Scheme aimed at training unemployed school leavers for self-employment. There were also conferences, consultations and workshops, and research programs.[20]

Currently a Peace Center has been established, and a diploma in Peace and Conflict Management is offered. They also have programs to help combat malaria, which is devastating in Africa. In June of 2005 an American Corner was established by the U.S. Embassy at a cost of $50,000. This is a resource center designed for anyone who wants to learn more about American society and culture, and offers an extensive book, periodical, and video collection, covering

---

[20]Information from a leaflet from the Mindolo Ecumenical Foundation, 1990.

diverse topics. The Corner offers free internet access and also other equipment to help in meeting the needs of users.[21]

The Pottery Project

I was grateful to be able to make use of the Dag Hammerskjold Library, named in honor of the Swedish UN Secretary-General who died nearby in a plane crash in 1961.

The Africa Literature Centre was also on the campus. It offered a diploma course in journalism and art. It was founded in 1958, one of the oldest Journalism and Art Training Institutes in Africa.

The Pottery Project was helpful to unemployed youth, and the sewing class at the YWCA, for women and girls.

Another institution on campus was the Theological Education by Extension in Zambia, a joint project of several churches. I introduced myself to the Director, Rev. R. W. Chongo. I was quite impressed with the study materials they had produced, and the TEE program which at the time was reaching more than 2,500 students, lay persons who were church leaders, and trained more than 800 tutors. Basic and standard courses were produced regularly, and advanced courses, obtained from South Africa, were offered for persons able to study at a more advanced level. All courses combined home study, weekly group meetings of one and one-half hours for twenty-four weeks, and practical work.

The training of lay persons was necessary as the churches were essentially run by the laity; this includes much of the preaching and leading of worship. The average number of churches per pastor was seven to ten, sometimes as many as twenty. The situation was (and is) much the same in other countries in Africa, but I had not seen as good a training program in any other country. They started in 1979, with three denominations. In 1990 there were five: Churches of Christ, Church of Central Africa Presbyterian, United Church of Zambia, Reformed Church in Zambia and the Zambian Anglican Council.

I had tea with the staff, and enjoyed meeting them and learning about this excellent program.

Other Events, Recreation

Though I was busy while in Zambia, I also had some enjoyable times. Rev. Helen Johnstone and Dr. Wendy Kilworth-Mason were friends who helped me out by taking me shopping with them. I also ate meals in their homes, and we went to restaurants together occasionally. The Rev. Paul S. Bwalya, Moderator of the Copperbelt Presbytery, and his wife Joyce were helpful in several ways, including taking me to the Mines doctor when it was

---

[21]See "Mindolo Ecumenical Foundation" on the Internet.

necessary. (Because I lived on the Mindolo Campus I was allowed to go there). She also helped to arrange for leaving. I taught Ellen and Rose how to play Rook, and we had several games together. (I sent each of them a Rook game after I returned home.) I also came to know some of the students' wives who lived on campus, and enjoyed the children.

Children of Students–
with Their Toys

And the Children's Band!

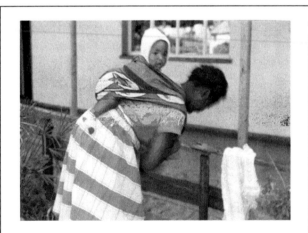

Cartildah Siyemoto, a wife of one of the students, demonstrated for me how
Zambian women carry their babies.

Frances Sombé became a good friend. She invited me to her home–a beautiful home, with a TV, VCR, and a swimming pool. Her husband, Rogers, was an accountant, the coordinator for Zambia-International. Frances owned a day nursery and worked part time in it. At another time we went on a picnic with another friend and their children; and she once brought me some cake and bananas. Her husband helped me by accepting a check from me for which he gave Zambian money.

Frances in Her Nursery School

Hilda Bandu and Frances–a Picnic

Rogers, Rogers, Jr. and Frances Sombé

Graduation was on June 2, and I was invited to it and other events at the end of the school year.

UNITED CHURCH OF ZAMBIA
Theological College

P.O. Box 20429
KITWE
REPUBLIC OF ZAMBIA
TELEPHONE 210218
2nd May, 1990

Dr. E. Megill
Theological College,
Kitwe

Dear Dr. Megill,

Although you have become almost one of our family, it nevertheless seems good that I should thank you on behalf of the College Community for the course in Christian Education you conducted towards the end of last term. I know from the responses of several of the participants just how much your work was appreciated and, on behalf of the College I would like to thank you very much for that.

Yours sincerely

(Signed)   Charles Helms

Fr. C. Helms

Acting Principal

[Hand written]

P.S. The College will hold its Graduation Service for final year students on Saturday 2nd June at 10 hrs. in Mindolo Church.

You are most welcome to join us and for the luncheon afterwards in the MEF Dining Hall.

Dear Sir/Madame, [Printed by hand: Dr. E. Megill]

Re. <u>GRADUATION PARTY 31-05-90.</u>

I greet you in the name of the Father, Son and the Holy Spirit.

I wish to most cordially invite you to the graduation Party of the fourth Year Students of the theological College scheduled to take place on the 31st May, 1990. This will take place in the Y.M.C.A. Buseko Hall.

You are most welcome.

Faithfully Yours,

(Signed)

<u>P. Kabala</u>

Student Council Secretary

[Handwritten]

Theological College Choir

c/o Theological College

P.O. Box 20429, KITWE

30th May, 1990

Dr. Ester Megil, [sic]

c/o Theological College,

P.O. Box 20429,

KITWE.

Dear Madam,

Re: <u>Choir Farwell Party</u>

The Theological College Choir will be having its annual farewell party this evening from 1900 hrs. to 20:30 hrs. This party will be held in class room number 2. On behalf of the Choir and of course on my own behalf, I would like to invite you to this important event.

The purpose of this party is to bid farewell to the Graduating Students who are at the same time members of the College Choir. We would have informed you in advance but the problem was that we weren't certain of the date. We therefore look forward to seeing you there.

Yours in Christ,

[Signed]

[Printed] Stanley Simunyola

Choir Chairman

The Graduation Service on June 2, which included the Commissioning and Licensing of the Probationer Ministers, was a solemn affair. The Rev. B. S. Chuba, General Secretary, gave the charge. I joined in the luncheon which followed.

Rev. B. S. Chuba, General Secretary, United Church of Zambia (Former Trinity College, Ghana, student)
Mrs. Chuba

The week before I left the All Africa Conference of Churches sponsored a consultation on "Women and Economic Development" at Mindolo Foundation. Women were there from about thirty different countries in Africa. I had become acquainted with some Sierra Leoneans who worked at M.E.F. and in the university, and was included in a dinner evening held by the Temples, Sierra Leoneans living there, for delegates from Sierra Leone. This included one of the women from the Women Aglow Bible study class and her husband, and other Sierra Leoneans. There was good talk and at about 9:00 p.m., delicious food. I enjoyed being considered a "Sierra Leonean" again.

On June 22 I went by bus to Ndola, and to the home of the Shaws. Just before 7:00 Graham took me to the airport to meet Dr. Pat Elmore, a friend from Mississippi, who had come to join me. We spent the night at the Shaws'. Pat and I took them as our guests to dinner at an Indian restaurant. We took a bus from the M.E.F. to Mindolo and home.

During the brief time Pat was there she was able to hold a nutrition workshop for the wives of students. (Pat taught home economics at the University of Mississippi.)

On June 25 we were part of a farewell luncheon for John Burgess from Theological Education by Extension.

On the 26th we had lunch with Helen Johnstone and Murial Sanderson, and on the 27th a farewell luncheon at the Sombés'.

Dr, Pat Elmore Teaching

Farewell for John Burgess

Helen Johnstone, Murial Sanderson,
Pat Elmore

Frances Sombe, Rogers, Jr., Pat Elmore

Leaving Kitwe

As has been indicated previously, the people in Zambia were living in a very depressed economic situation. I once overheard the Student Council discussing the eggs which Wendy and Helen bought and gave the students the chance to buy (cheaper than in the market). They were saying that they couldn't afford them, even at K4 each, when for K10 they could buy enough *nshima* to feed four or five childre--, a little more than the price of two eggs.

Then just before I left the government (at the demand of the International Monetary Fund) suddenly increased the cost of "mealy meal" (corn meal), the basic food, by 108%. One of the men who had just graduated from the Theological College and was waiting to go to his church said it would take one and one-half times a month's salary just to buy enough mealy meal for his family. He would get the equivalent of about $15.00 a month, if he were paid. (U.C.Z. ministers had not been paid since February.) The average salary in Zambia was the equivalent of about $18.00–a little more than the cost of a bag of mealy meal. The result of this sudden price increase was riots, curfews, tension, and some killings.

These made it difficult for us to leave. Joyce Bwalya took me to the air freight officeto weigh a suitcase I wanted to send on to Kenya, then to customs. Just as we finished, word came that there was rioting, and the shops were closing. So we rushed home. Joyce found a roundabout way, and we arrived safely. There was rioting in Chimwemwe, and shooting later that night. Pat and I were to go to Frances' for dinner, but we received a message that they couldn't come to pick us up. Regretfully, we had to cancel the last class for the Women Aglow, and postpone the dinner with the Sombés.

The next day Frances came with her friend Usha, who took me to Zambia Airways Cargo, where I finally was able to send my suitcase by freight. We also hoped to pick up our tickets for Livingstone, where Pat and I intended to visit, but the travel agency was closed. We stopped at Ushas for the dessert we didn't get the night before, and then went home.

Farewell to the Children

The next morning (June 27) we went to chapel and said goodby. I took Pat on a tour of the M.E.F., finished packing, and gave away food that was left. I said farewell to the children, and gave them some biscuits (cookies). We left the Theological College at noon, with some regret. We had been concerned about how we would get to Ndola to catch the plane, because taxis and other transportation were not going, But again Frances Sombé and her family came to our rescue, and offered to have their driver take us. We first went to her home for the postponed lunch–roast chicken and dressing, Jollof rice, salad, pawpaw

483

(papaya)–and chatted for a while. There were sad goodbys, and then her driver took us to Ndola, where we stayed overnight once again with the Shaws. The next morning we took a flight to Lusaka. I wondered whether Noreen Mapala would be able to meet us as planned, because of the turmoil in Lusaka. (The paper said that twenty had been killed, and that there was a night curfew.) But she was there, and we gave her our extra baggage to keep until we returned to go on to Kenya.

Tourists

The flight to Livingstone was fine, and we were soon in Musi-O-Tunya ("The Smoke that Thunders") Intercontinental Hotel. I could not help but think of the hungry students, pastors and others in Zambia, and the turmoil and deaths as we settled into, by comparison, a luxurious hotel.

We arranged with Eagle Travel for transport to various places, and for the Zambezi River "Sundowner Cruise." We left at 4:20 and returned at 6:20. It was beautiful and peaceful. We saw elephants crossing the river and one on the shore; the humps of hippos, birds, and a beautiful sunset.

Launch on the Zambezi

Elephants Crossing

On the next day, Friday, we were up at 6:00 and had a continental breakfast with fresh fruit and orange juice, though we shivered in the outdoor coffee shop. We then got a taxi and went to the entrance of Victoria Falls. Pat and I visited the Livingstone statue, erected in memory of David Livingstone, "Missionary-Explorer-Liberator," and then went over the bridge to Zimbabwe.

Livingstone Statue

Victoria Falls, the "Devil's Cataract",
from Zimbabwe Side

Rainbow Over Falls– Zambia Side

The Falls were magnificent, though we got wet because we didn't bother putting on our plastic rain coats. At noon at the Victoria Falls Hotel we had a delicious buffet lunch, then went to the craft shop, and got a taxi to the Zambia border, where the Eagle Travel man picked us up and took us back to our hotel.

The next morning we walked down to see the Falls from the eastern (Zambia) side. There was a beautiful rainbow over them, and we took pictures. It was pleasant and cool. We stopped at a Crafts Market, and bought a few things. A little after 10:00 the travel agent took us to the Livingstone National Museum. We had only an hour, and could have spent another.

When we returned, we checked out of the hotel and put our bags in storage. There was a leisurely, two-hour lunch, with barbeque, and traditional music.

From Livingstone we flew to Lusaka. The flight was one and one-half hours late, and when we got into the Lusaka Airport they were closing up–there was no snack, and no transport – because of the curfew. Due to the kindness of one of the women on the staff, and a manager who shared a private taxi with us, we were finally taken to the Baptist Guest House, where I had previously made reservations, and arrived at about 10:30. It was a comfortable room. We boiled water and had coffee or herbal tea, cheese and crackers, and cookies which we had brought with us.

The next morning was Sunday, and we were up at 6:30. We had a breakfast of crackers, coffee and dry granola. Noreen and a man from the Synod office came for us, and we went to the Trinity U.C.Z. for church. It was Harvest Sunday, and the church was packed, with people sitting outside. Some people brought produce, most money, as their harvest offerings. When the offering was taken a woman danced down the aisle with the offering basket and started a Bemba song, the most interesting part of the service.   We left just as they were beginning the communion service, and were taken to the airport. Noreen and Queen Sendoya waited for us as we checked our luggage (which took a long time because of excess luggage). We had a drink and finally a small sandwich and French fries. The cafeteria was not open. The waiter said the cooks hadn't come. The women gave me a Zambian tie-dye dress, from the office staff, which I appreciated. The staff had wanted to meet us to say goodby, but were prevented because of the problems.

We sat for over an hour and were finally on our flight to Nairobi. We had a welcome but small lunch of a small potato patty, a few pieces of chicken, a small piece of cake and orange juice.

I left Zambia with a warm feeling of friendship, thankfulness for the experiences I had, and a little ache for the partings.

Zambia Since 1990

Zambia has continued to have problems. After extensive protests President Kaunda realized that changes had to be made, and lifted the ban on political parties. This resulted in elections being held in 1991. They were generally regarded as being free and fair. Frederick Chiluba, a union leader, who led a political party called the Movement for Multiparty Democracy (MMD), won the election by a wide margin and the MMD won 125 of the 150 seats in the National Assembly.

Chiluba liberalized the economy, privatized state-owned enterprises, such as the copper industry, and removed the subsidies on some commodities, especially cornmeal. With a multiparty system, many expected a more democratic government, but this did not happen. Many opponents were imprisoned, and some countries withdrew their aid. In 1993 the government-owned newspaper, *The Times of Zambia* reported that there was a plan by UNIP (United National Independence Party, Kaunda's party) to cause industrial unrest and organize mass protests, and then to take over the government. Although this was denied by UNIP, the government responded by putting twenty-six people in detention, and of these, seven where charged with offences against the security of the state. One of these was Kenneth Kaunda's son.

In the 1996 elections UNIP formed an alliance with six other parties and Kaunda planned to run for president once again. The government then amended the constitution, banning people whose parents were not Zambian citizen from becoming president. This was aimed at Kaunda, whose parents had come from Malawi. In protest UNIP and its allies boycotted the election, so Frederick Chiluba won the presidency easily.

The situation escalated, and in 1997 an unsuccessful coup took place. Chiluba declared a state of emergency, and eighty-four people were arrested. Kenneth Kaunda and Dean Mungomba, leader of one of the opposition parties, were among them. There were accusations of torture. The arrests were condemned, both inside and outside of Zambia. Kaunda was released, but forty-four of the soldiers who took part in the coup were sentenced to death in 2003. Prior to the elections in 2001 Chiluba tried to change the constitution so he could run for a third term. There were protests from within the party as well as from the public, so this was prevented.

In the December 2001 election Levy Mwanawasa won the presidency by a narrow majority. Chaluba was arrested and charged with several counts of embezzlement and corruption. But by 2004 Mwanawasa began to show an authoritarian streak, when he deported a British citizen and longtime resident of Zambia who had published a satirical attack on the president, and his zeal to root out corruption had waned somewhat. Generally, however, the Zambian people viewed Mwanawasa's rule as a great improvement over Chaluba.

In 2006 more than 70% of Zambians lived in poverty and the per capita annual income was one-half of what it had been before independence. The country is now among the world's poorest. The country's rate of economic growth cannot support rapid population growth. Zambia is also one of sub-Saharan Africa's most urbanized countries. Almost half of the population is concentrated in a few urban areas and major transportation corridors, while rural areas are sparsely populated. Under and unemployment is a serious problem.

As is true in many African countries, Zambia is burdened with a foreign debt that it is impossible to pay. In 2000 the country qualified for Highly Indebted Poor Country Initiative (HIPC) debt relief, contingent upon meeting certain criteria. They were not able to meet the deadline given, but agreements were reached with the IMF and World Bank to delay debt forgiveness from late 2003 to early 2005. In order to accomplish this, the government drafted an austerity program in 2004, which froze salaries of civil servants and raised taxes. Many objected to this plan. By the end of July 2006, however, Zambia had reached the "Post-division point HIPC's."[22] The Zambian government is pursuing an economic diversification program to reduce reliance on the copper industry. They are seeking to develop Zambia's rich resource base by promoting agriculture, tourism, gemstone mining and hydro power.[23] By November of 2006 the International Monetary Fund (IMF) released a statement saying that the Zambian economy was continuing to perform well, and that economic prospects were favorable. The nation's greatest problem, however, is HIV/AIDS, with 17% prevalence among the adult population. The disease will continue to ravage Zambian economic, political, cultural and social development for many years to come.

According to the United Church of Canada, which is a partner church to the United Church of Zambia, in 2000 UCZ was the second   largest Protestant Church in Zambia, and was seeing membership increases of tens of thousands, as is true of many churches throughout Africa.

The Theological College in 2007 was asking the Canadian church to supply someone to teach church history.[24]

22

See the report by the World Bank on the web, of the HIPC's.

23

From *Wikipedia, the free encyclopedia.*

24

"Living the Experience: 75 Years in The United Church of Canada (1925-2000)," edited by Graham A.D. Scott and others. (On the internet.)

Chapter 5. Kenya
1990

Kenya is on the east coast of Africa, and is divided by the equator. It is approximately 200,000 square miles in size, slightly smaller than Texas. Its altitude ranges from sea level to more than 17,000 feet. Kenya has a multiracial population, representing fifty different African tribes, Europeans, Indians and Pakistanis and Arabs. More than fifty different languages and dialects are spoken, but the nation is united by Kiswahili, and English is spoken almost everywhere.

Kenya gained her independence from Great Britain on December 12, 1963, after eight years of fierce fighting, led by the "Mau Mau" freedom fighters. The first president was Mzee Jomo Kenyatta, who was in power for fifteen years, and created a solid foundation for the new nation. Daniel arap Moi succeeded Kenyatta in 1978 and was still in power in 1990.

The country is noted for its abundance of wild life. It produces some of the world's finest coffee and tea. Fruits and vegetables are also exported. Many Kenyans are skilled craftsmen and produce beautiful handicraft items.[25]

In 1990 Kenya was stronger economically than many other countries in Africa, but there were the same problems that one finds in all developing countries. There was a strong undercurrent of dissatisfaction with the one-party government, but little tolerance for those who dared to express a desire for change.

(Map courtesy of the University of Texas Libraries, The University of Texas at Austin. Provided by U.S. C.I.A.)

---

[25]From "Kenya in Brief," a tourist booklet published in July 1990.

My Time in Kenya

Pat Elmore and I arrived in Nairobi (the capital) on Sunday evening, July 1, at about 6:25 Kenya time (one hour ahead of Zambia). Sam Atiemo, my former student at Trinity College, then Secretary of Youth for Christ International, Africa Region, was there to greet us warmly. Because of the difficulty of buying food in Lusaka, we asked him to take us to a restaurant; so he let us out at an Indian restaurant, and we had the first hot meal we had had in about thirty hours–spicy, but good. Sam went on to the Methodist Guest House and put our baggage in the room reserved for us, and then came back for us. When we arrived at the Guest House, we found a beautiful large bouquet of flowers in our room–which Sam had provided.

The next morning after breakfast Sam took me to a Ghanaian woman who gave me a permanent. We then went to the Methodist Church headquarters which was nearby. After waiting for an hour we were able to meet, briefly, (Presiding) Bishop Lawi Imathiu. I had written him several letters before arriving, but had not heard much from him. After lunch we returned to the office, and Nicholas Kathingi, from the bishop's office, took us to try to

490

get the baggage I had sent by freight. However, we were too late to get it, so he took us to the guest house.

The next morning we had the adventure of catching a bus into town and to the Methodist headquarters. Again we went to the airport, but there was no sign of the baggage, so Zambia Airways sent a telex.

I had asked ahead of time for someone to get a doctor's appointment for me, and was able to see a doctor (an Englishman) that afternoon about my feet. He gave me a cortisone injection and enough medicine to last until I got home. When he had finished, the doctor rather apologetically said, "I'm sorry, I will have to charge you, because this is a private office." Then he said, "But–oh! you are an American, so you are used to that." The charge for the visit, the injection and the medicine was equivalent to $35.00.

During the time I worked in Africa I was frequently asked whether I had gone on a safari. Since we did not have safaris in the part of Africa I was in, I always had to say "no." So now that we were in safari country in East Africa, Pat and I made arrangements for one. Sam had introduced us to "Travel Free Ltd." managed by Florence Ang'awa. Caroline Ayah, her sister, worked with her. They arranged for a less expensive safari than it would have been elsewhere, and later made arrangements for a trip in and around Nairobi. Before we left, we were friends.

While in Nairobi we experienced local transportation and local food. We enjoyed eating an Ethiopian meal, a buffet, at the Africa Heritage Café. It was in a gallery where all kinds of handcrafts were sold. On one day Lois Olsen, a longtime friend from Sierra Leone days who was working as a volunteer in the hospital at Maua, arrived to spend the day. We thoroughly enjoyed our conversation, and she took us several places in Nairobi.

At the guest house I met Dot and Bill Anderson, whom I knew from missionary gatherings and teaching at Conference Schools of Christian Mission. They were in Kenya doing volunteer work for the Methodist Church. We enjoyed our time together. They told us that when they were in town that day (July 7) there was shooting and people rushing by the bus stop where they were. The government soldiers had broken up a meeting where they were to discuss the possibility of a multiparty government. Previously a lawyer and others had been arrested.

We finally learned from the office that we were to go to the theological school in Meru, which is about thirty miles from Maua, so I expected to see Lois again. We also met Tripp Helms, a recent college graduate from North Carolina, who had come to do volunteer work for six months. We still did not know when or how we were to get to Meru.

On Sunday Jonathan Njuki, the financial secretary of the Methodist Church, picked up Pat, the Andersons, and me and took us to the Lavington Methodist Church. We got in on the last half of the youth service (with communion), and all the main (English) service. It was the first church I had been in on my African trip that was not full, although there was a good congregation. The pastor, Tim Kogora, had studied at Perkins School of Theology and at Iliff. In his sermon he used the story of Elijah and the priests of Baal on Mt. Carmel, and preached about the problems in Kenya. "Where is the church?" he asked. "There are many Christians in Kenya but few Christian actions . . . the problem is which God we worship and the way we worship. God is Lord." There were also prayers of intercession for specific persons who had been detained by the soldiers or whose whereabouts were not known.

On to Meru

Finally, the next afternoon, on July 9, Nicholas took Pat, Tripp, and me to Meru, where we would be staying. We passed coffee and tea plantations, wound up into the mountains and then down a little. We stopped to buy fruit and discovered we had a flat tire. It was changed, and we stopped at Embu to get it repaired. The three of us waited at an inn while this was done, and had drinks.

We arrived at Meru at the bishop's house at nearly 8:00. After greeting him and his wife Florence, we were taken to the Kaaga Rural Training Centre/Methodist Theological Institute, where we were to stay. We were greeted by Silas Miriti M'Mworia and his wife, Damaris Kaari. They had just returned from the States, where they had studied at METHESCO (Methodist Theological School) in Ohio, so they knew Ethel Johnson. They took us to the flat and helped us to unload. It was very nice–the only drawback was that the electricity was off and it would be some time before it could be turned on. They fed us a good meal at about 9:00. We were really hungry by that time. We got to bed at about 11:30.

Meru is about 175 miles northeast of Nairobi, very near the equator, a mile high, and cool in July, but warmer and very pleasant by the end of August. It is the strongest center of the Methodist Church. Missionaries of the Methodist Church in England first arrived in Kenya in 1862. The Methodist Church in Kenya became autonomous in 1967, four years after independence. The United Methodist Church (U.S.) had had a relationship with them for several years, and provided missionaries and some funds.

Central Office. Draped with color, design of flag of Kenya, for a special occasion

Our neighbors, Silas and Damaris, were very helpful. Having only recently returned from the U.S., they were just getting settled themselves. However, they helped us by taking us shopping, arranging for a young woman to do our laundry (by hand), and sharing their television. When we went to shop, I bought a newspaper. It said that there were still riots in Nairobi, shops had been closed, and people killed. The government was very upset with the United States. A lawyer from Kenya had been given asylum, and the Ambassador had said that

Congress was becoming less inclined to give aid to governments that did not move toward democratization.

The Methodist Theological Institute

David and Betty Hinson, British Methodist missionaries, next door neighbors, took us shopping at times. Margaret Mburugu, who headed the Family Life Program for the Methodist Church, also became a good friend. Gina Chamberlain[26], a United Methodist Mission Intern, spent some time with Margaret. We at times played games together. We were able later to have them all for dinner in the apartment.

Pat and I did occasionally travel by *matatu* (a van with wooden benches for seats, and always full of people), but it was not easy to go to the market and bring back produce in them. I copied the following from a *matatu*:

A Speed Song

80 kph [kilometers per hour] [48 mph]: God will take care of you.
100 kph [60 mph]: Guide Me, O Thou Great Jehovah
120 kph [72 mph]: Nearer, My God, to Thee
140 kph [84 mph]: The World is Not My Home
160 kph [96 mph]: Lord, I'm Coming Home
Over 180 [108 mph]: Precious Memories

We were grateful for the transport provided us by friends or the Theological Institute or the Rural Centre. We also appreciated the vegetables from the Rural Training Centre farm. My suitcase shipped from Zambia finally arrived, after I got my passport to the office so they could get it. After we were settled, I talked with Miriti about the possibility for workshops. He was obviously rather in a quandary because the bishop hadn't given responsibility to him (or apparently to anyone else). I explained the possibilities to him, and he agreed that there could be a workshop that weekend on Bible study. He also arranged with the Hinsons to lend me a manual typewriter, and I began typing stencils for the workshop.

Esther and Pat

---

2. Gina spent 16 months with the World Student Christian Federation in Kenya. See her article, "Avoiding a Harvest of Violence," in *New World Outlook*, July-August 1992, p. 16 for her discussion of the place of women in Kenya.

Tripp Helms

Tripp sometimes ate with us, but mostly with the students at the Theological Institute. On Thursday of that first week he received a phone call from his parents, who were very worried about the situation in Kenya. They had contacted a friend who had been an Ambassador, who contacted the State Department. There was a visitor's warning for Kenya, and the Embassy wanted to know where Americans were. We phoned the Embassy the next day.

Workshops
<u>Meru</u>

Because there was no planning ahead, it took some time before I could do many workshops. With Miriti's help I had the first one on Friday afternoon, July 13, at the Theological Institute. I began the workshop on "Planning and Leading Bible Study," which was supposed to be for pastors. Forty-one attended the first session, of whom only five were ministers. Tripp attended, and said he was impressed. The next day there were only twelve, and

no pastors. I had only one person lead a Bible study. That evening two of the theological students, David Gichuru and Margaret Nakaluma, who was from Uganda, came over at my request, to see whether they would do further writing. David had already done another, which he read to me. Four others, two actually pastors, came to see me later.

Margaret Nakaluma and David Gichuru

Kaaga Synod

It was September 7-8 before I was able to have another workshop. This was arranged by Bishop Anonda (the bishop of the area–similar to United Methodists' district superintendents), with the help of the Youth Organizer, Rev. William Markiuki. This was a workshop for Sunday School teachers.

Only four had arrived by starting time, so we did not begin until 12:00. Finally fourteen people attended. Everything had to be interpreted, which took more time, and I am sure some things were not understood by those with limited education. But several responded well, and I did what I could. We had lunch and supper (I had *ugali* for supper, the corn mush staple dish in Kenya), and finished at 9:30. The next day we planned a lesson, as a group. Several people contributed, and, in the end, we produced a good lesson. I read them a story I had written for children about David's sparing Saul's life, and tried to show what I did to make an interesting story based on a Bible story.

There were questions and suggestions for follow-up for some time afterward. We didn't close until 1:30 and it was about 2:00 when we left.

Nkubu

The last workshop was for the Nkubu Synod, held at the Kaguru Farmers' Training Centre September 17-18. Bishop Gitonga (read "District Superintendent") of that synod took me to the Centre, just outside Nkubu. We started the Sunday School workshop at about 11:15, after tea. There were eighteen to start, and by late afternoon we had twenty-six. That evening I showed a film strip I had produced years earlier on "Play As Learning" (for young children). I shared a room in one of the dormitories with Charity Gakii, the Youth Patron.

Bishop Gitonga

Using Rhythm Instruments

Things went fairly well, although two did not understand English and I was not sure how well some of the others did. (I found less understanding of English in Kenya than in Zambia.) The entire morning the next day was spent in planning a lesson, and then evaluating the workshop.

495

There was a lively discussion, mostly in Kimeru. They seemed appreciative, and gave the traditional "vote of thanks."

Rev. Charity Gakii, Youth Patron

Lectures at the Theological Institute

On September 10-13 and the 21st I gave some lectures to the Christian Education classes at the Theological Institute. I was given little advance information, so it was a slow start. I had only four hours with each of two classes–the second year and the third year–so did not try to deal with lesson planning. Instead I worked on writing Bible studies. This enabled me to get to know some of the students.

One of the students, Julius Mbaya Makathimo, came one evening to talk to me about his research paper. Then he spent some time trying to persuade me to retire in Kenya. He said he would give me some land, the government would build a house which I could pay for monthly. I would be part of his family–his mother. He really meant it.

Rev. & Mrs. Julius Mbaya Makathimo

Later I visited his home in Gitugu, where I met his wife Tabitha and children. I kept in touch with Julius for some years, and helped him as I could. He was able to come to the States and study to be a chaplain. He had hoped to become a hospital chaplain, but they put him in charge of a church and the last I heard (2006) he was ministering to the Maasai people.

The Makathimo Family

One evening Stephen Makena, from Tanzania, came with his corrected Bible study, and told me how the Methodist Church had started in Tanzania. He said that a Methodist pastor from Kenya had come to their town near Lake Victoria and held a crusade. Stephen was then a student in a Catholic seminary. He and a Catholic priest were impressed by the pastor's preaching. It was decided that Stephen should go on and finish his seminary course. Then the Father said it was time to start a Methodist Church, and so they did! It was 1987. The church began to grow. By 1990 there were sixteen churches, one with a membership of three hundred. When the people in Kenya heard about a Methodist Church in Tanzania, the Presiding Bishop and others went to see how it had happened. The Tanzanians told them they didn't know anything about a Methodist Church, but they wanted to learn. So, the priest went to the Methodist Theological Institute in Kenya for six months, and Stephen was then sent for a year. However, he finished in seven months, and would soon return to his own country. He told me there were no other trained pastors. Some had applied to attend MTI, and others to a school in Uganda, but there was no money to send them. Stephen said he would hold seminars when he returned, if money was available. I later sent him copies of the manuscripts I had prepared in Africa.

On another evening one of the Ugandan students, Daniel Wandabula, a third year student, came to see me. Daniel had become a "born again" Christian in 1986, in the Anglican Church. He heard about a Methodist Church which was just starting, read about it, and attended at the invitation of a friend–and was "hooked." He organized a youth club, which cleared land and planted crops. He was very much interested in agriculture, which he considered the gift God had given him.

He talked about his sister, Patience D. Kisakye, who had been accepted at The United Methodist United Seminary in Dayton, Ohio, but needed $6,000 before she could go. I called

Bishop Imathiu to see if he would write a letter to the Women's Division (United Methodist Board of Global Ministries) to recommend her. However, he said he didn't know her. She hadn't applied to be a candidate for the ministry. Daniel said she had applied in 1988 to her local church and was approved. They had recommended her to the circuit, but because the girl's father was one of seven who wrote to the Bishop urging him to come settle some serious problems in the church, the minister, whose incompetency and dishonesty had caused the problem, refused to send her name to the Synod in Kenya. Daniel said that Patience felt committed to the ministry, and the family would raise money for transportation if other money could be found. However, there was no chance the Women's Division would take any action without endorsement from the bishop. He told Daniel that he would go to Uganda in December. We hoped he would talk with the girl and write the letter. Margaret Nakaluma, also from Uganda, was going to try to get a letter from the new co-pastor, who had just graduated from the Theological Institute. I never heard just how this complicated situation was worked out, but Patience eventually did get to United.

Sightseeing and Other Events

Although I had only one workshop before September, I continued to keep busy compiling, editing, writing and typing curriculum materials from the countries I had been in previously. Unfortunately, however, there had been no plans for any contribution Pat Elmore could make. Finally, in July, she was able to make one presentation to a women's group (arranged by Margaret Mburugu), and enjoyed getting to know Catherine Nkirote, the dietician at the Institute.

We did have other interesting events which kept us busy during this time. The Hinsons took us to the English-language church in town on one Sunday; on other Sundays we attended the Kimeru service at the Institute. There were Volunteer in Mission (VIM) teams from the Rocky Mountain and Yellowstone Conferences of The United Methodist Church whom we met briefly. One evening we went to the dining hall and saw the program the students put on for them. They had drama, music and speeches–a new experience for Pat.

A Visit to Maua

On Wednesday, July 18, Lois Olsen sent a car for us, and we stayed at Maua until Thursday afternoon. We arrived in time for lunch, and then Lois took us around the hospital. She was a nurse-midwife, and was giving two years' volunteer work there as a midwifery instructor. There was much talking and reminiscing, and after a light supper we went to the last of the reception for the Rocky Mountain Conference folks who had come over from Kaaga.

Pat and I stayed at the Nyambene Lodge, where we had a small room with no shower or toilet in the room. The women's toilet was the squat kind. It was later that we discovered there was a shower also. But the room was comfortable, and the $6.00 we each paid for the room included a light breakfast. Lois came for us, and took us to the hospital again. I learned some statistics there:

There were about forty tribes in Kenya. The population was about twenty-four million. Until the previous year it had had the highest per capita increase in population in Africa–4% per year. It had been reduced to 3.8%, and the government was serious about family planning.

The Maternal and Child Health section in Maua Hospital saw about 1,500 patients per week. There were seventeen outpatient clinics, but they were hampered by lack of a vehicle. They had about three hundred deliveries a month. In 1986 they had had 4,500. They also had a pediatric unit, where Sharon Fogleman was the doctor. Her husband, Lynn, was also a doctor.

There were male and female wards, and a dental clinic. A dentist from Louisiana was building the clinic, and came for two or three weeks a year to work. They were also planning for an eye clinic.

The nursing school, where Lois was working, had approximately one hundred students–one-fourth men and three-fourths women. The number they could take was determined by available dormitory space. The government required that there must be a certain number from outside the area.

Pediatric Patients

Dr. Lynn Fogelman

Lois Olsen with New Baby

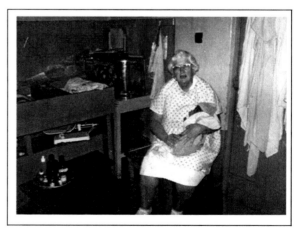

Dr. Lowell and Ruth Gess

Later, after Pat had gone, I spent another night with Lois, and met Dr. Lowell Gess and his wife, Ruth, who were there for a short time as volunteers. I had known them in Sierra Leone (and after), where I was his medical technologist. We visited, then went to the church service. (It was Sunday.) Lowell was in charge. Afterward we stood outside the church and talked to Bob and Sandra Harland, dentist and wife, who had had to leave Liberia because of the civil war, and had just arrived in Kenya. We were eager to hear from them about some of the people we knew in Liberia.

The Gesses joined us for supper at Lois's, and there was more reminiscing about Sierra Leone.

The Tea Plantation

Pat and I were able to get in on a tour to a tea plantation with the Rocky Mountain group. It was a long ride on a bus, up in the mountains and over some rough roads. We passed the equator, and stopped to take photos. When we finally arrived at the KTDA (Kenya Tea Development Authority) we found that we were not allowed to take photos inside this government-owned facility. We saw trucks pull up with large woven bags full of tea on hooks. They were unloaded and weighed, and a record kept. They were then put on conveyer belts and taken to flat vats, where an exact amount was spread out for withering, by blowing hot air from the bottom for sixteen hours. The tea was taken by conveyer to another part of the plant, where it was chopped and rolled. It was then graded into seven sizes by a huge round sifter.

From there the tea was packed into sacks. The finest was used for export. One of the M.T.I. students said that Kenyans could not afford to buy it.

A Tea Field

Entrance to the Tea Factory

A Lorry Loaded With Tea

One of the workers, a supervisor, showed us around. We learned from him that farmers were paid KS 2.60 per kilo[27] for the tea leaves (about 10.8¢), but the price had recently been raised to KS 3.00 (15¢). Only the tips were picked, and then they grew again. The government trucks picked them up at different points. Each bag held about thirty kilos. Farmers were paid by the month. The plants operated twenty-four hours a day all year round. The peak months were November to January; then the workers worked twelve-hour shifts, every day; in other months they worked eight-hour days. They were paid a little more than $1.00 per day, regardless of how long they worked. In addition they were supplied a house (unfurnished), with electricity and water. They were given twenty-four days leave a year, with perhaps emergency leave when necessary. The worker we talked to had not seen his family since December. Extra casual laborers were hired in busy months, then laid off. Some of them would get houses, some not, but more houses were being built. When I drink tea now, I sometimes think of how much it costs the laborers and how little the farmers get.

The Makena Textile Workshop

On the following day Margaret Mburugu arranged for us to go to the Makena Textile Workshop in Meru. We went to see Ruth Rinturi in the Ministry of Education, who was in charge of the teaching of Home Science in the primary schools. She took us to the Workshop, which was a women's cooperative. The women did weaving and tie-dyeing in order to earn money. They were paid for piece work and then a share of the profits. They carded and spun wool, wove rugs, and made beautiful tie-dyed materials. I bought some tablecloths as wedding gifts, and, even though I had many pieces of tie-dye, I couldn't resist buying one for myself.

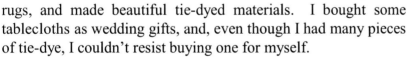

Carding Wool

Weaving a Rug

[27]The currency in Kenya is called the Kwasha. A kilo is 2.2 pounds.

Tie-Dyeing

The Shop

Afterward we took Ruth to lunch at the Springboard Cafeteria, where we had *chapatis* (similar to pita bread) and beef stew, a taste of a pastry with ground beef, and a pastry something like a doughnut. Margaret then met us and drove around the first Methodist Church which had been built, and is the center for the circuit meetings. In Meru we stopped at her house and had coffee and banana fritters and chatted for some time. She told us she had left her husband (a magistrate) several years ago because of his jealousy and physical abuse. She had two sons–Patrick Paul, who was a senior in medical school, and Alex, in Form 3 (high school).

At another time we had an interesting visit to the National Museum of Kenya in Meru.

Posters Seen in Meru

Elephants

There was a large demonstration farm at the Kaaga Rural Centre (from which we profited). One evening we heard the noise of banging pans and shouting, and were informed that elephants were coming. Gina went out to see if she could see elephants–we who were older just stayed in the apartment. I learned that elephants caused problems for farmers, because they would go through and destroy farms along the way. No one was allowed to kill elephants, and so all they could do was make a noise to try to frighten them away. One Kenyan said the problem was that people continued to farm in the migration paths.

The Safari

July 28 was Pat's last night in Meru. Of course she was mourning that this was her last night to carry a pan (with no handles) full of boiling water, to the bathroom for a bath!

The next morning we were wakened a little after 6:00 a.m. by Lois calling outside the window. She was taking us to Nairobi, since she was going there to the airport to meet Ted Stapleford, an Englishman whom we had known in Sierra Leone. We had expected her to be there at 8:00, have breakfast, and then leave at 9:00. But she had looked at Ted's letter again the night before and discovered that he was coming in at 9:15 a.m.. So we hurriedly dressed, finished packing, took a

The Norfolk Hotel, Nairobi

thermos of coffee and what bread and fruit we had, and left at about 7:00. We arrived at the airport at about 10:20, but Ted had been waiting less then ten minutes.

Lois took us to the G.P.K. (Church of the Province of Kenya) Guest House (Anglican), where we had made a reservation. It was closer to the main part of town than the Methodist Guest House, and a pleasant place to be. We settled in, and at 12:30 Lois picked us up for lunch at the historic Norfolk Hotel, a renowned hotel from the colonial period, after which we went to vespers at the Presbyterian Church. It was a small congregation, with good singing, and a warm welcome. As was usual, the service was led by the laity. During the sermon the following interesting story was told by Mr. Washington Muuya:

In 1955, during the Mau Mau rebellion, it was a very difficult time. He was an untrained teacher. The teachers took children from their village some distance to where the school was, and they had to carry a spear and a sword. When they were to return home at the end of the school day the other teachers went on to another place and told him he was to take the children home. He was stopped by government officials who asked where he was going. He said he was taking the children home. Then they asked where his sword and spear were–didn't he know he had to have them? He took his Bible out of one pocket, his hymnal from another and said, "This is my sword and this is my spear. As a Christian I don't know anything else–God protects me!"

And so they let him go.

After the service we enjoyed a meal at a Chinese restaurant.

The next day Pat and I set out with our driver and guide, David Muthee, for our long-anticipated safari. We were surprised to learn that, except for one short part of the journey, we were alone in the comfortable van–so we really had a personalized trip.

Our first stop was at the Outspan Hotel in Nyeri. We had a delicious buffet lunch–soup, then fish, three kinds of meat, green beans, and mashed potatoes. We didn't even see the salads until we had more than enough to eat, but we did have a little dessert, and strong Kenyan coffee.

From there we set out for the Tree Tops hotel, which sat on poles, thus near the tops of the trees. We had a small room, looking out over the water hole, where animals gathered. It was a leisurely afternoon, with tea, a lecture at 4:00, dinner at 8:00–smoked fish, a piece of cheese, a wedge of tomato, followed by consumé, then roast beef, mashed potatoes, carrots and green beans; a salad of tomatoes, pepper and mushrooms; the dessert was mixed fresh fruit and whipped cream. (We were certainly not on a diet on this trip!) During the afternoon and evening we watched for animals which came to the water hole–buffalo, warthogs, elephants, baboons, water buck, a lion at a distance. It was cold and we slept under three blankets that night.

Tree Tops Hotel

We were up at 6:15 the next morning, and were on the first van to go down to the Outspan,

where there was another delicious buffet breakfast, from which I chose a few items. We left at 8:30 or a little before, and arrived at the Sarova Shaba Lodge in the Samburu Game Park at 12:30. As we traveled, we saw a land with rather sparse vegetation, except for a few trees. The Umbrella (Acacia) trees were most interesting. Mountains could be seen in the distance. We had a luxurious room at the hotel–except that the electricity was off. We were offered another big lunch, though I skipped some of what was available. At 3:30 we went out to the Game Park with David, until 6:30. We saw a number of animals–giraffes, zebras, elephants, oryx, Grant's gazelle, water bucks, warthogs, baboons, and birds, many of them beautifully colored.

506

We went swimming at the Lodge in a delightful pool, and were able to do laundry.

The lights went out two or three times, and also during the night. So the next morning (August 1) we had to finish packing by candle and flashlight. After a light breakfast we left with David at about 7:50. We saw elephants, baboons, giraffes, zebras (two kinds), springboks, ostriches and camels along the long drive. We again saw a land with rather sparse vegetation, except for occasional trees.

Brilliant Blue Birds

Mt. Kenya

The dry country was home of the Samburu tribe, a subgroup of the Maasai. They subsisted on goats and cows. Their houses were small round huts, made of mud and wattle, with grass roofs. The dry country gradually gave way to greener landscape. We passed Mt. Kenya, and had a good view. There were some rough gravel roads; others were good tarmac. It was beautiful and green and warmer as we neared Lake Baringo, where we arrived at the Lodge, which was surrounded by trees and flowering plants. Mt. Kenya could be seen in the distance. We were greeted with cold orange juice, went to our room, and came back to lunch. I selected small servings from the Kenya dishes, salads, and deserts. We often had fresh fruit, which I especially enjoyed.

At 5:00 we went on a boat ride, where we saw hippos, crocodiles, penguins, storks, African fish hawks, and a number of other birds. We went swimming afterward, then read the newspaper for a while, looked in the gift shop, and saw the slide presentation on "The Birds of Lake Baringo." We had a light dinner and were in bed by 9:30.

Hippopotami

Malibu & & Yellow-Billed Storks

We were up at 6:30, ate breakfast, and were on our way by 8:00 to nearby Lake Bogoria, where there were hot springs and huge flocks of flamingos.

Lake Bogoria: Hot Springs and Flamingoes

We drove on toward Nakuru. On the way we stopped at a sisal plantation and processing plant. Pat was thrilled to be able to get pictures and samples, which she could use in her university classes. We learned it takes about three years for a plant to be ready for harvest, but they kept crops growing so that they harvested all year round. The tall stems were used for poles for building, and fibers were extracted from the bottom leaves. They washed and scrubbed the leaves to free the green outside, and the fibers were then dried over posts for eight hours. They were graded according to length. Those with dark spots were used for rope. The "waste" was dried on the ground and used for making ropes and mats. At a factory eight kilometers away they

508

were put into 50 kg. packs, then five of those pressed into one 250 kg. bundle for export. Lower grades were used locally.

Sisal Plant

The Sissal Plantation–Processing Plant

At Nakuru we stopped for a rest room and drinks, and then went on to Lake Naivasha, in time for lunch. Florence Ang'awa and her sister were there, and gave us changed information for the next day. The ornithologist was gone, so there was no bird watch. We decided we did not want to take another boat ride. So we read, slept, walked down to the lake and watched the birds, and wrote cards. We saw a video, the first and last parts of "Out of Africa," with dinner in between, and then we saw "Born Free."

Friday, August 3: Up at 6:30, ate breakfast, and at 8:00 left for Masaai Mara, with four other passengers this time–Basques (as they said, between Spain and France). We stopped at a curio shop and arrived at the Sarova Mara Camp at about 12:30. There we stayed in a tent–a fancy one! A tent was put up on concrete, in front of a regular toilet, and had a shingled roof. But it faced trees and a brook, so it gave the impression of being outdoors.

After the usual big lunch and rest, David took us on a game drive. We saw many wildebeests and zebras and some other animals. It started to rain, and we almost got stuck–four other vans did. It rained before dinner. We read, went to dinner, and came back to our cozy tent to read until bedtime.

The next morning we were again on a game drive, and there were many animals to see – twelve lions, hyenas, jackals, bat-eared

fox, ostriches, Malibu storks, Egyptian geese, gazelles, thousands of wildebeests, waterbucks, topis, wart hogs, buffalo, hippos, many zebras, various kinds of antelope. We finally saw some elephants, but no rhinos, cheetahs, or leopards.

Male Buffalo

Lions

Perhaps the most interesting part of the trip was our visit that afternoon to a Maasai village. At the gate of the village we each paid the Chief $20.00, and were allowed to see and photograph anything. (I felt a little uneasy about taking advantage of them, but realize that this was an important source of income for them. We were told that our entrance fees would probably pay for school books, uniforms, etc.) The Maasai is an indigenous semi-nomadic African group found in Kenya and Tanzania. They wander freely between the two countries. According to the *Wikipedia Free Encyclopedia* they always wear some form of red. (The adults we saw did wear something red.) Both males and females have their ears pierced and disked. They are also known for their beautiful beadwork.

There were dirt, and many flies, because the cattle stayed there at night. Milk is the staple of their diet, either drunk fresh or after it has fermented for a few days. Meat is seldom eaten, although on special occasions a cow, goat or sheep may be slaughtered. Blood from the cattle is an important part of the diet, and can be drunk plain, mixed with milk or cooked into porridge. They sell cattle to buy the few other things they need.[28]

The women build the small rectangular houses made of mud and sticks. They first put sticks in the ground, then tie cross sticks, and put a layer of small sticks inside, which are tied to the cross sticks. The roofs are made of sticks also. They then plaster inside and out with cow dung. Grass is put on the roof, then plastered with dung. An opening in the roof is made by inserting a gallon tin, with the top and bottom cut out, though the ones I saw were plugged. Raised platforms made out of sticks and covered with leather serve as beds. There are upright sticks at each end. Calves stay in a portion partitioned off at one end. There is storage for water and milk. Long gourds with plugs served as containers. There was a store for grains, a fire in the middle, and the adults' bed on one side and the children's on the other.

Young men move about with the cattle as they seek grass.

Interior of House, Unfinished

Interior of House

28

Information about the diet is taken from *Facing the Lion; Growing up Maasai on the African Savanna*, by Joseph Lemasolai Lekuton, in an article by Hermon Uniola, p. 118. National Geographic, Washington D.C., c.2003 by Joseph Lekuton.

Woman Working

Women and Children with Sale Items

I have seen much poverty in Africa, but I had never seen such poverty as I did in that camp.

Of course there were things to sell; I bought a gourd decorated with beadwork, with a plug in it. There were various objects made with beads.

It started to rain before we got back to the tent, but we had our usual quiet evening there.

The next morning we had our last breakfast at the lodge. As Pat was carrying some bananas we had purchased for our breakfast, she was startled by a monkey trying to take them away from her.

An Earring

We were off again, over some rough roads, the tarmac full of pot holes. On our return to Nairobi we drove along the Rift Valley, a

beautiful view, but too hazy for good photos. We arrived at the Methodist Guest House, where we would be staying, at about 12:30, and said goodby to David, with many thanks.

It was a dull, cold day, so after lunch we just read.

512

The next morning we put some of our suitcases in storage, and then went to town by bus, and walked to Methodist headquarters, where we left our accumulation of purchases with Nicholas. I had to make travel arrangements for Egypt at Menno Travel, and filled in forms for visas. We then ate lunch at the African Heritage Café, a delicious buffet of African foods. Pat visited the Home Economics School in the same building. We went to Travel Free and Florence arranged a two-day tour of Nairobi for us when we returned from Mombasa.

Mombasa

The next day Florence and her sister took us to the station for the overnight train to Mombasa. We had a sleeper and ate in the dining car. We were settled in by 6:30, and left at 7:00. We were glad to be in the first lunch call, where we had a meal for less than $6.00–vegetable soup, broiled lake fish, curried chicken and rice, with condiments; rhubarb crisp with custard sauce. Berths were made up when we returned to the compartment.

On the Overnight Train

Mombasa is the second largest city in Kenya, and has an international airport and port. For many years Arab, Persian, Indian and Chinese merchants traveled to and from the Kenyan coast, in pursuit of rhino horns, ivory, and other treasures. It was mainly Arabs, however, who settled there, intermarrying with the Bantu of the area. The people are known as Swahili ("coastal man" in Arabic), and are made up of nine ethnic groups who live along the coast. Today there are many hotels along the beach, frequented by tourists.[29]

We arrived in Mombasa at about 8:15 and took a taxi to the Manor Hotel where we had reservations, but had to wait to get into a room, so we went to get some Continental breakfast–only to discover we were in the wrong (first class) dining room! However, since I had already started to get food at the buffet, the waiter told us to stay.

Our room was a nice one with a refrigerator, and a safe we could rent. It started to rain by the time we had showered and hung up our still-wet laundry and added more. But the sun came out, and we walked on the beach and ate lunch at a grill. It rained again in the afternoon, so we finally went back to the room.

The next morning (August 8) we were ready for the Dhow Cruise for which we had arranged. The dhows for centuries had plied the routes along the east coast of Africa, the Persian Gulf, Arabian Peninsula and India. Of course the one we were in had an engine installed as well as a sail. When we got on the dhow, we sat around tables, and were given fresh lime or soda drinks, plantain and potato chips. We set "sail" (by motor), and it was smooth until we got outside the river and to the edge of the sea–then we had too much pitching and rolling for me! But before long we were in quieter waters and enjoyed the Zulu "warriors" from South Africa

---

[29]*Wikipedia Free Encyclopedia* and a tourist pamphlet.

who gave us contemporary African music, along with a keyboard and electric guitars. From the dhow we saw Mombasa from the sea, a river village, and a floating market. We stopped at a hotel and picked up lunch, and were back on land at 2:35, when we were delivered to the hotel. We swam in the Indian ocean that afternoon.

As previously arranged, Bill and Dot Anderson arrived soon and took us to a Women's Cooperative where Dot and Bill bought some tie dye. I had damaged my camera on the safari, and so Dot took me to a camera repair shop. The man there could not repair it, but said I could get it done in Nairobi. (But I lost a roll of film from the safari, and was not able to take more photos until after it was repaired. Pat Elmore supplied me with some of the safari photos and those taken in Mombasa.)

From there we went to the Wesley Centre. There was a church, the first one in Mombasa, and, a training school for school leavers (after the eighth grade), which taught carpentry and leatherwork for young men and sewing for women. The women learned to make their own patterns. They were day students, about fifty. Guest rooms were also there. The program was self-supporting.

The Andersons took us to the city bus station and we had the experience of riding the bus to the hotel, for less than 25¢. We had a quiet evening there.

Thursday was another sunny day. We were supposed to go on a city tour at 8:00, but the guide didn't show up, so finally a driver from the hotel took us to town and we picked up another one. Mombasa was a fascinating city, particularly the old city. We saw a Hindu temple as well as mosques. Fort Jesus was of special interest. The Portuguese took Mombasa in 1593, "and began at once to build a large fort to guard the harbor entrance. The Portuguese regarded

Main Street, Mombasa

themselves as representatives of Christendom rather than Portugal, and for this reason they sailed under the flag of the Order of Jesus Christ. Jesus was therefore an obvious name for the new fort."[30] The fort was fought over for centuries by Portuguese, Turks, and the English. We walked through streets in the Old City, then to the city market. Of course we stopped at craft shops along the way. I bought some spices at an Indian shop and nuts and mangoes at the market.

Street in the Old City

Hindu Temple, Old City

---

[30]From a leaflet, "Visit Fort Jesus Mombasa," published by the National Museums of Kenya.

515

I enquired about the possibility of getting to Mamba Village. The bus driver heard me, and offered to take us in his own car. So at 4:00 we left with him. We saw the Crocodile Farm, home for more than 10,000 crocodiles, and stayed until they were fed. We could have eaten crocodile meat at the restaurant, but did not have the courage to try any.

On August 10 we were again on an all night train to Nairobi, where we stayed this time at the Fairview Hotel, since there was no room at either of the church guest houses. I was able to get my camera repaired. On Sunday we walked to the St. Andrew's Presbyterian Church, this time to the morning service.

The Nairobi Tour

Our Nairobi Tour began the next day. We looked over Uhru Park and the city, saw the Parliament Building, Law Courts, and Kenyatta Centre, which was a conference center. ((Many organizations had their African headquarters in Nairobi, so the Conference Centre was no doubt frequently used.) I took a picture of the monument to President Moi's ten years, and one to Kenyatta, the first president; we went to the Railroad Museum and to the National Museum and the Snake Park. We saw the entrance to the city with the "Kenya Uhuru" (Freedom) gate.

The Uhuru Gate

Moi Monument

Statue of Kenyatta, Law Buildings

Parliament Buildings

***Conference Centre,
KANU Headquarters***

*25th Anniversary of
Independence*

Lunch was at the famous Carnivore Restaurant, where the meat (sixteen kinds) was roasted over an open fire and served on a three-foot long skewer and served on hot pewter dishes.

From there we went to see the "Bomas (music) of Kenya," dancers using traditional instruments.

August 14: We moved after breakfast to the CPK Guest House, since there was a room available. The driver then came and took us to Karen Blixten's house, of special interest to all who had seen the movie "Out of Africa," which was based on her book telling of her life in Kenya. From the verandah we saw the view of the Ngong Hills of which she often spoke.

Karen Blixon's House   *Interior*

A Candelabra Tree on the Grounds

Pat went to Kenyatta University in the afternoon to meet with people who taught Domestic Science (Home Economics) and had a great time.

Our time together in Kenya ended with a dinner with our travel agents and friends. The driver for "Travel Free' picked us up and took us to the Ayahs' home. We were surprised to learn that Florence Ang'awa was the wife of the Ambassador to Germany, and Caroline Ayah of the Minister of Foreign Affairs (similar to our Secretary of State). We were with quite important government officials that evening. It was a pleasant evening, and when we left they sent samples of Kenyan tea and coffee with us.

The next day, August 16, Pat Elmore left for the United States. Florence and Carolyn arrived at the hotel just as we were leaving, to say goodby to Pat. I went with her to the airport and said goodby there.

I stayed in Nairobi until I could get transport to Meru. In the meantime I made arrangements with Menno Travel to go on to Egypt, Israel/Palestine, and the Philippines on my return home. I obtained a visa for the Philippines. I had hoped to go to India also, but was denied a visa. It

Florence Ang'wa, Minister Ayah, Caroline Ayah

seemed that at that time the Indian government had decided not to allow Americans to visit their country.

519

I had just booked a seat on a bus to Meru for the 18th when a call from the Methodist Guest House informed me that Bishop Kanake (Maua) was returning the next day, and I should transfer there because he would be leaving at 7:00 a.m. So I moved over about 10:00 a.m., did some necessary shopping, ate, slept, played solitaire, wrote letters, and read.

On the 19th I rode to Meru with Bishop Kanake, I unpacked, ate, and Tripp and I played Rook that evening.

Back in Meru

On August 24 two more Americans arrived to stay in the flat at least part of the time–Arlene and Don Shannon (Volunteers in Mission who were preparing a video of church history). Murden Woods, on the staff of the Women's Division (General Board of Global Ministries, UMC), whom I had known in New York, was with them. She would be staying with the bishop for the time being.

On August 26 I rode with the Shannons and Bishop Gitonga to the final day of a revival, which 10,000 people attended, coming from all over the Eastern Province. It was held outdoors near the Kaaga Church. Those conducting the service (and visitors, including me) sat on a roofed, wooden platform. The people sat on the ground in the large open space, or on chairs they had brought with them. There was lots of movement in and out.

The service lasted for three hours. The speeches and sermons were all in Kimeru or Kiswahili. The first hour was spent in greetings from bishops of different districts and representatives of other churches. There were about four sermons, all related to Matthew 16:13–20, "You are the Christ." Many gave testimonies. One had been a drunkard, but was now a bishop, and another a witch doctor. At least two spoke out against corruption and bribes. One hundred ten people came forward to become Christians. Names were taken and given to pastors in their areas. They would have to attend Thursday night fellowship for some time before they could become members, and would be checked on by church members if they missed.

It was 3:00 before we returned home, to prepare a meal and eat together.

Dinner with the Bishop

September began with an invitation to dinner, along with the Shannons, at Bishop Imathiu's home in Meru. His wife and daughter were there, and distinguished visitors: Sturgeon M. Dunham III, editor of *The United Methodist Reporter*; and Arlene and Don Shannon. The Bishop and Sturgeon Dunham had just returned from South Africa, where they, with other Methodists, had met with de Klerk and Pik Botha. Don showed some of the video he had taken, and then taped an interview with the bishop. It was nearly 11:30 when we got home.

A Church "Opening"

The next day, Sunday, Nicholas came for the Shannons and me, and took us to the dedication

of the new Mbwinjeru Church building (a church "opening"). It was an attractive building, paid for by the people themselves. We were taken with other guests to a small room, and given boiled beef and soft drinks. (They poured water over our hands before we ate to wash them.) The Women's Fellowship met the bishop with singing and dancing, all wearing the same type of clothes of special "prints," as is the custom in many parts of Africa. The Boy's and Girl's Brigades and Sunday School children also danced as they greeted the bishop.

521

Boy's and Girl's Brigades

Women's Fellowship

Sunday School Children

Service Inside the Church

After 11:00 we were seated with other guests in front, under the outside shelter. We sat through the Kimeru service (with some translation) until 2:30. We were introduced, and I was asked to say a few words. The bishop and Spurgeon Dunham each told about their meeting with de Klerk and Pik Botha in South Africa. It was almost unbelievable–God's Spirit was surely at work!

At 2:30 everyone was served lunch, still seated–boiled beef, a slice of bread, a banana, and soft drinks. There was special music by different groups during this time. (I observed much more use of traditional dancing in Kenya, in praise of God–and the bishop.) At about 3:30 we finally went into the church. Again, we were seated on the front, and waited for the bishop and pastors to enter. Many were standing in the back, and many outside. There was another hour's service, including the history of the church and introduction of people involved in the building. The people surely have patience and endurance. One needs a tough bottom and a large bladder for these events!

I returned with Margaret, stopped for tea at her house, then came home.

522

A Move to Margaret Mburugu's

Esther Megill, Margaret, and Alex Mburugu

On September 3 Margaret told me that another couple, David and Marilyn Brenchley, was coming to do volunteer work, and they would need the apartment (He was to start building the University.) Margaret invited me to move over to her house before they arrived. I knew there would be electricity (at least most of the time), a refrigerator on most of the time, and hot water there! I was expecting a visit from Lois Olsen, and Margaret said she could stay there when she came, since she would be in Nairobi. The next days were busy with preparing for and holding workshops and teaching at the Institute, but on the 13th I cleaned the apartment thoroughly, packed, and moved over to Margaret's.

Lois came on the 15th, and the next day we went to church, ate lunch at the Meru Hotel, and then to Maua.

Margaret was frequently gone (because of her work), and even when she was there, I would sometimes cook. When she was gone I had to ask Julius Mbaya to light the fire for the water heater, a large mud block structure. It heated the water well, and we had warm water for a bath even several hours after the fire had died down.

The Church Under the Mango Trees

The bishop told me that I should experience not only the larger churches, but a small one in a village. So, on the last Sunday before I left Meru, Rev. Alfred Kuburu, who had just completed MTS, took me, along with a woman named Hilda, about 30-40 miles, part of it on dirt roads, to a mission church. Alfred pointed out other Methodist churches along the way. Although this had been Presbyterian territory, there were now twenty Methodist churches, started since 1985. (This developed after the Kenya Council of Churches declared the old comity agreements were no longer in force.)

The church to which we were going was the Kigiri Church of the Maaru Mission Circuit, one of six in the circuit. Although it was established in 1985, it was still meeting under a mango tree. There were five adults and twelve children who were members. Formerly, there had been a large congregation, but the people had dispersed when they could not build a building. The people who belonged were poor; they had depended upon growing coffee, and the depressed price of coffee on the world market had affected the growers badly. But, as I told them, the church is the people of God gathered for worship and service, not a building; and I worshiped with them under the trees. The Methodist order of service was followed, in Kimeru, the language of the area. There was much singing by the choir of six young people from the "mother" church, and the small group of Sunday School children. I gave a short sermon, on "What Is That in Your Hand?" which the pastor interpreted into Kimeru. Afterward they took me to see the site where they hoped to build a church, and to see the small pile of lumber they had managed to collect so far. (Of course, they hoped that I could help raise money for them to build the church.)

A Layman, Two Pastors, Esther Megill

Sunday School Children

The Visiting Choir

We also went to see where the women were cooking the meal, which they served in my honor. Of course they were not able to be in the service.

Afterward, the circuit steward gave the history of the church, and I was given gifts: a chicken, a beautifully woven bag, and a small beaded cross necklace from the children. They said that now I was a member of the church. I wished that I had money to give them to help build the church, but I didn't.

The experience only emphasized what it meant to be in a country where the church was growing faster than the resources could provide for their needs. The official figure for the Methodist Church was 135,000 members. One of the synod bishops said that he estimated it to be closer to 300,000. There were very few pastors; in one case one pastor supervised thirty churches. Again, one saw a church run by lay people. Money was in such short supply that they were unable to take a new class in the Theological Institute for the year which had just begun. There was not even money to buy paper on which the students would write their final exams. (Finally, the Methodist Book Store did let them have some, though apparently the bills had not been paid for previous supplies.)

Small churches had been established in Tanzania and in Uganda through mission work of the Kenya church. They were begging for pastors and financial help. Bishop Imathiu had to refuse a request from Ethiopia to start a church there, because they simply couldn't stretch their resources of personnel and money any further.

The Women Cooking

More Farewells

In the final days there was dinner with Bishop Gitonga and his family. His wife taught agriculture at the Teacher's College. There were three children: Timothy, Irene and Katherine. They were a lovely family, and we had a good time.

A dinner at Catherine Nkirot's of mashed potatoes, chicken and gravy, cabbage, carrots, chapatis, and fruit was all very tasty, and it too was an enjoyable time.

A farewell pot luck supper at Margaret's was the final event. Staff of the institutions, volunteers and visitors were present. The lights went out, so we finished cooking and ate by lamp and candle light. It was a wonderful evening of fellowship. They all said such complimentary things, and Miriti prayed a beautiful prayer as we held hands. My heart overflowed with gratitude for those friends.

Marilyn Brenchley, left; David Brenchley, right

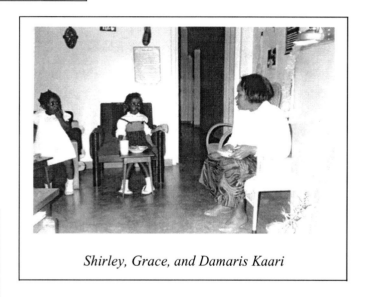

Shirley, Grace, and Damaris Kaari

Miriti M'Mworia

526

Margaret Mburugu and Gina Chamberlain

On September 26 Margaret drove me to Nairobi. She took me to the offices of the All Africa Conference of Churches and the National Christian Council of Kenya. I was trying to get up-to-date information that would enable me to revise the textbook I had written while in Ghana, and also talked with them about the possibility of publishing some of the material on which I had been working.

Margaret then took me to the CPK Guest House, and I had to say goodby to another friend whom I would probably never see again. (Margaret told me toward the end of my time that she wished she had known what I could do, as she would surely have kept both Pat and me busy.)

The next day Sam Atiemo took me to Uzima Press to see about possibilities of getting my textbook, *Education in the African Church*, (a revised updated version) published by them. We had to wait for an hour and a half to see the General Manager, Samuel arap Ng'eny. Sam tried to impress him with how useful he felt the book was. Mr. Ng'eny seemed favorably impressed with the book, and promised to evaluate it for a possible request for funding from SPCK. (Nothing ever came of this. A revised edition was published in Ghana in 1998.)

Sam also helped me get around to the travel agent, some of the embassies, and immigration, as I was preparing for my onward journey, and to KLM to get a suitcase sent to Phoenix (where my brother lived, and I expected to spend Christmas). I discovered that if I could send it the next day I would avoid the big price increase that would be in effect on Monday.

Sam and Pauline and I went to the Tintin Chinese Restaurant Friday evening. It was a very enjoyable evening.

When I was at the C.P.K. I suddenly recognized one of my former students from Ghana. He was on his way home after visiting Mauritius as a consultant in Christian education. He was leaving in a few days for Ghana, and promised to see what he could do to help get the kindergarten curriculum finished.

527

While I was at the C.P.K., which was near the center of town, I was able to take care of a good deal of business, including a permanent at a hotel, and a cholera shot. I also sent my manuscripts by DHL to the retirement home to which I would be moving–for $150.00! I secured a visa to Egypt, where I was going next, and arranged with the Menno Travel agent for transportation there and beyond.

After lunch on Saturday I took a taxi to the Methodist Guest House because a room was no long available at the C.P.K. There I met Murden Woods, who arrived just as I did. We then discovered there was no water! Because of the Agricultural Show, the City Commission had diverted the water from that section of the city. We walked to a shopping centre and bought bottled water and some juices. Later we talked to the manager. He was trying to get water, and thought there would be some yet that night. But there wasn't, so I went to bed dirty.

After breakfast I called the Heron Court Hotel and reserved a room, and arranged for a taxi to pick me up later. Murden went with me, and we ate lunch at the Buffalo Bill Restaurant while we waited for the room to be cleaned. There was the luxury of a hot shower and clean clothes.

We decided to take a safari in the game park in Nairobi, and made arrangements for it. In four hours one afternoon we saw baboons, a bat-eared fox, buffalo, bushbucks, crocodiles, various species of antelope, elephants, giraffes, Grant's gazelle, hartebeest, hyenas, impala, two kinds of jackals, lions, two kinds of monkeys, oryx, ground squirrels, warthogs, waterbuck (two kinds), wildebeest, zebras (two kinds), vultures, Malibu storks, cranes, ostriches, and many other birds, hippopotamuses, and one rare black rhinoceros.

Zebras

Eland

Black Rhinoceros

On the evening of October 3 I left Kenya, at the end of my volunteer work. However, before I left Africa I wanted to go to one more African country, where I had never been, and so I took a flight to Egypt. This time I was going as a tourist, not as a volunteer.

Kenya Since 1990

An article in the February 1991 issue of *Africa News*[31] quoted President Daniel arap Moi as saying, "Nobody should go around cheating the people [into thinking] that elections are on." The next election was scheduled for 1993, and he made it plain that he was not going to move it up, although there was increasing discontent with the one-party system and the lack of civil rights. The Kenya African National Union (KANU) had been the only party allowed since1982.

Local and foreign pressure continued, however, and in 1991 parliament repealed the one-party section of the constitution. Multiparty elections were held in December, but KANU won the majority of seats and Moi was reelected for a five-year term. There were ethnic clashes during this time also, with many people killed and property destroyed. The tribe to which the president belonged were the aggressors.

An article in the *Asheville* [North Carolina] *Citizen-Times* in 1997 reported that armed police had clubbed students and shut down the University of Nairobi as part of President Moi's violent campaign to silence demands for a free and fair election.[32] However, in 1997 he won another five-year term. He was barred by the constitution from running for another term, but he tried unsuccessfully to promote the son of the first president, Kenyatta.[33] "A rainbow coalition of opposition parties routed the ruling KANU party, and its leader, Moi's former vice-president, Mwai Kibaki, was elected president by a large majority."[34] In the years that followed Kenyans began to enjoy an increased degree of freedom.

In late December 2007 elections were once again held. There was a close election, with President Kibaki winning with a slim majority. There was some violence and fighting between tribal groups, but in the beginning the elections were declared "largely peaceful" by the Electoral Commission. However, in days following, many people were killed and villages destroyed. In spite of attempts by former UN Secretary Kofi Annan and other African leaders to effect reconciliation, at the time of publication there was still violence in Kenya.

According to the U.S. Department of State, from 1991-1993 Kenya had its worst economic performance since independence. However, in 1993 the government began a major program of economic reform and liberalization, with the help of the World Bank and the International Monetary Fund (IMF). In 1997 there was a period of stagnation. Kenya failed to meet commitments made to the IMF, and help was withdrawn. In addition, there was a prolonged period of drought. There was also a great deal of corruption, although in 1997 the

---

[31]*Africa News*, February 11, 1991, p. 8.

[32]*Asheville Citizen-Times*, Asheville, NC, July 10, 1997.

[33]U.S. Department of State, *Background Note: Kenya.*

[34]*Wikipedia, the Free Encyclopedia*, "Kenya, history."

government took some positive steps of reform. Under the leadership of President Kabaki the government began an ambitious economic reform program, and resumed cooperation with the World Bank and the International Monetary Fund. Kenya was chosen to be part of the Poverty Reduction and Growth Facility, which gave a boost to the economy. There is still need for more economic reforms and continued fight against corruption, however.[35]

In 1990 there was chaos in the local church at Maua, which resulted in a civil suit and a split.

There is now a Methodist University in Meru. From the *Wikipedia, the Free Encyclopedia* (internet):

Kenya Methodist University, often referred to as KEMU, is a four-year, liberal arts university located in Meru, Kenya. It is under the auspices of the Methodist Church in Kenya, and has over 1000 students. Founded in 1997, its first graduating class received degrees in 2001.

It is located about five miles from Meru Town on the road to Maua. Built on the site

of the former Kaaga Rural Training Centre, it offers degrees in Business, Agriculture, Education, Counselling, Mathematics & Computer Science, Computer Information Systems, Nursing, religious studies, History and other subjects. Plans are in place to build a teaching hospital and other faculties in the future, when a medical course for doctors will be instituted.

KEMU has received generous support from a number of foreign and domestic donors,

both for special building funds and operating expenses, to supplement revenues from tuition and fees. It educates students from all over Kenya.

On January 29, 2006 the World Methodist Peace Award was given to Bishop Lawi Imathiu at an award ceremony at the university. About 3,000 people, some of whom walked for hours, came to celebrate the occasion. The Award was given to one "who exemplifies the struggle for mercy, peace, justice and freedom."[36]

The Presiding Bishop in 2007 is the Rev. Dr. Kanyaru M'Impwii Stephen. Dr. Stephen wrote:

Our mission has continued to grow in scope. We are sponsors of other 200 schools, a hospital and many dispensaries. We also have agricultural training institutes, youth polytechnic, technical schools, special schools for the physically disabled and vocational schools. Our ecumenical cooperation has enabled us to have a united Theological College at Limuru. We also have Lavington United Church which is sponsored by the Methodists. The church now has 205 ministers, 1,000 congregations

---

[35]U.S. Dept. of State, op. cit.

[36]United Methodist Church News Archives, on the Internet.

with 300,000 members and a Methodist community of 800,000. We anticipate doubling our membership in the next five years. We have opened a Kenya Methodist University that will spearhead university education in our region. We have other programmes such as rural development programmes, community health, youth, women's fellowship, AIDs, lay training and family education. We are members of the All Africa Conference of Churches, National Council of Churches of Kenya, World Council of Churches and other fraternal bodies in the region.[37]

The hospital in Maua has been improved and grown, as it ministers to the health needs of many in the area.

The United Methodist Church in the U.S. continues to assist the church with personnel and funds, including projects to fight malaria and HIV/AIDS.

In May of 2006 Daniel A. Wandabula, formerly a student at the Methodist Theological Institute (see p.497), was elected Bishop of The United Methodist East Africa Annual Conference (composed of Burundi, Kenya, Rwanda, Sudan, Tanzania, Uganda). He had earned two degrees at Garrett-Evangelical Theological Seminary in Evanston, Illinois in the 1990's, and was ordained an elder in The United Methodist Church in 1994.[38]

---

[37] *Kenya, Methodist Church, Leader: Rev. Dr. Stephen Kanyaru M'Impwii*, on the Internet.

[38] United Methodist Church News Archives, on the Internet.

Chapter 6. Egypt
Oct. 4-11 (A Tourist)

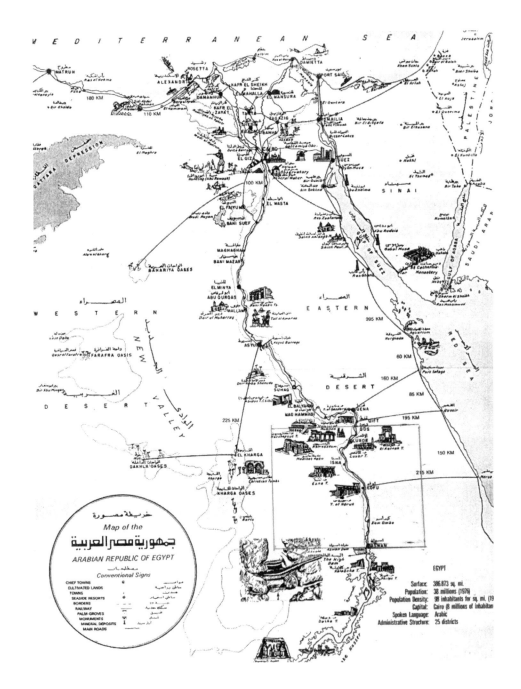

(Map from a paper given to tourists)

I arrived in Cairo at 1:20 a.m. October 4. I had discovered in Nairobi that it was impossible to book a tour there, since all tours seemed to start in the U.S. or Europe. I did, however, ask the travel agent to make a reservation in a hotel for me. As I was standing in line a friendly man from the Half Moon Tourist Company came up to me and asked if I was with a group, and when he discovered I was alone, whether I would like a tour. So he helped me through immigration, gave me a cold drink, and I signed up for some tours. He then sent me in a car to Bel Air Hotel where I had a reservation for one night.

Cairo

The tour began the next day. Soon after 10:00 a.m. Ashraf Amer of Half Moon Tours was at the hotel with the driver and guide for the day. The tour that day was in Cairo, where we went to the National Museum, and I had my own conducted tour. I saw there the Ramses statue which I had seen in Memphis when it was on a tour in the US. There followed a long ride to Giza, and at about 3:00 I had an Egyptian lunch. From there they took me to the pyramids and the Sphinx. I saw the pyramids of Cheops, Cephren and Micerinus. One can take no tour without being taken to the shops, and so some time was spent there, where I bought a few inexpensive items. I also saw an interesting demonstration of making papyrus, and bought a few small pieces.

Pyramids and Sphinx

The Sphinx

Camels at Giza

In the evening there was the spectacular "Sound and Light" show at the pyramids and Sphinx. Afterward, a Scots couple, Bill and Mary Flavell, who were working in Saudi Arabia for the Zoological Society of London, joined us. They would be on the tour the next day.

By the time I got to the hotel at 9:30 I was exhausted and famished. I ate, showered, and was in bed by 10:30

In my journal I wrote the following impressions of Cairo: A huge, crowded city. Most women with heads covered (Egypt is 80% Muslim, 20% Christian). Mosques (3,000 in Cairo alone). Camels, horses, donkeys. Bright, hot sun. Poverty–dirt–trash along and in the irrigation canal. Children playing in dirty water, men fishing. The Nile (crossed two branches). Friendliness of shopkeepers, who offered cold soft drinks, tea or coffee at each place. The ancient culture of Egypt, with names familiar to me from my study of biblical and other history.

The Old City

I had a good night's sleep, so was ready for a tour of the Old City at 9:30, joined by the Flavells. There were the Nile, Ramses Square, a view over the old city, and a visit to the Mohammed Ali Mosque, built in 1830. A clock in the tower was given by Louis Phillipe of France. We saw other mosques, the Military Museum, and an old synagogue (Abraham Ben Ezra), the oldest in Egypt.

A View of the Old City

Mary Flavell, our Guide, and Esther Megill

Inside the Mohammed Ali Mosque

Interior of the Mosque

View from Inside the Museum

According to the author of a booklet given to us, in the time of Moses, about 1392 B.C., Jews lived in the Land of Giza (Goshen Land) close to a synagogue where Moses used to pray and worship God. He said that Moses left "unmistakable traces or mark signs" which prove his existence in Egypt in those early days, and that the Jews who returned with their prophet Jeremiah during the reign of King Nebachadnezzar (606-538 B.C.) accidently found the "mark of Moses" and built a synagogue there. The synagogue was destroyed by the Romans in 30 B.C. In later years the Copts claimed the land and built a church on it, which was destroyed in the 10th or 11th century. In 1115 A.D. the great Rabbi Abraham Ben Ezra came to Egypt, and persuaded the rulers that the synagogue had been on their land, so the land should be returned to the Jews. So he rebuilt the synagogue, which is still called by his name. The synagogue was surrounded by twenty-nine mosques and twenty churches. There were about 133,000 Muslims, 10,000 Copts, and forty-two Jewish families in Old Cairo. "This population of different religions . . . are [sic] united and love each other as one family."

To the west of the synagogue is the Abou Serga (St. Sergius) Church, in which there is a crypt whose history goes back to before Christ. It was said that when Herod ordered the killing of the children, the Virgin Mary, Joseph and the Child Jesus fled to Egypt and were sheltered in this crypt for three months. Renovation was taking place, and there was a lot of trash and dirt. The buildings were crowded together,

The Sign at St. Sergius Church

St. Mark's Cathedral
According to tradition, the Apostle Mark
brought Christianity to Egypt

with narrow passageways between. We saw other Coptic churches also. Services were being held, but the main services were on Sunday.

We left the Flavells at the airport, since they were flying back to Saudi Arabia. The driver took me to a restaurant where I had another Egyptian dinner–Foul (foo´-ul) (mashed garbanzo beans), in olive oil; various pickled vegetables, unleavened bread. I was tired when I got back to the hotel, so I slept, went for a short swim and took a shower, then ate soup and ice cream at about 7:30. I had a quiet evening of writing letters.

The Nile

I was up early on October 6, and had packed, checked out, and eaten breakfast by a little before 6:00. A taxi took me to the airport to fly to Aswan. Then, as I was going through security, I realized I had not taken my things from the safety deposit box at the hotel. It was then 6:50, and the plane did not leave until 8:00. So I managed to get a taxi, made a mad dash back to the hotel, and was back at the airport just in time to check in and get on the plane.

The flight to Aswan was one and one-half hours. As we were about to land, they announced that the temperature was 37°C (98°F). We were now in the desert, with strips of green along the Nile–grass and palm trees. I was met by a taxi and guide, who took me to the floating hotel "Nora," by 10:00. I soon discovered that we would not sail until the next afternoon. Of course, they tried to sell me another tour, but I could not afford another. So I read and slept. The air conditioner was too cold. I was the only one eating in the evening (8:00 p.m.) and there were only two others at lunch. That night I went to another "Sound and Light Show," at the site of the transplanted temple to Isis. It was an interesting presentation of the mythology and history of the Nile.

"Nora"

By 5:30 the next day, at dawn, I was awake, and sat on the sundeck, waiting for 8:00 and breakfast. It was pleasantly cool, but getting warm in the sun. I watched a ferry come in, and the struggle three young men had to get a donkey to pull a loaded cart onto it. The donkey planted his legs firmly and would not budge, though they tugged and pulled. Finally, they unfastened him from the cart, and eventually got another donkey. They still had to lift up the front legs of the other and literally drag him on to the ferry!

After lunch I went on a tour with a young Australian, Darwen (Dare´-en), who was traveling alone too. We were the only two English-speakers on board–all the rest were German. This meant we were not provided with an interpreter, so we missed much on the tours. On that day we went to the Low Dam, built by the British to supply some of their industries, not to help the people; then to the High Dam, started with the help of the Soviets in 1960. It was supplying electricity to all of Egypt, and to Libya. In order to build the dam, President Nasser moved the Nubians out to new villages. The government provided schools–education was free and

The Aswan High Dam

The Unfinished Obelisk

539

compulsory through secondary school, and the University was also free. Medical care was free in government hospitals. Persons who went to private ones had to pay.

From there we went to the "Unfinished Obelisk" which would have weighed 1,267 tons. From these granite quarries came the granite for all the Egyptian obelisks around the world.

We then took the sailboat "Nefretiti" to Elephantine Island, where the mausoleum was of Aga Khan, who died in 1957. I chose not to walk the long way up in the heat to see it. We had tea when we returned to the "Nora," and later, dinner. Darwen asked to sit at my table, and we had a pleasant conversation.

On the Sailboat

Boys in a Boat on the Nile

Unfortunately, the next day I had to spend in bed, because I was afflicted with problems that I was told few visitors to Egypt could avoid. I was unable to go on the tour to the Temple of Komombo, home of the Crocodile God, so had to be satisfied with what I could see from the boat. I felt well enough to go to dinner to have some soup and orange juice. The next day I felt better, and did go on two short tours to the Temple of Horus at Edfu, where we were lucky enough to happen on a group of Americans with an English-speaking tour guide. Horus is reborn symbolically every day. The temple is sacred to those in childbirth and to women who want to have a child.

Temple of Komombo

Temple of Horus

Sacred Barque, Temple of Horus

In the afternoon at the Temple of Khoum in Esna we were not so fortunate, and I did not stay long. I had to battle my way through a long row of shops on my way back.

Temple of Khnum

As we floated down the Nile, I was interested in the irrigation system, used since ancient times. It is said that Egypt depends on the river in a way that no other nation does. 97% of Egyptians live on 2.5% of its area.[39] I was interested in watching as the lock and drawbridge were opened so we could pass.

Irrigation System

Raising the Drawbridge

---

[39]From "Ancient Irrigation," on the Internet, www-geology.ucdavis.edu.

Oct. 10: An exhausting day Darwen and I went in the morning on a boat tour to the Temple of Karnak. We were fortunate there to be able to connect with a Cook's tour with an English-speaking guide. Karnak is the temple dedicated to the god Amon, at the site of ancient Thebes. It is the largest temple supported by columns in the world. Sadly, the saltpeter is rapidly destroying the plaster. We saw a young man working at making drawings, with the help of a photograph, of a small section of a wall–very painstaking. This is the only way the heritage can be preserved.

From there we went to the Temple of Luxor. Luxor was for centuries the capital of the Egyptian kingdom. We had a guide, along with two nurses working in Saudi Arabia–one from Holland, one from Zimbabwe.

Luxor

Outside Luxor   *Avenue of the Sphinxes*

The Colossus   *Obelisk*   *Columns*

Temple of Queen Hatshephut

We were glad to go back to lunch and some air conditioning. At 1:50 we left for the Valley of the Kings. Here we were disappointed, for there was no guide, and all we could do was look. (No photographs were allowed.) It was terrifically hot (I heard later about 105°.) There was a lot of climbing and walking. From there we went to the Temple (Tomb) of Queen Hatshepsut, but with no guide got little out of it.

At 6:00 the travel agent met me, took me to the "Sound and Light Show" at Harnack, which was good, but there was more walking and climbing. Then he took me to a hotel to eat, and finally, at 10:30 I flew back to Cairo, arriving at nearly midnight, and was taken to the Gabaly Hotel -- rather crummy but not as expensive as the previous one.

Alexandria

I did not get much sleep that night, because just as I was falling to sleep at 1:30, the travel agent called to say I was to be ready to leave for Alexandria at 6:00 a.m. I was up at 5:15, packed, and ate a quick breakfast. The travel company representative met me and we drove across town, where we picked up a Greek Australian family–man and wife and four children. I sat in the back. It was hot and I could smell exhaust fumes. We left Cairo at about 7:00, and drove through the desert for three and one-half hours, as Arabic music played loudly.

The man who accompanied the driver confessed that he was not an official guide, but did give us some information. At one time, pointing to the left, he said, "There is desert," and on the right, "There is desert!" We asked about the white cone-shaped structures we saw, usually on the top of houses. He said they made nests for birds. People believed that if they provided for the birds God would protect them.

Upon arrival in Alexandria, we went to the Greco-Roman Museum–and were disappointed that no guide was provided for us. We were fortunate to find a young woman with one client, who allowed us to listen also. The museum was interesting. In conversation with my companions

I learned that Carol (the wife) was from Macedonia, home of Alexander the Great, and was perhaps a descendant; Bill, an electrical engineer, once did repairs on Onassis' ship.

From the museum we went to the Citadel of Qaitbay, a fort built by the Mamluk Sultan Qaitbay in 1477-1479 A.D., on the ruins of the old lighthouse of Alexandria. Everything was written in French and Arabic, and with no interpreter we didn't stay long. We saw a marine museum which did not amount to much, and then had an Egyptian lunch–the usual bread and dips, pickles of various kinds, shish kabob. Then back to Cairo. We felt that we did not get much for our money on that trip.

The Citadel

The driver picked up my luggage (after going nearly to the airport first), and then when we did reach the airport, took me to the wrong terminal, and the wrong side of that–and then left me, with my luggage. I had to struggle up and down stairs, and finally discovered I was in the wrong terminal and could take an airport bus. But the bus put me down a considerable distance from the entrance, and so by the time I reached the Israeli El Al airline, I was exhausted, hungry, and my feet hurt! At the cafeteria all I could get were a few slices of bread and cheese and a cola drink. There followed a very grueling experience at the Israeli airline–but that is another story, not to be told here. I was on my way to Palestine/Israel, and in for a life-changing experience.

Egypt
October 30-31

While I was in Palestine/Israel, I was guided by Dr. Romeo del Rosario, United Methodist missionary to Palestine and liaison with the Middle East Council of Churches. At my request, he was able to make arrangements through the Council of Churches for me to see some of the work of the Coptic churches in Egypt. I had a twenty-four-hour layover before taking a plane to the Philippines (the last leg of my journey before returning to the U.S.), and I was interested in seeing some of the work to which my church (United Methodist) contributed.

I arrived on schedule in Cairo on October 30. The travel agent who had planned the tour before saw me, and I used their van to go to the hotel (I had made a reservation at the Gabaly Hotel when I was there previously.) I think I must have received a lower price because of them–only $16.00, which included breakfast, and a decent room.

M.E.C.C. Projects

Leadership training and development

As had been arranged earlier, Mr. Ayad Henry, the Director of the Leadership Training Program for Diakonia and Development of the Middle East Council of Churches, met me at 9:00 a.m. the next morning. We went first to the MECC offices, where I called to confirm my flights. Mr. Henry had hired a taxi for me for the day–very cheap. The driver was a Christian. Mr. Henry went with me to see Dr. Maurice Fouad of the Bishopric of Public, Ecumenical and Social Services, Coptic Orthodox Church. They had a program of Vocational Training, Health Education, Family Life Education, Community Centers, Nurseries, and Rural Development Education.

He said that Egypt was about 10% Christian, although the government figures said 2%. The Coptic Church for a long time did not concern itself much with social work. (The clergy said it wasn't the church's job.) But development work began in the 1970s and had become well established in the previous five or six years. It was called the "Round Table Program." Emphasis was on partnership with donors and strengthening ecumenical relationships. The program was proposed in 1984 and started in 1985. There were ten sub-programs:

(1) Leadership training for communities. Entrance is through the churches, but there had been tension between the non-Christians and the churches, due to the evangelistic efforts of some groups. The program emphasized the training of local leaders, clergy and lay, for development work, and there had been growth in understanding of the importance of social work.

(2) Vocational or Employment Training. There was a horrible problem of unemployment They had loans to help people set up small businesses.

(3) Primary health care. Village workers and social workers were health-oriented; communities would submit proposals for projects such as latrines, pure water, or a cleanliness campaign.

(4) Youth Program. Villages were concerned mainly with developing local leaders among the youth. They had holistic programs.

(5) Women and Development Program; 20% of the budget was for this. They established women's centers, and programs for literacy teaching, needlework, etc. to help financially. They aimed to help illiterate young women to become good mothers. They sought to form a bond with the community; communication between the center and other community ventures was important.

(6) Nurseries for children, three to five years, were some of the best in Egypt. They had institutes to train leaders, and tried to help the family improve attitudes toward children.

(7) Education–literacy, working through other programs.

(8) Service activities–meeting emergency needs of marginalized people.

(9) Development loans. Priority was given to women's centers, vocational training centers, members of farmers' clubs. Loans (revolving funds) were usually to provide tools and equipment.

(10) Loot program–small projects which could not be put in other programs, which complemented them.

The third phase would be begun in 1991-1993, with emphasis on quality rather than quantity, and training local leaders.

There had been a great change in attitude among the clergy toward social work. An added problem at that time was the needs of those returning from Kuwait. (Kuwait expelled foreigners at the time of the first Gulf War.)

The Agape Center

We then went to visit Emad Kamel, the director of Agape Center, a Coptic Orthodox project. I saw one of the seven places in Cairo where the garbage collectors lived. These were people, whole families, who gathered garbage from the houses in Cairo, and then brought it there to sort out all that could be used–plastic, bottles, etc. Garbage (food) was given to pigs. (Since these were Christians, they ate pork.) They then transferred the rest to where it could be discarded. They used to use donkeys and horses to pull carts, until some people who were concerned about the appearance of Cairo for tourists got a law passed to outlaw them, and they were now fined heavily if they used them. But many could not afford trucks; sometimes several would go together to buy or rent one.

The city did not extend many amenities to that area–e.g., a sewage system, adequate schools. In that area, called Mo'attammedia, three to four thousand people lived.

Garbage Collectors–Where They Lived and Worked

The church's program had begun thirteen years before, through women's meetings, child care centers, development centers for young girls, Sunday School. It was six years ago that they centered the program on garbage collectors. Their program:

(1) Awareness program–Public meetings, A-Vs, day trips, etc.

(2) Economic development–They taught carpentry, electricity, gave development loans.

(3) Women's program–Development center, day care center (Montessori method). There were meetings in each subarea once a week.

(4) Leadership training–They trained deaconesses; had a Youth Club, where young people were taught how to live with others. Some were selected to teach health. They trained stewards to take charge of programs.

(5) Health program–Immunization, family planning, training for health workers.

(6) Community Programs–e.g., drainage scheme, electric power to pump underground water. They helped them to buy land rather than to rent, in order to build houses.

(7) Social Service program–Helped meet needs by giving money, clothing or loans.

The clergy were involved in these programs.

We went to see some of the projects–a Nursery School class, a girl's class where they did craft work and knitting. The girls gave me a necklace they had made. I hesitated to take it when they needed so much, but I knew that it would be an insult not to do so.

Many of the people lived in horrible shanties surrounded by piles of garbage, animals sometimes sharing the same "house." The stench was very bad, and flies were everywhere.

Next we went to meet Sr. Maria (Roman Catholic). We saw a sewing/cooking class for girls. They took turns preparing lunch, three girls each day.

Sr. Maria had purchased land, built the school (for the first three grades), and was building houses. People contributed labor and paid low rent, which eventually would buy a house. One man was weaving on a loom, one of the income generating projects.

Sr. Maria's Housing

Sewing Class

From there we went to the roof of the highest building and looked down on the deplorable housing (shacks) and garbage dumps.

Projects of the Coptic Evangelical Church

We then went to a project of the Coptic Evangelical Church–CEOSS (Coptic Evangelic Organization for Social Service). Staff members who were there were Nasim Saber, Community Coordinator; Evan Nabil, staff: Rev. Andrea Zaki, Associate Director of the Comprehensive Development Programs.

That program was for both Muslims and Christians. Each project had three phases:

(1) Partnership phase–Create community and volunteer leaders (5-10 years).
(2) Transition partnership–Would try to give some responsibility to local leaders. (3-5 years). (This is where they were at the time I visited.)
(3) Responsibility given completely to volunteers.

Programs: Literacy, Home Economics, Youth, Children, Women, Family Planning, Medical Treatment, Community Health, Vocational Training, Loans, Community-owned projects, Chicken Program, and Leadership Training.

There were four areas:

(1) Education–health, economic (for self-reliance), community councils formed, leaders trained. They developed community projects–e.g., an incinerator to burn refuse that was not usable; a clean water project, which was nearly finished, concientization Literacy classes–they had four classes for women and two for men.
(2) Home Economics–helped them to use their own materials
(3) Children's Clubs–taught skills, concepts, attitudes.
(4) Medical–Family planning. They had reached 80% of the population in the area with this.

They had purchased a truck, which took three or four trips a day, and also had the incinerator, in order to get rid of the garbage.

85% of the families had loans–
    –to increase income;
    –to maintain dignity (not providing services but doing development)
(Rev. Zaki obviously did not agree with Sr. Maria's approach. He said she "owned" the people.)

There was a government poster on the wall against female circumcision. I was told that Muslims were divided–some for it, some say it's not necessary. Christians had made no clear stand. Rev. Zaki felt it was a real problem.

Finally, we went on some home visits. I met two women who were local leaders. They were small, dingy homes, but an improvement over some. I took a picture of children in the second home, and of course they were delighted.

To the Airport

From the homes we started toward the airport, and stopped to get some foul, which we carried to the office of Sara Naphla, Ayad Henry's wife. She was Executive Secretary of the Development and Social Service Association of the Coptic Orthodox Church. We ate the foul and had a cold drink. It was time to say goodby, with many thanks. Then the taxi driver took me to the airport, this time to the right entrance. He charged me only half the usual price, but I gave him more–all the Egyptian money I had left. I hope it was adequate to express my appreciation.

It took two hours for the Emirate Airlines staff to get me checked in, but I was finally on the plane bound for Dubai, the first stop in my long trip to the Philippines.

Thus ended my "Return to Africa," probably the last time I would be able to visit the Continent where I had spent so many years–at home.

Bibliography

Africa News, February 11, 1991, p. 8.

"Aggrey, James Emman Kwegyir," in *Columbia Encyclopedia*, Sixth Ed., 2001-2005.

An address by the Al-Fateh Delegation to the Second International Conference in Support of the Arab Peoples, Cairo, January 28, 1969, in *Toward a Democratic State in Palestine*, General Union of Palestine Students, Kuwaiti Graduate Society, p. 1 (pages unnumbered).

Asheville Citizen-Times, Asheville, NC, July 10, 1997.

Atiemo, Sam. Letter by e-mail, on the "Queen Mother."

Barrett, David, "A.D. 2000: 350 Million Christians in Africa" in the *Christian World Encyclopedia*.

Butler, David W., "Tunisia," unpublished manuscript.

Chamberlain, Gina, "Avoiding a Harvest of Violence," *New World Outlook*, July-August 1992, p.16.

Chu, Daniel and Skinner, Elliott. *A Glorious Age in Africa*. Doubleday & Co., 1965. (Booklet)

Clarke, Rev. Dr. Stuart, Letter on the beginnings of the Theological Hall, Sierra Leone.

Facing the Lion; Growing up Maasai on the African Savanna, by Joseph Lemasolai Lekuton, in an article by Hermon Uniola, p. 118. National Geographic, Washington D.C., c.2003 by Joseph Lekuton.

Fyfe, Christopher. *A Short History of Sierra Leone*. London: Longman's Green & Co., Ltd., c.1962, Chapters 5 and 6.

Ghana Information Services, *Ghana Today No. 4, People of Ghana*.

Harker, F. D. *The Church Is There (In Ghana)*. Church of Scotland Foreign Mission Committee, Edinburgh, 1964, p, 10.

Independence! Daily Mail Guide. Sierra Leone, 1961.

Innis, Bishop John. Report to the Liberia Reunion in 2005.

"Kenya in Brief," from a tourist booklet published in July 1990.

Knoxville News Sentinal, Knoxville, TN. January 1, and January 3, 1982.

Kwakye, Mary. Letter about the naming ceremony.

Leaflet from the Mindolo Ecumenical Foundation, 1990.

NDEKE Tales, published for Zambia Airways, 1990.

New York Times, January 5, 1982.

Poulsen, Elisa. Article in *The New Mexico Daily Lobo*, May 5, 1982.

Program for the opening ceremony of the new Trinity College buildings at Legon, Ghana, January 23, 1965.

Quansah, Isaac K., "An Akan Naming Ceremony," unpublished manuscript.

Report of the Zurich Consultation (March 23-26, 1972) to the World Division and the European Boards.

Sierra Leone. Director of Information, Sierra Leone Government, n.d., pp. 1-6.

The Book of Discipline of The United Methodist Church, 2004, pp. 5-7. United Methodist Publishing House, Nashville, TN, c. 2004.

The Encyclopedia of World Methodism, Vol. II, p. 1697. Nolan B. Harmon, General Editor. United Methodist Publishing House, Nashville, TN, c. 1974.

"Visit Fort Jesus Mombasa," published by the National Museums of Kenya (leaflet).

Internet

ABC News (Australia), "Votes Counted in Sierra Leone Elections" (August 13, 2007) and "Election Violence Grips Sierra Leone Capital," (September 2, 2007).

"Ancient Irrigation," www.geologyucdavis.edu

"Elmina Castle in Ghana"

"Forts and Castles of Ghana"

"Ghana," in *Encyclopedia Britannica Almanac*, 2005

"Ghana–Timeline–the Gold Coast," The Crawford.dk Home Page and "Ghana on a Road to Freer Economy,"*Insight*, Sept. 12, 1988, Vol. 4, No. 37.

Historical Perspectives on Scouting, "BSA Hand Clap," "The History of the Left-Hand Handshake Comes from Africa."

Kenya, Methodist Church, Leader: Rev. Dr. Stephen Kanyaru M'Impwii,

"Living the Experience: 75 Years in The United Church of Canada (1925-2000)," edited by Graham A.D. Scott and others.

"Mindolo Ecumenical Foundation"

Moxon, Mark, "Ghana: The Prempeh Room."

Stevens III, William S., "Africa: A Place in the Discovery of the Americas," published in *Five Hundred Magazine*, Vol. 1, No. 1, May/June 1989. Coral Gables, FL 33146.

The Epoch Times (Reuters), September 17, 2007.

The United Methodist Reporter, January 29, 1999.

"Truth and Reconciliation Commission, Sierra Leone,"at
    htpp://www.trcsierraleone.org/drwegsite/bublish/indexshtml

United Methodist Church News Archives

U.S. Department of State, *Background Note: Kenya.*

Wikepedia, the free encyclopedia: "Algeria," "Tunisia," "Kenya, history," "Lake Bosumtwi," "Zambia," "Sierra Leone" (Civil War), and other articles as indicated in the text.

World Bank, report of the HIPC's, on the web.

Maps

Map of Africa: Licardo, Daniel, ed., *Prayer Calendar 2007*, p. 15. Women's Division, General Board of Global Ministries, The United Methodist Church, c. 2006 by the General Board of Global Ministries.

Maps of Algeria, Ghana, Tunisia, Zambia, Kenya by the CIA, Courtesy of the University of
    Texas Libraries, The University of Texas at Austin.
Map of Egypt from a tourist leaflet
United Nations maps:
    Liberia–No. 3775 Rev 6. January 2004.
    Sierra Leone–No. 3902 Rev. January 2004.
    Nigeria -Map No. 4228. October 204.

Index

A

554

556

G

Gakii, Charity 4 95,496
Galow, Clyde. 148,149,152,159
Galow, Gladys. 152,157
Gannaway, Bill 262
Gannaway, Bruce M. 244
Gannaway, Grace 262,286
Gannaway, Ollie 244,261,275
Ganta Hospital 112,125,129,136,138,
143,152
Garrison, Mark 362,365,266,370,375
Gasser, Elaine 411
Gaston, Fred. 152
Gaston, Margaret. 152
Gbanga Pastor's School (Ministerial
Training School) 128,130,132
Gbowonyo, F. H. 239
Gebhart, Bob. 18,23
General Board of Global Ministries (United
Methodist) . . i,55,103,197,219,258,
288,290,299,302,329,330,339,340,
452,498,520
Gess, Dr. Lowell 410,421,500
Gess, Ruth 500
Getty, Betty 140
Getty, Dr. Paul 112,126,135,140
Ghartey, Sam 239
Gichuru, David 494
Gilliland, Dean (Dr.). . i,58,60,73,75,84,89,
97,100,158,435,451
Gilliland, Lois. 60,73,84,98,158
Gisler, Emma. 10,23,27,28
Gitonga (Bishop) 495,520,525
Goebel, Brunhilde. 151,159

Good News Institute 305,310,316-321,
324,339,339,340,341,343,347
Gorvie, Emerson 406
Grau, Dorothy 197,216,217,218,296
Grau, Eugene (Gene)(Dr.) 197,201,202,
216,217,218,296
Gray, Ulysses (U.S.).. 110,141
Gray, Vivienne. 110,139,141

Greig, Alan 462,463,465
Grcig, Ruth 462,463,465
Griffith, Eric 27
Griffith, Janice. 9,21,27
Griffith, Lester. 9,21,27,28,29
Grove, Erma 305,308,323,325,359,366
Gruver, Loretta.. 112,136,137
Guanu, Pastor.. 111
Guinter Memorial Hospital. 87,90,151
(See Bambur Hospital)
Gulley, Jim & Nancy 96,460
Gumanga, D.Y.. . . . . .291.292.293
Gyan. D. F. 362
Gyang-Duah,C.. 292,293

H

Hache, Arlene (Lennie) 397
Hales, Hand. 16
Hamilton, L. 166
Hammerskjold, Dag. 180,182,476
Handy, Doris. 162,168
Hankins, Eleanor. 114,132,139
Hankins, Jim 114,132,141
Hansen, Arnie 112
Hansen, Ula-Britt.. 112
Harford School for Girls 6,152,153,
157,160,398,399,404,407,411,422
Hartranft, June 407
Hasselbad, Dr.. 126
Hastings, Father Adrian 184
Hein, Hilde.. 152
Hein, Kurt. 152,157
Heisler, Metra 151,152,157,160,229
Helms, Father Charles 463,479
Helms, Tripp 491,494,520
Henry, Ayad. 545,546,550
Henry (Epting), Marcia. 7,18
Hensler, Gesila 436,438
Herr, Arba 367,370
Hess, Doris 70,127,156
Heyer, Ed 152,156,160
Heyer, Jane 152
Hickman, Dr. Max 112

558

559

M

561

World Council of Churches . . 42,47,51,68,
69,72,89,119,172,185,219,532
World Division . . . . 25,31,36,37,43.44.
45,47,51,52,70,71,81,86,88,90,
92,95,96,111,117,119,120,121,
122,125,126,127,128,134,138,
148,152,159,160,162,163,164,
165,175,197,302,349,437

Y

Yakaka, James 435
Yambasu, J. K. 407
Yeboah, Edmond 201,202,242,246,247,
255,281
Yeboah, Marie 246,247
Young, Rev. 407

Z

Zaki, Andrea 549
Zumuntar Mata (Women's Fellowship). . . .
.   94,438

Printed in the United States
113285LV00001B/53-94/P

9 781434 375285